MY POOR ELEPHANT

—

MY POOR ELEPHANT

——

27 Male Writers at Work

EDITED BY
EVE SHELNUTT

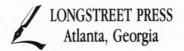 LONGSTREET PRESS
Atlanta, Georgia

Published by
LONGSTREET PRESS, INC.
2140 Newmarket Parkway
Suite 118
Marietta, GA 30067

Printed in the United States of America

1st printing 1992

Library of Congress Catalog Card Number: 91-77193

ISBN 1-56352-028-1

Lee K. Abbott's essay, "The True Story of Why I Do What I Do: An Essay," appeared in a slightly different form in *Puerto del Sol* vol. 23, no. 2 (1988).

Jim Barnes's essay, "On Native Ground," appeared in a slightly different form in *I Tell You Now: Autobiographical Essays by Native American Writers* (University of Nebraska Press, 1987).

John Haines's essay, "Within the Words: An Apprenticeship," also appeared in *GW Review* (Winter/Fall 1991).

"The Elephant" was originally published in *Ploughshares*.

"Ithaka," by Constantin Cavafy, was originally published in *C. P. Cavafy: Collected Poems*, ed. George Savidis. Copyright © 1975 by Edmund Keeley and Philip Sherrard. Reprinted by permission of Princeton University Press.

Design by Jill Dible
Wood engraving by Michael McCurdy
Marble paper by Margaret Amoss

Dedicated to the memory of
Emile Snyder

CONTENTS

PROLOGUE
The Elephant

I make an elephant
from the little
I have. Wood
from old furniture
holds him up, and I fill him
with cotton, silk,
and sweetness.
Glue keeps his heavy
ears in place.
His rolled-up trunk
is the happiest part
of his architecture.
And his tusks are made
of that rare material
I cannot fake.
A white fortune
rolling around
in circus dust
without being
lost or stolen.
And finally there are
the eyes where the most
fluid and permanent
part of the elephant
stays, free of dishonesty.

Here's my poor elephant
ready to leave
to find friends
in a tired world
that no longer believes
in animals and doesn't
trust in things.
Here he is: an imposing
and fragile bulk,
who shakes his head
and moves slowly,
his hide stitched
with cloth flowers
and clouds — allusions
to a more poetic world
where love reassembles
the natural forms.

My elephant goes
down a crowded street,
but nobody looks
not even to laugh
at his tail that threatens
to leave him.
He is all grace, except
his legs don't help
and his swollen belly
will collapse
at the slightest touch.
He expresses
with elegance
his minimal life

and no one in town
is willing to take
to himself
from that tender body
the fugitive image,
the clumsy walk.

Easily moved
he yearns for
sad situations,
unhappy people,
moonlit encounters
in the deepest ocean,
under the roots of trees,
in the bosom of shells;
he yearns for lights
that don't blind
yet shine through
the thickest trunks.
He walks the battlefield
without crushing plants,
searching for places,
secrets, stories
untold in any book,
whose style only the wind,
the leaves, the ant
recognize, but men
ignore since they dare
show themselves only
under a veiled peace
and to closed eyes.

And now late at night
my elephant returns,
but returns tired out,
his shaky legs
break down in the dust.
He didn't find
what he wanted,
what we wanted.
I am my elephant,
in whom I love
to disguise myself.
Tired of searching,
his huge machinery
collapses like paper.
The paste gives way
and all his contents,
forgiveness, sweetness,
feathers, cotton
burst out on the rug,
like a myth torn apart.
Tomorrow I begin again.

— Carlos Drummond de Andrade
　(*Travelling in the Family*, trans. Mark Strand)

INTRODUCTION

For some time I've loved Andrade's metaphor of the elephant for both the poet and poetry, so felicitous and melancholy at the same time, the "fragile hulk" going off with his cloth flowers and stitched clouds. Yet it wasn't until I was able to compare the essays collected here with those in the companion volume by women writers, *The Confidence Woman*, that I realized how supremely male the image is. Not Brazilian, necessarily, like Andrade, nor Portuguese, the language of his poetry, but unequivocally, splendidly, simply *male*.

It's true that most writers, male and female, search for stories "untold in any book," but what woman would imagine the writer's inherent vulnerability as a "tail that threatens / to leave him?" Or say of the writer's isolation: "No one in town / is willing to take / to himself / from that tender body / the fugitive image, / the clumsy walk."

In this collection of essays, you will be able to watch the elephant being made of "old furniture"; filled with "cotton, silk / and sweetness," and finally sent out with eyes "free of dishonesty" and tusks that cannot be faked.

Thomas Mann once remarked that American writers seemed to have little staying power. But not these writers. Clearly, "myth torn apart" is reassembled, a fact that seems so important in this vexing time of American social and political history. We need, perhaps more than ever before, *these* images of male writers, their elegant voices expressing their lives.

For, of course, the men whose work is represented by these essays live anything but minimal lives. I have been changed by their writing; in some instances by their generosity to me as a writer; and sustained more than once by their beginning again.

Why do we not have parades for our poets, which would exhibit America's uncommon bounty as nothing else could? Most of the writers represented here also teach in creative writing programs, master-artists to so many apprentice writers. Several are so known for their generosity to fellow writers, male and female, that the wonder is how they find time to write. Yet they do, out of uncommon hope.

Energy that comes from such hope is evident in the essays. It is a rare kind of energy, responsible, in part, for my having asked these particular men to write for the collection. They walk "the battle-fields / without crushing plants"—Andrade's line that admits with horrifying simplicity to battlefields' seemingly implacable existence, while simultaneously honoring the living world. The elephant's very clear-eyed balance is evident in the essays.

We say too infrequently how great a luxury it is to be able to write, but indirectly these essays say it often. They testify to *benign* power, and to love that "reassembles / the natural forms."

During the making of this collection, I talked and corresponded with the essayists, becoming aware again, as I had when editing *The Confidence Woman*, that for writers to write about their work is most difficult. Facts, "the thickest trunks," are, after all, what makes the elephant "yearn for lights / that don't blind." I am grateful to the contributors for their beautifully luminous facts.

What these essays can do for us seems to me immense, if we can listen to their style. Not having woven myths around themselves by being too much, too insistently, or emptily, outside, they speak with a rare humility and gratitude about "the clumsy walk" that writing is. Their essays, along with their poetry and prose, comprise "that tender body."

What we need in Washington and on the West Bank and in Belgrade, on every street and alley, over every desert, is a parade of elephants. The "veiled peace" might show its true face.

Eve Shelnutt
October 1991

Eric Feinblatt

*Born and raised in Tennessee, Madison Smartt Bell has
lived in New York and London and now lives in Baltimore, Maryland. A graduate of Princeton University
and Hollins College, he has taught in various creative
writing programs, including the Iowa Writers' Workshop and the Johns Hopkins University Writing Seminars. Since 1984 he has taught at Goucher College,
where he is currently writer-in-residence, along with his
wife, the poet Elizabeth Spires. His novel* Soldier's Joy
received the Lillian Smith Award in 1989.

ONE ART

One Taw, Two Taw . . .

My grandmother died last year. Among her last words, often repeated during the final weeks of her life, so my mother told me, was this jingle, which she had learned when she was a child in Mississippi:

One taw, two taw
Six taw, Sal
Ringtail, dominecker
dinktum, dal
Hajum Scajum
Virjum Maryam
Zinctam, zanctum
Boram buck.

Spellings are speculative, some of them anyway. I don't think the woman my grandmother learned the rhyme from could read or write. Her name was Aunt Mary, she was born in slavery, lived out her life as a family servant, and had a generous hand in the raising of a couple of generations of children in my grandmother's family. I know her only from the stories and from one picture which shows her sitting on a step, a lean, strong-looking woman, dark and hard as a nail, with an apron and headcloth clean and bright enough to cut you.

My mother told me that whenever Aunt Mary reached the end of the rhyme, punching out hard on Boram, *buck*, she would spit on the ground for punctuation. She also told me, after my grandmother's death, that I had better make sure I remembered the rhyme for the rest of my life. As an aid to my own memory I have been teaching it to my daughter, who is three months old. There is some irony, I guess, in a bunch of white folks enshrining a rhyme of an ancient black woman in this incantatory way, without having any notion of its original meaning. I suspect it may once have been a charm. Anyway, my daughter Celia thinks it does very well as a variation on the pattycake jingle. She puts up her hands and smiles when I sing it to her. Clearly this is one pretty good use for the thing. Eventually it may turn out to be one of the very first things she can remember herself, and something that sets her apart, by the tiniest measure, from others.

The Land

My grandmother married a Tennessee man and lived her married life in Nashville. When my parents married, they bought a farm. Land was cheap, then, in the middle fifties, out in Williamson County, or at least cheap enough. What were they thinking? My father was working in a Nashville law firm then; later he started his own practice in Franklin, the Williamson County seat. My mother had always taught riding lessons and she wanted room to have horses and to run a summer camp. They bought ninety-six acres, about half of it wooded, with an old saltbox house, built over a log cabin whose "foundation" consists to this day of round logs balanced on heaps of unmortared fieldstones. On the other end of the property was a tenant house which was soon occupied by Benjamin Taylor, a small, powerful, broadly talented black man known to us as Mutt. This was a nickname his friends had taken from the "Mutt and Jeff" comic strip for him, a comic reversal since Mutt, our Mutt, was so short.

For the first few years, Mutt and my mother ran the farm. My mother learned a very great deal from him. He could make or repair almost anything, manage most animals, make anything grow. He was a good enough carpenter to raise barns and he built a room on the house when I was going to be born. In that room and on that place I became whatever I am.

I was born in August, during summer camp, and came two weeks late. My mother conducted her campers on seven trail rides, seven hours on horseback, the day of my birth. It worked. Soon enough I was out horseback on the trail again, strapped to a papoose board.

In those days my parents had a big red Doberman named Wotan, who was as attached to my mother as a child might have been. How this dog would respond to my appearance was a subject of some concern. My grandmother, both my grandmothers, were upset about it. As it happened, Wotan easily transferred much of his love and loyalty to me. He came upstairs for the first time when I was brought home (he hated to climb stairs for some reason). When I was a little older my mother discovered that she could leave me in my playpen out in the yard, more or less under the dog's supervision, while she taught in the riding ring. Wotan would bring me trimmings of horse hoof, his favorite delicacy, and offer them to me through the mesh of the pen. I can remember the taste and texture of them, rather like a fingernail, but softer and chewier — not half bad for a teething baby, though my grandmothers were greatly distressed. Later on I learned to go out in the barn lot and lick salt with the horses from their block. This practice greatly horrified my grandmothers though it seems to have done me no harm.

By the time I was old enough to walk unsupported, the farm had become a quite serious operation. There were fourteen horses in the barn, hogs in the hog lot, two dairy cows. Sixty children were in the summer camp, whose proceeds funded fences and upkeep, and my mother taught riding every school afternoon except in the dead of winter. By then she had learned to can and freeze all the vegetables we needed year round. We had fresh milk and churned butter, killed hogs and under Mutt's tutelage cured the meat in the smokehouse.

With Mutt's great abilities and my mother's huge energy, the whole thing was kept going at a high rate of speed. Mutt did most of the outside work. He was a master of making do. For transport around the farm he used a drag sled, drawn on runners by a mule called Blue. Mutt also rode Blue in the mule race at the Iroquois Steeplechase every year, and usually won. He plowed with the mule also, and I can remember trying it myself, with his hands guiding mine on the handles, keeping the row straight. We didn't use the tractor much until later, when I was eight or nine, and Mutt, undone by whisky, the death of his first wife, an unfortunate marriage to the local bootlegger, whisky again, left the place for good. We found out then that he was irreplaceable, the last of his kind or one of the last. The last who'd ever live with us, for sure. Then much of the work he had used to do landed on my father and on me.

Mine was an atavistic childhood. I knew it at the time, because people told me, and it was obvious anyway. A generation before, it wouldn't have been so unusual to grow up as a child of educated, professional parents who were also real farmers. But at the schools I was driven to in Nashville there was nobody else that lived the way I did. The town children lived in their backyards, on the sidewalks, in neighborhoods. For the most part they had less work to do. I might envy them a little, as they would envy me for the horses, the pool, the big territory on which I was free and alone. But mainly I knew I was different from them, and already, in my way, I was proud of it.

Books

My mother taught me to read before I started school, which

changed my life deeply and forever. I think at first I wanted to learn to read for myself, but I had no idea how hard it would be until my mother sat me down at the dining room table and printed a capital A and asked me to identify it. No problem there. I had learned the alphabet off a tablet and could sing it for my grandmothers. She drew a typeface a and asked me what that was. Now since this character does not physically resemble a hand-printed capital A very much at all, I had no notion. What I began to suspect was that I had got myself in a lot deeper than I had really intended. This episode inaugurated a period of frustration and struggle for both me and my mother, at the end of which I was released into what is probably the greatest freedom I will ever know.

And by the way, I can scarcely remember anymore what it was like not to be able to read. Certain books will almost bring it back; if I look at an old Babar book, say, I can for an instant feel again how the few simple words were once thorny and irascible objects, so difficult to ingest. And in their absence, the images loom. . . .

Anyway, I mastered print, not without some difficulty, graduated from Babar and Peter Rabbit to books with whole paragraphs in them. I remember a few particularly, a big blue book about Indians, and several by Holling C. Holling, *Paddle-to-the-Sea* and another about a hermit crab whose name I have forgotten. By the time I started school I could read pretty good. That ability, like our general manner of living, was just slightly isolating. It put me just a little out of sync with the group—always in the wrong place in the reading circle, and so forth. To my first-grade teacher, more than a bit of a martinet, skipping ahead was a crime. She didn't believe I could read anyhow, the whole idea offended her. At the end of the following summer, I hid in the barn to avoid going back. But my next few teachers were kindly.

Well, I was ahead in the book. My classmates knew I could do it, and to them it was a mere curiosity, I think, like being able to balance a banana on your nose. But for me it was a reflection of the world in which I realized I could go much further, much faster, than I could in the real world. I think it was from learning to read, so early, that I first learned to reflect. In bouncing off the books I got some sense of who I was, or might be, those possibilities. It was also around this time, first and second grade, that I caught a habit which I still have to this day, of talking to myself, sotto voce but often audibly, rehearsing bits of dialogue and telling myself little stories. This particular bit of eccentricity was a little nerve-wracking to children who sat me near me in school. Also if some episode or conversation among school friends struck me as having dramatic possibilities I would begin to finish the lines by muttering "he said," or "she said," under my breath. If asked at that age what I wanted to be I would usually say cowboy, or a lawyer like my father, but I really wanted to be an "author."

Sick

I had severe chronic asthma from the age of two, caught bronchitis frequently, and was violently allergic to just about everything around me, especially the horses, which I continued to ride. The problem was serious enough that my parents at one point considered packing it in and moving to town. They had received some medical advice along those lines as I recall. I think they asked me. I said no.

There was nothing out of the ordinary about any of that for me. I couldn't remember not having the asthma, the allergies, the rashes and so forth. It was run of the mill, the way things were. I don't recall feeling sorry for myself or resenting it. Probably that is because my parents managed at least to appear to take it all very easily in stride and never made me feel as though I were pitiable.

The bad asthma attacks brought the doctor, first on house call with a literal little black Gladstone bag, later a trip to town. In either case there'd be a shot of Adrenalin, which as far as I was concerned was paradise in a syringe. The amazing thing was that it worked instantaneously, flooding me with a euphoria which was partly the relief of being able to breathe again, to relax, and partly the giddy edge of the drug itself, which seemed to make my thoughts and perceptions rapid and brilliant, and gave me too a false sense of extraordinary physical power.

Other attacks I learned to ride out on my own. The illness was with me like an animal, not a bad animal entirely but one that needed to be broken as one might break a horse. After a good two days of constant coughing I would feel as if somebody had been kicking me steadily in the belly for an equivalent amount of time. I would have to fight the cough, strangle it, swallow it back down the sore muscles of my diaphragm. With bad asthma the problem was I could never lie down. Any pressure on my chest or back seemed to shut off my lungs. I would lie, then, propped up on my elbows, with a book propped in between my arms, reading until I finally lost consciousness some way or other.

Whatever doesn't kill you makes you stronger. I felt that many years before I ever heard it. It's no better than a half truth but it certainly does have a ring to it. The odd thing is that with all this illness I seldom ever felt weak, at least, not psychologically speaking. It seemed that I was engaged in a terrific struggle but also that I had the resources to win, and this, in its way, made me powerful.

Books

Sick, I would usually be reading. Illness released me from the whole chore of going to school and doing schoolwork. Though I would usually work in a book from the school library every day then. My mother got good stuff in front of me. I read most of Gerald Durrell, most of Mark Twain, before I reached eighth grade. I would read these books over and over, sick or well, but they were especially comforting when I was sick, like talismans, charms even.

Also there were the Tolkien books, and C. S. Lewis's Narnia stories. When I was in the fifth grade, my obsession with the latter began to border on the pathological. I trained myself to wake up around two in the morning, when my parents were solidly asleep and unlikely to catch me, and I would reread the books until dawn. At school I was exhausted and for the first time began to do poorly. The reason for all this is still hard for me to grasp. I was rather unhappy that year, when I was awake and outside the books, but I had no real reason to be. I had somehow acquired a distaste for the mundane, for ordinary reality, and all I wanted was to get through one of those magic doorways and enter a world which was magic. I don't really remember how it stopped.

Dream of Power

It was a couple of years later, I think, that I had my dream. It was a dream of a sort that the Indians used to go on dream quests to capture. I had not undertaken any quest, at least not on purpose, but I got the dream anyway. It was quite brief, emotionally overwhelming, and I saw clearly that its purpose was to give me power, although, in the following days, when I thought about that, it seemed a little silly. It was hard for me to take it with perfect seriousness, but I did take it seriously enough that I told no one. I had read enough to know that if you tell such a dream you will lose it. At times, for a long time, I didn't think about it, but I never forgot it and I never told. It seems to me now that whatever I have been able to do as a writer really has been powered by this dream. So I am glad I never told it, and I never will tell it either, unless, someday, I am ready to surrender the power.

Childhood's End

Well, I am grown up now I guess. Ain't no dog going to offer me horse hoof now. If he did, I probably wouldn't take it. But I am grateful for that horse hoof. Everything else too. It was the making of me, whatever I am. Because I learned to read so early, I lived, all along, in a slightly different mental world than my schoolmates. Meanwhile the way that we lived on the farm ensured that I did not go quite seamlessly into the life of my time but stood just slightly apart from it. From such a separation one may see a little more vividly. Because of these circumstances, accidents more or less, I was enabled to start becoming the writer I wanted to be.

Books and the Land

I had a science-fiction phase that lasted two years, when I was twelve and thirteen. I'd buy and read a paperback book every day if I could get away with it. Some good and memorable stuff, and lots of genre junk, but maybe time well spent just the same. As George Garrett would later tell me when I became his student, it's not altogether a good thing for an apprentice writer to be fed a steady stream of masterpieces. In genre you can see more easily how the thing was put together, how the trick was brought off. . . .

But when I started high school I lost interest in sci-fi suddenly and completely and began to read almost exclusively fiction of the Southern Renaissance, beginning with Warren's *All the King's Men*, which I must have read a hundred times since. Then I read most of Warren's other novels, all Flannery O'Connor, Peter Taylor, Allen Tate, and Andrew Lytle, a good deal of Faulkner, though understanding this rather incompletely at the time, and some novelists of a younger generation, like Madison Jones and Harry Crews.

It made a difference that some of these writers were friends of my parents, members of a Vanderbilt circle to which they also belong. Madison Jones was their close college friend, and they knew Mr. Lytle, Mr. Tate, and Donald Davidson very well also. From when I was very small, I was in awe of these people because of what they were. Authors. It was Mr. Tate who seemed especially set apart, the swollen head wreathed in smoke with the cool dry voice coming out of it, as if almost already disembodied.

As for myself, I knew the Jones family very well, was good friends with several of their children. Mr. Tate died before I could have been much to him other than the child of his young friends. But I have had the good luck to know Mr. Lytle as a grownup and as certainly one of the best and sharpest readers I've ever had, who can cut straight to the core of any book I (or anyone else) have written, usually with a single sentence.

The rest of them lived in their work for me, and when I went off to Princeton my great ambition was to be a writer like them. I became a sort of scholar of Southern Renaissance literature, writing long papers about all the novels of Harry Crews published up to that time, and a thesis on the work of Madison Jones. A step away from my parents and the farm, I thought I saw that my life and theirs had, by whatever combination of accident and design, been played out as a realization of many of the ideas in *I'll Take My Stand*. That in taking up what economists call subsistence agriculture they had secured for themselves and for me a great many of the good things of an agrarian described by Mr. Lytle in "The Hind Tit." Not to mention a great deal of hard, grinding, absolutely unceasing work. . . .

When I had this insight, such as it was, I was rather excited, intellectually. It was almost as good as living in a book, which was something I had very much wanted to do with at least a part of my being. But there are drawbacks to success with such a project.

Sick

My plan to become a writer was completely unsupported by any attempt to write anything until the end of my senior year of high school. At this point I came down with a spontaneously collapsed lung. My doctor told me I could go into the hospital and have them cut me open or I could remain in my room without moving much for a couple of weeks and hope the lung came back up on its own. This was an easy choice for me. But it was an odd imprisonment. I didn't feel sick at all. There had been some quite extraordinary pain in the beginning, enough to send me to the doctor, but this stopped. Boredom set in. There was little to do. I was not even supposed to go downstairs. I discovered I could no longer read eighteen hours a day. I began to watch television, something I've never done very much of at a stretch. A strange stultifying experience, like a drug.

Out of desperation I wrote my first real short story, "Triptych," in which the deaths of a peacock, an old man, and a bull were pictorially juxtaposed. The style was imitation Hemingway. I wrote the whole thing out in pencil and hid it in a desk drawer. So much for that.

Some Formalities

It was always my notion that once I got to college I would set about becoming a writer. Princeton was known for its undergraduate creative writing program, but I didn't realize till I hit the campus that you had to apply to get into it. Intimidated by students I met who had apparently written huge quantities of fiction already, I took this requirement rather more seriously than necessary. There were other difficulties also and I dropped out of school for a semester, returned to Nashville, got a job on the Ingram Book Company's receiving dock, and tried to write some stories. I also got the old "Triptych" out of the drawer and rewrote in the manner of Flannery O'Connor, as best I could manage. The conflation of the two borrowed styles made the derivativeness of the whole rather less obvious, and I knew it was the best thing I had to show.

Later on, after six months at Ingram had helped me to understand that Princeton was not such a bad place after all, I showed the story to George Garrett. It was the end of the semester I had spent in his class. I had done some so-so work for the group, but I liked and admired George so much that I wanted to show him the best I could do. When he had read it he nodded and smiled and offered to publish it in *Intro*, of which he was then the editor. That was my first publication and for quite some time my last. In this way I went on the list which is at least a hundred or more long (no exaggeration) of writers who owe their first good start, and many legs up afterward, to George Garrett.

I had very good luck with the other writing teachers I had also, William Goyen, Stephen Koch, Rosanne Coggeshall, and Richard Dillard. They were all good masters, good examples, and there is much I owe them too. Although I was a stubborn student who usually wouldn't listen to anything or follow any advice.

Displacement

I do not think I would have amounted to much as a writer if I had gone to school down South, or if I had returned there immediately after school, for that matter. I wanted too much to be a Southern writer, and I understood, intellectually, too well what that was. I would have tried to make a career out of embroidering the great themes of others.

Another coincidence kept me from this: friendship with Alex Roshuk, a charismatic Russian of many genius abilities, a child prodigy filmmaker who came to Princeton to study engineering, and dropped out after a couple of years, returning to New York to become a wanderer there, a sometime street person, sometime street magician, virtually. I would have followed him anywhere, in those days. And I did follow him, for several years, into a great many interesting places. It wasn't my subject I found there — that's a more complicated matter. But I found a setting wide and deep enough to contain several books, and also, in some way, a context.

The Subject, Insofar as I Am Willing to Discuss It . . .

For writers to discuss their own work analytically is tempting and dangerous to the precise degree that it is self-indulgent. It's difficult to see one's own work that clearly anyhow. A lucid and complete understanding would usurp the work and take away the point of writing it at all. There is also a great temptation to lie. I am like most writers, I think, in that I don't want to make myself understood in a précis. I want the work to be read and apprehended as a living whole, in its essence. With these little warnings in mind I will nevertheless have a brief go.

First of all I will say that I have never wanted to write the same book over and over again, though I have lately realized that is exactly how to make a successful career in American literature today. I have tried to make my six novels as different from one another as possible. But I am far enough away from them now to see some general similarities.

Each book features some slightly or extremely isolated individual in a troubled relationship to a larger group. This person is usually embarked on a sort of spiritual pilgrimage acknowledged or not. Often he will be an apostle of some particular creed: voodoo, santeria, Islam, Russian Orthodox Christianity. . . . Anyway, there is a search going on whose intention is to resolve some spiritual unease or discontent.

Somewhat at odds with this general tendency is *Soldier's Joy*, my fifth novel, which was written with an explicitly political motive. I never thought I would do such a thing, and was a bit horrified to find myself attempting it. But now it seems to me that it is not quite so much an anomaly in the body of my work.

Many if not all of the problems of American society come from the effort to formulate and live up to a political conception of equality. The effort is continually breaking down because it is, in one sense, based on illusion. The fact is that people are not created equal with respect to their gifts. No matter what opportunities are thrown in my way I will never play the banjo as well as Bela Fleck. But all souls are equal under God. It seems almost impossible for this idea to find any viable expression in our political life. In a society so secularized as ours it becomes difficult to believe in the soul at all. Yet it seems to me that, regardless of whether a belief in God is possible, it remains vitally necessary to believe that we are souls, embarked on a pilgrimage, that this is exactly what it means to be human.

I am not a proselyte of any particular religion, far from it, I am not even a churchgoer. But I have sent character after character in book after book on a mission to discover such a religious vision of the world, in accordance with which an ordinary life can be lived in an ordinary way. In my last novel, *Doctor Sleep*, this character actually succeeds. He finds what he is looking for, under his nose all along as it happens, and comes home at last to a kind of wholeness.

What that means, of course, is that I am finished now. Shot, washed up. Done with it.

Rimbaud

I am not very interested in Rimbaud really. I had a brief infatuation with him in college, about which I now remember next to nothing. It is the picture of the Rimbaud who abandoned poetry that appeals to me now. He got through and he quit. Renunciation is a most appealing prospect — to abdicate from the dream of power, what a delirious sense of liberation that would bring! Become a chess player, like Marcel Duchamp. I could become a lawyer. Be a farmer again perhaps. A tax collector, even. . . .

Some thirty years after the publication of his last novel, his masterpiece, *The Velvet Horn*, Andrew Lytle was asked by an interviewer if he planned on writing any more fiction. His answer was the least evasive I ever expect to hear to such a question: "No. It's too hard, and I've said what I have to say."

He also said, in another context, that once you have made one masterpiece you are supposed to go on making them.

Music

I have been hearing it all my life. My father is a bit of a piano player, a bit of a guitarist, can play the accordion too, and is a fine singer. When I was little I heard all the old ballads and folk songs from him. Since then I have been in and out of rock and roll, the blues, jazz, bluegrass, classical, all sorts of music. I play a little, very little considering the time I've put into it—guitar and banjo. I've even composed a little music. Music has gone into my writing in a number of ways, directly as subject a number of times. It has influenced more subtly the way I make a sentence or a paragraph or even a whole book.

If I could choose to go back in the egg and come out again as something else I would want to be a real musician. I say that knowing full well that most of the professional musicians of my acquaintance lead much more straitened, vexatious, and difficult lives than the one I've been lucky enough to lead as a writer. I know also that I don't have the talent for it, nowhere near enough, and never will. Still it is a great pleasure to me to try to play as well as I can. And it has also put me constantly face to face with failure, an experience I still find extremely valuable.

One Taw, Two Taw . . .

Well, I see this thing is about over with and I have left a good deal out. I have not said all I meant to say. There is one ordinary lesson though. If you mean to learn something well, sing it yourself.

To believe in the unity of truth, I must also believe that everything is potentially revealed in any part. If I ever do understand that rhyme completely, absolutely, I will understand everything else in that same moment. The end is in the beginning, the beginning in the end. The angel said, *There shall be no more time.*

Books

The Washington Square Ensemble (novel). Viking Press, 1983. Penguin Contemporary American Fiction Series, 1984.
Waiting for the End of the World (novel). Ticknor & Fields, 1985. Penguin Contemporary American Fiction Series, 1986.
Straight Cut (novel). Ticknor & Fields, 1986. Penguin mass-market paperback, 1987.
Zero db (short fiction). Ticknor & Fields, 1987. Penguin Contemporary American Fiction Series, 1988.
The Year of Silence (novel). Ticknor & Fields, 1987. Penguin Contemporary American Fiction Series, 1989.
Soldier's Joy (novel). Ticknor & Fields, 1989. Penguin Contemporary

American Fiction Series, 1990.

Barking Man (short fiction). Ticknor & Fields, 1990. Penguin Contemporary American Fiction Series, 1991.

Doctor Sleep (novel). Harcourt Brace Jovanovich, 1991.

Anthologies (Short Fiction)

"Triptych." *Intro 9: Close to Home*. Hendel & Reinke, 1978. Also in *The Best of Intro*. Associated Writing Programs, 1985.

"The Naked Lady." *Best American Short Stories 1984*. Houghton Mifflin, 1984. Also in *Oral Interpretation*. Houghton Mifflin, 1987.

"Triptych 2." *New Stories from the South*. Algonquin Books, 1986.

"Zero db." *The Editors' Choice* (vol. 3). Bantam Books, 1986.

"The Day I Shot My Dog." *Homewords*. University of Tennessee Press, 1986.

"Monkey Park." *The New Writers of the South*. University of Georgia Press, 1987.

"The Lie Detector." *Best American Short Stories 1987*. Houghton Mifflin, 1987.

"Finding Natasha." *Louder than Words*. Random House, 1989. Also in *Best American Short Stories 1990*. Houghton Mifflin, 1990.

"Customs of the Country." *Best American Short Stories 1989*. Houghton Mifflin, 1989. Also in *New Stories from the South*. Algonquin Books, 1989. Also in *Amerika Porteller*. Den Norske Bokklubben, 1990.

"Witness." *Voices in Fiction and Non Fiction*. Long Ridge Writers Group, 1990.

"Getting Involved." *Words on the Page, the World in Your Hands*. vol. 2. Eds. Lipkin and Solotaroff. Harper & Row, 1990.

"Black and Tan." *The Literary Dog: Great Contemporary Dog Stories*. Atlantic Monthly Press, 1990.

Chapter from *Soldier's Joy. Literary Outtakes*. Ed. Larry Dark. Fawcett, 1990.

Periodicals

Individual stories have appeared in *America Illustrated, Antaeus, Atlantic, Boulevard, Crescent Review, Columbia, Green Mountains Review, Greensboro Review, Harper's, Hudson Review, Lowlands Review, North American Review, Poughkeepsie Review, Stories, Tennessee Illustrated, Witness*, and several foreign publications.

Fred Chappell

Educated at Duke University, Fred Chappell teaches literature and composition courses at the University of North Carolina at Greensboro. Among his most recent awards are the Bollingen Prize in Poetry, the Burlington Industries Professorship, the O. Max Gardner Award, the Ragan-Rubin Award, and the Thomas H. Carter Award. He and his wife, Susan, live in Greensboro.

FIRST ATTEMPTS

The real beginning of a writer's compulsion to compose is difficult to discover, and he must be a foolhardy author who will attempt to sound these strange, moiling, storm-lit depths in search of an origin. The first time he sets words on paper he has already forgotten why he ever desired to do so. The job before him, finding the best arrangement for the words his subject matter demands, is so taxing that his concentration must focus there — outside himself — and the vague longings and shapeless wishes and half-remembered regrets and dusky fears that brought him to this decision are sealed away, perhaps forever. The first serious pass a writer makes at a page changes his interior life so drastically he can never return to his incomplete earlier state of being.

He has been forced to be objective about something, to try to see it in a light that permits description, however fumbling and inaccurate. Even if this something is only his own subjective feeling, he has made the first step backward necessary to focus upon it. He has divided himself; he has learned that *to feel* and *to see* are not identical activities but complementary ones. If he continues to write he will understand that seeing is more important than feeling and that his emotion must be guided by what he is able to understand of his subject. This stage of development is analogous to that earliest breakthrough a percussionist makes, access to the complementary independence of different parts of his body, the ability to play separate rhythms with each of his hands and feet.

It is not so complicated or unnatural as we might like to make out. After all, this division of our faculties is one we all must resort to when we try to make important rational decisions about matters with which we are emotionally involved. We step back; we try to take account of our feelings and to see how they may be affecting our judgments. This division of faculties is not habitual with us, but it is hardly uncommon. For the writer, though, it must become habitual.

A more dangerous phase of development comes shortly afterward. There arise now two conflicting impulses: the need to write, and the desire to be a writer. The beginning writer — let us put his age at thirteen or fifteen or eighteen years — can hardly articulate and certainly cannot visualize the need to write. But *being a writer*: that is easy to imagine.

At least it was for me at age thirteen. And fourteen. Fifteen. Sixteen. I knew what I would look like as a writer. During my working day, I would wear a tan cotton shirt and trousers of vaguely Australian cut and sandals with broad thongs — because of course I would be living in a tropical climate. That was my working outfit. I would own a great many other costumes, being an enormously successful novelist. My wardrobe would include cowboy outfits, detective trench coats, suave tuxedos, spotless laboratory tunics, and all the rest; these would be the togs in which I gathered the raw materials for my writing.

I knew too what I was supposed to look like while writing. I was to sit in a director's chair before a steel-topped table and squint at the keyboard of my ancient and trusty Royal through a picturesque swirl of Chesterfield smoke. Without removing the cigarette, I would hammer out sentence after telling sentence, paragraph upon paragraph of breath-stopping excitement. For revision, of course, another atmosphere would be required. (Oh yes, I already knew that a writer revises.) To revise — no, to polish — the morning's work I would dress in tweeds and sit outdoors. During this process I would smoke a briar pipe and sip brandy. But I would be ruthless. The blunt red pencil in my tanned athletic fingers would tear through the awkward phrases and unnecessary adverbs like broadsword strokes; the new constructions would be written in beautiful tiny black calligraphy with Waterman's finest point. This draft of the manuscript would go to my private secretary for final typing. The salient points of this sexy girl changed from time to time, as I learned to appreciate a variety of females, but the worshipful gaze she cast upon my manuscript remained constant through all my daydreams.

But then the daydreams changed. I began to fancy that I had become serious about poetry; I was reading Shelley and Shakespeare by wholesale acreage and had bought a copy of Yeats's early plays for twenty-five cents from a junk dealer. As a poet I would have no leggy, adoring secretary. (Alas.) No wealth, no public acclaim. I would live lonely in a neat little cabin on the edge of Pisgah Forest. I would study the world's religions and sciences and philosophies, each in its original tongue. I would *commune with nature*. Wisely, sweetly, I would write long poems by the light of a kerosene lamp. My death would be little noticed and my poems unregarded for half a century. Then they would be discovered by a scholar; the critics would be astounded, the reading public grateful; my name would be carved on the lintels of libraries.

That was a heady sensation — to have lived happily but obscurely, to have died solitary and unappreciated, to have received at last my just acclaim, and, best of all, still to be alive at age fifteen.

I suspect that most writers are urged to their purpose by adolescent fantasies such as these, and that these daydreams do not entirely evaporate with adolescence. For even the most seasoned scribbler, there probably arises a pale green tender shoot of hope each time a new book is in the works. He doesn't dare think the thoughts fully, but the echo of his early glossy reveries rings faintly in his head. "This is the one, the one that breaks through to the green clover field of paradise where swarms of readers mass to my books like bees to lonesome blossoms." The steely frost of publication soon lays this pastel hope a-withering but never kills it entirely.

Even so, and even in his youngest years, the watchful writer tries not to indulge too freely in these fantasies. Already he feels that such daydreaming is antagonistic to his goal. Something has caught his attention — the look of a hillside in the moonlight, the white hands of a jeweler, an aunt's swollen ankle bulging painfully over the strap of her shoe, a locust fence post patched with lichen and crooked with weather, its rusty staples loose in the grain — and he wants to express what he sees and feels. He knows for a certainty — without knowing how he knows — that if he can fix the image of that fence post clearly and suggestively, if he can cosset it with his language until it replies in its own secret language, he shall have accomplished something worth doing, a step necessary in the development of his powers. He knows too that the image of himself as a writer of popular bestsellers or forlorn hermit stands between him and his fence post and that he must wipe away his wish as if it were breath-mist on a cool window pane in order to see the true lineaments of his desire.

The person who wants only to be a writer, who has no larger hope or finer design, may well become a writer and may well become no more than that. But the person who actually wants to write is almost guaranteed a more savorable existence than the other, if he will pursue faithfully the disciplines of the art. A religious person may find comfort in the Gospels and strength in prayer, but the person who puts himself through a regimen of spiritual exercises will possess a deeper life, happier and more tragic, even though it may not be his temporal life that he seeks to improve.

Yeats's poem "The Choice" is well loved, but my experience discovers its dichotomy a falsity:

> *The intellect of man is forced to choose*
> *Perfection of the life, or of the work,*

And if it take the second must refuse
A heavenly mansion, raging in the dark.

For me it is in the work that the final perfection of a life is lodged; the work is the life. One of the grand things about writing is that it never stops; the writer is not always sitting at his desk, but he is always writing. This fact also marks one of the most wearying things about the discipline, that there is no escape from it. The writer is sentenced to a lifetime of observation, of analysis, of emotional rigors; he is sentenced to a lifetime of sentences.

Perhaps when I come to be as wise as Yeats I shall agree with his poem, shall acknowledge that the intensity of focus demanded by writing debilitates one's natural charity. But I have not seen such attrition to happen. I have known any number of writers who were drunks, buffoons, knaves, clods, blowhards, sycophants, trimmers, charlatans, and egomaniacs; indeed, I can find episodes of my own life in which I have matched each of these descriptions and sometimes all of them together. But I cannot hold my writing to blame for my character faults, and in fact I believe these would be profounder if I did not write. I believe this of other writers too; insufferable as they are, if they did not write they would be worse, they would be justifiably exterminable.

Not that writers as a group are scurvier than other groups. Maybe it is a holdover from my adolescent glamorizing that I expect them to be better than other people, more considerate, self-effacing, decisive, brave, strong, loyal, trustworthy, and on their honor to do their best as Boy Scouts. I entertained the notion that the worthiest of vocations draws the worthiest of people — and then betters them. But it doesn't seem to work that way.

When I was a teenager the only contemporary writer whose personal life I knew anything about was Hemingway. *Life* magazine was always running photos of the animals he had slaughtered, the bottles he had downed, the movie stars he had companioned. He possessed exactly everything a writer was required to possess: global fame, wealth, athletic prowess, important friends, expensive gear, and a beard.

It didn't take long, though, for my fantasies to reject this figure; the image was too rich for my palate, and even as a teenager I suspected that the Hemingway of the photo journals was an unreal phantasm conjured up by press agents. His was a heady way of life but not for me; I foresaw that I would have responsibilities that I would betray if I tried to live like Papa. ("Papa" was what Marlene Dietrich called him, according to *Life*, and I knew deep in my soul that no movie star was ever going to call me Papa.)

What these responsibilities would be I could not say. It is characteristic of some writers to feel the brunt of their responsibilities before they have been able to imagine the kind of writing they must do in order to give rise to these duties. Somehow or other they hear the first throbbings of the tone they will be required to strike and then they begin to meander unsteadily toward that distant sound. I knew that I was not going to make a sound like Hemingway; I knew that the glamorized image of Hemingway stood between me and my fence post.

But if not him, then who? The only other writer of whose personal life one ever heard anything was Poe—and he was regarded as both scandalous and tragic. Whenever my parents, teachers, and ministers tried to dissuade me from a life of writing—as they did regularly and assiduously—it was the fate of Poe they threatened me with. They pictured him as a wild-eyed genius who was an alcoholic and drug addict, and they hinted too at darker vices and nearly incomprehensible sins.

Well, I could see that being Edgar Allan Poe had it all over being Ernest Hemingway, but Poe belonged to history. The past was irrelevant; I felt that no one in that fusty demesne ever encountered problems that shared any kinship with my problems. The model I was looking for had to be someone in a situation like my own who had overcome the same complex of drawbacks to become a globally acclaimed or fairly successful or even just a writer who had published something, damn it all to hell and sideways.

The trouble was that I on my side and my well-meant, minutely benevolent antagonists on theirs made too much of my ambition to write. To all of us it seemed such an exotic occupation, such a dangerous ambition, that when we tried to imagine the way of life a writer might trace we could come up with only the most lurid and improbable scenarios, scenarios that horrified and repulsed my elders while they attracted me with all the force a two-ton electromagnet exerts on a single crumb of iron filing.

If I'd been bright enough to look around me, I would have seen that my little drama was being enacted in the homes of many if not most of my friends. Our part of the world offered little opportunity for careers. If the good times kept rolling, a young man might take his father's place in the papermill—that kind of arrangement actually obtained—but he would have to wait for his father to retire. If his family owned a farm he could starve on his own hilly property. The usual jobs in selling, clerking, building, accounting, and so forth were soon filled up. So the boys decided to head out to Detroit or Pontiac or Flint; there were little Appalachias in those towns, whole settlements of "briars," as we were called, in the factory cities, and maybe they could find a toehold in the tenements. Others headed for the military; mountain boys were especially attracted to the air force, where they imagined themselves set down in the Elysian Fields of engine-tinkering. A lucky few were able to go to college. But in order to find careers, to make their lives, they had to leave their families and strike out into the unknowable world, and regret and disappointment, sorrow and anger, accompanied their leavetakings of their tight-knit mountain families.

What I didn't say was: "Well, look at Joey Swain. He's going into the army where he's got at least a chance of getting killed. I don't see how trying to be a writer can be any more dangerous than that." If I'd had sense enough to see the world around me in these terms, then my parents and the other friendly dissuaders might have been able to do the same. But none of us did, and the conflict continued and became less amicable as my high school years began to come to an end.

I think I understand now a little better this one particular source of the conflict. They too had once enjoyed fancies about undertaking careers of the kind I proposed and had rejected these ideas out of prudence. Perhaps they too had been advised by their parents that the stuff of dreams was not bankable, that the road that looked to lead to stardom actually led to starvation. Perhaps they felt that their present security in the world had been founded upon their early refusals to follow their desires.

I got an inkling of this possibility on the eve of my departure to Duke University. My father and I walked up the hill to my grandmother's house so that I could say goodbye to her. She had attended Weaver College and recalled it pleasantly. My mother had attended Carson-Newman College and then had transferred to the University of Tennessee. This evening my grandmother mentioned that some of my mother's "things from college" were still stored in that closet there. I rummaged and, sure enough, found textbooks, annuals, photographs, some letters and buttons and dance cards, and a school newspaper in which I discovered a poem signed Ann Mae Davis. When I showed it to my father, he at once devised a practical joke that seemed as tame as a butterfly. "Copy it down on a piece of paper," he said. "We'll tell your mother it's something new you've written. I'll bet a pretty she won't recognize it."

She did, though. As soon as I read the first line her face flushed scarlet and grew puffy and her eyes filled with tears. She rose from the table crying *No* and left the room with little choppy, heart-sickening steps. My father and I looked at one another ashamed. We had blundered terribly but we weren't sure how. It is obvious to me now that my mother had harbored literary aspirations and that the fond misery she had made of my adolescence (with a lot of help from her son) was in part an outcome of these thwarted desires.

She would not have been alone in her hopes. The desire to be a writer is a common one, after all — as common as the desire to write is rare. Among her friends and acquaintances there must have been other ladies and gentlemen with literary leanings. Some measure of literary learning has traditionally been part of a Southerner's makeup, and an Appalachian, not thinking of himself as Southern exactly, is likely to look to the Southerner as a model of cultivation. So here was another reason why she and her peers felt they had authority to try to turn me aside from literature: in their minds they had tested the possibility for themselves and found it lacking in substance. Or maybe they found it frightening. Usually the most daunting thing to people who want to be writers is the prospect of having to put words on a page, one word and then another and another, spelled more or less correctly and punctuated more or less sensibly.

When she came back into the room and resumed her chair at the supper table, she had recovered pretty well. The subject of her writing was not taken up again at that time or ever again in her mortal years. The memory of the expression on her face when she tottered out remained vivid in my mind, and in my father's too, I expect.

But she must have suspected something when my father asked me to read from my work. They never asked me to do that; they didn't want to hear what I wrote, they didn't even want to hear about it. My bedroom was too small to accommodate a desk and typewriter, but I had found a niche in the upstairs hall. When I set the Royal clattering, the sound could be heard all over the house. Visitors who asked about the racket were informed that Oh, that's only Fred working on his typing. Their embarrassment was just that acute; I was not trying to write, I was learning to type. Typing was a useful skill that might come in handy someday. Writing was impractical, and impracticality was worse than heresy, thievery, or some kinds of homicide. These were the tag-end years of the depression; it was imperative to be practical.

I'm making my parents sound like obtuse Victorians, like the parents of Beatrix Potter, say. They were not; they were sweet and decent people in difficult economic circumstances who were stuck with a wayward child. They indulged me in all sorts of whims and vagaries, some of them rather expensive, as when I decided that I might be taking an interest in photography or chemistry. Probably they hoped that in these passing fancies some fascination might arise that would supplant my determination to write. In the life of most families there comes a time when the offspring begin to assert their need for independence. As often as not the child fixes upon the one matter which represents independence in his mind and which his parents cannot abide. "Anything but this," they say. "We want you to be happy; you're free to do whatever you want to do. Except become a rock musician — or an artist — or a hang glider — or a homosexual — or a soldier of fortune — or — ." But for the young person, it is this, this one thing and no other, upon which his future appears to depend.

Some quality of self-pity always tincts a writer's memoirs as it does the memories of most other people who consider themselves successful in some degree. Those who look upon their lives as having failed are sometimes able to point to imperfections of their characters or to elements of their circumstances as being the causes of ruin, and they may examine these facts in a sort of complacent wonderment. But the successful person likes to picture himself as advancing triumphant over the obstacles that hindered his way; he likes to find a legendary outline in his career. He forgets those who aided him in ways that were hugely important at one time but seem less important as his self-satisfaction overcomes his sense of history.

In my case, a lot of people were willing to aid. I could write substantial tributes to Tom Covington, Lynn Hickman, my high school Latin teacher Mrs. Kellet, and to a few other high school teachers who knew of my ambition to write and found it, if not laudable, then at least harmless and fairly amusing. I have tried to write a lengthy essay about my beautiful friend at Duke, Dr. William Blackburn, and have twice failed. I wrote a sketchy tribute to Reynolds Price, but have never paid proper thanks to Hiram Haydn, James Applewhite, George Garrett, Peter Taylor, and others. The list of my literary creditors is impressive both in its size and in the prestige of its names, and it lengthens year by year. I owe more to scores of my students than I can ever say, however much I want to say it.

But most of these friends belonged to the future. Now I sat in the upstairs hall facing the tongue-and-groove pine paneling and clack-clack-clacked at pages of what I thought was fiction, what I hoped was poetry. It was stifling up there. Drops of sweat slid down my sides from my armpits; my hair matted, and I breathed with my mouth open. In wintertime, though, it was freezing, and I had to keep flexing my fingers and blowing on them.

I wrote mostly fantasies, ghost stories or horror stories or Arabian flights or science fiction — a great deal of the latter. It was not that I had no realistic experience to write about; there was God's grand plenty of realism on a farm. But I found it impossible to organize experience into any kind of shape; reality may have had the advantage of authenticity but it had the disadvantage of stubbornness, of sheer perversity. It didn't want to be whittled, rearranged, or even comprehended; it just wanted to sit laconic in an ungainly lump and refuse to differentiate into parts. The Canton High School library contained two books about writing, both with short chapters on fiction which set a lot of store by plotting. Plotting real experiences proved impossible; plotting what I made up proved to be fairly easy — a little too easy. So my stories were flimsy little contraptions with unexpected, often unexpectable, endings. The characters were colorless except for some single livid trait I laid upon them like the impress of a branding iron. The setting of any story was as insubstantial as a soap bubble, the characters' motives as murky as the vagaries of our foreign policy architects. Style was —

But there is no reason to go on in this vein, denigrating the literary effort of a hapless adolescent whose writing may be, for all that I can tell, not so much worse than mine is nowadays. It was not important that the writing be good; however good or bad it was, I would be forced to move away from it as my majority came on. The important thing about the writing was that it got onto the page. Wanting to be a writer was not standing in the way of my searching for words and patching together clauses, misplacing phrases and dangling modifiers, overusing dashes and whirling on as capricious with pronoun references as a March breeze with a girl's rayon skirt.

I learned to write more or less in the same manner that I learned to type: by doing it so dreadfully wrong so habitually often that now and then I would hit upon something acceptable by merest accident. Then I had to recognize what made my discovery useful, to try to repeat it and to build upon it. This was a process as painful as adolescence itself, but in my case just as necessary. My way of learning to write presaged the method I would pursue in learning anything else; an eon of trial was followed by an infinitude of error. I didn't fret, though. I knew that the climb was going to be long and steep; in fact, it was supposed to be. Writing was not something anyone could just pick up and perform perfectly from the start; it was different in that respect from ballet or skiing. Writing was a product of blood and toil, sweat and tears. I had invested enough of each of these, I thought, to insure my eventual success. Even if I failed, I was vindicated. In order for someone marvelous to succeed, someone like Henry James, say, whose *The Turn of the Screw* had become one of my favorite novels, then perhaps someone like me had to fail. And in cooler moments I recollected that I hadn't really shed any blood — my parents had only boxed me about a little — and had shed no tears either.

Because rejection was no great sorrow. I sent my stories off to *The Saturday Evening Post*, to *Story*, to *Astounding Science Fiction*, and, most frequently, to *Weird Tales*, and they were promptly returned to me with form rejections on little blue slips. I was not disheartened, but a little jealous when I heard that Tennessee Williams had sold his first story to *Weird Tales* when he was only seventeen years old, and when I saw a photograph in a fashion magazine of Truman Capote lying petulantly on a sofa and looking to be about fourteen. Science fiction was an especially daunting genre in this regard because so many of its famous practitioners — Isaac Asimov, C. M. Kornbluth, James Blish, and a lurid squadron of others — had begun to publish and to establish enviable reputations in their teenage years. It was true that in the 1930s there was much less competition in the field, and true too that one never found in the anthologies the earlier efforts of these authors, but they had accomplished the first main thing a young writer feels that he must accomplish: they had published professionally.

Before I went off to college I published only a very small amount in the professional magazines. I am not going to talk about that because by the time it happened it was already irrelevant to my goals. I published a fair amount in the amateur science fiction press, the fanzines, and these efforts were important to me because I got feedback about them. Soon enough, though, I lost interest in this whole side of writing. When I began to think seriously about poetry, I learned to think seriously about fiction too. The first story of any interest that I wrote came along in my senior year. As a story, it was dreadful, and I was wise to toss it away just as soon as I put a period to the final sentence. But it was lousy because it tried so hard, because it was original without attempting novelty, and because it was attached to a vision, one that I could not hammer into verse, no matter that this vision was the stuff of poetry, the real stuff, and probably not fit for fiction.

The vision I had was of seven marauder horsewomen in a snowy storm-whipped landscape. The women wore clothing patched together of animal skins and were barelegged and not at all clean. Their long hair streamed in the wind, blonde and greasy. Their horses were tall, white and black and dapple gray. These women preyed upon the hamlets and small settlements tucked away in the icy fastnesses, and in the saddlebag of the leader was the severed head of a man, a poet who once had dared to become her lover.

This vision was important to me for reasons I've never tried or cared to understand. If I made a losing job of the story, too bad. The necessary thing was that I recognized in it a subject imperative to write about. As soon as I junked it I began another story, this one about an adolescent boy troubled by vivid fantasies that enmeshed completely his real life and were beginning to disorder his mind. The vision was important, but more important was *stepping back* from it, finding a dramatic context that would give it meaning. I learned in those hours to subject my vision to analysis and to make the analysis part of the visionary process. The vision was incomplete without analysis, but without vision analysis was pointless.

I didn't know then what I had learned, of course, but I knew that I had learned something. When I packed up to go to the university, that story (from which the marauder women had disappeared) and a sequence of villanelles about farm life went into the suitcase. All the other writing of the five years past, hundreds of pages, went to a bonfire, without lament and without ceremony.

Books

Fiction

It Is Time, Lord, Atheneum, 1963.
The Inkling. Harcourt Brace, 1965.
Dagon. Harcourt Brace, 1968.
The Gaudy Place. Harcourt Brace, 1972.
Moments of Light (short stories). New South, 1980.
I Am One of You Forever. Louisiana State University Press, 1985.
Brighten the Corner Where You Are. St. Martin's Press, 1989.
More Shapes Than One. St. Martin's Press, 1991.

Poetry

The World Between the Eyes. Louisiana State University Press, 1971.
River. Louisiana State University Press, 1975.
The Man Twice Married to Fire. Unicorn Press, 1977.
Bloodfire. Louisiana State University Press, 1978.
Awakening to Music. Briarpatch Press, 1979.
Earthsleep. Louisiana State University Press, 1983.
Driftlake: A Lieder Cycle. Iron Mountain Press, 1981.
Castle Tzingal. Louisiana State University Press, 1985.
Midquest. Louisiana State University Press, 1985.
The Fred Chappell Reader. St. Martin's Press, 1987.
First and Last Words. Louisiana State University Press, 1988.

John Haines

Jo Going

John Haines lives and writes for a part of each year on a homestead outside Fairbanks, Alaska. He studied at American University and the Hans Hofmann School of Fine Art, and has held numerous positions as writer-in-residence and guest lecturer. His awards include two Guggenheim fellowships, a National Endowment for the Arts grant, a fellowship from the Alaska State Council on the Arts, a grant from the Ingram Merrill Foundation, and the Alice Faye di Castagnola Prize in poetry. His most recent collection, New Poems, 1980–88, *has won both the Lenore Marshall/Nation Award and the Poets' Prize for the best book of poems published in 1991.*

WITHIN THE WORDS:
AN APPRENTICESHIP

L et me begin at the beginning and attempt to say why I believe, against most current thought and practice, that poetry is neither a profession nor a career, nor can it in any genuine sense be understood as a choice, but comes, as it were, to the chosen, as a gift or, it may sometimes be, an affliction. In the true instance it becomes an obsession, something that cannot be refused. If this is not the case, then in all honesty I believe that it would be far better to have done some more practical and humanly useful thing in life.

I would trace my own interest in, my respect and love for, the spoken and written word back to my father, to his reading to me from the old tales: from *Treasure Island* and *The Jungle Books*, and on occasion from such weightier works as *Moby Dick*, though it was unlikely that at an early age I understood much of what Melville was saying. I listened to "Gunga Din" and "The Road to Mandalay," to stories of Br'er Rabbit and Tar-Baby, and to much else that was then considered reading matter for young people. This reading aloud was perhaps the finest thing my father did for me, though he did much else besides. I suspect that in that echo of a voice, of the words within the voice and the voice within the words, comes our earliest and most lasting sense of the language, its traditions and its possibilities. Certainly it was so in my own history. And from that followed an early interest in reading on my own, while I did not suspect for many years that I too might write and be listened to.

My second clue comes from a class in my junior or senior year in high school. I had a teacher, a man named Roy Burge, who loved English poetry and managed to convey that love to many young people in Coronado High School over the years. During one fall term we were reading Chaucer and Shakespeare, as well as other English poets. We were asked to read aloud and pronounce as well as we could those portions of the *Canterbury Tales* that were assigned to us. And one thing above all that Roy Burge did for us in that class sticks firmly in mind. One day he brought into class a record player and a disc on which a well-known English scholar read, with care and precision, selections from the *Tales* in Middle English. Thus, struggling along with the text as well as we could, we were treated to someone reading from the poem as an expert. Listening to that cultivated voice speaking the lines with their memorable cadences and inflections, I was entranced. For the first time it struck me that to be a poet must be something exceptional and marvelous; that poetry, the real thing, had within it a power that might change, if not the world, at least the life of an individual. And I was not alone in that impression; I recall more than one of my classmates taking a renewed interest in the poem, and reciting along with me some of the lines we had learned. Some years later, while at sea during World War II, I could recite, for my own consolation and for the entertainment of my shipmates, portions of the text — long passages from the *Prologue*. And without subsequent reference to the text, I could still do this many years later. Something in that music had caught me, and it never let go.

After the war, as much as I may have been attracted to the spoken and written word, I was still far from being decided on a life in poetry. Instead, with a related inclination, I was attracted to art, to painting and drawing, and to sculpture. And it was to this discipline that I began to devote myself soon after getting out of the service in 1946. If I read much poetry then, it was more apt to be Whitman or Tennyson, Omar Khayam, Kahlil Gibran, or someone else in a popular vein. I remember a long-ago girlfriend and I reading together one evening from *The Prophet*; or perhaps it was she who read and I who listened, not overly impressed, but for her sake attentive and respectful.

Then, before my first year in art school was over, came my decision to leave school, to seek adventure and a home in Alaska. From that decision and its consequences I date my beginning as a poet. For it was during my first solitary winter at the Richardson homestead that I began to write seriously for the first time.

When I had built my small house, had put up a woodpile, and settled in for the winter, I had time on my hands; time to read and, as I had thought, time to paint. At some point during that fall I had ambitiously built an easel. Now I looked over my meager art supplies, the canvas, paper, and paints I had brought with me. It seems to me now that I tried a few sketches, perhaps a watercolor or two. But with the advent of early winter the sunlight departed and the nights grew longer. Moreover, the outdoor scene with its snow mass and its slanting and fugitive winter light, its mountains and its icebound river, struck me as so overwhelming and dominant in itself that my halting efforts to reproduce some of it on paper or canvas seemed to me more and more futile. After a few weeks I grew despondent and cast about for something else to do.

That first winter, with all of its newness and mystery, its strange power, had a profound effect on me, and I had to find some way, aside from the more obvious and practical measures, of responding to it. I had built a house, the first true project of my young life. I had begun to explore some of the country around me, and I was coming to know a few of the older inhabitants of the area, individuals who were, to all appearances, still steeped in nineteenth-century life and in some important way representative of it. In all of this there was an intensity of impression and feeling, and without in the least understanding what I was letting myself in for, I looked about for some means of making my impressions clearer to myself if not to others.

I no longer remember what books I had brought with me. I could not have had many, but I did own a three-volume set of art history by the Frenchman Elie Faure, and I probably had an anthology of poetry, of romantic or conventional verses. Somewhere at mid-point during that long winter, and provoked by whatever internal sign, I began to write, and once begun I wrote steadily for some weeks. I have kept with me all of these years a few of those early efforts; they were long lined and prosy, made up from God knows what model, but it certainly wasn't Chaucer. I was attempting to set down, in what seemed to me then the only appropriate form, something of what I was seeing and coming to know, far off there and alone in a strange country. I was at the same time attempting to clarify, for myself and for some future reader, something of that loneliness and its effect on me, a thing at once painful and strengthening.

I wrote many poems; or I should say that I wrote a great many of what I thought were poems at the time. I had no one to show them to, no one to tell me that they were good or bad, promising or a waste of time. Looking at them now, some forty years later, I see a rudimentary form of the kind of poem I would later write with better success, and an unmistakable sign of the subject matter it would take me many years of work to clarify and embody in a true poem. What does impress me now in those early efforts is the abundance of energy and imagination, of the basic inspiration that seemed to drive me. Once I began, I found it easy to write, all too easy perhaps. There was nothing evident to tell me that I should write, no one to tell me what I should write about; but I sensed that this was what I had to do, at least at that moment, and the lines and homemade stanzas poured out. Only later did a self-critical faculty take firmer hold in me, and with that came an inevitable dwindling of motivation; or I should say that I learned to write less and became harder to satisfy. Nonetheless, that early motivation carried me a long way, and provided the necessary energy for many years.

In my second summer at the homestead, with a house built and nothing more of pressing importance to do there, and before me the knowledge that in the fall I would have to leave and return to school, I spent much time reading. While in Fairbanks one day I went to the one bookstore then in town and bought a hefty anthology of American poetry, edited by Louis Untermeyer or by another editor or critic prominent at the time. And for the first time I began to read and to pay close attention to poems I had not known before. Just who the poets were who most impressed me I am unable to say now, but certainly E. A. Robinson was one of them. I recall being excited by his long poem "The Man against the Sky," and before long I made my own attempt to write something like it, long-winded and philosophical. Of that brief summer period a handful of poems survive, written in one style or another, with little direct or discernible influence. Reading them now, I find them not embarrassing, only inadequate. I did not know how to say, nor did I yet know what it was I most needed or wanted to say.

That summer, prompted by some obscure impulse, I joined the Book-of-the-Month Club, and I acquired through the mail, among other things, a set of *The Great Thinkers*, and Sigrid Undset's long trilogy, *Kristin Lavransdottir*. I read these books during the long summer evenings, sitting on the screened porch of my house, with the sound of the river in flood downslope below me, and outside the screening an incredible whining from the worst mosquito infestation I have known in the north.

In the late summer of 1948 I left Fairbanks and returned to school in Washington, D.C. I enrolled in the art program at American University as a returning veteran and quickly became absorbed in painting and drawing again after a long absence. My girlfriend had taken up with a fraternity man in the meantime, and I was on my own again in a totally new situation.

Just when it was that I resumed writing poems I am not certain, but it must have been early in that fall. Many things—hopes, fears, loves, obsessions, discoveries, and deprivations—were stirring in me, and I had to find the means of getting them out. I assumed that I would be able to continue my art life and be a poet too. It required some painful and drawn-out time for me to give up that illusion—a long year in which I half-starved on my inadequate GI allowance and turned out poems, paintings, and two serious pieces of sculpture.

My return to the city opened up the book world to me, and I began reading furiously. What I read then owed much to one particular event. While still in Alaska I had sent to my former girlfriend a few of the poems I was writing. She in turn showed them to her mother, a woman who had become a good friend to me quite apart from my having been at one time a prospective son-in-law. This woman, intelligent and generous, far ahead of her time in being what has become known as "liberated," saw the germ of something in those rough and early poems of mine. When I returned to Washington, she suggested that I show my poems to the poetry consultant at the Library of Congress. Robert Lowell had just departed from the post, and his place had been taken by Leonie Adams, a poet of whom I knew nothing at the time. I was myself far too diffident to approach such a person, but my old friend, not at all hesitant, called and arranged a meeting. This meeting took place late one September morning in the office occupied by the consultant.

Leonie Adams was a shy, quiet woman. After some brief conversation I gave her my sheaf of verses, and we all sat there in silence while she looked through them. She had little to say about the poems in detail but was quick to appreciate what there was of merit in them. Inevitably, she asked who I was reading. I don't remember what I replied to her, but it was bound to be obvious that I knew next to nothing of modern poetry. She asked me if I had read this or that poet, and named a few of them, famous at the time: Eliot, Ransom, cummings, Frost, and others. She then did something for which I will always be grateful. She put a recording on a machine that stood against the wall in her office and played for us brief moments of these poets reading from their own work. We listened to Frost, to Ransom, and to several others whose names have slipped away. These voices, unknown to me, and unlike anything I had read before, stirred a new interest in me. Before we left her office she wrote down for me a list of the poets I might find worth looking into.

Such is that obscure, almost accidental service we render to others at the right time in life. I took her list and her comments with me, and in no time at all I launched myself into modern poetry with an appetite born of long deprivation. It was to be quite a while before I met and talked with another poet.

I lived then, an impoverished art student, on the top floor of a rooming house on N Street, near Dupont Circle. I occupied one room with a skylight and a closet, with a bath across the hall, for twenty-five dollars a month. I had a single bed, a small table, and a hot plate to cook on, donated by my father and his second wife, who lived then a few blocks up Connecticut Avenue. N Street was then a fairly cheap and bohemian neighborhood. On the other side of the street and half a block down, under the green copper dome of St. Matthew's Cathedral, was St. Matthew's Court where Peter Blanc, an older artist I came to know, had his studio. A few blocks away, across Connecticut Avenue, the Phillips Gallery was within easy walking distance. And not far up the avenue was Whyte's Bookstore where, as I soon learned, almost everyone in literary and artistic life in Washington came to browse and might be met there. I recall now one early fall evening at the bookstore a reception for someone in the area. Wandering around the store, listening to people I did not know, I heard from a corner of the room where a handful of people were gathered, the voice of T. S. Eliot reading from *The Wasteland*. My ear was caught by that music and the tone of that voice, as obscure as I found the verses then, and I was soon deep into the work of that poet, echoing his imagery and his cadences, composing from moment to moment and from day to day my own version of an urban wasteland, one I was to know all too well before I was finished with my art studies in Washington and New York.

It was an intense year and a half. With the energy left over from reading and studio work, I wrote poems almost automatically, with the cadences of one poet or another running in my head. I would stop, as it were, in midstride while walking the streets, to jot down a line or an idea, while at the same time thinking of the artwork I had begun or was to do. I had no car, and I rode the bus and the trolley between N Street and American University. My friends and fellow students were all in one way or another seriously occupied with art, intent on becoming painters and illustrators, perhaps headed toward a teaching career or, in one or two instances, a museum directorship. I knew no other writers. All the same, it seemed to me that I found ample fellowship among the people I studied with, many of whom, like myself, were veterans recently returned from the war.

Once again I was fortunate in having an outstanding teacher, one who gave me, in example and encouragement, precisely what I needed at that time. Leo Steppat, who taught both drawing and sculpture, was a refugee from Hitlerite Austria. He was highly intelligent, a good artist in his own right, and dedicated to the teaching of art. He was also literate, knew German poetry well, and was one of the few people to whom I could show my poems and receive an intelligent comment on them. He gave me exactly the hearing I needed, and something more: an adult companionship at a critical time. It was not that I needed encouragement; I would have prevailed, I think, had the whole world been stone deaf. It was something more than that, and of profound significance in human life: that individual who appears to us as a guide and a guardian, at a time when we are, if not lost precisely, perplexed and needing confirmation and assurance. Leo Steppat, with his own perplexities, his nail biting, and his perpetual migraine headaches, was that to me.

There was also a girl, a fellow art student, with whom I became involved, and whose interest in me, I now understand, was that of a fairly conventional person attracted to someone who appeared to be anything but conventional. She brought me an intermittent joy, much pain, and finally an intensity of emotional abandonment when she lost interest in me. But she also gave me the first good poem I was to write. It was influenced by the voice and the imagery of Dylan Thomas, but was still a poem I could call my own, stricken as it was, filled with images of late autumn and of doomed love — all the classical symptoms, in fact, and in the background a student garret where we met and loved and finally took leave of each other.

I was somewhat older than many of my fellow students, and may have appeared to my instructors as more serious than the average. But for whatever reasons, I often fell into company with a few of the older artists and teachers during that period, and I was sometimes invited to events and gatherings not often attended by the other students. And this fact led to a brief meeting with the poet Charles Olson.

Caresse Crosby, of Black Sun Press, at that time kept a gallery off Connecticut Avenue and within a block or two of the Phillips. I recall stopping by the gallery one day to talk to her about something or other, and to look at a show of paintings by the French Surrealist Robert Delaunay. She also kept the press going and had recently issued a small book of poems by Olson, called *Y & X*, and illustrated by an Italian artist. As I understood it, Olson was then working as a postman to support himself, his wife, and small child. One evening in late fall I was invited to a gathering to be held at Olson's home somewhere in the northwest section of the city. The purpose of the gathering was, in part, to raise money for some medical expense concerning Olson's wife. Along with the fund-raising, there would be a film showing and a reading by Olson from his new book.

Many people from literary and artistic Washington showed up that evening; there was a good deal of talk and drinking. We were shown the Cocteau film *Blood of a Poet*, and I seem to recall one other and briefer film. After the film showing, Olson rose to the center of the room to read. He read two of the poems in a ponderous and pontifical manner, staring out over the small audience from behind his eyeglasses, looking rather like a stranded walrus. It was my first poetry reading, and I found the poems for the most part impenetrable.

After the brief reading, copies of the book were auctioned off. As it turned out, there were only one or two bidders among the audience, and I found myself wondering at the lack of interest and concern in these people, at their unwillingness to contribute. I felt ashamed for them, and after some hesitation I raised my hand and voice and bid, as I recall, ten dollars for a copy of the book. That was a lot of money to me then, money I could ill afford, but on looking back on that evening I am glad I made the gesture. Olson signed my copy for me, looking up at me from where he sat, as if he did not know quite what to make of me. Somewhere in my dislocations of the past twenty and thirty years I seem to have lost that copy, and where it ended I cannot say. I did not see Olson again, and it was only many years later that I read of his visits with Ezra Pound who at the time was still confined to St. Elizabeth's Hospital, not far from the city.

I did not seek the company of other poets and knew none while I lived in Washington. So far as I could determine then, painting and sculpture were to be my field of work, and poetry would be something I would also do on the side. I spent the winter of 1948–49 in a fever and grind of work, of study in art and poetry, my energies divided between them.

To live then on a GI allowance without other means was extremely difficult. I worked intermittently as a draftsman for an architect I knew, but most of my time was spent at school, working in one of the studios, and otherwise at home in my small, skylighted garret on N Street. It was a year of privation, materially as well as emotionally, but it seems clear to me now that the poet in me was nourished and strengthened by that condition.

Later, when the school year was over, and I had taken a temporary job with the Navy Department, my feelings were in serious conflict. For some time an old friend and fellow art student had been urging me to move to New York where all that mattered in art was then taking place. My mood shifted about from day to day and from week to week. New York City, what I had seen of it in one brief visit, terrified me. But there in Washington my energies were increasingly consumed by my job as a statistical draftsman, and even the better part of my weekends went to the Navy Department in a hectic postwar period when the armed services were being unified and each of them was competing with the others for their funding. Whether I wrote more than one or two poems during that summer and fall I cannot now be certain. I recall one isolated episode: while waiting for my girlfriend in a doctor's office one morning, I had a sudden flash of inspiration and wrote down some verses I still have a copy of; they were dark and passionate, filled with foreboding.

For a time I entertained the notion that I might remain at my job, keep a studio, and do my artwork in my spare time as some with whom I worked in the office managed to do. I went so far as to rent a separate living space while keeping the upstairs room as a studio. But in the end I was able to do very little creative work during that summer and fall, working a long night shift and saving my money.

Like many plans in life, mine, as tentative as they were, eventually ran up against abrupt reality. I was called into my supervisor's office one day and informed that after December my contract would not be renewed. I no longer remember the reasons given for this decision, but it was the signal I had been waiting for. I decided to leave Washington and move to New York. In early January of 1950 I took the train from Union Station, and a whole new phase of my life began.

I went at first to live with my old friend and his wife in a rundown three-room apartment on Stanton Street, near the Williamsburg Bridge. Soon afterward I enrolled as a student in Hans Hofmann's School of Fine Art on 8th Street, in the Village. It may have been a month, or a little more than that, after a few sessions at Hofmann's school, that I decided to abandon art and devote my life to poetry. At what moment, motivated by what particular event, I made this decision, would be impossible for me to say now. But there was one striking fact connected with it: for some time I had suffered from severe headaches of a migraine sort; it seemed significant that once I made my decision, the headaches vanished.

Many pages might be written on my two years in New York, on the summers spent in Provincetown on the Cape where Hofmann's school moved for the season; on the people I met with, and about the changes that were taking place within me. With the abandoning of art came a renewed passion for poetry and for literature generally. I continued to attend classes once or twice a week at Hofmann's, to draw from the model and participate in his occasional and half-puzzled criticism of my drawings. I say puzzled, because Hofmann was never able to understand why I did not bring in more work to be viewed and discussed. I could hardly tell him why, and simply avoided classes as much as I decently could. My thoughts were no longer in art except as a witness.

I spent my days walking the streets, visiting libraries and book-stores, reading voraciously, muttering to myself verses from other poets or some lines of my own in formation. I steeped myself in the atmosphere of the city, or as much of it as I could know. I lived nearly within sight of the East River and its famous bridges, and I read Hart Crane with a kind of religious passion: "The Harbor Dawn," "The

Bridge," and many other of his poems. I read Whitman also, and rode the ferry to Staten Island and back. I walked from the Battery and the Fulton Fish Market uptown to the Museum of Natural History, and back; and I came to know firsthand the silence of Wall Street on a windy and freezing Sunday. I knew that my time in the city would be limited, that once my government subsidy was exhausted I would have to leave; and I knew also that one day I would return to my house and land in Alaska, to a project looming though still far off.

Sometime during that year of 1950, Dylan Thomas gave his first American reading, at the Y. I went with an artist friend to hear him, and we listened enthralled to that sonorous voice reading from Hardy and Yeats, from Auden and Edward Thomas, and finally from his own startling poems. Inspired, I was soon writing in a new style — needless to say, one not yet my own.

Other poets came to read from time to time, at the Y or the New School, and I was privileged to hear, long before I knew their work well, Edith Sitwell, cummings, William Carlos Williams, Mary and Padraic Colum, and once Carl Sandburg, who sat on a stool with a guitar and, along with a reading of his own poems, sang for us a few of the old ballads. Besides these, there were the gallery openings and receptions, the student gatherings, and other events of the art world in which I mainly moved.

When school moved out to the Cape for the summer I went along, like many others, to escape the city heat. That first summer I lived in a tent on the dunes, and walked the three miles into town over sandhills and through a scrub oak forest. With the sound of the ocean in my head day and night, I began reading *The Four Quartets* for the first time. The poems I wrote were long and sequential, filled with the sea wind, with the cries of gulls, and with occasional news from the town itself. I wrote continuously, and destroyed the better part of what I wrote.

After Labor Day nearly everyone returned to the city and to school. I stayed on alone for a few weeks, haunting the empty streets and the beaches, composing my verses, aware of my slow progress, but aware also that I was learning to write and that the time would somehow be sufficient for me to find myself.

I had no declared or public ambition to be a "writer," only that more secret ambition to learn as much as I could from the example of poets from the recent past as well as from the contemporary writers I had become familiar with; and, finally, to render justice to all that I was seeing and coming to know, the evidence for which I somehow understood was far more universal than my own limited experience of it. There was a voice, or so it seemed, not wholly mine, and through which I might learn to speak if I lived long enough and continued to write and to learn.

I made little effort to publish. I read my poems to friends, but seldom sent them out to magazines. I was more or less ignorant of the entire literary culture of magazines, editors, and schools of writing. I published one poem, my first, in the summer of 1950, in a small magazine called *Gale* that originated from New Mexico. The one poet of importance whom I met in my two years in New York was Weldon Kees, who showed up at a reception one evening in Hofmann's 8th Street studio. I knew Kees not as a poet but as a figure in the art world, a painter and a critic. My friends and acquaintances otherwise were painters and sculptors; some, like David Smith, Franz Kline, Willem de Kooning, and Jack Tworkov, already well known, others about to become so, and many who would never be.

Poetry for me was something that might grow of its own accord and in its own time, fed by whatever experience life sent my way, and nourished by the poets I was reading and whose work I was slowly absorbing and making in some way a part of my own potential aesthetic. And not only the poets but writers of fiction also, the writers everyone was reading in those days: Mann, Joyce, Proust, Kafka, Gide, Hamsun, and the prominent English and American modernists. It was an intense and fruitful time, the best of times, possibly, to have lived in New York.

What I have described here, as incomplete as it is, is the sum of one individual's early experience. To what extent it will prove valid for poets generally, I will leave to others to ponder and decide. I know that it does not describe the normal course for a poet nowadays, located as most of us are within the university.

As for vision, that abused and illusive word, I am convinced that it cannot be an acquisition. It is given, along with the elementary talent, in a confused and rudimentary form, to be nourished and struggled with, clarified through experience, and verified by the example of others. It is part of the world in which the poet lives and of which he too is a part, some portion of which may be realized and given form in a poem or a book.

What one's vision amounts to in its completed form, as incomplete as it must remain, will be mostly up to others to determine. Inevitably, one will feel at times that he has fallen short of his best inspiration, that the utmost in him has not been realized. Yet, in all fairness and generosity, the effort has not been wasted. Finally we have done the best with what we were given, have not held back from the required commitment in a conventional safety. In art, as in love, only the whole thing, the complete and consuming passion, really works.

It goes without saying that one must do something in order to live. How one chooses to live may to some extent be a matter of deliberate choice, as was Williams's decision to become a doctor, or Stevens's choice of insurance law as a profession. But the choice in such cases is surely related to the original impulse and cannot be arbitrary. When one is lucky and driven toward a goal he cannot see, the choices are apt to be the right ones, even when we cannot be certain that they are. It is a matter of faith, of steadfastness, along with a certain indifference to fashion. One's models are the great poets, the great examples, and no others.

It follows from what I have said, and drawing again on the example given us by the great work of the past, that we are the better for knowing many things, and for having immersed ourselves in life, in the world of people and events. One's sensibilities require not specialization but amplitude and depth in order to be nourished properly.

The sum of available knowledge for a poet has diminished considerably in recent times, and with this has come, inevitably, a reduction in resources. We have lost much of the ancient material of poetry, nearly the whole of its mythological background with all of its natural and supernatural transformations and embodiments — dragons and demons, metamorphic types, and so forth. That we can no longer look into the night sky and see there gods and heroes, whole constellations of beasts and actors, means that the world as imagination has been reduced in scope and value. It is in part the mission of poetry to keep these and all related things alive, to renew their character and their meaning, and in so doing keep alive the language we speak to ourselves and to others, and keep fresh also the heart and the spirit from which the words must come.

Books (since 1985)

Stories We Listened To. Bench Press, 1986.
Meditation on a Skull Carved in Crystal. Brooding Heron Press, 1989.
The Stars, the Snow, the Fire. Graywolf Press, 1989. Paperback edition, 1992.
New Poems, 1980–88. Story Line Press, 1990.
Rain Country. Mad River Press, 1990.

Periodicals

"Meditation on a Skull Carved in Crystal" (poem). *ZYZZYVA* (Fall 1987).
"Mudding Up" (prose). *ZYZZYVA* (Fall 1988).
"Notes from an Interrupted Journal" (prose). *Ohio Review* (Summer 1988).
"Interview" (with Robert Hedin). *Northwest Review* (Summer 1989).
"On Robinson Jeffers." *Gettysburg Review* (Summer 1989).
"Letters and Reflections" (prose). *Ohio Review* (Summer 1989).

Other Essays

Foreword. *Travels in Alaska*, by John Muir. Sierra Club Books, 1987.
Preface. *The Story and the Fable*, by Edwin Muir. Rowan Tree Press, 1987.
"Shadows." *Essays, Memoirs & Reflections*. Graywolf Press, 1987.
Foreword. *Season of Dead Water* (anthology of poems and essays on the Valdez oil spill). Breitenbush Books, 1990.
"Early Sorrow" (essay). *Ohio Review* (Spring 1992).

Reginald McKnight

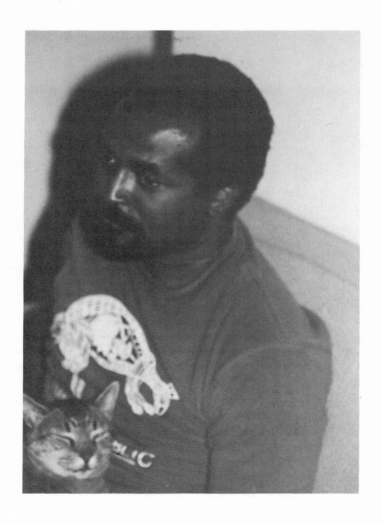

Reginald McKnight earned his master's degree in English from the University of Denver. His honors include a grant for literature from the National Endowment for the Arts, the Kenyon Review Award for Literary Excellence in fiction, the O'Henry Award, a Bread Loaf fellowship, the Drue Heinz Prize for Literature, the Bernice M. Slote Award for Fiction, and a Thomas J. Watson Foundation fellowship. Having taught at numerous colleges and universities over the past ten years, he currently teaches at Carnegie Mellon University in Pittsburgh.

IF YOU DON'T KNOW ME BY NOW

1. Get up! Stand up!

... in the 1980's many black writers of quality have come into conflict with the demand from without — responsibility as orthodoxy — and have begun to negotiate the right to their own inner interpretation of the essential gesture by which they are part of the black struggle.
— Nadine Gordimer, *The Essential Gesture* (1984)

As a black writer I must ask myself these questions. For what am I responsible? To whom am I responsible? What is the role of the black writer at the present time? (Why do I write and what should I write?) And what is the difference, if any, between the role of black writers and the role of writers who are not black? I cannot avoid asking these questions. Black people are in so much trouble, says Addison Gayle, Jr., critic and author/editor of *The Black Aesthetic* and *The Way of the New World*, that every black person, particularly our writers and critics, must commit him or herself to the amelioration of these problems. I must admit I am somewhat uncomfortable with any critic who demands that artistic works be shaped to heal social woes, but Gayle is not an isolated voice. Not only is his voice in harmony with a significant number of critics, but also with Hoyt Fuller, Larry Neal, Alex Laguma, Ngugi wa Thiong'o, N'tozake Shange, Brenda Marie Osbey, Langston Hughes (to a degree), Don L. Lee, Ishmael Reed, Ayi Kwei Armah, and Richard Wright. Because of my admiration for all of these writers, I cannot take his ideas lightly. Gayle argues that the Western literary tradition is too rife with Western bigotry and decadence to be of any value to black artists, writers, critics, and the black audience. He says that black Americans must "de-Americanize" themselves in order not to become as bigoted (self-hating) and decadent as those of the dominant culture. Gayle believes that black critics should discover images and ideas most relevant to the black audience and point them out to black artists. In short, he calls for the fomentation of a black aesthetic.

In his essay "Black Literature and the White Aesthetic," Gayle defines the black aesthetic in relief. He briefly discusses the "white" aesthetic from Aristotle to Nietzsche, citing black images in Western literature as those which connote evil, death, etc., and white images as those which describe goodness and purity. Gayle does not say specifically what black writers can do to remedy the problem. Instead he leaves us with:

> The acceptance of the phrase "Black is beautiful" is the first step in the destruction of the old table of the laws and the construction of new ones, for the phrase flies in the face of the whole ethos of the white aesthetic. . . . Black critics must dig beneath the phrase and unearth the treasure of beauty lying deep in the untoured regions of the Black experience. (Gayle 44-45)

While he does not give us much, he does suggest that there is something iconoclastic, revolutionary about a writer saying that black is sublime and white is base. But is it so revolutionary? Might it not be something akin to changing the order of the squares on a checkerboard from red-black-red to black-red-black, but not changing the rules of the game? After all, the rules to the game of literature are imbedded in the language in which it is written. Can one, under the auspices of a particular aesthetic, remove from the word *niggardly*, for example, its negative connotations? Won't *brilliant* continue to connote that which is full of light? I suppose this depends on how a writer handles these things, and I do realize that my questions are rather puerile. Gayle isn't merely asking us to eschew "bad" words or reverse their meanings. What he's asking black critics and writers to do is discover new images as a bulwark against an aesthetic system that denigrates black people. But as Henry Louis Gates says in "Criticism in the Jungle," "Black people have *always* been masters of the figurative: saying one thing to mean something quite other has been basic to black survival in oppressive Western cultures" (Gates 6, emphasis mine). But will any amount of signification, figuration, any kind of reversal, foment a renewed consciousness in those who read certain works? That's much harder to say. "To think oneself free," says Gates," "simply because one can claim—can utter—the negation of an assertion is not to think deeply enough. . . . It is to take the terms of one's assertion from a discourse determined by an

Other. Even the terms of one's so-called 'spontaneous' desire has been presupposed by the Other" (ibid. 7). Gates insists that critics concerned with black literature "seek to define *black* forms of language and literature peculiar to the black tradition, traditions of language-use related to, but distinct from, Western literary traditions" (ibid. 5). He does not say, however, that discovering such forms will perforce create a change in consciousness in those who read these works, though I can't believe he would term his close readings of literary works and his deep analytical thought as mere "play." It goes without saying that writers may bend and squeeze the language any way they please so long as the language maintains the essence of what makes it what it is (whatever it is), as long as it retains its power to move the reader, or as long as the reader is able to find meaning in it. But as T. S. Eliot says in "The Social Function of Poetry," the poet's (any writer's) duty is primarily to his or her language, and only secondarily to his or her society:

> *[H]is direct duty is to his language, first to preserve, and second to extend and improve. In expressing what other people feel he is also changing the feeling by making it more conscious; he is making people more aware of what they feel already, and therefore teaching them something about themselves. . . . [H]e can make his readers share consciously in new feelings which they had not experienced before. . . . [H]e discovers new variations of sensibility which can be appropriated by others. And in expressing them he is developing and enriching the language which he speaks. (Eliot 9)*

On the surface, it would appear that Gayle and Eliot are in agreement. Both are concerned with the social function of literature, and both believe that literary works can change society. But Eliot says that literature's influence on society is "very diffused, very indirect and difficult to prove" but that it does "in proportion to its excellence and vigor, effect the speech and sensibility" of a whole society (ibid. 12). Gayle, on the other hand, believes that the question for black critics and writers "is not how beautiful is a . . . poem or a novel but how much more beautiful has the poem or . . . novel made the life of a single black man" (Gayle xxii). The black aesthetic for Gayle is not concerned with art, but is "a corrective . . . a means of helping Black people out of the polluted mainstream of Americanism" (Gayle xxii). Ron Karenga, in his passionate, restless essay "Black Cultural Nationalism," concurs with Gayle. He says that "all [black] art must reflect and support the Black revolution, and any art that does not discuss and contribute to the revolution is invalid" (Gayle 31). He goes on to say:

> [A]ll Black art, irregardless [sic] of any technical require-
> ments, must have three basic requirements which make it
> revolutionary. In brief, it must be functional, collective and
> committing. It must be functional, that is useful. . . . we cannot
> accept the false doctrine of art for art's sake. (Gayle 32)

He says that black art must "expose the enemy, praise the people and support the revolution" (ibid. 32). His opinion was tempered in the heat of the black political struggle of the 1960s, and I must admit that, though I too warmed myself at those rhetorical fires, I now find his words vague and untenable. For I am black, shaped by the vicissitudes and exigencies of black life in America. And I am no Phillis Wheatley, no Alexander Pushkin or Henri Dumas, one of those blacks whose literary works reflect the "commonly shared hopes and expectations of the culture in which they were raised" (Wright 111). Isn't my work, no matter what its content and form, as black and "relevant" as it could possibly be? And even if my work does not toe Karenga's or Gayle's or anyone else's ideological line, does it not, nevertheless, express a valuable facet of black reality? Black people should revel in the fact that being black does not hold them to strict patterns of behavior, attitude, and belief. Diversity in the black world may result in factionalism, from time to time, but it adds depth to black culture. Without diversity black culture(s) would lack the critical internal dynamism to develop and grow, leaving them prone to be effected by external forces only. Black culture is primarily a series of cross-generational, cross-geographical, multiclass dialogues; as inextricable as the subatomic world, it is a perpetual search for the meaning of blackness, a palimpsest of sorts, where no single opinion is fully substantialized or meaningful without its opposite or alternate. I do not think it is, as Karenga and Gayle would have it, a set of givens which must be extolled or reshaped by critics and artists.

Conflict and struggle against the white world and the legacy of confusion and despair best characterizes the preponderance of black literature in content, theme, and purpose. From the idyllic if not atavistic strains of the *negritude* poets like Senghor and Diop to the sometimes vicious, sometimes visionary works of writers like Ayi Kwei Armah or Richard Wright, it is possible to trace the strong, developing veins of a nascent black political and social (and perhaps spiritual and emotional) identity. Black writers cannot help but relate some aspect of their blackness in their works. They would have to lie, or at least consciously inhibit themselves to do otherwise, much like Frank Yerby, who, for the most part, considered himself a literary purist. No matter how privileged and pampered a black person might be, there is no escaping the unique pains, problems, and quandaries of blackness. As Richard Wright says in "The Literature of the Negro in the United States":

> *I think you can readily see what it is that makes the difference between American Negro writing and just plain American writing.... [The] tradition of lament ... roll[s] down the decades, swelling, augmenting itself, becoming a vast reservoir of bitterness and despair and infrequent hope. This tradition of bitterness was to become so complex, was to assume such a tight, organic form, that most people would think, upon examining it, that all Negroes had embedded in their flesh and bones some peculiar propensity toward lamenting and complaining. (Wright 118)*

Black writers, regardless of political hue, are aware that their psyches have been shaped by their blackness perhaps more than education, nationality, or religion. I am not implying some sort of genetic predisposition. But I do insist that black people have to deal with life, either individually or as a whole, in the context of a world controlled by white people, white people who have generally feared, despised, humiliated, and brutalized them. Can any black writer venture forth simply as an individual?

2. Standin on Shaky Ground

In 1984, Rick Atkinson of the *Washington Post* wrote an article on the strained relations between Democratic presidential candidate Jesse Jackson and American Jews. Atkinson claimed that Jackson, while speaking with a group of black journalists, referred to Jews as "Hymie" and New York City as "Hymietown." Atkinson is white, and few readers, black or white, were surprised that he had reported Jackson's slurs. What did surprise many readers was that Atkinson learned of Jackson's remarks from Milton Coleman, a black journalist from the *Post* who had been in that group of journalists to which Jackson had made the "Hymie" remarks. The controversy sparked by Atkinson's report raged for nearly three months (and may never be forgotten by Jews — and many others — of voting age at that time).

White readers were upset because Jackson's remarks exposed him as possibly too insensitive and bigoted to be a viable candidate (as if the good reverend had had a prayer in the first place). Many blacks had the same concern, but what mostly concerned them was the rightness or wrongness of Milton Coleman's reportage. For many blacks, the majority, I dare say, the reaction was immediate and visceral: Milton was wrong, they said. Many called him a traitor, an Uncle Tom. A few made death threats against him and his family. Many blacks asked him whether he considered himself "black first . . . or . . . a reporter first" (Coleman 1-C).

Coleman is, of course, a journalist, but the question is every bit as relevant to fiction writers and poets as it is to journalists, peace officers, lawyers, politicians, military officers, educators, or any black person in the public domain. We are, in a sense, the leaders and the voices of black society. Are we not, as Addison Gayle says, responsible to blacks first? Should we, given the economic, political, spiritual, and social crises in which we find ourselves, expose our weaknesses and faults to those of the dominant culture, many of whom are only too happy to exploit these weaknesses in any way possible? Coleman, in defense of himself, says that in post–civil rights, post–affirmative action America, the question "Which side are you on?" is no longer relevant. We are functioning on the "next level" (ibid. 8-C), he says. I do not know exactly what he means by the "next level"; he does not explain. It is my guess that he means that because American blacks are legally free to vote, live where they please, and so on, we are, for the most part, pretty much like Americans of the dominant culture.

But I am not so sure that Coleman's assessment is accurate. Black people are still economically, educationally, and politically far behind those of the dominant culture. A few years ago I read somewhere that though the majority of the black population in the United States are middle class, 90 percent of that middle class are employed by the federal government. This makes some blacks feel more like wards of the state rather than a solid, self-sufficient middle class. Furthermore, says Harvard economist Glen C. Loury in an article for the *Chronicle of Higher Education*, "After rising during the 1970s, the percentage of college students who are black has actually begun to decline" (Loury 100). The May 6, 1991, issue of *Newsweek* says that "College enrollment among black 18- to 24-year-olds was 15.5 percent in 1970; in 1989 it was 23.5 percent . . . [and] in 1976, 6.6 percent of all master's degrees went to blacks; only 4.6 percent were awarded in 1989, . . . [and] Only 811 doctorate degrees were awarded to blacks in 1989, compared to 1,056 in 1979 ("New Politics of Race" 27). There has been, according to another relatively recent article in *Newsweek*, "an ugly resurgence of racism around the country, from the hazing of a black student at the famed Citadel academy in Charleston, S.C., to the beating and death of a black in New York City's white community. In Arizona . . . Gov. Evan Mecham revoked his predecessor's proclamation of the [Martin Luther King, Jr.'s birthday] holiday; in Georgia, 300 rock-throwing Ku Klux Klansmen broke up a 'brotherhood march' through all-white Forsyth County" ("Uneasy Festival" 24). I don't point out these facts to illustrate black victimization for its own sake, and I'm not saying that blacks don't occasionally do egregious things to nonblacks as well as to one another. I'm simply suggesting that there's little evidence of Coleman's "next level" so far as I can see. Coleman himself may be on the next level, and therefore immune to "inside" language such as "Let's talk black talk" (Jackson's purported preface to his anti-Semitic words), but I feel quite certain that most blacks are not.

I do not consider Coleman a traitor or an "Uncle Tom," his specious defense notwithstanding. But I do not think I would have done what he did. My reasons are too lengthy to discuss in this paper. But my own hypothetical behavior aside, I must admit that I am happy, in a way, for what Coleman did, for it added another inevitable dimension to black culture, deepening it, expanding it. And while some would argue that Coleman's behavior is no more "expanding" for black society than freedmen who betrayed escaped slaves, I would counter that the two acts are substantially different. For the former could only improve the lot of black people in the long run, if it forces our political leaders to regard others as they themselves want to be regarded, but the latter proved to do not one speck of good for anyone, black or white. As each of us moves toward that "next level," we are incrementally freed from behavior which is based on racial imperatives. We become less narrow as a people, in attitude and aspect. Coleman did not report Jackson's epithet merely because he is a journalist. There were several other black journalists in the meeting that day. He did what he did because his world is not strictly black. He has been touched and changed by his contact with the dominant culture, and other social groups besides. Perhaps he truly does engage the world from a different level.

Coleman seems to have benefited (if "benefit" is the right word) from the same sort of expansion that Matthew Arnold advocates in *Essays on Criticism*. Arnold argues for keeping literary criticism separate from ideological intent because political predisposition enfeebles artistic and critical thinking. Arnold demands that critics "see things as they are" so they are not tempted to narrow their view of what is artistically sound and aesthetically pleasing:

> *For the practical [read prejudiced] man is not apt for fine distinctions, and yet in these distinctions truth and the highest culture greatly find their account.... [A] thing which he has always been used to look at from one side only ... looked at from another side may be beneficent and beautiful. (Buckler 433)*

Arnold could be described as a cosmopolitan. He claims to eschew anything that would narrow an artist's or critic's grasp of that which is both aesthetically perfect and also lies outside the sphere of purely factional concerns. A literary work, in his opinion, must express the human experience in the broadest terms possible. He praises the ancient Greeks for focusing their poetry on noble, larger-than-life characters (whatever that means) and placing emphasis on their actions while keeping expressions subordinate. Such broadness of scope, Arnold insists, gives classical Grecian poetry a universality to which all readers, regardless of culture, historical place or ethnicity, could relate. There is no room for elitism, bigotry, jingoism, or chauvinism. The critical/artistic mind must be given room to explore or it loses its creative force. If it loses its force, it cannot expand the field of ideas through which artists must sift for their creative work. Ideas seemingly maleficent, and ideas seemingly beneficent must be treated evenhandedly, "without any notion of favoring or injuring, in the practical sphere, one power or the other" (ibid. 438).

Addison Gayle, however, is uncomfortable with such a formula. It is his claim that this sort of eclecticism actually stifles black creativity. He sees the urge toward objectivity and universality, in certain black artists, as nothing more than the impulse to be white:

> *He [the black writer] attempts to gain acceptance as an American by arguing that there are not two separate cultural streams dividing the two races. There is, he supposes, only one giant cultural ocean in which white and black experiences have been churned into one. The result of such assimilation is the transformation of black men into carbon copies of white men. (Gayle 386)*

He goes on to say that the problem of the color line is insoluble, that the idea of the American melting pot is archaic, and that black writers ought to give up their hopes for assimilation and speak directly to black people. And I must admit that his argument is compelling, given the rise in racial antipathy in recent years. But there is a logical leap in his argument. Cultural division does not necessarily determine artistic orientation, though it may certainly affect socio-political beliefs which, in turn, may determine one's choice of subject matter. Even if we do not accept the fact that black writers will ever be accepted as Americans, why should they be, how could they be, precluded from the ranks of world literature? I realize that I share similar or identical experiences and impressions with many other black people. And I know that the black reading audience may very likely understand many of my works with a clarity, empathy, and depth much greater than nonblack readers. I realize that my people are the only ones likely able to judge my work in terms of its importance to black culture. But whether I can or should create works that can help "de-Americanize" black people, expose the enemy, or support the revolution, is hard for me to say.

Ezekiel Mphahlele says in his 1974 essay "The Ethnic Imperative" that revolutionary writers take it upon themselves to create new imperatives for the masses. He commends their intentions, but sees no way to accomplish this on any level other than the "educational process in the uniqueness of the individual's emotions in the response to art" (Mphahlele 18). His opinion on the employment of art as a guide to social action, however, is less than optimistic:

> When some ... say that literature can help the working class in determining the specific goals of revolution and moving towards that end, we know they are romanticizing the worker. Those we conveniently call the working class ... spend their leisure time in ways that do not include literature at the level where we analyze it. They have their own poetry, their own spiritual pursuits. I do not see how we as writers can play around with symbols and images and fantasies and mirrors and representations at a level that does not correspond to that of the working class and yet ask of its members to decode those verbal messages for use in the class struggle, wherever this latter may be found. Do we then, after the hypothetical revolution, call them back to peaceful order with different symbols ... ? I think this is romanticism carried to the point of arrogance. (ibid. 19)

Critic Simon Gikandi (countering both Arnold and Mphahlele) says that the insistence on the part of some writers and critics that literature can move the worker to revolt is a "misconception nurtured by both 'vulgar' Marxists and their ideological sparring partners, that art can be reduced to specific political and philosophical forms of consciousness; hence ideology tends to be taken as dogma" (Gikandi

112-13) and by consequence reduces literature to tract. And he goes on to say, being prompted by Terry Eagleton, that true ideology is a mode of perception which permits us to see the world in an articulate way, a system for grappling with the various mystifications of our seemingly "fragmented" unreadable and chaotic world. He says:

> It [ideology] is an instrument for understanding creations of culture and of relating these creations to their specific social and historical structures; it is a mode of consciousness that helps the artist analyze patterns in the experiences he is writing about and accord them some meaning. . . . [Also] a literary ideology enables the novelist to shape and rationalize the world in his novels; it functions as a philosophical referent, what Karl Mannheim calls "the ultimate and fundamental interpreter of the flux in the contemporary world." We can thus argue that the limitation of the modernist novel as an interpretation of contemporary reality is the author's assumption that he can represent a fragmented world without ideological mediation. (ibid. 113)

Gikandi does not specifically say what his ideological leanings are, but it's quite clear, given the sources in his short essay, that his inclination is decidedly Marxian. There's no doubt that Arnold would label him a "practical" man, were he able to. And if we are to be honest we must admit that Arnold himself is no more or less a "practical" individual than either his Greek artists and critics or Simon Gikandi, or Mphahlele, for in our age it is very much a truism that all human activities and all human relationships are political, and I will make no argument with this issue. This entire essay, though it means to extricate the writer from the demands of those like Gayle and Karenga and even Gikandi, is really no more than a defense of my own political position. My own literary works have a definite "shape and rationale" which may bring either joy or discomfort to those who read them. Yet wherever one might find me or place me on the political spectrum, I remain quite certain that my work is not a gun that I can aim at this or the other target.

Writers can no more define reality for the "masses" or define their conscience or propel them toward revolution than they can feed them with words. Those who read fiction, poetry, and drama read either to entertain themselves or to confirm what they already believe about the world, or to learn something new. But they won't change unless they permit themselves to be changed. I am sure that black writers hope that, while being entertained, their audience gets a fuller grasp of the black experience. The black reading audience should (and when I say "should" I am expressing a hope rather than an admonition) read as many black writers as possible in order to reap the vast wealth of black being. They should be hungry to know what it is "like" to be black and female, black and poor, black and West Indian, black and homosexual, and so on. They should take a deep interest in both the future and the history of the black world.

The black writer has the potential to awaken or deepen that interest. As I have said, there is no ultimate definition for blackness; it can only be explored, expanded, revealed. Blackness begins and ends with the separate experiences of each and every black person. It cannot be defined within the walls of a single ideology. Am I in some way, by insisting that the only definition of blackness is to be found in the experience of every black person, but not venturing to say what makes an individual black, equivocating, begging the question? Perhaps so, but my only answer to that is the same thing I am told Louis Armstrong said to the woman who asked him what jazz is. "Lady," Satchmo said, "If you have to ask, you'll never know." I must accept the various expressions of blackness as they appear to me. I may not like all of them, but then I shouldn't be expected to, either. Yet in experiencing each of them I discover a great deal more of who I am. I discover the boundaries of blackness, which at present, appear to me to be infinitely distant from where I, as an individual, stand. And, at the same time, very close. In my work, I'm hopeful that some reader out there will find a blackness she did not know before. If she happens to be black, I hope she'll find something in the work that will allow her to see that we are much more than she ever thought we were.

I wouldn't mind having that kind of effect on the nonblack reader as well. The influence of the nonblack reading audience has been both a boon and a hindrance to the evolution of black literature and has tended to obfuscate the role of black writers. Many black writers, both American and African, at one time wrote chiefly to express to whites their humanity, their potential and desire for full citizenship. Richard Wright, in his essay "The Literature of the Negro in the United States," refers to this type of black literature as the Narcissistic Level of expression:

> [T]here were some few Negroes who, through luck, diligence, and courage . . . [rose and made] the culture of their nation their own even though that nation still rejected them; and, having made the culture of their nation their own, they hurled pleading words against the deaf ears of white America until

> *the very meaning of their lives came to be in telling how and*
> *what the rejection which their country leveled against them*
> *made them feel.... Negro writers were condemned by Amer-*
> *ica to stand before a Chinese Wall and wail that they were*
> *men like other men, that they felt as others felt. It is this*
> *relatively static stance of emotion that I call the Narcissistic*
> *Level. (Wright 124)*

European and American publishers, particularly in the 1920s and the 1960s (two decades when blacks were more or less *en vogue*), were eager to publish either literature which did little more than beg the question of black people's humanity, or that which would "tell it like it is," or that which gave white audiences the new, the mysterious, the exotic. They gave the white world what it believed to be the inner workings of the "black mind." The writers themselves knew that they were mainly speaking to a white audience and rarely gave the audience other than what it wanted to hear. Perhaps they consoled themselves with the notion that limited expression was better than none at all.

I'm sure that in some sense there really is something that could be called the "black mind," but I can't say I would ever want it encompassed by either the language of philosophy or literature. Several years ago I was in a graduate-school writing workshop listening to student after student discuss a story of mine entitled "The Honey Boys." It was a rather mundane discussion and I was listening with but one ear. Then one of my fellow students read a line of dialogue by the narrator, who is black. After reading the line, the student said, "This just doesn't seem to be something a black person would say." I vehemently interjected with: "Which black person? Are you saying there's something out there in the wide world that a guy can't think or feel just 'cause he's black?" The student never got a chance to answer me—though I know he felt terrible about what he'd said—because the professor told me to shut up. He didn't permit you to speak up in class if your story was being discussed. Moreover, I didn't talk to the student after class because the professor summoned me to his office immediately after dismissing us. The professor asked me to sit down, and then he looked me square in the eye. "Look, Reg," he said, "you can't let yourself get rattled like that about criticism. You're big, you're black, and you're intimidating (though you don't intimidate me—I worked with lots of black students in Milwaukee) and I won't permit that kind of intimidation in my classroom. It's not conducive to free speech." I tried to explain to the professor that my anger had absolutely nothing to do with the student's "criticism" but his idiotic presumption that blacks appear to be predisposed to certain behavior. I tried to say that "This doesn't seem to be something this character would say," is criticism, but "This doesn't seem to be what a black guy would say," is racist.

The professor was having none of that. He fixed his stare upon me again and said, "You know, when I taught in Milwaukee I had a lot of black students, and not one of them ever made an outburst like yours. Not even remotely. You're too sensitive." And then he suggested that it was probably a result of my class and upbringing that made me this way, and that if I'd been raised in the ghetto, I'd be a lot tougher. I was so angry and astonished that I could not speak. I gave up on reiterating my objections to the student's words. I gave up on trying to explain to the man that I was no "rich boy." My father had been a mess sergeant in the air force. My mother worked as a cook in a nursery school. I decided to give up on trying to explain anything to anyone for the rest of my tenure at the University of Denver. That afternoon, I simply stood up, mumbled an apology, and left the professor's office. That's the black mind for you.

3. What You See Is What You Get

As I stated earlier, writers must resign themselves to the fact that even the most well-wrought novel, poem, or play, though it may be stuffed with social truths, does not have the capacity to elicit more than individual response. And how it will affect the individual reader is beyond knowing. This does not mean literature has no social function; quite the contrary, for art, according to Raymond Williams in *Marxism and Literature*, "is not a special kind of object but one in which the aesthetic function is dominant. . . . [A]t the same time the aesthetic function is not an epiphenomenon of other functions but a codeterminant of human reaction to reality" (Williams 53). In other words, art is not a separate category outside reality; it is reality. It is individual response which makes art appear to turn back on itself. Williams goes on to say that:

> *If we are asked to believe that all literature is 'ideology' in the crude sense that its dominant intention . . . is the communication or the imposition of 'social' or 'political' meanings and values, we can only, in the end, turn away. If we are asked to believe that all literature is 'aesthetic,' in the sense that its dominant intention . . . is the beauty of language and form, we may stay a little longer but still in the end we turn away. . . .*

> *Some people will lurch from one position to the other. More,*
> *in practice, will retreat to an indifferent acknowledgment of*
> *complexity, or assert the autonomy of their own (usually*
> *consensual) response. . . . But it is really much simpler to face*
> *facts of the range of intentions and effects, and to face it as a*
> *range. All writing carries references, meanings and values.*
> *(Williams 155)*

In April of 1981, at Colorado College in Colorado Springs, novelist Elie Wiesel gave a lecture entitled "Remembering the Holocaust." Wiesel, a survivor of several Nazi death camps, told his audience at one point that he was always filled with the feeling of failure upon completion of each page because he expected them to burst into flames as he wrote them. Because none of them ever did, he felt he had not fully elucidated the horrors of the most vile crime committed against the human race. There is probably no writer who, in some way, does not understand this feeling of inevitable failure to recreate reality. But as Williams suggests, it is not just the inadequacy of writing itself but the range of consciousness which interprets it, the range which makes up society. Each of us fills a space in the hermeneutical range as readers and writers.

Haki Madhubuti (Don L. Lee) expresses a notion similar to Wiesel's in one of his early poems:

> *I ain't seen no poem stop a .38*
> *I ain't seen no stanza break a honkie's head*
> *I ain't seen no metaphor stop a tank.*
> *(Henderson 332)*

Writers seek to capture the essence of their society in terms of its language, physical makeup, religious/spiritual beliefs, politics, aspirations, history, humor, pathos, sense of beauty, etc. This demands not only total commitment to art, but a sort of cohesion, an intimacy with one's society as well. Even those writers (probably most of them) who find themselves at extreme odds with society, wishing either to change it, excoriate its institutions, or expose the enemy within it, must realize that their work: 1) finds its fullest meaning within the context of the writer's own society, 2) helps to support the writer's society because of its intimacy with it. The work, as I have said before, is, if nothing more, certain to add a fuller texture to society, thus enriching it, and 3) could very likely be embraced by those the writer means to castigate if readers interpret it in ways that are paradoxical to the writer's intentions. "All art," says Hayden

White in his essay "Historical Dialectic," "is ideology . . . and . . . all ideology is Utopian" (Davis 158). But the same maxim applies to interpretation. And interpretation is a two-edged sword.

I am always surprised and disconcerted when someone, having read my short story "Rebirth," says of it that if one didn't know that the story's author was black, one might think him white, and not only white but someone who very much supports the world view of Theodore Treadwell, the principal character. I am dismayed when those who read "Peaches," "The Honey Boys," and "Gettin to Be Like the Studs" say to me, "You know, man, I agree with your idea that we and they [blacks and whites] just can't ever be friends or lovers. It's the stone truth, man, the stone deal." And I am still crackling with anger at the reader from the *Bread Loaf Quarterly* who said of "How I Met Idi at the Bassi Dakaru Restaurant, "If you . . . did more with the anticolonial racism of Idi, that would make for a more interesting story as a whole." A more interesting story indeed. Anticolonial racism indeed. Yet I must admit I find this reading fascinating. I had always perceived the story to be about Africa's desire to master Western ways, Western technology, while preserving her cultural integrity, a sort of large-scale calquing. I intend it to be a story about African pride, not African racism. What fascinates me about the editor's peculiar response, as well as the various responses to any of my stories, is the bizarre mutations a story goes through in the hands of a reader. Shock, dismay, and anger notwithstanding, I must accept these comments at face value. A text is more than what its author says it is. According to Wolfgang Iser, all texts are actually two texts. The first, of course, is the "artistic" text, that which is created by the author. The second, the "esthetic" text, is that which is realized by the reader:

> *The work is more than the text, for the text only takes on life when it is realized, and furthermore the realization is by no means independent of the individual disposition of the reader — though this in turn is acted upon by the different patterns of the text. The convergence of text and reader brings the literary work into existence, and this convergence can never be precisely pinpointed, but must always remain virtual, as it is not to be identified with the reality of the text or with the individual disposition of the reader. (Davis 377)*

This is a very important phenomenon for any writer to be aware of. Reading is an imaginative, participatory, creative process. Once a story enters the consciousness of the reader, it ceases to be the product of one mind, that is, the writer's mind. "A literary text," says Iser, ". . . must be conceived in such a way that it will engage the reader's imagination in the task of working things out for himself, for reading is only a pleasure when it is active and creative" (Iser 377).

There is little that I can do to make Theodore Treadwell of "Rebirth" less sympathetic without being unfair to him or without reducing the story to a tract, thus condescending to my reader. As I see Treadwell he is mad, funny, sad, vicious, lascivious, and weak. But if there is someone out there who, after having read the story, feels compelled to emulate Treadwell, so be it. That is the scatter shot of literature. There is little that I could do in terms of "improving" the story in hopes of turning anyone away from racist sentiment. Such a story probably wouldn't make her less a racist, and such a person probably would not be less disposed toward racism because of one short story or another. If your "getting" (getting what I hope you get) "Rebirth" is contingent on your knowing that the author is black, I may despise you, but it is your story as such as it is mine. There is little I can do to bend you toward my will.

As for "Peaches," "The Honey Boys," and "Gettin to Be Like the Studs," my feelings are not so unambiguous. After all, each story deals with a relationship between a black person and a white person, and each of those relationships falls apart. But I write about relationships whose dynamics I am familiar with. I was raised in a military family; most of the neighborhoods in which I was raised, most of the schools I attended, and most of my peers were white. These relationships I write about in my stories do not fall apart because there is some immovable cultural wall between blacks and whites which keeps them from being friends, though I am to some degree trying to express that there may be something wrong with our society, which poisons amity between the so-called races. But beyond this, I am trying to say something about friendship in its "purer" sense. In "Peaches" and "The Honey Boys," both sets of principal characters (Rita and Marc, Spider and Caspar) could have all been the same color and the same breakdowns still could have occurred. The word *nigger* in "Peaches" and the punchline "pizzas don't scream when you put them in the oven" and the other insensitive remarks Caspar makes in "The Honey Boys" have relatively little to do with the dissolution of each friendship. They fall apart because they, like most other human relationships, are built on misapprehensions. Rita decides to drop Marc, principally because Marc reveals too many of his weaknesses to Rita as he badgers her for the kind of relationship he wants. "What's wrong with me?" he asks again and again, opening himself up for damning scrutiny—and, secondarily, because of the way she interprets her father's little speech about peaches. So, it is not merely the "race" issue that fuddles their love, but Marc's youth, his insecurity, their different classes, and so on.

Caspar's and Spider's friendship never really takes off because the utilitarian Spider, perhaps because of his rootlessness, perhaps because he is a son of a bitch, is incapable of love. And he is not incapable of love and friendship simply because he is a black kid living in a mostly white world. Caspar doesn't fit in well either, yet his heart is full of an oafish, ham-handed love. This story is, more or less, the same story as "Gettin to Be Like the Studs": two socially marginal adolescents befriend each other, then split because one discovers he is able to move up "a couple of notches on the popularity scale," provided he leaves the other behind. Kids do this sort of thing all the time. In my experience color has little to do with it. All three of these stories are fleshed out (no pun) by the black/white themes; that makes each perhaps a little more interesting. And as I have said, I am comfortable writing what I know—not only comfortable with it but responsible for it. But I hope these characters are deeper than skin deep. Nevertheless, the gap between my intent and any potential reader's response is broad enough to allow for a wide variety of interpretations. Whether I agree with any of these interpretations does not preclude the fact that they have an effect on rewritings or on ideas for new stories. One way or another, they affect my work, helping me to consider its power, its weaknesses, or its ambiguities. I am in a dialogue of sorts with my reader. Sometimes we hear each other, at times we do not. Who can figure it? As Nadine Gordimer puts it, "The writer is eternally in search of entelechy in relation to his society. Everywhere in the world, he needs to be left alone, and at the same time to have a vital connection with others; needs artistic freedom and knows it cannot exist without its wider context; feels the two presences within—creative self-absorption and conscionable awareness—and must resolve whether these are locked in death struggle, or are really foetuses in a twinship of fecundity" (Gordimer 299).

I honestly don't know what to make of my work with regard to social or ethnic imperatives. For though my writing is as black as it can possibly be, it is nevertheless an expression of my blackness, a blackness that is both solitary and communal. But my writing is more than black. I, like most black American writers, am a cultural mulatto. And I do not mean that I am some sort of mongrelized mishmash that is neither one thing or the other. I mean that I am metablack. I express all that has touched me, and all that I am. Some of the things I write may very well improve the life of some black woman or some black man (or some nonblack person), but I won't take credit for it. The way people interpret my stories invariably mystifies me.

I began writing twenty-one or twenty-two years ago, and the first and only person who ever read my work then was my sister, Regina, who'd always tell me my writing was beautiful and that I should keep at it. Later, I found the courage to put my work in the hands of my friends, some of whom also wrote, and they would say things like, "weird," or "cool," or "humpf," or "Didn't read it," and hand it back to me, looking thoughtful and bemused. Still later I'd let my teachers look at what I was writing (for myself and on my own) and they'd let loose with the red ink—pints of the stuff—and use words like "fascinating!," "intriguing!," and every teacher's favorite "promising!" Then in college I took my first workshop and I started hearing things like "interesting story, but . . . ," "great potential, but . . . ," "reminds me of your other story but. . . ." In graduate school people started asking me to explain my stories, to interpret and defend them. And someone once even said to me, "Why even write a story like this?" I couldn't then and I cannot now even begin to explain or defend or justify why I write what I write, or simply why I write at all.

I write for all sorts of reasons. I write because a couple teachers and my sister told me I had a knack for writing. I write because some other people told me I had no talent for it at all. I write because my grandfather, my father, and my mother filled my head with stories from the time I was old enough to ask questions. I write because I am a bullshitter and don't mind being paid for it. I write to exorcise my fears and anxieties. I write for revenge. I write because there is a Niagara of words in my head and I feel much better when I can pour them onto paper. I write because I enjoy writing, and if I do not satisfy this critic or that editor, I know that just around the corner, and perhaps with a rewrite or two, or ten, there will be others who for some reason or another I will satisfy. There is a distinct and intractable tension between the writer's ability to make his or her audience perceive, and his or her ability to prompt an audience to act upon those perceptions. When all is said and done, writers must admit that their work is really peripheral to the lives of the public. We lack the force to translate vision into action.

Force is the domain of politicians, not writers. Politicians create laws which regulate lives and temper our social realities. Literature may very well propose, but politicians dispose. I am not suggesting that literary visions cannot seep into the realm of social reality, for as I said earlier, literature is real. Because it is capable of increasing our capacity to perceive, the greater is our capacity for insight. The greater the insight, the greater the willingness to question one's relation to the outer world. Literature may not move the masses in any direct manner, but it does place the burden of knowledge on them. But what my audience does with my work is out of my hands.

Works Cited

Buckler, William E., ed. *Prose of the Victorian Period*. Boston: Houghton Mifflin, 1958.

Coleman, Milton. "When the Candidate Is Black Like Me." *Denver Post*. April 2, 1984, p. 1-C.

Eliot, T. S. *On Poetry and Poets*. New York: Noonday, 1961.

Gates, Henry Louis, Jr. *Black Literature and Literary Theory*. New York: Methuen, 1984.

Gayle, Addison, Jr. *The Black Aesthetic*. New York: Doubleday, 1971.

Gikandi, Simon. *Reading the African Novel*. Portsmouth, N.H.: Heinemann, Inc., 1988.

Gordimer, Nadine. *The Essential Gesture*. New York: Knopf, 1988.

Henderson, Stephen. *Understanding the New Black Poetry: Black Speech and Black Music as Poetic References*. New York: William Morrow, 1973.

Loury, Glen C. "Why Preferential Admission Is Not Enough for Blacks." *Chronicle of Higher Education*. March 25, 1983, p. 100.

Mphahlele, Ezekiel. *Voices in the Whirlwind*. New York: Hill and Wang, 1974.

"The New Politics of Race." *Newsweek*. May 6, 1991, p. 27.

"An Uneasy Festival for Martin Luther King." *Newsweek*. January 26, 1987, p. 24.

Wright, Richard. *White Man Listen!* New York: Doubleday, 1957.

Books

Moustapha's Eclipse. University of Pittsburgh Press, 1988.
I Get on the Bus. Little, Brown, 1990.
The Kind of Light That Shines on Texas. Little, Brown, 1992.

Periodicals

"Gettin to Be Like the Studs." *Leviathan*. (1981).
"Rebirth." *Leviathan* (1981).
"First I Look at the Purse." *Players* (1984).
"Uncle Moustapha's Eclipse." *Prairie Schooner* (1985).
"Mali Is Very Dangerous." *Massachusetts Review* (1986).
"The Kind of Light That Shines on Texas." *Kenyon Review* (1989).
From *I Get on the Bus. Callaloo* (1989).
"Roscoe in Hell." *Black American Literature Forum* (1989).
"Quitting Smoking." *Kenyon Review* (1991).

Anthology

"The Kind of Light That Shines on Texas." *Prize Stories 1990: The O'Henry Awards*. Doubleday, 1990.

William Logan

Deborah Brackenbury

William Logan is a graduate of Yale and the University of Iowa. He has received a grant from the National Endowment for the Arts, a grant from the Ingram Merrill Foundation, and the Amy Lowell Poetry Traveling Scholarship. In 1989 he received the Citation for Excellence in Reviewing from the National Book Critics Circle and the Peter I. B. Lavan Younger Poets Award from the Academy of American Poets. He lives in Cambridge, England, and Gainesville, Florida, where he directs the writers' workshop at the University of Florida.

WEIRD SCIENCE

16 Woodedge Lane, Braintree, Massachusetts

In the summer of 1953, when I was two and a half, I set out to discover the world. I was accompanied on this journey by the faithful Moey, who as it happened was a dog; and we took as provision against the cold of alien climates a heavy if somewhat small blanket. After a time we came to a vast entablature of field and brush, soon to become the tidy yards of damp pastel houses. Beyond us lay a forest and a dire swamp. We took counsel with ourselves on this zone of the forbidden; but as we were preparing to enter it, we were discovered and dragged back to a home we had forsworn.

In these penal years, before I was able to read, certain local mysteries arrested me in my ignorance. There were, for example, the boulders which had imposed themselves, like conversation pieces, on scattered backyards. On ours, for instance. Our boulder presented various faces, as was appropriate to this mild community, and geometry had left its sundry angles in acute and imprecise relation, as if Escher had been employed to design the Precambrian Age. The glacier which had deposited this coarse evidence had left no other trace, having been closely followed by herbivorous bulldozers and cheap architects. The houses looked frailer than the boulders, and we looked frailer than the houses. On this modest cul-de-sac — shaped like a bulb of mercury, but called hopefully a "lane" — I was introduced to the dark resources of reading. I was drawn — I couldn't have been more than four — to an uplifting moral text whose purpose was to discourage the young from household accident. This it hazarded by detailing the mishaps of three well-regarded young ducks who attempted certain ingenious acrobatic feats, such as changing a light bulb while standing on a rickety ladder. What attracted me to this text was not its transparent lesson plan for misadventure but the author's remarkable comprehension of zoological anatomy; in falling, each duck broke a particular bone, and the bones were, for example, the tibia and the fibula.

I reached two conclusions from this authority. First, that there were words more intransigent than "horsey" and "bunny," words which might drop into the backyard as easily as, say, a boulder. Second, that ducks had not only an uncommon vocabulary but a skeletal structure recognizably human. I later realized, after a course of empirical research which involved the minute digestion of certain close relatives of these ducks, that I had been over-hasty in my second conclusion. From the carcass of a Christmas turkey I deduced, in rapid succession, that all moral texts performed their devotions at the risk of fiction, that all texts were moral texts, and that there was no God. I was, however, a compliant student, and I memorized the book, under the impression that this was what constituted reading.

Religious training: Episcopalian, or Methodist if the
    Episcopalians had raised their church more than five
    miles away
Years effectively lost to organized religion: 11 (ages 5–16)
Reason for leaving church: Poor supernatural comprehension
Belief in a god (as %): 0

1868 Main Road, Westport Point, Massachusetts

My father had been an aluminum salesman, with a route that snaked upward through Massachusetts and possibly a little farther into New Hampshire and Maine. By the time I was five, however, he had been given a desk of responsibilities in Providence, taking direction from the "home office" — that mysterious phrase which caught in our determining ears. My father was neither provident nor improvident, and went through life with four hundred dollars in his savings account.

The little realm of my childhood, that childhood, was bounded by the ocean, and the ocean for our intents was the long duned shore of Baker's Beach. John Baker lived behind our house, down the hill we used to sled in winter, through the piney edge of his property. He was a bachelor, perhaps fifty when I first knew him, and because he was not intolerant of children I was permitted to visit him. His house was sparely furnished, the rooms crimped and, as I remember, without rugs.

The striking thing about Mr. Baker — the attaching aspect, the nexus of fascination — was that he never seemed to work. In the summer he could be seen in genial occupation of his beach, where he performed no service or labor. He was, in a robust way, seigneurial. In the winter he went on vacation, and might send me postcards from Utah or Stratford-on-Avon. During the day he was often at home, a large man doing odd jobs or cooking himself some dinner. He was unstintingly kind to a bothersome, inquisitive child. In his roll-top desk he had an ancient album of stamps, dog-eared and held together with a rubber band. I had a modest stamp collection myself, which he used to improve with small gifts of old definitives — the beauties of Scott A168 and A172. He had a store of other treasures, and some rough faculty as a teacher. Once he unwrapped a cheesecloth to show me his set of brass knuckles — I had no idea what they were, scratched and scarred like a fistful of wedding rings.

In this innocent hour I was allowed to visit whomever I liked, and to roam. I plucked dandelions from the gloomy yard of the old ladies next door, who made me weak lemonade. One owned the house, beyond a high stone wall, and the other had come for a visit in the forties *and stayed*. I used to visit Mr. Baker's older brother, who lived in a whaler's cottage across from us. He and his wife were travelers, and entertained me with plates of small cookies — they told me dozens of stories, but I remember only the dry, sweet cookies. Once they offered me, like a slice of cake, a black wedge of lava pried from the slope of a Hawaiian volcano.

Our house was protected by its own stone wall — on which, in summer, I used to lay wilted garden vegetables for sale — but I had my quiet, undisturbed freedoms. Often I would wander down Main Road a mile or more, past the general store with its metal soda chest and its tempting pocket of bottle caps, past the closet of a post office where you could still buy commemoratives a dozen years after their issue, down to Lee's Wharf where the boats sailed in with lobsters and swordfish. I trailed past the bins of squirting clams or lobsters with pinned claws, listening to the high scream of sea gulls. In the fish markets of Paris or Venice the salty, almost rancid smell still conjures up for me that weathered gray-shingled building, with its driveway of crushed clam and oyster shells, the brilliant purple and white shards of mother-of-pearl.

I passed first and second grade at the Point School, a two-room schoolhouse a few houses down Main Road. Mrs. ——— presided over the first grade; Mrs. Pilkington over the second: the first guileless and queenly, the second lean and hungry. Mrs. ——— died young of cancer; Mrs. Pilkington expired deep in old age. I taxed them both, as I taxed the patience of numerous teachers thereafter. I was sent into the exile of a spidery corner of the second grade for impertinently reading a book during the Pledge of Allegiance. Like most children, I was utterly bored by school, eager for work and quarrelsome as soon as the work was finished, anxious to recover the delicious edge of vocabulary hinted at, distantly glimmering, in the *tibia* and *fibula* of my memorized book. But the books we were given had a vocabulary that would have insulted slugs, that did insult slugs. This was a decade when America decided it could raise a race of rocket scientists on the adventures of a Dick and a Jane and a Spot. Our grandfathers had read Emerson and Milton and the Bible; we were condemned to the secular lobotomy of Dick and Jane.

My parents were not great readers. When I scan their faded library, on the shelves of an out-of-the-way corner of their "den," there is little beyond the Book-of-the-Month Club selections of the fifties and sixties. My grandmother — my mother's mother — was a reporter and a playwright, active in Little Theater and author of a number of children's adaptations. Now in her nineties, she still receives an occasional royalty from her version of *Treasure Island*. I was a greedy reader from an early age, which gave her some pleasure. My taste was entirely unformed, and I am pained to come across my boxes of childhood paperbacks, which ran to the story of the Malmedy Massacre and the biography of the hangmen of Paris.

During recess at the Point School, I learned every cruelty of childhood, some applied to me, some to others. I was a pipsqueak of a boy, and I banded together with an equally diminutive friend with whom I reveled in the mean application of our early linguistic powers. We were small, and smart, and almost all our leisure was spent cheating at marbles. We applied ourselves, many of us applied ourselves, to this pitiless game of commerce and thievery; and by our secret cabals I amassed, by the time I left Westport, a hoard of a thousand marbles stained by this infant green capitalism. All around the schoolyard we preyed on the weak, and when the strong could catch us they preyed on us.

Collections (many abandoned or defunct)

the stamps of Ghana and the Gold Coast
four-leaf clovers
Liberty Head nickels
clam shells
daguerreotypes
Waring Blendors
ketchup bottles
everyday items marked with the names of poets (e.g., a milk

bottle labeled Borges Sanitary Dairy)
black-market Roman jewelry
books
Formica tables
pre–World War I electric toasters
Afghan war rugs
coaching trunks
railroad and steamship dishes
shoeshine boxes
ancient glass
early pornography
houses

1536 Hazlitt Road, Pittsburgh 37, Pennsylvania

Because this is not a *Bildungsroman*, I feel no obligation to provide a picture window over the landscape of ages nine to nineteen. There were certain quarrels, and certain curiosities, which developed in ways neither predictable nor predictive — they merely tumbled forth. I passed most of these years, the fraught creature of education, in the suburbs of Pittsburgh and New York, in a house so new it had no grass and a house so old it was built on a foundation of boulders. There are few whom the shallow vacancy of the suburbs does not completely corrupt, and in these suburbs of stable marriages and social drinking I was not among them. My parents had grown up in a Pittsburgh still rough and ethnic — my great-grandfather had been engineer of the Pittsburgh-Columbus run of the *Spirit of St. Louis*. My schooling in its suburbs was in a world where blacks and Jews did not exist, where even the rites of Catholics were mildly suspect. I therefore fell in love, when I was of an age to love, with every beautiful black and Jew and Catholic I met.

The remnants of my father's family lived in Pittsburgh, particularly two great-aunts, doughy and formidably bosomed, who cosseted my sister and my brothers and me. One ushered us into her "club" each Christmas for a magic show, usually given by a thin, pasty-faced magician who had trouble with card tricks. The other lived in a grand house somewhere downtown — I remember a huge, musty entry hall, perhaps with a suit of armor, and an angular stairway which swept importantly up one wall, then another. The house was the last remnant of family wealth, derived from a Pittsburgh funicular railway once owned by another great-grandfather.

Though we lived in a neighborhood almost without history — it had been a farm not half a dozen years before — two of my great-grandparents were buried in a cemetery across the street, and three or four generations had farmed within fifty miles. In Braintree and Westport we had often visited my mother's grandparents in Marshfield Hills. They were already very old, though my great-grandmother loved to bake us ginger cookies and scold us around the house with her cane. They lived in a fine old Marshfield house, built by my great-great-great-grandfather, a North River packet pilot and friend of Webster. One of my aunts had inherited a magnificently ugly couch, reputedly Webster's own. History, to us, was a hideous couch.

Occupations

Father: salesman, executive (Alcoa, Con Ed), Realtor
Grandfather Logan: salesman, office manager (Westinghouse), hotel clerk
Grandfather Damon: executive (Quaker Oats)
Great-grandfather Logan: railroad engineer (Pennsylvania Railroad)
Great-grandfather Oakley: riverboat rat, banker, company president (Duquesne Incline Plane Co.)
Great-grandfather Damon: livery-stable owner
Great-grandfather Drew: bank clerk, general-store proprietor (failed), landscape gardener
Mother: radio continuity writer, Realtor
Grandmother Logan: housewife
Grandmother Damon: reporter (*Boston Evening Transcript, Providence Journal, Boston Herald, Boston Traveller*), playwright
Great-grandmother Logan: housewife
Great-grandmother Oakley: housewife
Great-grandmother Damon: housewife
Great-grandmother Drew: tea-shop proprietor

9 Private Road, Huntington, New York

I can find little evidence of a poetic education in the midnight car rides, the underage drinking, or the shy thwarted fumblings with girls which constituted the full expression of high school on Long Island. Our rival high school, which we were encouraged to hate, had been thrown up a mile or so from the poet's birthplace, and so was called Walt Whitman. I had no taste for the poetry anthologies we were supplied with — their timid ventures into the twentieth century stopped with a sentimental version of Frost (not for us the darker, unpleasant Frost), and their pages were filled with the anodyne verse of Witter Bynner, Arthur Davison Ficke, Carl Sandburg, Laura Benét, Christopher Morley, and Lola Ridge. Walt Whitman did not appear at all. It is not surprising that I disliked English classes, and those who found salvation in them.

I required a knowledge harsher and bleaker, something more condensed and atomic than anything English literature — as it was known to me — could provide. I might have taken the appropriate lessons from Shakespeare, but Shakespeare for my teachers was a plot, not a language. We were fortunate to be dragged, hostile but docile, to Stoppard's *Rosencrantz and Guildenstern Are Dead*, then on Broadway, and to a certain memorably comic Stratford (Connecticut) production of *Julius Caesar*, in which plastic packets of blood flew grotesquely around the stage during Caesar's assassination.

I was a difficult adolescent, pleased with solitude even with my brothers and sister — I was surprised to be called "aloof" by a childhood friend. I suppose that like some children of a certain mind, not wholly of the world or in the world, I was drawn to the sciences for their purity and isolation, the clean intellectual fabric of test tubes and formulae, and particularly to the hierarchies of math, each discipline unfolding out of simplicity into distant, barely apprehensible complexity, a life of one devouring chess problem after another, each with the promising finality of solution. I know more about the blindness of science now, the approximations of method, but the myths of solace and discipline are still powerful.

Many of the debts I owe to structure I owe to Thomas Garbrick, who taught me molecular chemistry, and to my teachers of advanced algebra and calculus. I have never enjoyed, or endured, the same intellectual pleasures since — there is a certain fine high tuning possible when the scientific imagination is young, and never possible again. It seems to me most easily accessible through a mathematical understanding, though I have felt faint echoes of it in the clicking of meter, especially when the meter comes right in the language by a kind of grace, or by a gratifying accident.

In the summer after my junior year, I was invited to apply myself to a long reading list prior to entering the advanced course in English, called by its kindly, fussy teacher "The Peacock Class." I mused over this reading list, down by our battered mailbox, and then threw it away and did not take the class. There was more than a little cowardice in this, but such was my distaste, a distaste I carried into college, where I missed the chance to study with Maynard Mack,

Cleanth Brooks, Robert Penn Warren, W. K. Wimsatt, R. W. B. Lewis, and the other venerable ancients then coming to the end of their tenure at Yale. I was caught up in an unfortunate desire to examine the mathematical underpinnings of political relation and political action, and was thick in the conjugation of numbers in graduate courses in probability theory and game theory.

I cannot now disentangle the various misunderstandings and false motives which had led me to this course of study. The spring of my deepest intent was overshadowed, overwhelmed, by the illegal Cambodian bombings and the murders at Kent State. I realized, in one of those slow accesses of understanding so rarely visited upon me, that I had neither a taste for politics nor a confident belief in its mystery. My secret pleasures had long since passed to literature, but that was not an admission I could afford to make, or afford to understand. If the mythologies of memory serve at the expense of accuracy, this revelation occurred the night I squatted with a desultory crowd listening to the lugubrious chants of Allen Ginsberg, who sat cross-legged on a makeshift stage on the Old Campus. It came the instant clouds of tear gas rose over the mock Gothic walls.

Left to discover, in my two years remaining at Yale, some direction, some shift not just of intelligence but of intellective will, I found myself beached. I deposited my now worthless courses in one of Yale's drift-net majors. I was sick at heart as well — first after an affair whose complex betrayals approached soap opera, and then after another in which my infatuation quarreled with her bewilderment.

That I emerged from college with any small design is due to two workshops I took in the spring of my senior year. The first was with Richard Howard, then forty-two, almost new to teaching, full of the magniloquence of monologue. I listened to him for twelve weeks and wrote the poems he commanded us to write. We were not asked or encouraged to talk; we were permitted to listen as he ranged among various literatures and the technical valences of those literatures. The monument that rose above that spring was his lecture on enjambment and the Colossus of Rhodes. He was a mannered, shrewdly poised lecturer — every sentence whirled as if on gambols — and a chaste and sympathetic critic. Our assignments were never returned to us. We handed them in, and a week later he might read one or two aloud at the beginning of class, almost in surprise that anything plausible had emerged. Some weeks we were wicked and hopeless and were met with silence. We received no comments and were tasked and ruined by each new assignment, with its peculiar commands and injunctions, its imposed theme, its crippling form — a few had allegedly been suggested by Auden. They were not always serious — we were once asked to reembody a poem whose individual lines had been snipped apart, and once required to compose a dialogue on the typewriter, using only the left-hand keys for the first voice and the right-hand keys for the second.

Howard believed that, in the impositions of pure technique, form extracts from the imagination what the imagination wishes to suppress. This seemed a perverse argument, but each week my poem contained something I did not control, the language or the idea of a more capable imagination, tricked out by his demands. The poems were the creations of his intelligence, and yet I was responsible for them. I had taken a couple of workshops from other writers without acquiring any poetic understanding — I might have been a dog trying to learn speech. Howard was the first of my teachers for whom poetry was a serious demand on the intellect, for whom it was a matter of high order as well as continual absorption. This had the force of revelation. The possibility of applying to literature the ingenuities, the bearings, the responsibilities seemingly central to science, would not have seemed, perhaps to any other student, so devastating a discovery. The poems the course drew from me, which he drew from me, were the foundation of all my later work.

My other workshop was overseen by David Milch, then twenty-six, a figure already secure in campus mythology, protégé of Brooks and Warren, former scriptwriter for "Peyton Place," gambler, law-school dropout. He possessed the finest analytical mind I was exposed to at Yale, and only once since then have I heard someone lecture with his presence or command. His class was held in an underground seminar room, lit by two leaded windows high on the outside wall. The light was thin and watery — we might have been in a Venetian palazzo. Each week he sat with a novel in front of him — Faulkner, Hemingway, Conrad, Kafka — and talked for an hour, broodingly and electrically, without a note. He almost never managed more; often the lectures were over in forty-five minutes. Once he talked for an hour and a quarter, tapped his watch with a sense of triumph, and said, "See!" I don't think any of us completely understood the disposal of terms by which he made his analyses, but in transverse angles he gave glimpses of the conditioning of narrative by form and what he called the "strategies of indirection" by which the writer gains access to the reader's imagination. He did not discuss student work in class, except on one or two rare occasions.

Richard Howard was a distant presence, detached from us by age and manner, taking the train from New York each week for his one afternoon with us, like Henry James — whom he had begun to resemble — arriving grandly in America. David Milch was an example immediately before us, waving us in for long conferences in an office — not even his — which grew shabbier during each week of his occupation. Once he pulled the arm off an old office chair while trying to make a point. His precise dissection of my poems was expansively considerate (he did not have a shred of condescension). He was able to convey, brilliantly if obliquely, the demands of thought, the activity of an intelligence openly engaged when considering a problem. The attention his lectures required was frightening — even now I cannot read the stray phrases I took down in my notes without a lingering sense of inadequacy. Had he not been drawn into another field, he might have been a philosophical critic with the power of Kenneth Burke.

This was the end of my poetic education — the education that occurs in the classroom — except for three seminars in graduate school under the hawk-like glare of Donald Justice, whose acute receptiveness to the weight and balance of words was a necessary refinement to the broader and more violent understandings of Howard and Milch. Justice, with his finicky care, was apt to pursue implication wherever it went, sometimes reversing his course, sometimes reversing it again — he was likely to overturn any settled judgment with a sentence beginning, "On the other hand." His own teachers had been Lowell and Berryman, and sitting in his class a young poet felt, however grandly and erroneously, part of a tradition.

Justice's attention to every shimmer of poetic meaning bordered on a moral virtue. He had a superb practical imagination and a richness of opinion and judgment — argumentative, severe in his treatment of sloppiness or cant, he never advocated a style or a school. He approached each poem with a cool (rather than, say, a suspicious) equanimity, and tried to conceive his criticism in the poem's terms, even when the poem he found before him was half considered, a blank imitation of a current mode, or without the discernible twitch of a meaning. It's hard to convey the effect of exposure to such trust in the adequacy of poetic language, or the standards and confidence it gradually imposed. In Justice's workshop I was first unleashed as a critic of poems, though not to the transparent delight of my fellow students. At forty-eight, he was the oldest of my teachers, but perhaps the closest in spirit or attitude — we shared the cynicism of atheists, and perhaps some of the wry self-satisfaction as well as mildly opinionated disposition. I would not prefer to discuss movies with anyone else, other than, say, Wittgenstein. He understood intimately the responsibilities of Coleridge's "armed vision."

Before my college workshops, I had had poetic ambitions but no access either to the ventures of my reading or to the recesses of imagination. I can't blame my education for this — I have recognized similar thwartings in some of my students. I was incapable of absorbing lessons not imminently factual, and impermeable to those lessons of style or emotional force which might have saved me time. The fear of influence is debilitating to a younger writer. It was a mark of jealous disrespect, no less than of impatience at their mumbling, that I walked out of poetry readings by Auden and Robert Penn Warren during college.

I had had poetic ambitions, but their source is mysterious. I came to the form all desire and inchoate emotion, and without such teachers I would have become, say, a competently vicious corporate lawyer. I've never felt a similar gravitation toward prose — the language of narrative prose is as blank to me as Linear A, and the writing of criticism might be mistaken for a mild sort of masochism (some, I realize, would call it sadism). I've never felt any desire to tell stories — I wanted a form of possession, the temporary control of the form itself, and by the form itself. In the intimacies of the verse lyric, in the intense, even explosive, charge of a few threads of language, I believed I had found a complete exhaustion. Perhaps this seems too absolute, merely a displacement of the wish for scientific absolutes. I have struggled to contain, to keep in fruitful tension, an unfortunate anarchic desire lurking beneath a belief in humane value. Poetry offers the rage of the imagination (the flaw of the scientific tendency), the profound conditions of disorder, chance, and imperfection — the lure of the unsystematic.

As it happened, the influences on my poetry were men — this was largely an accident of the workshops in which I found myself. But the influences on my life have often been women — my first- and sixth-grade teachers, my fencing coach in high school, one of my best friends in high school, and most of my close friends thereafter. It would be wrong to say that I prefer the imaginations of women (though I'm not sure how wrong), but I do prefer the ways in which the world goes wrong for women to the ways in which it goes wrong for men. And the poet, the woman, I have lived with for seventeen years has had her own influence.

Poetry has served as the form of my comprehensions. My comprehensions have been radically imperfect and often distant from the ease of "personality" which is the medium of almost all our poetry. I have been more interested, more appealed to, by the moral actions of language. There I must discharge my obligation to my father, who despite material failures which were sometimes comic, and sometimes nearly tragic, served as the principal of my moral architecture.

It is fine to read about actions but crucial to watch the casual courage which begins them. After we had moved away from Westport Point, John Baker fell into argument on his beach over the salvage of a boat. Words were exchanged, and he shot a man. When Mr. Baker was put on trial for murder, my father flew back eight hundred miles to serve as a character witness. He was not required to do so, and as far as I know Mr. Baker had not asked him to do so. But my father thought it was right, and he went. My father was a tall but not particularly formidable man, though he knew the advantage of temper. Some of my tempers of language have made use of my admiration.

Books (poetry)

Sad-faced Men. David R. Godine, 1982.
Difficulty. David R. Godine, 1985.
Sullen Weedy Lakes. David R. Godine, 1988.

Limited Editions

Dream of Dying. Graywolf Press, 1980.
Moorhen. Abattoir Editions, 1984.

Christopher Merrill is editor of the Peregrine Smith Poetry Series and a freelance journalist. He and his wife, violinist Lisa Gowdy, divide their time between Santa Fe, New Mexico, and Portland, Oregon.

PERMISSION TO SPEAK

The story may be emblematic: born tongue-tied, I can speak clearly — according to my parents — thanks to a retired military doctor, a family friend whose rough-and-ready surgical technique (honed on the USS *Hope*) had followed him into private practice, He wasn't our doctor; his methods were too brutal. Yet he freely offered advice, once counseling my mother to provoke arguments with my taciturn father. "Silence isn't healthy," said the doctor. "He'll live longer if you fight." And when I was nine months old, he noticed the fold of skin under my tongue was too short to allow for proper speech; before my parents could stop him, he splayed me across our kitchen table and, wielding a pair of rusted scissors, cut my frenum. My tongue flopped in my mouth, like a fish dangling from a hook.

That I didn't speak until I was nearly two may come as no surprise: raids on the inarticulate, as Eliot understood, are often accompanied by acts of violence, psychic and/or physical; the repercussions may last forever. Writers are products of such wrenchings out of the ordinary — every poem or story, in fact, depends on raiding silence — and I see my life as a series of uprootings and severings, each one of which articulates a new relationship to what Stephen Spender calls "a language of flesh and roses" — that is, to poetry. "O taste and see," Denise Levertov writes, a line I cherish; for writers taste the world, the bitter and the sweet, and out of each tasting issues vision — and the word. I am indebted to that doctor who granted me both the freedom to taste and permission to speak without impediment; no doubt I write to honor his legacy, his gift, as well as to obey the imperative rooted in poetic speech: the obligation to transform the language — and the world. In an early poem I paid homage to that "operation":

Tongue-Tied

I forgive my tongue's clipped wings,
The rusted scissors, the nod;
The cluttered kitchen table
On which they laid me down;

The smoke in the doctor's eyes;
The bourbon shaking his hand;
My father, who fainted twice;
And my mother, flecked with blood,
Who should have known better;
For my blood tasted like milk,
A birdcall swelled in my throat,
And my first words let me fly.

(reprinted from Workbook*)*

Other rendings and other flights followed in due course, the effects of which may have been exacerbated by the fact that I was raised in what may seem like idyllic circumstances — in an upper-middle-class family, in a village ninety minutes west of New York City. My father was a banker, my mother a homemaker and volunteer at the Mental Health Association, and I grew up surrounded by an unspoiled version of nature. When I was a child, there were twenty-five farms in Brookside, countless apple orchards, miles of woodland, and no more than 1,800 people, most of whom I knew at least by name. I fished (without a license) in any number of streams and ponds, rode horses down to the commercial center of town (which consisted of a grocery store, the post office, a Congregational church, and the elementary school), caught snakes and frogs and rabbits. In the neighboring woods I followed the crumbling tracks of the long-abandoned Rock-a-Bye railroad, where I found rusted spikes as well as arrowheads left by the first settlers of the area, the Indians of the Leni-Lenape tribe. And I knew where quicksand was, patches of shifting earth deep in the swamps that fed my imagination, the marshes coloring my dreams, leading me to believe I lived almost like a pioneer.

Something else for my imagination: history. Brookside was lined with houses dating back to the Revolutionary War, General Washington's winter headquarters were nearby, and over the hill from my grandparents' home was the Wick estate — hundreds of acres of orchards and pastures and possibilities for a boy who liked to daydream. Here was the legend of Tempe Wick, a buxom young woman who in the coldest winter of the American Revolution stood up to the rebellious troops of the Pennsylvania Line. Quartered on her father's grounds, drunk and angered by the paymaster's inability to pay them their last month's wages, these "patriots" revolted on New Year's night, 1791. They captured General "Mad" Anthony Wayne, prepared to march to Princeton, and tried to commandeer all available supplies, including Miss Wick's favorite horse. But she hid the mare in her bedroom, and the soldiers never found it. Hers was an act of heroism, which took on symbolic importance once the short-lived mutiny fell apart. I thought about it constantly.

I would bicycle to her house and walk in her gardens, wondering what had prompted her to face down those soldiers. I would study the wooden fences zigzagging like a slalom course along her fields, each post set three feet to either side of an imaginary straight line, and the makeshift huts and redoubts that had housed the freezing plotters, and the log cabin used as a hospital, and the tiny room in which she had hid her horse. I would dream about her show of resistance, her courage in the wake of her neighbors' capitulation to these encroachers (who were supposed to have been on her side), and her imaginative approach to saving what was dearest to her.

Did her example inspire me and others to take our own stand against what we considered to be another form of encroachment—the developers carving up farm after farm? Perhaps. Or it may be that we were simply bored children determined to be vandals. What was clear was that our village was changing: in the place of woods and pastures now were surveyors' stakes for large housing tracts; one by one our secret and sacred groves vanished. I knew the genuine carpenters in Brookside, craftsmen like Ernie Maw and Ed Radtke who would renovate old houses and build only one or two new houses a year, artisans who had no interest in shoddy workmanship; their floats in the annual fourth of July parade customarily won all the prizes. I didn't know the developers, the nameless figures who were supposed to bring prosperity to our village, the shadows who always lived elsewhere. They were the ones who had to contend with the missing stakes.

I don't know who started pulling them out and throwing them into the woods—probably the older brother of one of my friends. Nor do I remember anyone being punished for destroying the surveyors' work, though I have a clear memory of our town's only policeman grilling me at length about my involvement with other boys known to have pulled stakes. What I know is that our actions, which had nothing to do with pulling up stakes in the proverbial sense of lighting out for the West, didn't stop the destruction of prized farmland and forests. I know, too, that what we did was wrong, much as I believe ours was an intuitive effort to reclaim part of a pastoral life we knew was rapidly disappearing. Yet it was, and remains, equally wrong to lay waste—in the name of progress—to agrarian ways of life and the native habitats of any plant or animal. No wonder the only wilderness preserve in our village came to be called Dismal Harmony.

Within a few years Brookside became a bedroom suburb of New

York City, its population more than doubling, all but three of its farms gone. A shopping center complete with an indoor tennis club, a nursing home, a high school that resembled a prison, townhouses and condominiums, traffic problems, a rising crime rate — these were just some of the developments the land rush produced. Soon the domestic problems associated with affluent suburbs began to crop up: ten years ago, to take only the most melodramatic example, seven high school students killed themselves — in a matter of weeks. Brookside, old-timers agreed, had lost its soul. Once a village where a young blue- or white-collar family could make its start, now it was a fashionable place where in the 1980s the average plot of land sold for half a million dollars. Who could afford — who would *want* to live there?

I was already on my way out long before the Wick estate was turned into a national monument. (Fittingly, the Park Service refuses to acknowledge Tempe Wick's famous escapade, because it is "only" a legend — that is, it belongs to the world of poets, not administrators.) There was first of all our month-long family driving trip around the West, where the steep slopes of the Rockies, Grand Tetons, and Sierra Nevadas, and the gorges of the Grand Canyon, and the vistas of the desert, left me — at the age of fourteen — with a vision of another way of life. More, my parents could afford to send me to a day school in Elizabeth, then to a small liberal arts college in Vermont. Everything, it seemed, was conspiring to loosen the chains of my attachment to that village. Even my parents were planning to leave; and after four years of school along the New Jersey Turnpike, where each fall I watched the sky turn red from the glow of burning chemical swamps in Bayonne, I realized I too had had enough of the Garden State. Middlebury College simply reinforced that conviction: my parents and sisters had moved south, and faced with the prospect of attending graduate school at Brown, Columbia, or the University of Washington, I chose Seattle — one of my wisest decisions.

For I wanted to be a writer. Which is to say: I wanted to claim part of an imaginary landscape — in word and deed. I believed I could do that only by forging a new life in the mythic Northwest. How was I to know that such a decision would result in the written discovery of my old life? And how could I foresee that my journey west would take me back — at least as far as my imagination was concerned — to Brookside? Yet that is precisely what happened. Call it homesickness, or nostalgia, or acceptance of the validity of my own life and story — whatever the reason may have been, once I moved to Seattle I started writing about the village of my childhood, the only landscape and lives I knew. Perhaps this was another version of what Richard Hugo calls the phenomenon of "the triggering town," the process whereby poets find it easier to write about their home towns when they visit other places, thus gaining enough distance and perspective on their material to trigger a poem into life. Certainly in the Northwest I felt free to invent and improvise on the facts of my own history. That freedom allowed me to write *Workbook*, my first collection of poems, as well as a handful of short stories.

I made another important discovery in Seattle, thanks to the example and teaching of David Wagoner, the poet and novelist. He suggested automatic writing as a way of beginning poems and fictions: one might surrender to the language, writing down whatever came into one's head, giving oneself over to every impulse — reasonable and unreasonable, concrete and abstract. It was, of course, a means of granting oneself permission to speak from the heart, the depths of one's unconscious, the edges of the language. And Wagoner's advice dovetailed with my own readings of the French Surrealists, poets like André Breton, Paul Éluard, Robert Desnos, and Benjamin Péret, fearless explorers of the unconscious, adventurers in the language: they were the ones who first drew attention to the glories (and the dangers) of automatic writing; their work, their example, gave me the courage to grant myself permission to speak and write as crazily as I wanted. Octavio Paz, one of the most important figures in my literary pantheon, notes of automatic writing that "it is a psychic exercise, a convocation and an invocation meant to open the floodgates of the verbal stream." Such a regimen, he explains, "destroys the conscious self. Poetry does not redeem the poet's personal self: it dissolves it in the vaster, more powerful reality of language. The practice of poetry demands the surrender, the renunciation of the ego" — a practice I wanted to make a permanent part of my life.

These discoveries — Brookside as a subject, automatic writing — enabled me to learn, by fits and starts, that "language of flesh and roses" articulated — in scores of different ways — in the works of the poets and writers I revere, what Thom Gunn calls "my sad captains": Chaucer, Shakespeare, Donne, Herbert, Milton, Pope, Smart, Blake, Wordsworth, Keats, Thoreau, Dickinson, Lautreamont, Rimbaud, Hopkins, Eliot, Breton, Francis Ponge, Kafka, Stevens, Marianne Moore, Henri Michaux, Paz, Elizabeth Bishop, Brewster Ghiselin, Yannis Ritsos, Vasko Popa, Italo Calvino, W. S. Merwin, and on and on. I turned to these and other writers to hear that language of desire and grief in all its "lovely orders." In their poems and fictions and essays I caught glimpses of the unknown, discovered ways in which the familiar might again become strange, and began to make sense of my own life; their work continues to encourage me to write. "Poaching," a poem from my first book, is a meditation on the various sources of my art:

Poaching

> *"You'd have to be able ... to see what steals I've made and used."*
>   *— Charles Wright*

At dusk, in the rusted light of August, I hummed like a wire
Along the fence dividing the widow's land
Into thirds, into the past,
        present, and future perfect
Tenses of the verb to have *in its holy trinity*
Of greed, and skimmed
        my voice across the pond, the warm air,
The waves and watery tops of timothy and alfalfa,
To scare her horses imported from Russia
        and the black men poaching in our woods.

———

In Fergus Tufts' field, shucking ears of corn
And whistling through the skins: a buck and a doe,
Feeding nearby, looked up, and didn't scare
Until I slipped away, the stalks stripped clean,
Our dinner tucked underarm, like a newspaper.

And when I climbed the bridle path, holding
The fence to keep from sliding down the muck,
The gully of horseshoes, and broken rails,
And cigarette butts scuffed into hoofprints,
A host of spirits tracked me through the woods,

Singing a song of the grief stitched, like stripes,
Into the fabric of my innocent needs.

———

Thus a scattering of seeds plundered from memory's husk —

At noon, through the trees, the way the light's riptide
and roll confuse the story line:

A bundle of oil-soaked rags, or the smell of singed flesh;

Names like Clarence Nagro, "Mad" Anthony Wayne, Tempe Wick;

A horse hidden in a bedroom, corn and apples rotting under
the floorboards, and soldiers plotting in the snow;

A barn fire and Tanya's stallions galloping into the sky; —

And then, at dusk, the way the round heads of red clover
bob in the wind, marking the far side of silence.

———

"If you mean to kill me, shoot me now!"
Cried General Wayne, opening his coat. "Here's
My heart." And his drunken soldiers reeled away
With fixed bayonets, fifes and drums, the cannon,
And a hundred head of cattle from the compound —
His Pennsylvania Line, knee-deep in snow,
Veering barefoot between Vealtown and Princeton.

New Year's night, 1791 —
Talbot and Bettin dead; Henry Wick's daughter
Stopped on the road, then followed home (her horse,
To the men's chagrin, vanishing along the way);
And now, an unpaid month of building and
Rebuilding huts and redoubts ending in
Revolt, a volley fired — overhead — at him . . .

Still, he chose to ride with them, who'd lived
On dogs, birch bark, roasted shoes. "Their business was
With Congress" — not with him. They'd worshipped him,
Like sons, this band of laborers and bounty-
Seekers; and so, like the helpless father who
Must watch his children make their own mistakes,
He headed for Princeton and imprisonment . . .

———

For memory invents its own network of new connections —

At daybreak, from the footbridge, I watched Tanya's friend
lead a white horse down to the stream, and shoot it.

All afternoon the stench of rotting flesh staining the air,
the swamp grass, the stones.

" . . . Because Clarence is illiterate," my father explained,
explaining nothing.

But when the rank water filled our pond, the clouds' boats
sailed past without signaling, stranding me there.

And when their barn burned down that fall, I saw a fleet of
slave ships blazing in a distant harbor.

—Then I heard the beginning and the end of speech and song.

———

But here invention flags before the facts:
When Sam Tufts (volunteer fire chief, Babe Ruth
Team coach, and plumber) choked a black-robed boy
One Fourth of July, honoring the war
In Asia and the memory of his nephew—
Fergus' son—by protesting the students'
Protest of our parade (their coffin lay
In pieces near the judges' stand), the sun
Burned through the fittings in the clouds, and burst
Into the students' song . . . Soon a horse-van came
To spirit them away, and the firemen raised
Their hands. My first pitch rattled the batting cage.

———

Smoke drifted overhead. The woods blazed
With signs: scars on a stranger's face. And when the last thread
Of light broke in the sky, and a gust of wind
Swept the smoke away, I knelt in the blackberry brambles
And wept. I licked my wrists. Tasted juice. Blood. Then footsteps,
Voices whispering beyond the fence, and my heart,
Like a fist, opening in the dark,
To lead me home again.

(reprinted from Workbook*)*

Yet I am reluctant to write exclusively about my past. Because I am a poet for whom the musical possibilities of verse — formal *and* free — are of the highest importance, I find that rhetorical strategies, metrical patterns, the dictates of the imagination, and the language itself take me far beyond a poem's initiating image, phrase, or idea — the seed from which almost anything may grow. Rooted in autobiography, whether from my past or from the lives and landscapes surrounding me now, each poem takes on a life of its own, and as I write it out, pacing around my house and chanting lines, I am obliged to honor that life, that mystery at the heart of any creative act. Writers know that mystery is everywhere: inspiration ignores all borders.

True, in my work I hope never to leave Brookside behind: it is a rich subject, an inexhaustible subject, and if I spent the rest of my life writing only about that village I am certain I would uncover no more than a few of the lines embedded in its "central poem." But it is also true I have made emotional and imaginative investments in other places besides those of my childhood, having spent the whole of my adulthood living in the West — first in Seattle, then in Salt Lake City, and now in Santa Fe. Surely some of the pleasure I derive from making my life in a canyon filled with apple orchards and horses stems from my attempts to write about my new surroundings. Because my wife, Lisa, a violinist, and I are caretakers of a small estate along the Tesuque Creek, we have more than passing obligations to this place: there are gardens — vegetable, wildflower, perennial, and cutting — to tend, trees and shrubs to prune, an irrigation ditch called an *acequia* that must be monitored, wood to cut and split for the winter, snow to shovel. And those obligations, which are as much familial as work related, and which have political as well as aesthetic ramifications, lead me to write increasingly about the West. I expect to continue to address the lives and landscapes from my childhood, that which shaped my vision of the world. But I also want to make a contribution to the emerging literature of the West, a tradition concerned in large part with the creation of myths running counter to prevailing notions of "a frontier mentality." Indeed, much of *Fevers & Tides*, my second collection of poems, as well as the work I have completed since then, is centered in the deserts, mountains, and coastal areas of the West. I hope to add to the literature of those determined to understand the limits — political, economic, spiritual, and aesthetic — we must now live within.

But how am I to describe these landscapes with the same authority I might feel about Brookside? Shirley Kaufman, an American poet who has lived for many years in Israel, asks: "How long will it take for 'what is out there' to 'move inside' and be authentic?" Is such authenticity even possible? I sometimes ask myself, wondering how to write about arroyos and ponderosa pines, coyotes and green chile. For guidance in western matters (and manners?) I look to the work of writers like Wallace Stegner, Brewster Ghiselin, Frederick Turner, William Kittredge, N. Scott Momaday, Richard Shelton, Leslie Marmon Silko, Theodore Roethke, Marilynne Robinson, Edward Abbey, and David Wagoner. For answers to the questions raised above I turn to an early poem by the Greek poet Constantin Cavafy; addressed to Odysseus at the outset of his long journey home from the Trojan War, "Ithaka" is one of my touchstones, a poem I read whenever I become confused about my vocation.

Ithaka

As you set out for Ithaka
hope your road is a long one,
full of adventure, full of discovery.
Laistrygonians, Cyclops,
angry Poseidon — don't be afraid of them!
You'll never find things like that on your way
as long as you keep your thoughts raised high,
as long as a rare excitement
stirs your spirit and your body.
Laistrygonians, Cyclops,
wild Poseidon — you won't encounter them
unless you bring them along inside your soul,
unless your soul sets them up in front of you.

Hope your road is a long one,
May there be many summer mornings when,
with what pleasure, what joy,
you enter harbors you're seeing for the first time;
may you stop at Phoenician trading stations
to buy fine things,
mother of pearl and coral, amber and ebony,
sensual perfume of every kind —
as many sensual perfumes as you can;
and may you visit many Egyptian cities
to learn and go on learning from their scholars.

Keep Ithaka always in your mind.
Arriving there is what you're destined for.
But don't hurry the journey at all.

Better if it lasts years,
so you're old by the time you reach the island,
wealthy with all you've gained on the way,
not expecting Ithaka to make you rich.

Ithaka gave you the marvelous journey.
Without her you wouldn't have set out.
She has nothing left to give you now.

And if you find her poor, Ithaka won't have fooled you.
Wise as you will have become, so full of experience,
you'll have understood by then what these Ithakas mean.

(trans. Edmund Keeley & Philip Sherrard)

Determining what "these Ithakas," these various homelands, mean may shed light on the problem of authenticating one's experience of a new landscape. The advice Cavafy offers is sound not only for Odysseus but for every traveler, including writers heading west. And here I must try to say what counsel I take from these lines.

This poem—the first draft of which was completed in 1894, years before the poet hit his stride—marks a crucial moment in Cavafy's artistic development, delineating a stance he will have to assume, an attitude he must adopt in order to find his "voice," and become the poet of Alexandria, one of the twentieth century's most significant literary figures. Thus he affirms the need to open himself up to experience; transcending the deadening effects of routine, he may begin to appreciate the complexities of his chosen place and shape his vision of the world, a vision at once sympathetic to the victims of history and ironic with respect to the modern human condition.

"Ithaka" is a didactic monologue, a form Cavafy all but avoids in his mature work, where his instructional voice gives way to narratives, dramatic monologues, and lyrics. A didactic monologue teaches both the reader and the writer, as it does this reader and writer; "Ithaka" can accommodate the occasional intrusion of a preacherly tone, because it is a function of the speaker's character: perhaps only a god or goddess—Pallas Athena?—can say to Odysseus, "As you set out for Ithaka / hope your road is a long one, / full of adventure, full of discovery." And those instructions apply to everyone: Ithaka, in figurative terms, is the homeland awaiting us at the end of our days.

I take heart, too, in the way Cavafy rewrites the ancient myth to fit his modern sensibility—a familiar strategy throughout his career. Juxtaposing the virtues of the Greek warrior with an artistic view of man allows the poet to pay homage to another set of values, celebrating the emotional, spiritual, and sensual aspects of life. Odysseus, we recall, didn't want to leave Ithaka to fight alongside the Greeks; once the Trojan War was over, he wanted to return home immediately. But "angry Poseidon" had other plans for him — the trials and tribulations of a long voyage back to Ithaka. Only by the strength of his will — and with help from Athena — does Odysseus survive his perilous journey home, where he must rid his hall of Penelope's suitors before he can again become king of his country. Cavafy, though, approaches this story from a different angle, diminishing the role of the will. Odysseus' voyage, which in Homer's epic tests his spirit, becomes for the modern poet a spiritual quest. Wisdom is the new goal: Ithaka is the path to enlightenment; hence the prayer for a long journey, since wisdom is not easily won. And Odysseus must not will his way home; rather, he must give himself over to the *experience* of travel, difficult as it may be. Pleasurable, too, insofar as our pilgrim revels in his journey, learning from it instead of pining for its end. The traveler's rewards, according to Cavafy, cannot be measured in monetary terms; what Odysseus may earn from the wealth of his experience is wisdom. Thus he must thank Ithaka for the gift of his "marvelous journey," which is the gift of life itself.

Ithaka, of course, is a far cry from Brookside, and Seattle, and Santa Fe. But Cavafy's instructions to Odysseus can serve me, too: if I want to write about the West, I must experience it with the whole of my being, with my senses on fire, learning the names of everything around me — flowers and trees, birds and animals, rivers and mountains, neighbors and customs. I cannot spend my life mourning the fact that I no longer live in my native place: there is too much to praise in my new surroundings. Ithaka, or whatever one may call "home," may well represent our death: keeping that in mind may help us approach our lives and the landscapes we encounter in a different light, in a spirit of reverence. Ithaka, which is the end and the beginning, is always close at hand — as I learned in "Erosion," the first poem I wrote in New Mexico:

Erosion

Past the salt flats, the grave of the sea, the sky divers
In a free fall, twisting and turning, the way stones
Drop through water — they heard only the whine
Of the wind, the drone of the airplane flying home.

Their chutes erupted like an argument, and up

They floated for a moment, till they saw
Smoke rising from the distant city, houses reclining
On the benches of the mountains, and rain

Evaporating on its way down. They carried their own clouds
Into the desert, the rippling cloth and cords
Trailing them, like debts, like children
And beliefs. And once they landed on the mesa,

Splashing into the sand, they could feel the past
Dissolve. Thus they praised the action
Of their chutes settling, like snow, over the stunted trees,
Over all the shrubs and flowers they would have to name.

They praised the ebbing wind, and the silence,
And the taste of their own salt. They praised a cactus
In the shape of a cross . . . Yet it was a dead place
To these disciples of the future, these

Pilgrims gathering potsherds and petrified
Chunks of wood. They damned the dry gullies. Damned
The heat rooted in the red earth and the hidden
Barbs of the prickly pear . . . Then it began.

In arroyos and on the hillsides: a hissing and
A heaving, like the sea. Or was this just the memory
Of the sea? they wondered, waving at the sky.
They scanned birds' nests, gopher holes, anthills, ants:

Nothing. One laced up his boots. Another
Took a shovel from a pack. A third tried to pray. Soon
Waves of diamondbacks were breaking against the mesa,
Eroding the shore beneath their feet.

The shoreline separating sea and sand, past and present, known and unknown, is constantly eroding underfoot, wherever we walk: every moment has its tides. And my task as a writer is to bear witness to that mystery, that wave washing over all of life, that ebb and surge and flow I glimpse from time to time. To do that I must serve the language I learned as a child—filtered through the prism of my reading, my loves and griefs, my life in the West. I need to listen not only to the voices in my memory but also to the accents of the wind rustling through New Mexico, and the diction of the water draining from the Rio Grande, and the stories of the people I live among. I will carry to my death the landscape of my childhood, a vista that will never stop informing and shaping my experience. Surely a measure of my happiness in living here stems from the fact that as I look out the window from the room in which I write I see three horses grazing in an apple orchard: a primal image for me. It is comforting to discover reminders from my past, in what is in almost every respect an alien landscape. Such signposts allow me to plant in this red earth my feet as well as my imagination, orienting myself until I have no choice but to write — with varying degrees of authority — about these arroyos and mesas, these scudding clouds and cacti, this light, this language. In short, they free my tongue:

Because

variation on a theme by Yannis Ritsos

Because the Dead Sea released its hostages — the taste for salt,
*   a rudder and a sail;*
Because a band of Roman slaves, disguised in their master's robes,
*   fled across the Continent;*
Because one manuscript, one waxen shoal of words, burned a monastery
*   down;*
Because the sun spurned the Black Forest, and windmills ground
*   the peasants into the earth, into the air, into the voice of*
*   the boy who cried wolf;*
Because the crowd hissed at the empty stage, and the prompter drank
*   himself to sleep, and the diva hid in the pit;*
Because we let barbed wire replace our wooden faces and fences;
Because a scream left a trail through the ruined air;
Because I followed that trail into the woods, where my hands dissolved
*   in smoke and rain;*
Because I wandered for days, weeks, until I found myself outside
*   a walled city, a city abandoned hundreds of years ago;*
Because I couldn't scale the walls, nor could I find a way to return
*   to my homeland, and so I settled along a river in the desert;*
Because the river changed course, and its banks crumbled into the dry
*   bed, where I was on my knees, speechless and afraid;*
Because whenever I hike into the desert I talk and talk and talk;
Because I have never been to the desert;
Because I refuse to follow any trail whose markings are not completely
*   clear;*
Because I distrust signs, guideposts, land- and seamarks;

Because on my single visit to the ancient city I rifled the ruins for
   potsherds and stone tools, and was warned never to return;
Because I heed all warnings, all directives from the crowd;
Because I won't listen to anyone but myself;
Because I love to cry wolf;
Because everything I read smells of smoke;
Because sometimes I wake at night to find my hands covered with salt,
   my sheet wrapped around me like a sail;
Because I can't tell if this is the desert or the sea;
Because I never learned to read the stars, and don't know where
   we're heading;
Because of this and more, much more, I hid your name in the well . . . and
   here it is again, filling my cup.

(reprinted from Fevers & Tides*)*

Books

Workbook (poetry). Teal Press, 1988.
Fevers & Tides (poetry). Teal Press, 1989.
The Forgotten Language: Contemporary Poets and Nature (editor). Peregrine Smith Books, 1991.
From the Faraway Nearby: Georgia O'Keeffe as Icon (biography), with Ellen Bradbury. Addison-Wesley Publishing Co., 1992.
The Grass of Another Country: A Journey through the World of Soccer (nonfiction). Chelsea Green Publishers, 1992.
Constellations, by André Breton (translator, with Jeanie Puleston Fleming). David R. Godine, forthcoming.

Periodicals

Poetry, fiction, essays, translations, and reviews have appeared in the following publications (a partial list): *Antioch Review, Carolina Quarterly, Chelsea, Cincinnati Poetry Review, Columbia: A Magazine of Poetry & Prose, Denver Quarterly, Mississippi Review, New Virginia Review, New England Review and Bread Loaf Quarterly, Paris Review, Pivot, Poetry East, Poetry Wales, Poetry Northwest, Prairie Schooner, Pushcart Prize XV: Best of the Small Presses, Seneca Review, The Journal,* and *Tyuonyi.*

Emile Snyder

A NIGHT AT THE OPERA

Had Rimbaud not existed, the French would have invented him. In any case, Baudelaire, a quarter of a century earlier, had already provided *le frisson*, with his *Fleurs du mal*. The French middle class (the solid money, that is) had always had a surreptitious taste for the peripheral, for the *voyage imaginaire*, as long as it was really *imaginaire* and did not threaten the structures of its power and expectations. Thus the children of that bourgeoisie found the books their parents had locked in a case, looked at pictures they should not have looked at, and read novels and poems they should not have read. They entered into the world of the poet, they closed their eyes and traveled, without having to leave the solid contours of their ostentatious bedrooms.

In retrospect, I feel that my meeting with poetry came from a contradictory desire: to introduce some rationality into my life. From the early days, my life appeared to me (for good reasons) so irrational that I tended to find in literature—and specifically in poetry—the aesthetic balance to deal with looming threats.

Everything seems to have conspired to make me an *outsider*, some sort of delinquent living under false pretenses, with a false passport and a false identity card. The early image I have of myself is that of a frightened rabbit pursued by hungry wolves. I was a Jew who could not be a Jew while unable not to be a Jew. There is a classic Jewish story of a mother bringing a present to her son. He opens the box and finds in it two neckties. He takes one in his hand, looks gratefully at his mother, and tells her that it is beautiful, to which she answers reproachfully, "And what is the matter with the other?"

There was always something the matter with my young life; some parts of me I could not—was not allowed to—integrate into a cohesive picture. My mother was one of seven daughters (it sounds like a joke; one would have thought that after the fourth, her parents would have given up . . . but in those days, a boy!), seven girls born of Rumanian Jewish parents who had migrated to France ahead of, or after, the last pogrom. By the time I came to be fully aware of them, the six sisters had married, each to an Eastern European Jew. My uncles and aunts, in themselves, would have constituted a bustling society: there was a shopkeeper, a salesman, a tailor (my grandfather, Daniel), and some representatives of other blue-collar professions. I was to belong to the second generation who produced lawyers, physicians, heads of industry, and a university "professor" who would write poetry.

What, in retrospect, fascinates me about that extended family was (and still is) their precise sense of hierarchy. At the top of the ladder were the German Jews, closely followed by the Russians, somewhere in the middle were the Rumanian (not exactly flattering to my grandfather), and at the bottom of the ladder were the Polish Jews whom my Aunt Renée (herself dutifully married to a Russian Jew) called the dregs, or ironically, *les juifs*!

Where did my immediate family and I fall in this pecking order? Nowhere. My mother had married across the line (which the family privately considered up the line), had married an American who was a *goy*, of the Catholic kind, *weh's mir*!, who could not be integrated into the geographical schema. My father's diaspora was the result of his having joined the American army in World War I and afterward remaining in Paris where, it could be said, he had prospered.

> *In contrast to their husbands, who drifted from the pogroms of Rumania, Russia, or Poland, my father, himself a stranger in France, nevertheless radiated with legality. And this American, surprising because his accent was unblemished, because he was blond, because he drove a Talbot, craved applesauce with his pork roast, and fell into ecstasy before my Aunt Renée's gefulte, filled the entire family with awe.*
>
> *Still, he was suspected of being snobbish, of making you feel he was too good for this story.*

(from La Troisième voix, trans. Kate Hancock)

My mother saw in this American the chance to disappear as a Jew. After all, weren't all worthy French bourgeois Catholic? I tended to think so. In my early days I recall, with shame, how in our grammar school a child had been singled out as being *un protestant*, and together with my friends, I looked at him as if he had two heads and spit fire through his nostrils. We lived on rue Tronchet near the Madeleine, a plush section of Paris, while many of my aunts lived in the populous *12ème arrondissement*. My parents socialized mostly with non-Jews, which gave me the opportunity to "assimilate." Ironically, this was never a complete metamorphosis, for, quite often, we would join the rest of the clan for dinner with Grand-Père, or for some ritual occasion like a bar mitzvah, a wedding, or a funeral. Then, once again, I would be plunged into

> *... the opulent gestures, the shrill cry of the*
> *circumcised, and the noisy rain of monnies, and the*
> *stuffed carp, the eggplant, and the unleavened bread*
> *under the skullcap of light*
>
> *and also grave*
> *and sad those profiles where the race had bled*

My relationship with my father was distant. I believe that we did understand each other, and perhaps too well, but that we did not like what we understood. He frightened me a bit (although he never hit me), and I must have disappointed him a lot. He was so American, so physical, the perfect movie image (maybe that is why he liked James Cagney films so much) of the self-made man. Not very tall, but still taller than I, he was a powerful man. At the first opportunity he would show you a photo, taken at the beach, where in a Herculean fashion he had lifted two men suspended on an iron bar. He had no formal education, and from what I occasionally gleaned (in my generation, one did not ask one's father, or mother, what they *did*), he might have been an athlete, a boxer, a bouncer, or some kind of entrepreneur, to put it politely. Finally he had enlisted in the army when America entered World War I and had remained in Paris afterward.

I was never quite sure whether or not he was telling the truth, and I believe that my mother had resolved, a long time ago, not to inquire too deeply. We lived in a sumptuous apartment, which, from the occasional arguments I heard at night, was difficult for my father to afford. Nonetheless, he had expensive tastes. All of his suits were of fine English cloth, cut by one of the best tailors in Paris; his handmade shirts were of imported cotton or silk, always white ("color is vulgar," he would say), and of course he traveled through Paris in his elegant Talbot, or in a taxi, as he considered *le métro* too vulgar a mode of transportation. At the opera or concerts — which he didn't like but felt that he should sometimes attend — he would sit near the orchestra, or in the first loge, convinced that the upper tiers were for the "riff-raff."

It is ironic that this man who, to my knowledge, never read a book — there wasn't a single one in our apartment, except for the ones in my room — encouraged me to read and even facilitated it. Once a month I would be allowed to go to the bookstore downstairs and choose a book. My father paid for it later, although he seemed to have no curiosity about my selections. A few times, when he saw me with a book of poems in hand, he would exhibit the forlorn expression French people have when something is beyond their comprehension, and they mutter *"mais c'est pas vrai, c'est pas vrai!"* Silently, he watched me go to my room, perhaps feeling that I was entering into a world he would never know.

That was the time I began to read poetry. In France one can develop a very special relationship with one's *libraire*. He was more than a simple bookseller; he was an adviser, a teacher. Very soon he would get to know your taste, the kinds of authors you liked, the literary genre you seemed to seek, and he would steer you toward the right shelves. Thanks to this marvelous man, I began serious readings in Lamartine (the romantic poet was still *en vogue*), in Baudelaire (although I was still too young to understand the overtones), and Verlaine, who seduced me with his sad music. After I had selected the book, I would ask him to wrap it carefully, then I would walk home, holding it preciously in my hands as if it were some talisman. Once in my room, I would carefully unpack the book and begin to read. I was losing myself in it, forgetting all my funny Jews, and my sad father and mother tearing each other apart. Unlike many youngsters who seek in literature—in poetry—an escape from the doldrums of their predictable lives (Rimbaud being a prototype), my meandering in poetry was a conscious effort to *understand* the crazy world of my parents and the reason why my history was not like that of other children.

My parents had registered me (together with my sister) in the ballet school of the Paris Opera. I became what is called a "petit rat," in deference to the numerous rats which inhabit the sewers underneath the opera. We had our *lycée* integrated with the demands of a full artistic life—that life being comprised of regular ballet classes, rehearsals, performances (as supers) in the opera—I can still sing the entire act of the Kermess in Gounod's *Faust*.

My life was totally different from that of other boys my age. I never lived the life of a *lycéen*. Now, when I see teens coming out of the *lycée*, noisy, bouncing, a cigarette in their mouths (even kids that seem to be no older than 12 or 14), I realize that I never had anything in common with them. I grew up caught in the mythology of the body: everything revolved around it, depended on its perfection. Our lives acquired meaning through a repetition of *grand-jetés*, *barre* work, and the threat of a pulled tendon or a fracture. Our satchels were filled with pieces of resin, rubbing alcohol, bandages, makeup, sweaty ballet tights, and ballet slippers.

My first serious entrée on the stage of the Paris Opera was in

Wagner's *Lohengrin*. I appeared at the very end as the young Duke of Brabant (who had been turned into the knight of the swan and was restored to his legacy), taken into the embrace of the opulent Elsa (my mother) as the curtain fell. I did not realize at the time the irony of my presence in this very Aryan opera (one of Hitler's favorites), an irony which took on a life of its own as, a few years later, Hitler drove down the Champs Elysées, and I was dismissed from the opera for being a Jew. My world had collapsed. Thanks to my father, who had had the good sense to register me (and my sister) at the American Embassy when we were born, I grew up with a double citizenship. Because of this, prior to America entering the war, I was able to "escape" from France — unlike my maternal grandfather, Daniel, who died in a concentration camp.

The ship landed in New York at dawn on the fifth day of January, 1941. My newborn life began. New York was to me like a fabulous stage set. I had never seen a skyscraper (except in American movies), and they appeared to me as giant monsters spitting light. I was fascinated by the yellow taxi cabs and by the revolving doors of Horn and Hardart, where, if one inserted a coin in the slot and pushed a particular button, the "machine" would eject a sandwich, a piece of pie, some hot food, and even transparent coffee. I spoke no English, except for a few words I picked up on the crossing: yes, no, so sorry, and come back again.

During my first six months in New York, I lived in silence. My father had the ingenious idea of enrolling me as a senior in the local high school where I sat, class after class, not understanding a word of what was going on. American high school students fascinated and frightened me. In Paris, I had grown up with the illusion that, at five feet four inches, I was of average height, something which does not even hold true today, thanks to the beneficial introduction of milk and sport into the life of young *lycéens*. Suddenly, in that high school, I found myself surrounded by screaming sequoias. I was rediscovering (for I had already felt it in my father) an aspect of American life which frightened me: an unpredictable virility, a physical impunity, the sense of a threat. I felt small, vulnerable, alien.

What troubled me most was the perception that French, my native language, had now become obsolete. But my brief *séjour* in the high school was not entirely negative. I retrieved from it an introduction to English and American poetry, an unsuccessful meeting with *The Rime of the Ancient Mariner* (of which I hardly understood a line), and a pleasant encounter with Walt Whitman, Hart Crane, and Carl Sandburg, whom I found at the time approachable and interesting.

America went to war. I enlisted in the U.S. Navy and "saw some action" at sea. This episode of my life was one of maturation. Moreover, it helped (unequivocally, it is true) to establish a sort of rapprochement with my father:

> *My father loved*
> *to parade down Broadway with his military son. The small*
> *decoration of ribbons that I wore on my uniform swelled*
> *him with pride. He would take me by the arm as if*
> *escorting a celebrity: a possessive, yet respectful,*
> *gesture.*

(from La Troisième voix, *trans. Kate Hancock)*

After my navy discharge, I had hoped to resume my career as a ballet dancer. However, the situation was quite different in America. There was no national theater, only ephemeral ballet companies that went broke after a year or two, and there was, of course, the Broadway stage where dancers found some means of making a precarious living. Naively, I would present myself at auditions, together with some hundred male dancers vying for a dozen chorus parts in such shows as *Song of Norway*, where, with my short height and dark complexion, I stuck out like a Pekingese among Great Danes. I also was hampered by the fact that, as a ballet dancer, I had committed a transgression: I loved to read — not only the glossy *Life* magazine, but *literature*!

My first attempt at writing poetry was at Harvard, as a graduate student in comparative literature. It was then the age in academia — and especially in the Ivy League — of Auden, Eliot, and Pound. They were the *monstres sacrés* in our poetic horizon. Pound angered me, baffled me, with his vicious racism, yet I had to come to terms with myself, ask myself fundamental questions for which there are only ambiguous answers. I thrilled at Pound's translations from the Provençal, his lovely adaptation of Li Po's "The River Merchant's Wife," and the astonishingly beautiful "pull down thy vanity" from the Pisan Cantos, an awesome moment of poetic humility . . . but with what magnificent language! In short, my years at Harvard (which in many ways I detested) were when I began to take literature seriously. I had befriended George Steiner, himself a graduate student after a Rhodes Scholarship and some additional honors. Although George was too young for his devastating intellect — which accounted in great part for his quasi-ineptitude in human relationships — he and I established a warm relationship. Perhaps what tied us in friendship was that we were both exiled Jews from Europe, and we related to each other in French. I owe to George the first serious criticism I received of my poetry. I was then a beginner and had little objectivity. I had just written a poem which seemed to me magnificent, with a sublime line which had to do with "a black snake slithering across the wild blackberry bushes." I had just finished reading Joyce's "Ana livia plurela," and I was seduced by Joyce's repetition of sounds. This particular line about the black snake had fallen (I should say slithered) into my lap one night while I was taking something out of the refrigerator.

George and I were at Howard Johnson's having those wonderful (and now departed) lobster rolls for lunch, and I thought that it was a propitious moment to show him my poem. He read it and said between two bites of lobster, "*dis-moi*, have you ever seen a black snake slither?" I was forced to admit that, being mortally afraid of snakes, I wouldn't have taken the time to observe whether it crawled, slid, or slithered. George continued, "Tell me about wild blackberry bushes." Raised in Paris and New York, I had never seen that animal nor tasted of those fruits. Then George administered the *coup de grâce*: "Then why do you write about what you don't know?"

I hated George at that moment. He had done irreparable harm to my poem and especially to that line which *le hasard*, as Breton would have called it, had generously brought to me in the middle of the night at the refrigerator. I thought that our friendship would not survive.

The next morning as I was shaving, I saw in the mirror a face that looked much like me, except that it was laughing. The famous line about the snake came back to me, and I realized that, given my boundless ignorance in the matter, my slithering snake was suddenly idiotic. I owe George for having taught me over lobster rolls that one should beware of lines written in the middle of the night, and especially if they appear to you as sublime.

At Harvard, it was also the first time that I heard a poet read his poem, and what a poet! Dylan Thomas was then quasi-unknown in America. He had not yet begun to record his poems. But word had spread that he was a great bardic poet, a consummate drunk (which wasn't really true; that came later when Thomas began to really act "Thomas"), and a magnificent reader of poetry. Thomas arrived about an hour late, being driven from some other nearby college where he had just read. Between that college and ours were a significant number of bars where Thomas ordered his "protector" to stop. That burly man walked nonchalantly to the platform — swaggering a bit — brushed back a lock of hair, and without bothering to open his book, began "The Refusal to Mourn the Death, by Fire, of a Child in London." Thomas's voice, now like a dirge, now like a passionate love song, rose and we were all shaken by it. I then learned that *politics* could be supremely poetic, the most frightening example being Paul Celan's *Death Fugue*, about the Nazi extermination camps.

After my M.A. at Harvard, I went to the University of California at Los Angeles to work for my Ph.D. I see some significance in the fact that, after a B.A. in English and an M.A. in comparative literature, I was now reentering French literature. The return as an angry prodigal son. I was to discover, under the guidance of Professor Oreste Pucciani, the world of Jean-Paul Sartre. Pucciani was the first serious interpreter of Sartrean existentialism in America. He knew Sartre and Simone de Beauvoir. It is fashionable nowadays to attack the Sartrean system, and indeed there are vulnerable points. However, for young French intellectuals of my generation who had seen France disintegrate — all traditional values (whether good or bad) rendered impotent by the Nazi occupation, honor and cowardice wedded (those who fought in the Resistance and those who collaborated), and the infamy of the concentration camps — Sartre's voice and writing were inspiring.

Few people today realize the impact of Sartre's prefaces: "Black Orpheus," presenting the works of African and Antillese "Francophone" poets, his analysis of anti-Semitism, or his preface to Henri Alleg's book *La Question*, in which Sartre revealed and condemned the use of torture by the French paratroopers in Algeria during the war. Many young French intellectuals of my generation found in Sartre the possibility of a new, secular humanism. Oreste Pucciani was a marvelous teacher — inventive, provocative, what the French call un *maître à penser*.

I had sent a poem to the *California Quarterly*, an excellent literary review based in Los Angeles — a somewhat "neutral" poem about the death of a seagull off the Santa Monica pier. The review had accepted it, and I was elated. It was to be my first publication. I couldn't wait to tell my "regular" group in the coffee shop. One of them, though, had a unexpected reaction. He informed me that Thomas McGrath, one of the editors, had been singled out for his political views and that the *California Quarterly* was being accused — by the witch hunters — of being communist. Whether that was true or not (which it wasn't), my friend pointed out that it wouldn't be "wise" to publish there. I confess that I became scared and leaned toward withdrawing the poem. But first I wanted to talk it over with Oreste Pucciani, my mentor. I called him that evening. He invited me over, and during coffee, I explained about my relationship with the *California Quarterly* and asked him whether I should publish *there*. He began by saying that, in the final analysis, it wasn't for him to decide. I would have to live with that decision. Then he added, "You realize, don't you, that if because of coercion, you were now to withdraw the poem, then the next time a group you belong to, or a publisher, or a well-meaning friend were to pressure you to withdraw or amend your text, what would you do then?"

He sent me home with those disturbing thoughts. The next morning, after a night of vigil, I decided to let the *California Quarterly* publish my poem. It was perhaps the most important decision I ever made in my life, and I never thanked Oreste for his guidance. I do so now.

I entered the academic profession (this sounds so pompous — I could have said the circus, or what the French call *le panier de crabes*) at Dartmouth, which was then referred to as the biggest prep school in the East. I understand that since it has become co-ed and now offers some graduate degrees, the atmosphere has matured. I didn't like their clannishness (moreover, in those days you hardly found a Jew or an African American in French departments); they didn't like my clothes. So we were even, and I have no resentment. I am, in fact, grateful to Dartmouth, for one day while browsing in the library — which was quite good — I stumbled upon Léopold Sédar Senghor's *Anthologie de la poésie nègre et malgache d'expression française*, with the provocative "Black Orpheus" essay by Sartre. At the time, with Jack Hirshman, a young poet and instructor in the English department — and who shared my opinion about Dartmouth — we began a poetry review, *The Hip-Pocket Poems*, which lasted two years. It gave us the freedom to publish barely known international poets, and I began to translate and publish Francophone African and Caribbean poets. This experience was to redirect my entire academic life.

Above all, what struck me about what was then considered "Third World poetry" was the conjunction of poetry and politics, poetry and human rights. This had a special reality for me, when some years later I was invited as a visiting professor to the University of Tanzania. Dar es Salaam, the capital, was then the base for most Southern African liberation movements: Angola, Mozambique, South Africa. In Dar, I had just met Eva, a young (much younger than me) Swedish woman. We fell in love. I began to feel happy again, after years of turmoil in a difficult marriage. In Dar, we had befriended Edouardo Mondlane, the head of Frelimo, the Mozambique Liberation Movement. One morning we learned that Edouardo had been killed by a letter bomb. Mondlane's death, in the midst of my newfound happiness was an unbearable paradox. There was something monstrous in his dying, something shameful in our love: "*Eva /*

Je t'aime et des hommes meurent [Eva / I love you and men are dying]."

My poetry is an attempt to legitimize my presence in the world and to speak for those unable to do so. Auden's line "for poetry makes nothing happen" has always appeared to me either as deliberately flippant, or as morally obscene. What makes what happen? Is poetry really excluded from the process? And if it were so, why would so many governments burn books, put writers (including poets) behind bars, torture and kill them? What is so indelible about the published poem that it sustains generations? The Nigerian poet Wole Soyinka, the Nobel laureate, recalls that in his Lagos jail, he found strength to survive by writing poetry on toilet paper. Archibald MacLeish told me that after the liberation of France he met again with his close friend Leon Blum, a former French statesman. Blum, a Jew, had been interned in a Nazi camp. He was already an old man, and MacLeish asked him how he had managed to survive the hardship of detention. Blum answered that in the most debilitating moments of his incarceration, when he was ready to "let go," he would recall a poem of Baudelaire, and this gave him the strength to hold on.

Poetry remains for me a way out of exile, a newfound relationship with Nature,

> *Your body resting on the rocks my penis on the edge of a sea shell the smell of salt and dill*
>
> *I begin to understand the shy radiance of the rose-hips along the path that leads to the water*

a coming to terms, after heart attacks and two open-heart surgeries, with what Camus called "the betrayal of the body [*la trahison du corps*]."

> *the hospital is writing me again*
> *"within the past months have you*
> *experienced difficulties in breathing"*
> *I am tempted to write "ever since*
> *the day I was born" but there is*
> *no such answer on the multiple*
> *choice*

the celebration of love when the couple truly becomes the couple. "I have lost so much time in not touching you the right way / we shall have to try again more *tenderly*." Above all, poetry is a meditation between words and Silence, birth and death, myself and myself, the flight of Icarus

> *a clean line with no*
> *smudge a horizontal*
> *line leading nowhere*
> *but to defeat and the*
> *irrevocable beauty of*
> *the search.*

Books (Poetry)

Return to My Native Land, by Aimé Césaire (translator). N.p., 1968.
Cadastre, by Aimé Césaire (translator). Three Continent Press, 1973.
Faux-papiers. Editions Saint-Germain-des-Prés, 1973.
La Troisième voix. Editions Saint-Germain-des-Prés, 1976.
Un Matin le temps m'est venu. Editions Saint-Germain-des-Prés, 1985.
Méninges. Editions Le Hameau, 1988.

Periodicals

Numerous poems, translations, and essays have appeared in *Beloit Poetry Journal, California Quarterly, Chelsea, Comparative Literature Studies, Dalhousie Review, Folio, Literary Review, New York Quarterly, Ohio Review, Poésie 1, Poetry Australia, Presence Africaine, Quixote, Sulfur*, and *Western Review*, among other American and foreign publications.

Jim Brown

Robert Flanagan was born in 1941 in Toledo, Ohio. He earned a B.A. in English at the University of Toledo and an M.A. in English at the University of Chicago. He also studied theology and literature at the University of Chicago divinity school. His writing awards include a National Endowment for the Arts Fellowship in fiction and Ohio Arts Council fellowships in poetry, fiction, and playwriting. He has taught at the Central YMCA Community College in Chicago, Slippery Rock State College in Pennsylvania, Thurber House in Columbus, Ohio, the Marion (Ohio) Correctional Institute, and Ohio Wesleyan University, where he is now director of creative writing.

LIFE'S FICTION, FICTION'S LIFE

Attention

Writing is a matter of attention. At the simplest level this means getting attention. Like children, writers want people to notice them. Look, look at what I made!

The people in my family were talkers. Their lives pared down by hard times, they entertained themselves by playing word games, mocking their supposed betters with sly jokes and recounting past family exploits to a point that they took on mythic status. If you wanted to hold your own at those late-night, boozy, kitchen table confabs, you had to know how to tell a story. When you had judged your listeners' interest and patience correctly, dropping the punch line at just the right moment, your reward was a burst of laughter. And family pride. An uncle might clap you on the shoulder and compliment your grinning father, "Red, this kid's no dummy."

At a deeper level writing is a way of paying attention to the world. Translating the coded messages behind the slogans we live by is hard work that requires conditioning the self to be acutely and painfully conscious.

As a boy in Catholic schools I was forever being told to "Pay Attention." It seemed that frequently I would float off somewhere in my head. At the end of my teens I was called to attention — "Ten-hut!" — in the marines. There, the veil of familiarity stripped from things, I began to take notice, and to question.

At still another level writing is a way of deflecting attention from the performing self onto the subject. In fiction, since subject matter most often is character, this may mean calling attention to others.

When I was younger I wrote to escape my reality and to parade my talent. Sinking deeper into fiction over the years, I became less concerned with self-display and more interested in calling attention to those who commonly go unnoticed by society. "Attention must be paid to such a man," I'd say, quoting Miller, although it was my father's fate, not Willy Loman's, that spurred me to work.

Writing holds surprising rewards. The act of creation which spirits you away from family and community may in time return you to them as you learn to pay better attention to things beyond the self. But there are costs as well. Fiction that aims at truth is very demanding of the writer. It calls everything into question. It requires a balancing act between the private and public self. Like the writer, it contains its opposite and is created at tension.

The Glass Center of the World

I was born and raised in the Ohio city that makes the scales used to weigh in prizefighters ("He tipped the Toledo's at 159 and ½"), the home of Owens-Illinois and Libby-Owens-Ford, companies that owed their success to old Mike Owens, my Dad liked to point out, an immigrant Mick who taught the high muckety-mucks a thing or two and made a bundle in doing it; the Glass Center of the World, as its billboards bragged, where the triple-A ball club for a time bore the bizarre moniker the Glass Sox; an industrial town of workers' neat houses clustered feudally about Willys Jeep and Autolite, Spitzer Paper Box and Pinkerton Tobacco, and the Champion Spark Plug plant where my mother worked as a machine operator for twenty-five years.

My father's father, John, and his father, Thomas, came to America from Aghoo village, County Roscommon, Ireland, in 1890. They left behind John's sister Bridget to scrabble a living out of the eight acres that was insufficient to support them all. I don't know how long the farm had been in the family, but it was a long time. When I went to Ireland in 1978 to see the stone homestead, now tumbled and roofless and part of the Martin dairy farm, I was moved to hear the Martin brothers remark that some of their cows were up in "Flanagan's field." John, son of Thomas Flanagan and Honorah Mattimoe, married to Mary Cody of Hugginstown, County Kilkenny, set up residence on City Park in Saint Patrick's parish, a Toledo neighborhood crammed with Irish who kept a goat in the backyard and a bin full of potatoes in the cellar. Thomas took his shovel and got work on the streets, and John joined the police force. My father, Robert, was John's second son. Hard times ended his education at the sixth grade. He went to work as a bellhop at the Boody House hotel to help his father support a family of nine on a policeman's pay. The oldest child, Mayme, had died suddenly of pneumonia, and Jim, the older son, couldn't be looked to for help; despite the captain's frequent use of the razor strop, Jim ran with a bad crowd of cornerboys, and Earl, the youngest son, was a precocious drunk. But no one worried much about Rob's missed schooling; a flame-haired bundle of energy, quick-witted, skilled at tap dancing, acrobatics, and boxing, he was a go-getter sure to make his mark in a land of opportunity.

My mother's family came from Redruth, Cornwall. Her grandfather, Samuel Treloar, was a tinsmith with an attached cottage on Foundry Row. He emigrated to Canada, where he started up his own foundry. His son Charles left Canada for the States and became a traveling insurance salesman; in Georgetown, Ohio, he met and married a schoolteacher, Almona Robinson. They settled on a sixty-acre farm on Summerfield Road near Petersburg, Michigan, struggling to provide for their six children. Despite persistent poverty, Charles Treloar thought of himself as an aristocrat whose talents and abilities went unappreciated by his country neighbors. His youngest daughter he named Minnie, after a prosperous sister who failed to reward her brother with a monetary gift for the honor. Devilish and lively, Minnie seemed unafraid of the tyrant father the rest of the family shied from. She tried to cure his stiff neck by sneaking up behind him and giving it a sudden jerk. She substituted sand for sugar in his coffee to see if he could tell the difference. Hearing a new phrase at school one day she skipped all the way home past neighbors' houses chanting at the top of her lungs so as not to forget it: "Son of a bitch, son of a bitch!" Minnie began high school but collapsed with a severe case of tonsillitis. A bleeder, she was sick for months after her tonsils were removed, at times coughing up blood so thick it looked like chunks of liver. In those days if you didn't pass the year-end tests you were charged a fee for the otherwise free schooling; the Treloars couldn't afford to pay, so upon recovery Minnie stayed at home to help her mother with housework. Resenting her father's heavy drinking and bad temper, she refused to surrender to his rule. She dropped what she felt was a rube's name, Minnie, in favor of her middle name, Jane. She shocked the family by getting her hair bobbed. Finally she packed her things and in a new flapper dress caught the interurban train to Toledo, where a red-headed tap dancer offered to help carry her bags.

Our family rented a one-bedroom apartment on Monroe Street near Detroit Avenue. It was above Maloney's Bar & Grill, which stood between the Do-All machine shop and Ideal furniture store. "Here we are," my father would joke, "living on the far side of Ideal." He took the bedroom, my mother slept with my sister Mona Mary, ten years older than I, in the Murphy bed that pulled down from the living-room closet, and my bed was against one wall of the small dining room which also held my desk and toys. Swayne Field, home of the Mud Hens, was a half block away and we could see most of the playing field from our back porch. I stood out on Detroit Avenue summer nights waiting for home-run balls to sail over the right-field fence.

Dad was a disabled veteran, a shell-shocked World War I U.S. Marine Corps machine gunner, one of the Devil Dogs who'd broken the German advance at Belleau Wood and Château-Thierry. His veterans' compensation check barely paid the rent. Sometimes he held down a sort of job, part time or short term. When he was short-order cook downstairs at Maloney's we had jumbo pickerel for supper on Fridays; he'd run it up the back stairs wrapped in his apron. But it was Mom, ten years younger than Dad and tall and wiry where he was short and stout, who supported us. Soon after I was born, when we were without light and heat due to unpaid bills, she got hired on at Champion Spark Plug as part of the World War II industrial effort. As Dad said, or I think I remember him saying, "Best thing that ever happened to this family was the Japs hitting Pearl Harbor." She worked second trick, making five thousand aviation plugs every night, and came home about midnight five nights a week completely exhausted. I waited up for her. "Oh Laws," she would say, "I'm so tired I could just die." Dad never cracked any jokes right then and was quick to pour her a beer. In the afternoons when he was sleeping, I sat with her at the kitchen table as she got ready for work, watching her tape her fingers to keep them from getting cut up by the freshly tooled cores. I took pride in her endurance and in her ability to handle such demanding work. Years later when I learned how to tape my hands for boxing, making sure to pad the knuckles and to cross over to support the thumb, it was my mother I thought of, hoping I'd prove to be as brave as she was.

But this was long before it became chic for women to drive bulldozers and men to be liberated to laundry, and my dominant feeling was one of shame that my father stayed at home, jobless, while my mother headed off to the factory. At school a nun scolded me in front of our class because on the student information form in the space provided for *Father's Occupation* I had written "housewife." She thought I was being a smart aleck, and maybe I was. I learned early on to use a stinging wit, like a jab, to keep the nuns and my fellow parochial-school inmates at a safe distance.

At times Dad crawled under the table if a car backfired in the street. When he was in the veterans' hospital at Brecksville, his hands shook constantly; to drink coffee without spilling it he held one end of a towel with the fingers that gripped the cup's handle, then with the towel looped about his neck he'd tug on it with the other hand, guiding the cup to his lips. Once when he'd lost still another job he came home and locked himself in his room and plucked out his eyebrows and the front locks of his red hair. For some time after, he covered his head with a white kerchief knotted at the four corners.

Rarely did I bring a friend to the apartment. I didn't want anyone to see my father walking around in his old blue robe dusting the furniture with wadded tissues or burning canned soup for our supper. Mom and Mona had jobs, so mostly it was just Dad and me at home. All the while he cooked or cleaned he was telling me, or maybe himself, stories of the heroic past. My grandfather, Captain John Flanagan, once shook hands with the great John L. Sullivan himself and was in the police cordon about the ring at the Dempsey-Willard fight, July 4, 1919, in Toledo's Bay View Park. Helping the bloodied Willard from the ring, he had to beat back sore losers trying to sucker-punch the man they'd bet on. My uncle Francis Delora, lieutenant detective, kicked down a door in a hail of tommy gun fire to shoot it out with the notorious Cowboy Hill.

Not very often, but sometimes, Dad talked about his own neighborhood scrapes and boxing matches, but never about the war. It was hard for me to imagine him in combat, although I'd seen for myself his Purple Heart and Presidential Citation and, in the bottom drawer of his dresser, the gas mask and the dented green helmet with a red Indian head on the front, an insignia he had painted on the helmets of his whole platoon. My father was nearly fifty when I was born, an old and broken fifty, and seemed more like my grandfather. Listening to the tales of his past, I'd try to match up the pot-bellied skinny-armed man before me with the battler in the story. Sometimes I thought he was making it all up. Generally, though, I believed his story because it was so clear that he believed it. And because I wanted to believe it. I was hungry for a sense of personal history, as if that might confirm my worth, of which I was in grave doubt.

One of the things I learned at home was that though our people hadn't come up in the world, we were a damn sight more interesting and had a helluva lot better stories to tell than the bloodless types who were better off. Another thing I learned, a teaching confirmed later by church and military, was that I was special because I was part of a select unit of humankind; yet I was a very undeserving part of that unit and could be expelled.

When he wasn't talking about the grand past, Dad was whipping up visions of a wonderful future. One of us would do something to hit it big and we'd all be on easy street. I was clever, it could happen to me, I could be the one.

As a young boy I wanted to be a cowboy or a priest, a cop or a boxer. While entertaining such fantasies, I spent my time, a fat kid with a hernia, constant throat infections, a heart murmur and touch of rheumatic fever, drawing and coloring and modeling clay. When Mom went to the bank she would bring home in her big purse thick packs of white Toledo Trust checking deposit slips. I used the blank backs to make cartoon books filled with bright colors and stories of miraculous rescue or heroic violence. I spent whole days making clay figures — usually cowboys and Indians; I was no great shakes at originality — and using them to act out adventures I made up as I went along, saying my characters' lines aloud. Dad spoke with pride of my artistic talent. But I caught the doubt in my mother's eyes. I knew she worried that my "art" was only a way of hiding from the world, and that she feared I would turn out like my father, a man too afraid of life to go out into it, hiding behind an unprovable illness, sleeping away the days in a small airless bedroom with blankets tacked over the windows, and prowling the apartment at night like something caged.

I'd be a success at something, I told her, although secretly I felt sure to fail at anything I tried. How could I hope to match my grandfather and my Uncle Frank for courage? What could I hope to do to strike it rich and save our family? And, at another level, I wasn't even sure how hard I was supposed to try. The message I got was mixed. On the one hand we Flanagans were nobodies in a world where being somebody meant that you were corrupt. Our poverty and obscurity were proofs of our virtue. "Look at her," my mother would say of someone dressed too fancily at Sunday mass, dismissing the pretender with a sniff. She scorned the man who owned our building, a fellow whose only interests were money and lording it over others. Her goal for me was that I'd hold a steady job — at Champion Spark Plug if need be, though maybe I could get in at Owens-Illinois, where my sister Mona worked, or better yet at the post office, where you didn't get laid off. On the other hand our family played Monopoly with a passion, Mom and Dad bet the slots and numbers in hopes of making a killing, and Dad's chatter was filled with envy of those in power. "I'll bet you that you might turn out to be rich and famous," he'd say to me, always when Mom wasn't home, and usually when he wanted me to feel better about some trouble at school or an argument we'd had that he couldn't patch up by giving me a bowl of ice cream, his standard remedy. "No, really, it could happen, Bobby. You just have to have an idea. Like the Parker Brothers." Over the years that became his repeated hope for me: "Maybe someday you'll have an idea."

Back then I never thought of being a writer. Dad had been a writer, briefly: a crime reporter for the old *Newsbee* and, partly due to his flowing Palmer Method handwriting, an executive secretary to the Toledo *Blade* editor. Where had it gotten him? (Of course, where had anything gotten him? He'd been a salesman for a meat company, a used-furniture store owner, a bankrupt, a dock worker in a tobacco warehouse, a short-order cook, a patient in a veterans' hospital, and finally a recluse. It was not a history to give his son confidence.) And although we were a talky family, we weren't literary. We told jokes, we played word games (Twenty Questions and What's Your Trade), we recited Thomas Moore songs my father had learned from his father and I from him, "Oh believe me if all those endearing young charms," and we admired the newspaper columns of Jim Bishop and the delivery of Don Dunphy doing the Friday night fights. The only reading materials in the apartment were *Ring* magazine and *Police Gazette*, Dad's paperback copy of Dale Carnegie's *How to Win Friends and Influence People*, and Mom's *Laugh with Leacock*, a hardcover which I think had belonged to her father. How religiously we took Carnegie's American principles of business success. How hard we laughed at the Canadian Leacock's parodies, from which Dad might read aloud some nights when he'd had a few, as in "Gertrude the Governess" when the romantic Lord Ronald, rebuked by his father, Lord Knotacent, the Earl of Knotacentinum Towers (pronounced Nosham Taws), "flung himself from the room, flung himself upon his horse and rode madly off in all directions." "Oh Laws," my mother would cry, wiping away tears and struggling for breath, "that darn fool!"

I did some reading on my own, mostly *Men at War* and *Classic* comic books. I owned two real books. My aunt Margaret, a schoolteacher, gave me the first one for Christmas when I was nine, *Boru: The Story of an Irish Wolfhound*, and I read it again and again. On my tenth birthday in April, maybe because I'd been begging for a dog despite the rule against pets in the apartment, Dad gave me *Wild Animals of the World*, a large-size dictionary of wildlife with beautiful, realistic illustrations, many in color. I'd never seen anything like it. I just about memorized the book. Dad liked to quiz me on it to impress my uncles. Quagga? "This partly striped animal believed to have been related both to the zebra and to the wild ass is now extinct." Tapir? "The Tapir has been picturesquely but unscientifically described as a pig that started out to be an elephant and then changed its mind." Seeing me reading and rereading the same two books prompted my sister, Mona Mary, who studied art at Notre Dame Academy, was the proponent of higher culture in our family, and was often put in the role of mother, to lead me to the Dorr Street branch library. There I found books that fed my desire to escape into dreams of power: Jack London's *The Call of the Wild* and *White Fang*, Rudyard Kipling's *The*

Jungle Book, Mark Twain's *A Connecticut Yankee in King Arthur's Court*, and, one of my favorites, Henry Gregor Felsen's *Street Rod.* Some years later I picked up the family Bible, which I'd never seen anyone open, and got lost in Old Testament battles. I would lie on my bed reading Judges and Samuel and Kings. My father kept asking me if everything was all right; behind my back he told my mother he was afraid I'd gone off the deep end.

It wasn't only my Bible reading that worried him. If I wanted to buy a paper route, or to join the Boy Scouts, he immediately sensed danger and predicted disaster. "Now why do you want to start something like that?" he'd complain. "Why can't you just leave well enough alone?" Out of fear, he actively encouraged me to do nothing. Because things were sure to turn out badly, the safest tactic was to keep still. Part of me came to believe that, and often I felt nailed in place. But another part of me resented and resisted inaction. In my late teens, to my father's dismay, the active part of me more and more took over. I sent away for Charles Atlas's *Dynamic Tension* body-building book and ordered correspondence courses in cartooning and gun repair; I took up the guitar; I won a St. Genesius medal (the patron saint of actors) for Best Actor in a Catholic Youth Organization drama festival; I did sit-ups until my hernia was declared healed and I could throw away the hated leather truss; I practiced with handgun and rifle and became a crack shot; I thumped the heavy bag and made the light bag dance; I drag-raced "borrowed" cars like a maniac.

Yet the fear was there, all the same. Especially if I let myself think about Uncle Frank.

Francis Delora was six feet four inches tall and weighed over 250 pounds. Retired from the force after forty-six years of service, 1908 to 1954, he still was a formidable figure. In fact, he was my image of God. He had a huge lion-like head with silver hair brushed straight back, a broad leathery red face, and hands that would make two of mine. He wore gold-rimmed glasses, a gold wedding band, and his gold retirement watch. Even in retirement he often packed his service pistol, a 32.20 Colt Police Positive.

The events that follow still confuse me, as they did when they occurred. I can't say for certain what happened; I only know what I think I remember, a memory distorted by pain.

One night when I was sixteen and had just come home from a high school dance, Dad got a phone call from his sister Nora. A great-hearted, fat-billowing woman who suffered from cataracts and hardening of the arteries, Nora was upset because she "couldn't get Frankie to wake up." Dad began hunting his car keys and fumbling around for a pair of trousers. Mom was due home from work at any minute. I went on ahead, running up to Frank and Nora's apartment on Lawrence Avenue. When I knocked, Aunt Nora opened the door a crack and said to come in. I pushed on the door but it stuck. Finally I squeezed through, stumbling over Uncle Frank. He lay on his back just inside the door, his neck bent and head propped on the baseboard. Aunt Nora had wedged a pillow behind his head to make him comfortable. She moved off down the hall, saying that she was cooking Frankie a hamburger; he'd feel better if he'd only eat a little something. I could smell whiskey on him. I called to him and pulled on his wrists to get him to sit up. He was so heavy I couldn't move him. His big hands felt cold. Greasy smoke and the smell of charred meat floated in from the kitchen. My fingers touched the back of his head. It felt pulpy, like a smashed melon. My hand came away covered with blood.

Dad and Mom showed up, and the police. Frank had been in a fight with his brother Hank in a bar. Hank was every bit as big as Frank and they were tearing up the place. It took a half dozen officers to get them calmed down. Then, as a courtesy to Frank, a squad car had run the Delora boys home. Both brothers were banged up, the Polish police captain told us, but Frank must have been hurt a lot worse than he looked. It was a terrible thing, though it'd be best to call it a fall, an accident. We wouldn't want to start something that could get the man's own brother charged with manslaughter, would we?

At home Mom and Dad called Hank and talked, then sat at the kitchen table saying it had to be the cops. Everybody knew the way Frank bullied patrolmen, and how hard he was to handle when he was on the sauce. One of those rookies, Dad said, had used a sap harder than he'd meant to, that was the truth of it, then they panicked and dumped the body and got the hell out of there, the lousy lying murdering bums. There wasn't one damn thing we could do about it either.

For some time after, I lay awake nights imagining myself tracking down the rookie to ambush him with Frank's own pistol. In school I'd daydream about getting the Polish captain too, making sure he recognized me before I let him have it. But finally I just tried not to think about Uncle Frank. Whenever I let myself dwell on it — so much power so easily destroyed! — I'd feel my father's paralysis creeping over me.

After high school I went to work. I worked as night watchman at the Family Fair department store at Bancroft and Auburn, 10:00 P.M. to 7:00 A.M., Monday through Saturday. I liked the job because I was left alone and got to carry a gun; it was a .38 American Bulldog, one of

Uncle Frank's revolvers that Dad had handed on to me when Aunt Nora died. I worked as janitor at the truck terminals out on Tractor Road, day laborer for a landscaper, and utility man at Republic Steel. I worked as dishwasher at the Waffle Inn downtown by the Town Hall Burlesque. The strippers would come in for coffee and donuts in the afternoon, sexy, scary women with hard faces and harsh, smoky laughs. They called me Kid and said why didn't I drop in and catch their act. I wanted to, but was way too leery of them. After washing dishes, having taken up boxing as a manly alternative to the neighborhood streetfights I dreaded, I'd walk to the Y and work out. I'd lost enough weight in training to be taken for a middleweight, a coach told me I had a snappy jab, and one wonderful afternoon a sparring partner went down after bouncing off the ropes into my defensive, stiff-armed right. I thought maybe I'd found my calling and talked of going into the Golden Gloves. This despite the fact that I had no power, possessed a suspect jaw and small breakable hands, had worn glasses since the fourth grade and saw my opponent in the ring as a moving blur. Getting coldcocked a couple of times cleared my head of that fiction.

When I'd quit a handful of dead-end jobs in the year since graduating from high school, and when I had no idea what I was doing or where I was going, and was scared that I was proving to be just like my father, I had a beer with a high school buddy in a bar on Toledo's east side. He told me that first thing in the morning he was going downtown to join the marines. I said, "Pick me up."

It seemed to me that I was doing something to show how different I was from my father, the ex-marine, by joining the Marines. Why I thought that then I don't know now.

At Parris Island I got to talk to guys who'd gone to college (because my friend and I had joined the reserves) and I noticed that they didn't seem that much smarter than I was. As soon as I finished my six months' active duty, I enrolled at the University of Toledo, the only college I'd heard of except for Notre Dame, home of the Fighting Irish, whose fight song we'd copied for ours at Central Catholic High.

It was then that I began reading seriously. The works which most influenced me at that time were the stories of Frank O'Connor, so natural sounding I might have been hearing them told around our kitchen table, the plays of Eugene O'Neill, which seemed to spring right out of the Old Testament, and James T. Farrell's Studs Lonigan novels: *Young Lonigan*, *The Young Manhood of Studs Lonigan*, and *Judgment Day*. In Farrell's work I recognized the characters I saw around me every day, and it struck me that I might write about the people in my own life, even in Toledo.

At twenty-one, I started writing some poems and stories of my own. I didn't write many because I was going to college days and working nights and spending as much time as I could with a great girl I'd found, someone who was good looking and spunky and took me seriously.

I read Jack London's *Martin Eden*, which excited me so much I decided to make my living as a writer. I knocked out a dozen stories and rushed them off to men's magazines and they bounced right back. The stories for the most part were accounts of things I'd seen, like a guy in a diner smacking somebody with one of those heavy, glass sugar dispensers. I'd never thought of using something like that as a weapon, and I wrote a story about an unarmed man trapped in a diner by a punk with a knife. I got John Brick, a visiting instructor at U.T. and, published novelist, to read it and he said, "Okay, but the only thing that happens in this is that one fellow hits the other with a sugar jar." I said, "Right! Like it?" He suggested that I sign up for his fiction-writing course the next semester, which, thank my lucky stars, I did.

Also in those first bursts of work I wrote a play and got the chance to put it on at the university. Entitled *The Discontent*, it was imitation O'Neill with some Ibsen tossed in and presented as the symbol of a family's despair an heirloom music box that had been wound so tight that it finally snapped. I directed the production as well as played the lead role of the father, a failed artist. I also helped to build the set, a kitchen, and hauled in a real sink as a final, convincing touch. The play, which dealt with art, history, war, love, courage, the family, and alcoholism, ran a bit long for a one act. The action consisted mainly of declamatory speeches which sounded like blank verse and gave the work, I thought, a certain tragic dimension. After the performance, the doyenne of the theater department stopped by to say "Well, Flanagan, you put in everything *and* the kitchen sink."

My first published work, a poem entitled "The Rift," was inspired by a break-up with my new girlfriend. I'd written it in the middle of the night in a Bancroft Avenue Laundromat, conditions which struck me as romantic and artistic. That the poem depended upon a metaphor based on cows, animals I knew nothing about, didn't matter. My girl and I got back together and the poem was published in *The Small Pond*, a little magazine in the east. Such publication, I thought, confirmed my calling.

In my junior year of college, at twenty-two, I quit breaking up with my girl and married her. Kathleen Rose Borer was from Ottawa, Ohio, where she'd grown up poor in a family with a troubled, troublesome father, and had come to Toledo to take her nurse's training at St. Vincent's Hospital on Cherry Street. At the time she had it in mind to become an air force nurse and see the world. I'd met her on a blind date arranged by some friends who'd gone to Central Catholic with me and were in training with Katy at Saint V's. Maybe they thought I needed a nurse to care for me; in those days, and for too long after, I acted as though I did. I'd ride around nights with two other aspiring writers from Irish families, talking literature and drinking and looking for trouble; one night we took a tiny Fiat cross-country over the Ottawa Park golf course as I fired my .38 at trees. Whatever the nursing students' motives, they did me a great favor. I've never known a person of deeper patience or more genuine independence of spirit than Katy; her understanding of people has helped give some depth to my fiction's characters.

Two years after our wedding, expecting our first child in three months, we left Toledo for Chicago, the literary turf of James T. Farrell and Nelson Algren and Richard Wright and Theodore Dreiser, writers I regarded as gods, and of a fairly new guy I thought showed promise, Saul Bellow. Why would anyone ever go to New York when there was Chicago? I could not believe my good luck. I had won a full fellowship in theology and literature because George Guthrie, my philosophy professor at Toledo, had taken me aside one day after class to inquire about my future. I thought I'd stay on at the city streets department, I told him, driving weed mowers and trucks, and would write at night. It shouldn't be long before I made some money; I'd already had a poem published. He told me that I ought to consider graduate school. I said okay, and applied to the one place he mentioned, his alma mater, the University of Chicago.

When Katy and I drove out of town in a U-Haul truck, we passed a billboard proclaiming The Glass Center of the World. Despite the promise of our future, I felt the truth in that phrase. It was what I had learned growing up. Everything about you was breakable.

It's that knowledge which informs my fiction.

Writing Life

A young marine from Detroit wrote to me about my novel *Maggot*: "Sir, thank you for having the balls to tell the truth!" That's the greatest praise I've ever gotten for my work.

Yet if at times I find truth, I more often lose sight of fact. I confuse what actually happened with what I've imagined or feared. Like a scavenger at a community dump, I'll pick up something from another's life that seems too good to waste. Saving it means putting it into fiction. To do that I need to emotionally live through the incident or anecdote, often to the point that it takes on the feel of personal experience. Sometimes my father's or grandfather's doings, which I've heard recounted in such vivid detail so often, seem to be my own. Or, if what I'm writing is based on something I actually was part of, I'm likely to forget that it didn't happen to the extreme that it does in the story.

For instance, I was only a "summer marine" yet I got more out of the experience by brooding about it afterward than did many marines who lived it for a four-year hitch or longer. The fact that I wrote about it to such an extent, as with my meager boxing experience, or my erotic fantasies, may lead one to imagine me to be more marine, boxer, or Casanova than in fact I am. By "one" I don't mean only my reader, whoever that may be. Often I'll catch myself feeling depressed or excited, or generally guilty, about something that upon reflection I realize exists only in my fiction. Yet it felt so real that I have to remind myself: Look, you just *write* this stuff; you make it up out of things you wish or fear you might do.

Sometimes I ask why I tell stories at all. I'm a fairly healthy, passably competent person. Why don't I just live life? This question most often occurs to me when I'm stuck on something I'm writing. Suddenly the entire enterprise of literature seems suspect. Why should I hide away in a little room making up adventures like some kid with plastic soldiers? Although unlike my father's bedroom it has no blankets over the windows, my study can come to seem a sanctuary unfit for a man who claims an interest in real life.

Maybe I should pedal my bike downtown to Delaware's Hamburger Inn (fictional Olentangy's Swope's Cafe) to drink coffee and catch up on local gossip, overhearing perhaps some farm woman remark of her recently passed-away father (as one does to the lawyer Owen Moore in "Local Anaesthetic"), "Things just wore him to a fragile"; or a father-in-law complain about the abusive bum his only daughter married (as handyman Dewey Grooms does in "Father's Day"), "The thing of it is you can't talk to the boy." Or I could take a ride in my truck along the back roads flanking the Olentangy River (past the limestone millworker's cottage where wild Shelly Gold lives alone in "All Alone and Blue"), or head north on Route 23, making the two-hour drive to Toledo to stir bittersweet memories by looking at the place that once held Maloney's Bar & Grill and our family's apartment, the landscape of the heart, now an on/off ramp for I-75 North.

Then again I may as well stay at my desk and hope to fill some pages. Because even when I'm not writing I'm thinking about writing. Although I would wish this not to be the case, it's generally not enough for me to live in the present. I want life to be narrated, to be witnessed. The lived moment has a felt value in itself, of course, but it has added value and the pleasure of form when it becomes something written.

Not that there are no rewards to life as lived. There are many times when I don't give a thought to writing. Playing in a handball tournament is not something I do in order to fashion a narrative from it. When I'm teaching, which I enjoy, although I'd enjoy it more if I could do it less, I'm thinking of the students' work or the work we're studying, not mine. At fifty, I no longer hunger to escape my known life for the illusory salvation of fame. I've fought through to a point where I can say that it's all right if the world regards my work as small potatoes. What's important to me is that the potatoes are cared for, are not let go to rot, and prove nourishing. I am fortunate to have a decent job at a small college where I respect and enjoy my colleagues; I give thanks for a marriage that has not only endured but continued to grow for nearly thirty years; I feel pride in going to New York City to act as audience for the talents of our daughters, Anne's in a play or Nora's in a photography exhibit. None of these experiences derive their value from being potential subject matter for fiction.

Nor has my life as lived lacked dramatic conflict. There was a time, after a long and painful, failed biracial adoption, when it didn't look like our marriage would last. There were other times, during my drinking days, when it didn't look like I'd last. I went roaring and swinging after four Puerto Rican teenagers in New York City one night when they passed a remark I took as an insult. I flew a car off the road into a cornfield at ninety miles an hour. These incidents aren't fictional, although I wish they were. And then there are things that I'm not sure if I really remember or only think I remember because I have reconstructed them, like fiction, from my own scraps of recollection and from what others say happened, such as the night I told a bartender who had a shotgun leveled at me that he didn't have the guts to pull the trigger. My line in this scene is the same as the one my father was said to have said the night he stood blocking the door when his brother Jim, hopped up on heroin and gripping a loaded pistol, tried to force his way into our place. Did I unconsciously repeat my father's dauntless remark, which I am assuming he actually said, or did my memory later rearrange the shotgun scene to include it? I no longer know.

However dramatic or tawdry, it's not the event that most interests me as a writer. I want language to become style and so to work the magic of transformation on raw experience, to validate it, even to redeem it. This is a childish expectation, perhaps, or a residual Catholic habit. Loving word power, however, is a major part of what it means to be a member of the tribe of writers.

As far back as I can remember I have delighted in language. At home my father's stories were punctuated by phrases that served as refrains in a formal verbal performance: Oh for crying out loud, Not for all the tea in China, As God's my witness, Mark my words, He's only small potatoes. At church I was a willing altar boy because I loved the sound of the Latin mass: *Introibo Ad Altare Dei, Dominus Vobiscum, Ora Pro Nobis*. Not that I was overly solemn about it. I joked that I knew the pope's phone number, *Et Cum Spiritu Tuo*, and in choir for *Ora Pro Nobis* sang "All blow your noses." But on the altar, in a setting of marble pillars and white candles that made me think of the art museum, I took pride in being prompt with my responses, keeping pace with the priest, matching him line by line in an incantatory dialogue that approached drama. (When the English Mass came in, the magic was gone and so was I.) In the gym, I loved the mix of archaic formality and salty tang in boxing speech: Pronate the blow!, a coach might shout, meaning, Turn the punch over from the shoulder to gain power; Lift it up and knock it off! meaning, raise your opponent's head with an uppercut and follow with a hook; and that gem of a maxim on handling an adversary: Make him miss and make him pay. In the service, I discovered the poetry of profanity, how a simple-four letter vulgarity could be used like salt in cooking to flavor any saying, and how richly metaphorical ordinary speech could be. A drill instructor warning me that the next time I lipped off he was going to punch me would say, I'm gonna put out your running lights; meaning, the eyes in the Jeep of my head, or in other words knock me out. You didn't stand close enough to your razor this morning, a sergeant would tell a grunt with five o'clock shadow; Put some glass in that hole, one boot would yell at another to get him to close the window. On a morning run, our platoon would chant, I gotta gal who lives on a hill, if she won't then her sister will; You hadda good home but you left, you're right. As clearly as any image of these experiences, the sound of them stays with me.

Often I will say my work aloud as I write. I listen for pattern and tone. The first paragraph of "Close Dancing," for instance, at least in part works on tone. The story deals with the conflict between institutional power and the individual conscience. The power is the Catholic Church, represented by a formidable nun, and the individual is a fatherless, scrappy boy who refuses to take the blame for something he has not done.

> *Word came down from Sister Mary Annunciation, their*
> *eighth grade teacher and principal of Saint Sebastian's. As*
> *usual, it had to do with trouble and Doolan.*

What pleases me about this is that it opens on *word*; in the beginning was the word, in this case literally so; also that Sister Annunciation is the moving power at the start of the paragraph and moves that power through Saint Sebastian's on down to Doolan who, coming last, bears the weight of the paragraph. And as I said it aloud I was aware of choosing low-frequency vowels: word, down, from, Annunciation. usual, do, trouble, Doolan. This gives a blues note to the story's music. Someone told me at a conference that they liked how the boy's name signified his combative nature, his *dueling* with the church. I had to admit I'd not thought of that. I'd gotten the name from a fishing village on the west coast of Ireland where I once waited out a storm before catching a boat to the Aran Islands. Doolin: I liked the sound of it, quiet, with sort of a mournful softness to it, yet solid and enduring, like stone in rain.

Language tone is one thing, emotional tone another.

Many times I've had it pointed out to me, by reviewers or concerned friends, that I most always write about defeated people and that even those works of mine that are comic, are darkly so.

Why do I tell the stories I tell?

It's not my habit to ask myself this. It makes me very uneasy to start digging around the springs of my inspiration for fear that they may dry up. Although a quick look might do no harm.

There was so much horseplay and laughter in my family, why are my stories so dark?

Maybe because my father's family had such a knack for loss. None of them made money or a name for themselves. Dad's mother died young, as did three of his four sisters, his police captain father turned to drink before his heart gave out, his uncle Tom mistook a bottle of carbolic acid for his whiskey pint hidden atop the medicine cabinet and died screaming and kicking on the bathroom floor, his brother Jim, drug addict and armed robber, was shut up in the Ohio state pen, and his other brother, Earl, a wino who walked out on his wife on their wedding night, took a nap on a flattened cardboard box in the basement of a neighborhood shoe repair shop and never woke up. And there was also the memory of Uncle Frank's brutal end. Although Dad was never without a joke at the ready, beneath his sustained patter—Frick and Frack routines, Johnny Juniper jokes, Burma Shave recitations—there lurked a view of life as a losing game.

Then why aren't all my stories grim? Why do they hold so much humor, verbal and physical?

Maybe because of my mother's high-spirited hijinks. Although she might refer to herself as the dummy in her family, she did so with a devilish grin that told you she knew darn well that she was the liveliest and best-looking one of the bunch. She refused to admit that she'd made a mistake in picking a husband. When he was right, she told her schoolteacher sisters, Red was the life of the party. Mom was a practical joker who'd dump ice water down your shirt or jump from the closet to scare the living daylights out of you. A fierce competitor, she played tag with me, frantically racing through the apartment, dodging, laughing, knocking things off tables, anything to keep me from catching her, as Dad stood at the door to his room, calling for us to know when to quit, and wanting to know had we finally taken leave of our senses. She and I entertained ourselves some Saturday nights by making prank phone calls. I usually settled for corny jokes: "Hello, is your refrigerator running? Then you better go catch it." "Eagle Laundry? How much to get my eagle cleaned?" Mom did characters in various dialects, Polish, black, Irish, Jewish; she'd call bars, asking for some name she made up, then threatening the bartender when he said there was no one there by that name. "Listen buster, I know he's in there," she'd say, as I stifled my giggling. "Put him on the phone this minute or I'm coming down there with a baseball bat and knock some sense into his head *and* yours." Irresponsible, but a world of fun. Yet her humor could take a bitter twist, especially if she thought someone was laughing at her or her family. She really did think of herself as "just another dumb factory worker," and was painfully ashamed, although fiercely protective, of her poor sick brothers, Hume and Fenn, who even though they weren't Irish could not stay off the bottle.

I grew up with the sense that if life is sad it's comically so, or sadly comical, and that most people are fools, God bless them, so don't be too hard on them.

Yet I also sensed that our family's laughter often sprang from mockery or envy. The point of a joke would be to bring down the smug or pompous with a snide crack. I recognize this trait in myself. It's evident in "Comedy of Eros," my story about a Hemingway fan living the singles life in New York City, a stalwart facing front-line duty in the battle of the sexes. The story's opening parodies that of *A Farewell to Arms.*

In the late summer of that year I lived in an apartment on the West Side that looked out over Columbus Avenue. On the avenue there were yellow cabs and gassy busses and platoons of cyclists with whistles in their mouths and roller skaters along the curb. They streamed toward midtown where business towers stood like fortresses. Dust, stirred by the traffic, rose and fell. Secretaries and receptionists and editorial assistants marched past on Adidas and Nikes, their office heels stowed in nylon backpacks.

Smart-alecky, but not necessarily a cheap shot. Papa deserves to be ribbed for that stiff-lipped elegiac tone, so self-consciously brave, that nearly conceals his incurable sentimentality. Whether it be stoic or madcap, I don't care for fiction with an overly simplified emotional tone. My experience has given me to understand that each of us contains his or her opposite, and I believe it's the writer's task to get in touch with all the elements of the self. Despite the darkness of much of my work, I don't see my characters as losers. They have hard times, true, and they are not always the most upbeat people, but I think that they win more often than not, although they may not win in the most obvious or worldly ways. In "Smoker," my story about boxing in the marines, Billy Troy, a reluctant combatant, loses a smoker bout in which he was way overmatched but summons the courage and skill to go the distance. Afterward, as he is being chewed out by Sergeant Schramm, a drill instructor who believes only in winning, Troy is unexpectedly cheered by a recognition regarding his late father, a gutsy, all-offense prizefighter who took fearful beatings for little money, for which his son pitied him while feeling guilty for doing so.

> *Schramm starts in on me again. He's got so many words for loser, he must sit up nights studying his Thesaurus. But it all blows by me. Now I know why Dad could grin. He kept his own score.*
>
> *To think of all the yapping I did back then. Tell them how it is, make them see, yap yap yap. And when Dad held his peace, I'd been foolish enough to think he was a fool.*
>
> *"You think you're really something, don't you, Troy?"*
>
> *Light and bouncy, I show the sergeant my bloody teeth.*

If I'm to learn anything from my writing, I'd have it be this: to behave in times of trouble like Billy Troy, a character I made up out of my own actions and wishes. I want to keep my own score. Faced with defeat and rejection, life's hard shots, I hope to keep smiling.

Books

Not for Dietrich Bonhoeffer (poetry). Crossing Press, 1969.
Maggot (novel). Paperback Library, 1971.
The Full Round (poetry). Fiddlehead Books, 1973.
On My Own Two Feet (poetry). Fiddlehead Books, 1973.
Three Times Three (stories). Ithaca House, 1977.
Once You Learn You Never Forget (poetry). Fiddlehead Books, 1978.
Naked to Naked Goes (stories). Charles Scribner's Sons, 1986.
Loving Power (stories). Bottom Dog Press, 1990.

Plays/Screenplays

Jupus Redeye (play). Contemporary American Theatre Company, 1985.
Teller's Ticket (screenplay). Produced and directed by Sheldon Gleisser, 1990.
Volleys (play). American Theatre of Actors, 1991.

Anthologies

"Not for Dietrich Bonhoeffer," "The Captain," "Bicycle," "After Him." *Doctor Generosity's Almanac: 17 Poets.* Ed. Ray Freed. Doctor Generosity Press, 1970.
"State Message: A Midwestern Small Town," "Atlas," "Heirloom." *Heartland II: Poets of the Midwest.* Ed. Lucien Stryk. Northern Illinois University Press, 1975.
"Whitman's Song." *Walt Whitman: the Measure of His Song.* Eds. Jim Perlman, Ed Folsom, and Dan Campion. Holy Cow Press, 1981.
"All Alone and Blue." *Best Ohio Fiction.* Ed. Larry Smith. Bottom Dog Press, 1987.
"Teller's Ticket." *The Norton Book of American Short Stories.* Ed. Peter S. Prescott. Norton, 1988.
"Reply to an Eviction Notice." *An Introduction to Poetry.* Ed. X. J. Kennedy. Scott, Foresman/Little, Brown, 1990. Also in *Literature: An Introduction to Fiction, Poetry, and Drama.* Ed. X. J. Kennedy. HarperCollins, 1991.

Periodicals

Stories

More than a dozen stories have been published in *Bird Effort, Black Ice, Chicago, Confluence, Cornfield Review, Fiction, Ohio Review, Kansas Quarterly,* and *Orpheus*.

Poems

Numerous poems have appeared in periodicals, including *Aisling, Beloit Poetry Journal, Buffalo Stamps, Contempora, Descant, Folio, Great Lakes Review, Hanging Loose, Hierophant, Hiram Poetry Review, Illinois Quarterly, Kansas Quarterly, The Little Magazine, Measure, Midwest Quarterly, Mill Mountain Review, Monmouth Review, New England Review, New York Arts Journal, New York Times, Nimrod, Northeast, Northwest Review, Outposts, Poetry and Audience, Poetry Northwest, Poetry Now, Sumus, Tennessee Poetry Journal,* and *Western Review*.

Conrad Hilberry

Conrad Hilberry teaches literature and writing at Kalamazoo College. His poems have won the Emily Clark Balch Prize from the Virginia Quarterly Review, *the Iowa Prize from the University of Iowa Press, and two fellowships from the National Endowment for the Arts.*

GRIEF'S ALLY

In *Writing a Woman's Life*, Carolyn Heilbrun argues that biographers have not been able to write confidently and subtly about women's lives — and, more important, women have not been able to imagine rich and varied lives for themselves — because literature and culture have not supplied the stories, the stock of narrative patterns that would allow us to think about the shapes that a woman's life might take. "The choices and pain of the women who did not make a man the center of their lives seemed unique, because there were no models of the lives they wanted to live, no exemplars, no stories." Her book supplies some of the missing stories: those of George Sand, Dorothy Sayers, Maxine Kumin, Anne Sexton, Adrienne Rich, and Heilbrun herself. Eve Shelnutt's anthology *The Confidence Woman*, predecessor to this volume, supplies a great many more, a series of intense, open, analytic, exuberant stories written by women who are now in the middle of those autobiographies, making them up as they go. Somehow these stories, though often painful, seem more full of juice and joy than Heilbrun's stories, probably because they are told from the inside, in transit, with many of the directions and achievements still to be decided — and probably because the other stories have come before and been assimilated, making way for the dashing histories that these writers are inventing for themselves right now.

My colleague Tony Hoaglund observes that men need fresh and promising stories now at least as much as women do — perhaps more, since women have been inventing life stories and telling them to each other for the past twenty years while men lumbered on, assuming that they already knew the plot. To be sure, the quest story, which has been male property for a long time, still seems able to give shape to qualities like courage, respect for something distant or unknown, and even magnanimity. But the success story or the denial-of-blame story or the comic failure story, the story of grand self-assertion or of cool reasonableness — these seem hardly more inviting than the stories of female subordination, and more dangerous. We all hope for more imaginative stories from the men gathered in this book.

But my own story, as I begin telling it to myself, seems singularly unimaginative. Summarized in the usual way, my career reads like this: I studied English at Oberlin College, did graduate work in English at the University of Wisconsin, taught English for seven years at DePauw University, and since 1962 have been teaching English at Kalamazoo College. To make it worse, my father was an English teacher before me. (I wonder if a person has ever refused to die simply because he was embarrassed to think how boring his obituary would be.)

My childhood, too, was calm, limited, satisfactory. I grew up in Ferndale, Michigan, the first suburb north of Detroit, a city of streets at right angles, small houses, and vacant lots. As I think about it now, it seems a suburb without distinction of any kind: no hills, no river, not even a downtown, except for the string of stores along Nine Mile Road and Woodward Avenue. But at the time, of course, it was just where I lived. My brother and I played touch football in the street and high jumped in the backyard. Some of the children I went to kindergarten with were still classmates when we graduated from high school. Tom Boyd, Jim Morrish, Mary Beckwith. None of them had names ending in vowels, and none of them were black. (There were black students in Lincoln High School, where I went, but I knew only one of them, a little. Incredibly, if I remember right, there were no black students on either the basketball team or the track team. This was 1942 to 1946.) I was sports editor of the newspaper and a good student, but not so good that I seemed peculiar. I ran the high hurdles on the track team and was utterly incompetent around girls. In short, mine was your standard midwestern, middle-class, white boyhood, relatively free of surprise or injury.

My parents, too, were intelligent, calm, easy to live with. My Swiss mother was more concerned with order than with expression of feelings, perhaps, but both parents, though they didn't talk about it much, were proud of me and my brother and willing to let us take our own directions. (To be sure, we didn't really put them to the test.) My father's father had been a Methodist minister in northern Ohio, moved from parish to parish every five years at the discretion of the district superintendent. As a child, my father felt uprooted, separated from his friends every time they moved, and he intended not to impose that sort of disruption on his sons. As it turned out, he spent his whole career at Wayne University in Detroit, coming there as an instructor in 1931 and retiring as president in 1965. We lived in the same house all the years I was growing up. My mother's father, a first-generation Swiss farmer in Illinois, died before I was born. My mother said she wished he had been as a good a man as he was a manager. What she referred to was alcoholism, his violent drinking bouts every few weeks and then humiliating fits of remorse. With alcoholism on one side of the family and Methodism on the other, ours was a temperate household. My parents never served anything alcoholic, even later when they had moved into the president's house at the university and hosted official parties.

I wish I could talk with my parents again, especially my father, who died at sixty-three, my present age. I wonder how he felt about his career, which steadily became more and more public. I wonder how it was for him to be a parent. (I am probably the only reader of *The Confidence Woman* who identifies with the parents in each story — a painful but illuminating way to read the book.)

I have sometimes felt that my childhood was so reasonable, so steady, that it supplied me with no experiences, no character. When I read Philip Larkin's "I Remember, I Remember," recounting everything that did not happen to him when he was growing up in Coventry, where his "childhood was unspent" — and ending with the lines "'I suppose it's not the place's fault,' I said. / 'Nothing, like something, happens anywhere'" — when I read that, I thought, that's Ferndale, Michigan, that's me. But I couldn't work up the bitterness that Larkin evidently felt. In my case, *something* had happened. I did have a character, of sorts, and an urgent sense of anticipation. In truth, my childhood had given me an unusually clean starting place, as though the past were a clear pine board on which events to come could write their happiness or grief without old pitch seeping out of the knots to discolor everything.

Happiness and grief came soon enough. Oberlin College, like many other schools in the late 1940s, was vividly alive. I had just graduated from high school in 1946, but many of my classmates were back from service in Europe or North Africa or the Pacific, full of experiences and opinions and drive to get on with the lives they had been postponing. They knew who they were, or so it seemed to me, and could be funny and brash and intellectual all at once. Occasionally, when I was growing up, my parents gave parties, inviting to our house husbands and wives from the Wayne English department. The talk there was unlike anything I had heard anywhere else — loud, witty, fast, ranging over everything I wished I knew. Sometimes when I was supposed to be in bed, I would sit on the stairs just out of sight and listen. I remember one long discussion of moon madness — it seemed to be something that everyone knew about, sailors standing watch in the full moon, wolves howling. When I went up to bed later, the light of the full moon had crept halfway across the floor. I was sure it would climb up my bed while I slept and make me mad. Anyway, that was what it felt like much of the time at college — as though I were on the stairs, listening in.

Things began to happen. After my sophomore year I spent the summer in Mexico with the American Friends Service Committee helping to make a road down to the river in the town of Mixquiahuala, where many of the people had hardly seen a North American before. After graduation, I taught for a term at Hiwassee College, a junior college in the hills of eastern Tennessee; I was more or less fired after I took what I believed to be a principled stand on some local issue. I went to Wisconsin for graduate work and met Marion Bailey, an English teacher who had also worked in Mexico with the Quakers, a different summer. We found we had plenty to talk about, fell in love, and almost immediately got married, to my surprise and pleasure. We had two daughters, Katharine and Marilyn, while we were in Madison and a third, Jane, while I was teaching at DePauw University in Indiana. The teaching was hard — twelve or sometimes fourteen hours of classes a week with student papers always stacked up by the dozens, long overdue. And very little money. But we had friends, all of us living close together in prefabricated houses on Observatory Hill, enjoying talk, our children, books, our complaints about the university. I wrote some poems and tried them on my friends. The girls grew up easily. It was happiness, though we might not have thought to say so at the time.

Then came the grief. Before we had reached Madrid on a Fulbright appointment to teach in Zaragoza, Katharine was killed in a railroad accident. She was nine years old — perfect, as nine-year-olds tend to be. We were racked with grief and guilt. This must be the most painful of losses: not just our loss as parents and her sisters' loss but the loss of the whole life that should have been Katharine's.

We came back to Greencastle and our friends. After a month or so, I took a one-year job in Chicago so that I might have something to do besides suffer sadness and remorse. It helped, but living in Evanston must have been more difficult for Marion and Marilyn and Jane than staying in Greencastle would have been. Marion says she's not sure; in Greencastle she saw Katharine in every group of children walking home from school. We moved to Kalamazoo College the following year, had another daughter, Ann, and kept going, making satisfying lives, with waves of sadness flooding over us from time to time. Our daughters grew, turning out to be very different from each other, each of them remarkable, we thought. For Marion and me, they were, and are, the focus of our love.

Their childhoods were not as smooth as mine. When they were in school, racial tensions were high, classrooms locked sometimes to keep disturbances from spreading from the halls to the rooms, etc. They were calm about this, outwardly at least, seeming to understand what was at issue. We moved around, too — two years in Yellow Springs, Ohio, a year in Berea, Kentucky, and later, when only Ann was with us, a year in Mexico. The towns, all smaller than Kalamazoo, seemed congenial. All three daughters took up folk dancing in Berea, Ann learned Spanish (and many other things) in Mexico, and all of them, plus Marion, seemed to me gifted at making and keeping friends. Our lives went on at a brisk pace, but the sense of loss never completely went away. Only now, decades later, are we finding out how deeply Marilyn and Jane felt Katharine's loss and how inadequately we attended to their hurt, being stunned by our own.

What about writing, then? I wish I could report that art assuages grief. So far as I can tell, nothing does that but time — and more life to be lived. In fact, grief and art seem to be allies in one way. We all spend a lot of time traveling neither inside nor outside our lives but on a middle ground, on a sort of Business Loop, the well-marked, manageable route through town, where we accomplish things but discover little about the world around us or about ourselves. Shopping, cooking, planning the week's work, writing memos, gardening, grading papers, selling, toting up the accounts — all this is necessary, perhaps restful, perhaps challenging. It can be very satisfying because, with practice, we can accomplish a lot in practically no time. We writers know the pleasure of zipping off a memo with all the relevant information, raising no distracting side issues, keeping the tone just right so that the recipient is almost sure to do what we're asking. It's a skill, an achievement, but well within that middle range where we know our competence. Like spotting a sale in the paper, tooling out to the mall, laying hands on exactly the pair of pants that will do the trick, putting them on the MasterCard, and being home in half an hour.

My examples sound more trivial than I intend. Almost all the world's work gets done in this way and much of our self-respect comes from this solid, practiced competence. It's what we get paid for and what we expect from others. But we could not stay on the Loop indefinitely even if we wanted to. Events push us off into unmanageable encounters with ourselves and with the world outside. Sudden grief or love or betrayal, situations that ask for action beyond the range of any skill we have on hand — those accidents lead us into ourselves and the world, offering confusion, a dark woods, when we thought we knew the way.

And so does art, if it's the real thing. A piece of art is always a new conception, so no one knows in advance how to make it or respond to it. A writer who can whip off a business letter as fast as her fingers can move becomes muddled and silent when it's a story asking to be written. How do these characters talk and think and feel? How does she feel about them—and about herself? On a minor scale, it's the dark woods again, and the desk fills up with false starts and hopeless paragraphs.

The rest of this essay will be mostly about writing and reading, what words can do. I have not made my living as a writer. I have taught, as intensely and inventively as I can, and I have been in on the daily workings of Kalamazoo College, a place I enjoy and believe in. The writing has come during vacations and leaves and occasionally during terms in which I have traded money for time, teaching less than a full load. But writing, like any other preoccupation, creeps in. It makes use of the feelings stirred by marriage and children and work, and, ideally, it leaves a healthy resinous smell on those other parts of life.

I would like to claim that from the beginning my interest in poetry had to do with the widening of experience. It didn't. At first, it could hardly have been narrower. My father had a woodworking shop in the basement, and my brother, who later became an architect, was good at making things. Almost everyone I know is handy at some craft. But I've always been clumsy enough so that the effort seems out of proportion to the results. But with words I'm all right—awkward and silent in conversation but OK on paper. It was this impulse, to build something out of words, that first attracted me to poems. I got started late. My family all wrote poems to go with Christmas presents, but I was out of college before I wrote on any day but December 24. And then the scale was small. I would tinker endlessly with four lines, determined to make them perfect, when, of course, there was nothing there to perfect—no insight, no presence. If I remember right, one of my first lines was "like icing on the night."

To my credit, I soon discovered Philip Larkin's *The Less Deceived* and Richard Wilbur's early books, especially *Ceremony* and *Things of This World*, and spent days and weeks trying to do what they did, to write those sinuous, flexible lines with everything in place, the rhymes all where they belong, the metrical patterns honored and used to control the movement of the poem—and yet the lines sounding natural, like talk in Larkin's case, the sentences running over the ends of lines so that you might not even notice that there was a formal pattern if you didn't see the poem on the page. I'm still moved by that technical virtuosity. (I didn't understand at the time that Wilbur's illusion of perfect control is often subverted and complicated by his images, as in "The Beacon," which gives us the wild, incomprehensible sea-in-itself, where the "booms, rumors and guttural sucks / warn of the pitchy whirl / at the mind's end.") I treated words as though they were objects, fitting and joining them. The satisfactions of this kind of cabinet making are pale compared to the excitement of the moment when an unexpected insight or image rises up out of some great pond of meaning and presents itself, already half clothed in words. But the two things don't exclude each other. And without construction nothing solid gets made.

Any art worth bothering about must enrich and intensify experience, must alert or alarm us, forcing us out from our familiar rounds. It does this, we say, by infusing the artist's vision into the subject matter — or into the medium itself, so that a subject becomes almost irrelevant. Literature is expression, making objective the flux and turmoil, the shadings and contradictions of human experience seen from the inside. I feel the force of this line of thought, as anyone must. My own poetry, I hope, has become more and more open to what I don't understand about my own feelings and perceptions, to the way my own voices contradict each other. Still, I'm not comfortable with too exclusive an emphasis on the shaping imagination or the inner life of the artist. I don't want to slight the stubborn, vivid facts outside ourselves, the literal world that gives us objects and characters, patterns, contrasts, places to begin and end. Words are remarkable in that they look outward and inward at the same time; they represent and express simultaneously. For me, that doubleness gives literature its toughness and surprise.

From time to time, I have undertaken what were essentially journalistic projects. I'm not sure about my motivation, but I'd like to think I took on these projects partly as a way to pay my respects to actual people and events, trying to do them justice, to get them right. As the staff person for a study of liberal arts colleges in the mid-1960s, I wrote profiles of Antioch College in Ohio and Wheaton College in Illinois, schools as unlike each other as any pair in the country — and unlike any colleges I had seen up close. Antioch was in the turmoil of Vietnam War protest, drug experimentation, student invasions of Board of Trustees meetings, "nude-ins" at the swimming pool, ambitious racial integration, the McLuhanization of consciousness, brilliant filmmaking, and smaller ventures like communing with trees. Wheaton, one of the intellectual centers of Evangelical Christianity, was, at the same moment, in turmoil of a different sort. Members of the faculty had organized an "origins symposium" that brought together Evangelical scientists from across the country to discuss ways in which the doctrine of creation could be accommodated to the data of biology, geology, etc. They were discussing, for example, the possibility of "theistic evolution," the belief that life and humanity were created over a period of time by a God-directed process. The trustees, hearing of this, were inflamed and passed what came to be called the "Adam and Eve Footnote," an addendum to the doctrinal statement that faculty members were required to sign every year. They had to affirm their belief in God's creation of Adam and Eve in the Garden of Eden. In both schools, I was drawn to the issues, the arguments, the drama, but also to the way in which the tension focused and intensified the education of some students.

A more elaborate project was a psychological study of two brothers who grew up in Kalamazoo, each of whom became a serial murderer. I interviewed each of them at some length in prison and talked with acquaintances, prison officials, and the woman who had been married to each of them. I was interested in the psychology of the two men, very different from each other, in the reasoning by which each of them justified or denied murder, in the workings of the Michigan prison system, and simply in events more violent and bizarre than any I had been close to before. At first, I thought I could write an objective account, keeping myself out of it, but it soon became clear that my own history, my feelings, my reasons for being there would have to be acknowledged. I would have to be a frank participant in the book: the project had turned inward as well as outward.

In each of these pieces of reporting, I knew that no account of the events could be interchangeable with the events themselves. Still, the main interest for me and surely for the readers was the reality I was trying to be faithful to. The conflicts, the wild details (a skating chimpanzee figured prominently in the murderers' story), the passions, the careful logic — all this was out there asking to be recorded, artfully put together, I hope, but deriving its force from the world.

A convincing reflection of reality is a less central virtue, perhaps, in poetry than in journalistic writing or fiction, but it is still important. No matter how much epistemology and literary theory call in question the conjunction between the word and some lived experience, we can't help looking for that connection and valuing it, as readers and writers. I return to Stephen Dobyns's "Canto Hondo" partly because of the engaging, deceptively ambling sentences and the speaker's painfully sharp self-awareness, but also because I believe in the two Antonios, the goat, the teeth, the epileptic mailman who sings. As I believe there is such a place as Granada province, I believe these figures populate it, and I thank the poem for delivering them to me. The same for Richard Shelton's desert. Underneath the fluid energy of the words, there is the desert, austere and beautiful. Out of that real soil spring those prickly poems, and the poems lead me back to the soil.

Mexico has meant a lot to me, in person and in poems. I want to respect the literal country, insofar as I can see it and understand it, and I'm moved by the mystery and threat and ritual that cling to the simplest events there. Here's a prose poem set in San Miguel de Allende, the town where we lived.

The Photographer

It has been raining hard for an hour, and the water, having no other place to go, roars down over the cobblestones carrying tree limbs, Pepsi bottles, socks, clumps of alfalfa, the plastic body of a doll. Drain pipes throw streams of roofwater into the center of the street. Three children flatten themselves against a door, and a flatbed truck sloshes slowly up the street like a river steamer.

Now an old woman, head covered by a rebozo, turns the corner into the full force of the rain. She pauses a minute on the narrow sidewalk above the cascading water, then steps in cautiously, starting across. If you don't get this picture, you deserve doorways and sunsets the rest of your life. You grab the Leica from the back of the chair, make a quick guess about the exposure, and walk out into the downpour. The woman is hardly fifteen feet from you, feeling her way on the slick stones, the water piling up against her heavy skirt, her shoulders curled, her face creased and dripping. You focus and shoot. As the water surges almost to her knees, she staggers a step backward, loses her footing, and falls. You shoot. She sits on one hip in the flood, bracing herself with her left arm, while the water plunges into her lap and presses her chest. One of her sandals floats downstream behind her. You shoot. She clambers up, crouching, one hand in the water ready to catch herself if she slips again. But she makes it to the curb where you offer her a hand, help her onto the sidewalk. She pushes past you, bending into the storm. Why not, you think, and shoot again, catching her dark shape against the wall. She pauses, steadied, you like to think, by the clear eye of the Leica.

The street is real, and the storm, the children, the woman, the sandal. I watched it all from a second-story window. The photographer is fictitious — or, rather, I am the photographer, turning the scene into a poem. The literal Mexico is there, urging itself on me and asking what, if anything, could justify my detachment.

I have been insisting on the place of the external world in what we write, journalism or poems. Words, of course, look inward, too. Poetry is the medium that we traditionally count on to pull us out of the safe, rational, daily loop into ourselves, into discovery and exposure of longing or anger or regret that we didn't recognize or have words for. How does the poet, as a person, figure in this process? As readers, we have learned to refer to the "speaker" in a poem, not identifying the poem, which we know, with the poet, whom we don't know in any full way. While recognizing the appropriateness of this scruple, we can't live with it wholeheartedly. We know that the voice in the poem is at least one of the voices of the poet and we can't help hearing it as coming from a live, suffering, joyous, or reflective person. As a reader, I'm like everybody else, drawn to poems and to the person who emerges through the poems — and willing enough to fill out the poems with biography and gossip. (But the poems continue to have a kind of authority, as though they were truer than information from other sources.) I don't feel apologetic for looking through the poems to the fiction of a person, whom I willingly make into a real person. Why not? The small-scale experience of individual poems may coalesce, imperfectly, into an experienced presence, a person from whom we can learn things as we would from a friend. I get angry when people who have read a good deal, myself included, do really stupid or insensitive things. We should have learned from all that vicarious experience. Admittedly, it often fails to work. But when I read poems about parents and children, Lucille Clifton's, Alicia Ostriker's, Linda Pastan's, Lisel Mueller's, Stephen Dunn's, they slip over from art to life and I think of myself, my wife, and our daughters. When Gregory Orr writes of an accidental death and his responsibility for it, I think of another death and my responsibility. I live through his hard, slow coming to terms. I have met Orr only once, at least twenty years ago, and yet I feel close to him, not just to his poems but to the man I have constructed out of his poems. If I were to meet him tomorrow, I would want to embrace him as a friend.

As a writer, I am less concerned than I used to be about the way family members or friends might take the apparently personal references in poems or in the miniature stories I have published lately — though, in truth, I have always been somewhat reticent. I think ordinary readers tend to be quite sophisticated in this matter. They know that individual poems create their own speakers distinct from the poet, no matter how many *I*'s there may be. And they know that in a larger sense the poet does appear behind the poems. In John Donne's work, for example, behind all the postures and attitudes, the outrageous seductions and satires and protestations of devotion, behind all those speakers, we sense Donne's own restless brilliance, his love of argument, his deep seriousness, his reckless self-dramatization, his bitterness at the fickle world and his intense longing for some permanent love. We see this presence as "Donne's own." How could it not be? This is the poet whose autobiography we begin to read behind all the dramatic poses, the man whom we admire or mistrust or both.

I have mentioned Richard Wilbur, Philip Larkin, Lucille Clifton, Gregory Orr, Sharon Olds, Stephen Dobyns, Stephen Dunn, and John Donne. There's great variety in that list, yet all those people write poems that are sharp edged and ordered — though in subtle and complex ways. As I look for poems, mine and other people's, to draw me into deep water inside or outside the self, I have a weakness for the illusion of lucidity. I like poems whose sound and syntax and imagery invite me in, as though there were nothing to it, but then the tone shifts, the connections move beyond the logic they have seemed to promise, or the implications ramify, refusing to let go. I'm thinking of poems like Robert Hass's "Heroic Simile" or Wallace Stevens's "The Final Soliloquy of the Interior Paramour" or Elizabeth Bishop's "Pink Dog" or many sections of Galway Kinnell's *Book of Nightmares*. The combination of clarity and suggestiveness is possible on any scale, I think — even in a miniature poem like this new one written for our fortieth anniversary.

An Anniversary

This is a dress
made of forty
ragged words we've
sewn together
haphazardly. Yes,
it fits, but now
it's time to rip
the seams, undo
the syllables one
by one until you
are naked again
in my hands.

Poems are remarkably versatile. If confusion seems overwhelming, they may provide a momentary stay against it, a shaping of our uncertainties and anxieties into something formal with parts and an ending, something we can think about, something we can show to friends and even strangers. But they can serve the opposite function, too. Though our raw experience is unimaginably rich and complicated — the immense jumble of sense impressions we are taking in at any moment, with memory and mood and thought playing over it, coloring and remaking it moment by moment — though our raw experience is utterly unmanageable, we blithely manage it. We simplify the world, as we must, to a plan for the day, an observation, an opinion, some good advice about how to season the soup or win the election. We reduce the world to the sentence we are speaking or writing. We have to do this in order to live, but there's a danger that we will come to mistake our simplifications for the real thing; we will come to believe that the world is orderly in a way we can describe and understand. We may come to live in a smaller and smaller slice of experience, a world shrunken to our own daily abstractions. One of art's functions is to counteract this over-simplification, to remind us of the astonishing welter of our own experience, to bring us back to the concrete particles that refuse to be abstracted into pattern, to show us again how much richness we have been excluding. Without saying it, without even being aware of what it is doing, art forces us back toward the live turmoil of concrete experience.

Fortunately, it can do this for the maker as well as the receiver of art. I myself am midwestern, Protestant, German-English, and white — which is to say orderly, reticent, hard working, and inclined to feel guilty about everything. In seventh grade, I loved grammar; in high school my favorite studies were algebra and plane geometry, where, with patience and ingenuity, a person could prove and solve and straighten out everything in the book. The qualities that seem to come naturally to me are useful in the making of poems: patience, a sense of structure and economy, a willingness to let things be implied, a conviction that there's always another way to do it if the first way doesn't work. But other, and opposite, qualities are needed if a person is to make true and moving poems: the ability to call up a fresh flow of images and words and memories, a respect for improbable connections, an alertness to one's own feelings and a willingness to hear them out, the recognition that remarkable creatures live in the vast bogs of idleness and accident. In order to write, I have had to become, momentarily at least, another person. And I imagine the same thing might happen in reverse for a poet who came with qualities opposite from mine. An utterly open, spontaneous, disorganized writer, for whom imagining is as natural as walking, might be brought through poetry (or fiction) to greater control, selection, reticence even, to steadier concentration and a clearer sense of structure. If I am right, this is an impressive advertisement for writing: it needs everything, and so it draws from each of us not only the qualities we have but also those we lack.

Books

The Poems of John Collop (editor). University of Wisconsin Press, 1962.
Encounter on Burrows Hill (poems). Ohio University Press, 1968.
Struggle and Promise: A Future for Colleges (with Morris Keeton and others). McGraw-Hill, 1969.
Rust (poems). Ohio University Press, 1974.
The Third Coast: Contemporary Michigan Poetry (anthology, edited with Herbert Scott and James Tipton). Wayne State University Press, 1976.
Housemarks (poems). Perishable Press, 1980.
Man in the Attic (poems). Bits Press, 1980.
The Moon Seen as a Slice of Pineapple (poems). University of Georgia Press, 1984.
Jacob's Dancing Tune (children's story). Perishable Press, 1986.
Luke Karamazov (case study). Wayne State University Press, 1987.
Contemporary Michigan Poetry: Poems from the Third Coast (anthology, edited with Michael Delp and Herbert Scott). Wayne State University Press, 1988.
The Lagoon (poems). MellanBerry Press, 1989.
Sorting the Smoke (new and selected poems). University of Iowa Press, 1990.

Anthologies

"For Katharine." *Poems for the Dead*. Ed. Greg Kuzma. The Best Cellar Press, 1984.
"Mstislav Rostropovich," "Crickets and the Rain," "Sorting the Smoke," "On the Promontory," and "Self-Portrait as Bank Teller." *Contemporary Michigan Poetry*. Eds. Michael Delp, Conrad Hilberry, and Herbert Scott. Wayne State University Press, 1988.
"The Woman Who Was Ready to Die," "Harry Houdini," and "Poet." *Vital Signs*. Ed. Ronald Wallace. University of Wisconsin Press, 1989.

"The Frying Pan" and "Tongue." *The Bedford Introduction to Literature*. Ed. Michael Meyer. St. Martin's Press, 1990.
"The God in Winter." *Passages North Anthology*. Ed. Elinor Benedict. Milkweed Editions, 1990.

Periodicals

Poems have appeared in *Antaeus, Antioch Review, Atlantic Monthly, Beloit Poetry Journal, Carleton Miscellany, Chowder Review, Epoch, Field, Ironwood, Kenyon Review, Missouri Review, New Letters, New York Times, New Yorker, Ontario Review, Poetry, Poetry Northwest, Saturday Review, Shenandoah, Three Rivers Poetry Journal, Virginia Quarterly Review*, and others.

Robert Watson

Robert Watson was educated at Williams College and Johns Hopkins University and later taught at both institutions. He attended the University of Zurich as a Swiss-American exchange fellow to study art history. At present he is Professor Emeritus of English at the University of North Carolina at Greensboro, where he lives. Robert Watson has received awards from the National Foundation of Arts and the American Academy and Institute of the Arts.

LUCK AND CHANCE

W hy I became a writer of poems and prose fiction I don't know. And I don't know at what age in life my writing began.

When I was a young boy I loved sea stories, *Mutiny on the Bounty*, *Two Years before the Mast*, and works by Joseph Conrad, who was both a writer and a sailor. When I was sixteen the Japanese bombed Pearl Harbor. In a perverse way I was elated: the war would give me opportunity for wartime adventures at sea. A few days after my seventeenth birthday I joined the U.S. Navy, but instead of sending me to boot camp and then to sea the navy decided that I should enter a new program for training officers, so I spent two years in the navy without ever going to sea. The war ended before I received my commission, and I was given a discharge even though I pleaded with my commanding officer to let me remain. Over two years without ever putting a foot on the deck of a ship!

In 1946 I crossed the Atlantic from New York to Le Havre, a two-week journey in a very small French troop ship on its way home to be converted into a passenger ship. I was seasick during the entire voyage. That trip, in those pre-Dramamine days, ended my desire to follow in Conrad's footsteps.

My clear alternative was to become a lawyer in my grandfather's and father's law firm. In the 1930s my father had a varied practice of both civil and criminal matters, and for a time he was a special prosecutor in Passaic County, New Jersey. He handled several sensational murder cases which made me feel that being a lawyer was almost as exciting as being the captain of a ship. For a time, after several death threats against him, my father hired a bodyguard, Harry Boyle, a retired county detective, who wore a derby and bought all his clothes at Brooks Brothers, a very fashionable men's clothing store in New York City. The much-older sister of a boy in my class consulted Dad when their father and brother were arrested in New York City after holding up a meat-packing company with a submachine gun. The pair were eventually caught after a running gun battle with the police. Even in my hometown there was adventure. The law had an excitement for me that made it an attractive profession, a marvelous source of stories, but law was well below the navy or merchant marine on my list of career choices. Later in life I rejected the law as a career because if I became a lawyer it would make the best sense for me to join my father's practice. He was affectionate, but so domineering I knew I would be under his thumb until he retired. He never did retire until he was eighty . . . and I was fifty-three.

As a small boy I was anchored in the humdrum world of home and also in the imaginative worlds of reading and radio. I would listen each night to programs such as "Tom Mix" and "The Shadow." My parents had no objections to my eating supper on a tray in front of the radio in my room. I was also an avid reader, encouraged by my family's giving me books as presents or as consolation when I was sick. Both my mother, Laura Watson, and my paternal grandmother were compulsive readers who would much rather stay home to read than go to parties. My grandmother, Mary Watson, loved Proust and was also swept up in the philosophy of Ouspenski and Nicoll.

I don't know what my mother's favorite books were because she never talked to me about them. When I grew up I know there was a period when she marched through Russian literature. Mother was also good at foreign languages, which she studied at Vassar, and she tutored my sister and me in Latin. Clearly, though, my mother's greatest gifts were in sculpture and wood carving. She did a bust of me in clay and cast it in terra cotta, but most of all she loved carving animals out of wood. I can look across this room in which I am now writing and see a beautifully carved head of a goat which is highly stylized and looks much like a goat that Matisse would have carved, if he had ever made one in wood.

In growing up, then, as many children do, I led two lives. When my daily life of home and school became too boring or painful I would retreat into fantasies made from fragments of my reading, radio serials or stories my Dad told about his deeds as a lawyer. One day when I was about seven or eight I saw a pirate with a beard, sword, and peg leg walk out of a neighbor's garage and down the driveway toward me. I ran fast as I could. I never told my parents or friends because I knew they would not believe me. I was a boy in search of adventure, trying to find in the world of Passaic, New Jersey, the excitement I found in imagination. Some days I walked a few blocks to the Lackawanna railroad tracks, where I watched the steam engines and dreamt of places the trains would carry me since I thought that anything distant from our house would be wonderful. Soon when I was about twelve, I began taking trains or buses into New York City on Saturdays, where I enjoyed the spectacular carnival of Times Square.

At Thomas Jefferson Junior High School I fell in love with Joanne

Werling, a Titian blonde at least two inches taller than I. She was especially alluring to me because her family had moved to Passaic from Ohio. Ohio, imagine that; in my imagination it seemed as far and beautifully strange as Tibet. Joanne was my Beatrice, radiant and pure. Although I went out with her later on movie dates, I don't think I ever knew anything about Joanne, so blinded was I by my imaginative conception of her. She did, though, inspire the first poem I ever wrote, a poem about the glories of Joanne whose red hair I compared to . . . what else? A sunset.

In high school, where I continued to adore Joanne, but in a somewhat diluted fashion, I had great luck in my senior year in having Miss Helen Hall for my English teacher. She had in retrospect an excellent taste in poetry coupled with enormous enthusiasm. Her special interest was in modern poetry: Yeats, Frost, Eliot. Miss Hall made us memorize a short poem every week which we then had to recite to her. The class detested memorizing poems. What I didn't count on at the time was the delayed reaction to this chore. When I finally began to write poetry I found that in memorizing poems for Miss Hall the musical elements stayed in my mind. I did not have to count syllables to write blank verse.

At Williams College I enjoyed browsing in the library stacks, especially in the shelves of modern poetry where, for example, I first discovered the poetry of Wallace Stevens, specifically a book called *The Man with the Blue Guitar*. I couldn't understand his poetry, but I was bowled over by his odd diction and his strange and grand imagination. At Williams I also suffered a setback in confidence. I made a mistake by giving a batch of my own poems to my English teacher who dutifully read them and also brought in a colleague for a second opinion. They both agreed that the poems had limited merits and that I did not have the ability to become a "genuine" poet. My mistake was in believing this verdict was correct. I was very disappointed and decided that, even though I could never become the "real thing," I would continue to be a closet poet, writing scraps and fragments for myself alone. I changed my major from English to economics.

One Saturday afternoon in December of my last year at college, I was taking a nap in my dormitory room. Even then I hadn't the foggiest notion of what I would do after graduation. I was awakened from my nap by Nelson Bushnell, the acting chairman of the English department. Would I, he asked, teach two terms of English as an instructor in the spring and summer sessions? After World War II with the veterans returning from war there was a surplus of students and a critical shortage of teachers in the colleges and universities. I said yes, not out of enthusiasm but because the teaching would postpone any decision on a career. I could then delay making application to law schools.

After two terms as an instructor, I sailed for Le Havre, seasick, as I said earlier, during most of the crossing. The harbor was glutted with sunken ships the allies had bombed. The passengers took a train to Paris where I stayed two nights in a hotel only one step up from a flophouse. Paris in 1946 had a severe food shortage and an enormous crop of streetwalkers because the government had closed down the brothels a month before my arrival. I was going to Switzerland, where I had won a fellowship to the University of Zurich to study art history. I had won the fellowship, I later learned, because I was the only one who applied. My German was almost nonexistent, but in art-history lectures one sees slides, and the professors use pointers to identify words with pictures — one way to learn the language.

My interest in the lecture courses was minimal since I was more interested in writing a novel. My teachers at Williams had said I'd never be a "real" poet, not that I could never become a novelist. Zurich, I thought, was a magic potion, for didn't James Joyce live here and die here? Didn't Thomas Mann live here at periods of his life, and wasn't Herman Hesse living in Zurich in 1946? I wrote the first sentence of my novel. And wrote it again and again. No second sentence would form itself. The muse of Zurich never appeared to me. What would I do with my life? I didn't know, so I took skiing lessons in Arosa and stared at a nearby tuberculosis sanitarium in the Alps, I thought perhaps the same one used by Thomas Mann in *The Magic Mountain*. It wasn't.

I decided not to go to law school, much to my father's disappointment; instead I enrolled in the English department of the graduate school at Johns Hopkins. In two terms at Williams I had found that I liked teaching, and I loved to read books. Why not be paid as a college professor for doing what I most enjoyed? I grew, though, to dislike the English department at Hopkins: the professors had little if any interest in teaching; they were, in my estimation, uncaring if not sadistic with the graduate students; and literature was little more than raw material for the production of scholarly books and articles. The teachers there were mainly vain, self-important grinds. At Williams, even though I was not encouraged to write, the department was staffed with professors who loved literature and were passionate teachers. I might have dropped out of Hopkins if I had had a clear calling to any profession other than teaching, but I had another reason for not dropping out: I had wanted to finish my training in the navy and became an ensign; I had wanted to write a novel and had only completed one sentence. My fear was that if I did not get the Ph.D., I would never complete anything of importance in my life, so I stuck it out at Hopkins, where to make life bearable I again led a double life. At the university I was a good dog; I would roll over and hold up my paw to beg, and best of all I learned to heel. The other Robert Watson roamed the streets of Baltimore, where he visited secondhand bookstores, strip joints, movie houses, and the docks where alcoholics were sprawled out, seldom returning home before three in the morning. I suppose I wandered around parts of Baltimore where the lost and helpless lived because I felt like a failure and was there among failures. My solace was reading and in that sense I was a good and dutiful graduate student. I read and read and read.

In the second year at Hopkins, I played a game in order to keep my sanity. I pretended that I did not exist, that Watson was not alive, that he was a ghost. I began to feel a confusion, that I didn't understand anything at all. If I could invent fictions myself instead of only reading them, I might be able little by little to understand the world outside my own mind. My game, one that actors and children play, was finding out what people are like by imitation. I decided to sit, stand, walk, and talk the way my models did. To duplicate their mental processes, I slipped in and out of others' lives, mostly people on the fringes of society. Only later did I realize that I was also imitating novelists, playwrights, and poets who write dramatic monologues. Chaucer, Shakespeare, Browning, and Frost, for instance, developed powers to become other than themselves, finding expression, as we know, in spectacular character creation.

This game of pretending I was someone else made it possible in future years for me to write poems where the speakers were my own invention, such as a prostitute ("Whore with Trick"), a judge ("The Judge Winds His Clock"), a parsimonious old woman ("Callers"), a middle-aged, middle-class housewife ("So, So"), a child rapist ("The Child Raper of Chelsea"), an astronaut ("Planet Eight"), and enough more to populate a small town. Then in my reading throughout the years I found many extraordinary Americans from the past who seemed forgotten. I tried to give them voices: "Victoria Woodhull," the first woman who ran for the presidency; "William Rimmer, M.D.," the first artist to make a fully nude male sculpture, who was also a famous anatomy teacher; "The Last Wild Indian," the last member of his tribe, who finally lived in a museum in San Francisco.

Not only was I fascinated by these people but I was also interested in the physical world in which they moved, realms beyond this earth, as in "The Radio Astronomers" and "Swan X One."

In my mid-twenties I married an artist, Betty Rean. At that time she was an accomplished painter and I was still without a completed poem or story to my name. I was intrigued with her pictures and how she made them. Her paintings taught me to look more carefully at the visual world and its structure. Many were of nudes, people stripped of all worldly trappings, all disguises. Often she had me pose for her. Posing is boring because the model must look in one direction only, and it is also difficult physically to hold a pose for very long, so most models attempt a kind of self-hypnosis. I found often in posing, cut off for a time from all worldly distractions, that my mind was composing poems, poems that would need much work when I began to commit them to paper. Many of these poems were directly inspired by Betty's paintings: "Odalisque," about an artist and his model; "Our Portrait," a description of two nudes, a man and a woman flying through the air, and others inspired by art, such as Veronese's "Mars and Venus United by Love."

In 1953, a year after our marriage, I received a job at the University of North Carolina in Greensboro (then called the Woman's College, or W.C. for short.) I can't name a place that was better for an incipient writer to work. In the English department were Randall Jarrell, Lettie Rogers, and Robie Macauley, and soon to come were Peter Taylor, Eleanor Taylor, and Allen Tate. Robert Lowell was a frequent visitor as was Robert Frost. What university or college then had an array of imaginative writers to match those at Woman's College in the fifties and early sixties?

The academic atmospheres at both Williams and Hopkins were stifling for imaginative writers and visual artists. Though the pay was low and the work load heavy, the atmosphere on the University of North Carolina campus was bright and clear for a painter and for a writer who was having a late beginning. Within a few months I was writing poems, though I had little confidence in them and let them pile up in a drawer. The pleasure for me was in the writing; I was thrilled that no matter how good or poor the poems were, I could at least write them. In those days and for years and years later I composed mostly on foot, where the rhythm of walking fed the rhythms of my poems. Usually I carried a pencil and used envelopes in my pocket so that I could write down the lines that came to me, often on the hood of a parked car. No poem ever flew into my mind that was complete and didn't need extensive repairs. I had no urge to publish, yet I was very curious to know what other writers might think of my poems. At last I gave a batch to Randall Jarrell, afraid he would reach the same verdict as my English teachers at Williams. Randall was an awesome critic whom almost everyone in the literary world feared. Randall said he thought that one of my poems was so good any poetry editor ought to publish it, but poetry editors were mostly not very good at judging poems, he continued. He liked two more of the poems and then dismissed the other dozen as "fifth of a watch poems." Where were the other four-fifths of each of these poems, he asked? I was jubilant that he liked three of the poems. And my life changed. After that conference I was not the same person I had been an hour earlier.

When Robert Lowell came to town a few months later, Randall suggested that I show him some of my poems. "Can you write in blank verse?" Lowell asked. I told him that half the poems he held in his hand were in blank verse. "I think you ought to go by what Randall says," he said. During his stay in Greensboro, Lowell was soliciting the comments of Jarrell on the poems that would shortly become *Life Studies*. "You ought to begin publishing your poems," Lowell concluded. "Publishing will lift your spirits and help you find your direction."

I thought I would give a third batch to Dr. William Carlos Williams, who for a while was both my sister's and my wife's pediatrician. A short time before I saw him at his home in Rutherford, New Jersey — which was only two or three miles from the home where I grew up — he had suffered a stroke. When I saw him he lamented that he had been forced to give up his practice of medicine because he could not readily remember the names of the drugs he would prescribe. Dr. Williams found it both difficult to read and sometimes to fish from his mind the word he needed. When he couldn't say Ezra Pound's name I filled it in for him. The stroke in no way, though, impaired his intelligence nor, oddly, his ability to write poems. He asked me to read my poems to him and then spread out the pages in rows on a table. "I like that one the best," he said, pointing to the one poem that had lines of different lengths scattered over the page. "You write very well for a teacher of English." He disliked academics because he found them both hostile to the kind of poems he wrote and favoring T. S. Eliot's poems, which Williams detested.

After these discussions of my poems with Jarrell, Lowell, and Williams, I began to have much more assurance and never sought advice on my poetry. My career as a poet developed swiftly in the next few years: first *Poetry* accepted a poem; next *The American Scholar* gave me a prize for another. The editor of *The American Scholar* was Hiram Haydn, who was also editor-in-chief at Random House until he left to become a founding publisher at Atheneum. After I won the prize Hiram asked me to send him a manuscript for a book of poems, which he published under the title *A Paper Horse* in 1962. When Hiram Haydn left Atheneum, my editor there became Harry

Ford, who published the next few books of my poetry. No writer ever had an editor better than Harry Ford.

Along with so many upheavals in the sixties almost every poet of stature was afflicted by alcoholism or insanity or both. Many of them committed suicide. Among the afflicted were John Berryman, Robert Lowell, Theodore Roethke, Anne Sexton, Sylvia Plath, Dylan Thomas, Randall Jarrell, and others. Madness was then a contagious disease among poets, or so it seemed. Poets were criss-crossing the country giving reading after reading. Many seemed to thrive on plane flights and partying, but not I. After giving countless readings myself, I felt that the frantic pace was unhinging me — I couldn't seem to slow down. The easiest way to keep my sanity and general health, to keep writing at top performance, was to limit stringently the readings that involved travel. This decision may have diminished the sale of my books, but it gave me the freedom and peace I needed to write.

I am often asked whether I have a religion or philosophy or hold to a specific aesthetic theory. Poets often do have aesthetic theories; mostly I've noticed they have taken their practices in poetry and turned these practices into theories, then with advancing age turn the theories into absolute laws. William Carlos Williams, for one. I have no system of aesthetics, no denomination in religion, embrace no philosophical system. What I have tried to do is keep an open mind, succumb to no dogma. Do angels exist? My answer is maybe, just as UFOs may exist. Probably not, but they might. Philosophy makes life hard to see with clarity. "It is the systematic befuddling of the mind in a language especially created for that purpose." All systems of philosophy are conjecture, not one is the truth. And as to religious systems, they seem mostly to be the cause of wars.

When I was about fifteen, I rode in an elevator with my paternal grandfather to the top floor of the Passaic National Bank Building where my father practiced law. My grandfather, a well-to-do man, had retired when he was about forty-five, then spent his days reading philosophy and history when he wasn't traveling to places such as Budapest, Casablanca, or the French Riviera. The elevator man was very old, bent over, and had hands that trembled. When we disembarked at the top floor Grandfather said, "Did you see that poor old man who runs the elevator? He was in my class in high school. I don't have to work because I am financially independent. You probably think that I was smarter than he or worked harder than he. No. Not at all. It's all luck. I've been extraordinarily lucky. He has been unlucky. Life is luck and chance. Don't you forget it." And as I grew older I began to agree that luck and chance may rule our lives and also rule the entire universe.

This is a universe of luck and chance. Galaxies
Spin in flight like snow, rattle in space and are gone.
For a while light lives, sound lives

Spinning through valleys and mountains of empty space;
God in sound, the great gambler sending in flight
The dice, the stars, the snow at 4 a.m. in Utah.

A universe of random events? I am not sure. And I am not sure about many events in my life and the earth I inhabit.

I feel that the poet's job is to be a seer, not a fortune teller or predictor of things to come but a person who can shed his prejudices and see life, maybe only very small bits of it, through an uncluttered mind.

Throughout my writing career there have been subjects I didn't know how to transform into poetry. I began to turn some of these thoughts into fictional prose, two novels and many short stories. Another way of putting it is: when, for some reason I can't fathom, I can't write poems, then I write fiction, and when I can't do either I write discursive prose, essays, and reviews, which I find a chore. Writing poems or prose fiction I find exciting, even exhilarating, like nothing else in life. When if for extensive periods of time inspiration abandons me, I feel depressed.

Writing has been a way for me to understand not only my life but the lives of others; my works are seldom autobiographical or confessional. I like to be lifted out of myself, not turned inward. "Know thyself." Well yes, but not to the exclusion of outer life. Many writers who swear by Freud tend to lock themselves in the prisons of themselves.

Let me end with a note that serves as a preface to my *Selected Poems*. I'm sorry if this seems impressionistic. Nevertheless, it represents my thinking:

NOTE

These poems are not arranged chronologically in order of composition or publication. They are evoked in clusters. His-torical time to me is an illusion. I can never remember how old I am or what happened in what year, so I hold to simultaneity rather than continuity. Clock and calendar time exist, I guess, and I know when I look in the mirror; yet Chaucer and Homer, to me, seem young contemporaries while Milton and Wordsworth seem like elderly gentlemen. What appears out of time is the elegant; what is ordinary is the grand. A naked man and a naked woman in a sunlit garden present culture in its highest form. A garden is not a wilderness, anymore than a poem is. History must not be neglected, yet should not be thought of as linear. Stars and snowflakes are great stabilizers for lovers, as are flowers in vases. So lyric poetry is one of the better defenses against the barbarities of war and politicians, a counter rhythm to sequential time. We all live and die in ways teachers, governors, clergy, press and philosophers rarely recognize, tone deaf to rhythm. To govern is to misunderstand, to follow is to be diminished. Considering particular lives, though, what else can most individuals do? Gamble? A dice game, two lovers, a city, a small child; each has, as the seasons, the planets, its own rhythm, in time, out of time. And so these poems have varied rhythms — and varied forms or shapes, hopefully not imposed but arising out of the nature of the subject and of language.

Books

A Paper Horse (poetry). Atheneum, 1962.
Advantages of Dark (poetry). Atheneum, 1966.
Three Sides of the Mirror (novel). Putnam, 1966.
Christmas in Las Vegas (poetry). Atheneum, 1971.
Watson on the Beach (chapbook). SB Press, 1972.
Selected Poems (poetry). Atheneum, 1974.
Island of Bones (chapbook). Unicorn, 1977.
Lilly Lang (novel). St. Martin's Press, 1977. Pocket Book Edition, 1979.
Night Blooming Cactus (poetry). Atheneum, 1980.
Victoria Woodhull (chapbook). Coraddi, 1980.

Plays

The Hoax. Privately printed, 1959.
The Plot in the Palace. First Stage, 1964.

Anthology

The Greensboro Reader. Ed. Gibbons Ruark. University of North Carolina Press, 1967.

Periodicals

Poems, stories, essays, and reviews have appeared in these and other publications: *American Scholar*, *Antaeus*, *Beloit Poetry Journal*, *English Literary History*, *Georgia Review*, *Harper's*, *Kenyon Review*, *Miami Herald*, *Nantucket Review*, *Nation*, *New American Review*, *New Yorker*, *New York Times*, *Poetry*, *Sewanee Review*, *Shenandoah*, *South Carolina Review*, *Tri-Quarterly*, *Victorian Studies*, and *Washington Post*.

Mark L. Shelton

Mark L. Shelton was born in Chicago and earned degrees from Western Michigan University and the University of Pittsburgh. A former editor for both Ohio *and* Pittsburgh *magazines, he resides in Athens, Ohio, where he teaches occasionally at Ohio University and writes the rest of the time. He is married to the writer Eve Shelnutt.*

MY WRITER'S LIFE

I

It is as easy as it is deceptive to look back over one's life and seem to see a narrative that leads, inexorably, to the present. Taking stock in this fashion makes the notion of free will seem absurd: how, we wonder, could it have been any other way? Yet no one's life (least of all one's own) can ever be that simple.

That I *am* a writer is, of course, a fact, and one not solely unconnected from the narrative of my life and experience. I can easily find a common thread; I tug, and the formative events follow, one after the other. In the macrocosm, this narrative is seamless.

But how deceptive to see a life as so linear! Instead, a word occurs to me, one that I have often used in a slightly different context, a word I use to describe what makes a good journalist. Good journalists are disposed toward observation, disposed toward awareness, disposed toward curiosity. Disposition is organic, accretive only in the way, say, a body grows (seemingly everywhere all at once); disposition is at once predestiny, suggesting as it does, the way one *is*, and free will, as in being disposed to act.

Thus, I would say that my "disposition" toward being a writer has made me a writer, a disposition that has worked in consonance with certain decisions and events, with luck, with the influence of several people, with both destiny and free will.

I sit here, in Athens, Ohio, in a clever little office over Dave Smart's barber shop, an office that is mine to write in. I am not only a writer, I am *only* a writer, and when I tug on a thread that is labeled "my writer's life," I inevitably tug on all the other threads, too; my history appears seamless. I don't know if it would be good or bad to be able to account for one's life in twenty or thirty pages, but I do know that I cannot.

Instead, what I conjure up are a few parts of my life that seem to lead to the disposition, rather than simply to the circumstance, an act that pretends that everything of my life is part of this story, but that only a few moments have their denouement in the writing of this essay.

II

My father, Ross Shelton, worked for fifty years on rotating shifts, such an anomaly in this age that the term needs glossing—one week, he would work from four in the afternoon until midnight; the next week, from eight in the morning until four in the afternoon; the following week, from midnight until eight in the morning. His two days off were always sequential, but only randomly on Saturday and Sunday. He crept around this odd calendar for half a century, as his five children (four daughters and a son) grew up and learned which hours of the day to themselves creep around the house, lest they disturb his sleep.

I describe this situation not only to illustrate something important about my father, although his job, which he was hired to do in 1926 and which he held throughout the Great Depression, throughout World War II, through every earthshaking event of the twentieth century, was the central fact in our household, the point around which everything else revolved. Rather, I describe my father's schedule as a way of introducing my mother, Rose Shelton, who among the many, many things she accomplished in her life, engendered within me both a sense of time and a sense of language, such that I could be disposed to spend one involved with the other. In my childhood home, there were two senses of time. One was the schedule determined by my father's work, both the hours he was gone and the mirror hours when he was home; when he worked the four-to-twelve shift, "dinner" was at about 2:30 in the afternoon; when he worked the day shift, dinner was at five, and so on. That was one way of seeing the time that we all had. Then there was the time that my mother kept, which was such that all things seemed to happen in their own time. In her own time.

It is difficult even now, ten years after her death, for me to write about my mother, simply because I can think of so much to say. I begin with her, however, because it is from her that I, as one of my sisters phrases it, "inherited" my love of words, of writing. The way that my sister uses the word implies a sort of genetics, like height or dimples, but I appropriate the word more in the sense of a legacy. My mother lived as much as she could in a world of words, a world of delight to her, and to all of those around her who wished to share it. From a very early age, I wished so, and so I did. I was able to in large part because the schedule of my father made for many times in the house when the house needed to be quiet; he would sleep during the day when he was on the midnight shift, so every third week the house would be quiet for six days. It was, as my mother discovered, I am sure, long before any of her children were born, an excellent time to read.

The picture I have in my mind is something like this. It is sunny, the afternoon sun coming through the living room windows of the family house, the only house I ever lived in until I went away to college in 1976. In the living room were low bookshelves built into either side of the fireplace, underneath narrow casement windows. The shelves were always full, not with books selected to look presentable but with *books*, real books, books that were meant to be read, books acquired to be read.

Titles I remember: Rumer Godden's *In This House of Brede*; Bartlett's *Familiar Quotations*; *Papillon*; a romanticized life of Tchaikovsky; another, equally romanticized, of Robert and Elizabeth Barrett Browning; a novel called *Joe, the Wounded Tennis Player*; a biography of Warren G. Harding, *The Shadow of Blooming Grove*; two travel books by Supreme Court Justice William O. Douglas; Camus' *The Stranger*; John Galsworthy's *Forsyte Saga*; the poems of Emily Dickinson and of Marianne Moore; e. e. cummings's autobiography, *The Enormous Room*.

In a chair, my mother sits, reading. Next to her on a table is an ashtray and her Pall Mall cigarettes, and a white china coffee mug. She generally holds the book in one hand and turns the pages, sips coffee, holds a cigarette, with the other. She is in repose. Upstairs in the small bedroom, my father sleeps, so the house is quiet; if one strains to listen, one might hear the odd, pendular groan of the kitchen clock, or the refrigerator cycling on and off. The windows are open, but the neighborhood tends toward quiet. And my mother reads. Around her, often, might be chores of various kinds — sometimes, for example, ironing, or laundry to be sorted, or sewing (my mother made most of her own clothes), tasks that she would interrupt to sit and read for a while. Later, as dinnertime approaches, she will rise and go to the kitchen to fix the evening meal, or finish the sorting of laundry, or the hemming of a dress, but for now, she is reading.

I used to sprawl on the floor of the living room on many of these afternoons and read as well. There was something . . . convivial about reading in the living room when my mother was reading. Often, for reasons inexplicable to me ncw, my preferred position was on my back, with my head and shoulders underneath a plain square coffee table, of dimensions just slightly wider than my shoulders, holding a book up in both hands directly above my face; a skill I developed was an incremental movement of my right thumb to let one page hang, in correspondence with a reach of my left thumb, to turn a page. I can remember doing this with small books, children's books, but as I grew, the books grew as well: an illustrated *Robinson Crusoe*, *Treasure Island*, the biography of Tchaikovsky, and for one entire summer when I was perhaps eight or nine, volume after volume of the *Encyclopaedia Britannica*, perhaps the one family possession that I still covet once or twice a week. One of my sisters, who has two small daughters, has it, should have it, will gain much for her daughters from it, but I can still feel the shiny black bindings, the somber weight of those volumes, the slick paper, the signed entries, and I wish they were mine.

A paraphernalia of reading accumulated around my mother over time: a dozen magazine subscriptions (*Saturday Review*, *National Geographic*, *The Nation*, *The New Yorker*), newspapers like the *Christian Science Monitor* and the *National Observer*, great stacks of magazines purchased at neighborhood sales — *Punch*, *Commonweal*. And because my mother wrote, off and on for years, for various suburban Chicago newspapers, we received all the local newspapers: the weekly Oak Lawn *News* (where she was editor for several years), the Blue Island *Sun-Standard* (where she was a reporter, writer, editor, and page-maker), the Worth-Palos *Reporter*. And of course, books.

Although my mother cooked all the meals, did all the housework, raised five children (spanning almost twenty years between oldest and youngest), and in general, ran the family from rides to the swimming pool to help with homework, it never seemed effortful, in large part because she had the gift of settling down comfortably in the small interstices of each day, and reading.

Years after these sorts of afternoons, when I stood as a freshman outside the door of my English professor's office, I was struck mightily by a picture postcard he had affixed there. It was a photograph — real? staged? — of what appeared to be a bomb-struck bookstore in London. Standing among the blown-to-smithereens timbers and window frames of the shop are several shelves still full of books. And at the shelves are two or three men, in suits and hats, bumbershoots hung over their forearms, browsing the volumes, reading, as though they were in their clubs. This was the repose my mother had with a book; I remember now a particular gesture, in fact, that sums up her reading. She would be sitting in a chair, book before her, and the phone might ring. She gathers herself to rise, begins to rise, begins to move the book away to set it down (I never saw her dog-ear a page), but all the while reading, one last sentence, one more word, as though she could hardly put it down. But she would. But she would also, invariably and when she could, return.

To my mother, words and books and writing had a presence — were,

I theorize many years after the fact and in a time when confirmation is impossible, an integral part of the world in which she lived. Like her in some small way, I have always since had books, owned books, gathered them, shelved them, stacked them around me, browsed them, stared at their spines while daydreaming: I have never, since I became old enough to have books of my own, lived in a room without books. I like to think I have books the way my mother had books, an inheritance beyond calculation.

I used the word *amiable* to describe my mother, a descriptive that holds both in general and in the particular, in the context of her relationship to language. She had an amiable and felicitous relationship to words, even the words she used to write up the doings of a small town council meeting. Her headlines were invariably punnish, allusive, playful: "Dredging Project Hits Snag" is one I remember; another, over an editorial about the methods of the Illinois Tollway System, was "For Whom the Road Tolls."

She loved Tom Swifties, wordplay, Scrabble, cartoons about writers and their Great American Novels; one year for the League of Women Voters, she wrote a satire on the local political structure in the form of a musical comedy, based on the movie *Camelot*, about a land (this in the era of the Seven-Up ad campaign for the "uncola") called "Camel-Un." And she wrote it in a handful of evenings, on her old Royal manual set up on a card table, chuckling as she framed the politicos in marvelous and baroque puns.

The picture, the narrative, that I see here now is clearly one of a certain disposition of my mother toward words, toward language, that seems at once highly visible and almost subversive: my mother was well liked, was well respected in a certain tiny community for her felicity with words, but the world did not define her, really, as a writer: she had no "career." It is odd, some twenty years after she left her on-again, off-again relationship with professional writing, and ten years after her death, to remember again the fundamental role that language and words played in her life through the prism of language and words in my life. It is as though I am reaping the rewards of her relationship to language. And I will always wonder: Did she know what she engendered within me?

III

I can ask the same question about a dozen or so other people, teachers of mine. In a grand gesture of simplification, I could make a case for a sort of conspiracy among them; if I were ghost writing the sort of romantic biography about me that I once read, sprawled on the living room floor, of Tchaikovsky, I would rope into the conspiracy a number of people who I am sure not only have never given me a thought in years, but who I suspect didn't give me much of a thought at the time. So perhaps the disposition was always present, or had been engendered by the time I went to school. I have an urge to list their names, a romantic indulgence, but instead I refer to what they did, which was to permit me to read. I think of myself at that age — six through fourteen — as somehow being an irritating child, in large part because I irritated the sisters closest to me in age by being so different from them, and one learns many things at home. I don't know that I irritated my teachers by my habits and predilections, which involved mainly finishing my assigned work as rapidly as possible and then waiting, antsy, for the rest of the class to catch up. I was a consummate jumper through hoops, first through, fastest through, and then I would wait, with an attitude of boredom. At age seven or eight or nine, I was a little snob. It is my impression that nowadays such behavior is seen in schools as bordering on the antisocial, or anarchistic; in my era, the solution hit upon was as simple as it was, I think, subversive. I was sent to the library to get a book and read. To other students, I am sure this often looked like punishment of some sort; for the teachers, it solved a "problem" by giving me something to do.

By the time I finished grade school, I had read perhaps 80 percent of the books in the grade school library, and a good portion of the books at the public library as well — in eighth grade, I would go with a friend of mine every day after school to the public library, where we would browse and read and check out books until five o'clock, when his father (a municipal official) would drive us home. I had read many books many times, had begun thinking of books as having something particular to do with *me*, as though they had been written expressly to fill my hours. It is not surprising, then, that by the time I reached high school, reading was as ingrained in me as handedness, or speech.

I have thought a great deal about the relationship between reading and writing; in short, I believe it is, to a point, almost one to one. By this I mean that reading opens up a world of possibilities for language, for thought, that otherwise remains unexplored. When reading becomes, as it did for me, the primary method of acquiring information and perspective, it does something to a person: language becomes the means by which the world is assimilated and refracted. It is then, I think (and again, with the caveat "to a point"), a short step toward using language to both expand and *tune* one's way of seeing the world: Bacon said that "reading maketh a full man, . . . and writing an *exact* man" [my emphasis], and while I don't tend to agree that often with Francis Bacon, I do believe that this is true. To a reader, writing is the way that one comes to explain what it is he or she knows.

I remember very clearly the time when this relationship between reading and understanding became apparent to me. It was the summer of 1972, when I was fourteen years old. Through a series of events too complicated to explain (they had to do with an almost forgotten linguist named Benjamin Whorf), I ended up with a book in my hands by Noam Chomsky. The book was (and I am saddened to think that this title will be unfamiliar to most people) *American Power and the New Mandarins*, a book that remains one of the most clear and meticulous and detailed indictments of America's role in Vietnam ever written. It not only politicized me, it *galvanized* me: if what Chomsky had written were true, then most of what I had been taught to believe must be false. If *writing* could produce such a reaction, could call into question the very foundations of the world as I thought I knew it, then writing, clearly, could do anything. Before that, I think I read mostly for what? Information? Entertainment? Curiosity? The world as I knew it suddenly seemed a quaint fiction. A month later, I was working for George McGovern's presidential campaign (hanging literature on doorknobs) and reading with what I can only describe as a vengeance, examining as critically as I could the minds that suddenly seemed on display in books. Writing was a way for a mind to bring to light all the ideas contained in it, and that seemed as though it were what minds were *for*. It would be presumptuous in the extreme to say that that summer, I "became" a writer; of course I didn't. But it was a time when it became clear to me that I could be a writer, because I was bursting with ideas that needed, I felt, to be given voice.

IV

I leap ahead a decade or so at this point, to talk about two or three decisions I have had occasion to make that were, concretely, connected with "becoming" a writer. In some ways, I suppose these are the real points of this essay, but without (at least in my own mind) the groundwork of engenderment and disposition, they would seem overly literal, overly concrete, because the facts of the matter are that I have decided on at least four occasions in my adult life to become a writer. Oddly, they all in one way or another took, too.

The first time was in high school, and I mention it only because it seems to coalesce quite well the points I've made here thus far; I saw myself becoming a journalist, the sort who wrote for a newspaper like the Chicago *Daily News*. (When the *News* folded, it affected me the way the folding of the New York *World* in the 1930s and the New York *Herald-Tribune* in the 1960s affected writers on those papers, although I was only about sixteen at the time; the *News* was a "writer's paper," and thus the sort of paper that writers aspired to work for. No child dreams of writing for *USA Today*. No one dreams that small.)

In part, I am sure this was due to the affection I had for my mother's newspaper work, as well as the spirit of the times — it was the post-Watergate era, when reporters were finding out all sorts of interesting things. To report like Casey Buckro (the environment reporter on the Chicago *Trib*) or Zay Smith (an investigative reporter with the Chicago *Sun-Times*) and to write like Noam Chomsky seemed a worthwhile pursuit. (Woodward and Bernstein were good reporters, but the *Post* was never a writer's paper.) I did all the usual things: wrote for and edited the high school paper, strung for a couple of suburbans ("School Board Lets Cafeteria Contract"), volunteered a half dozen nights a month on a senior citizens weekly, doing layout, pasteup, headlines, and captions, considered journalism school at Northwestern, the University of Illinois, and the University of Wisconsin. And then I changed my mind and decided to try for medical school.

That's the sort of sentence that should open a very bad semi-autobiographical novel (one, I hasten to add, I will never write), and while it is unquestionably a part of my larger story — another thread to tug — it is a different story than the one I am telling now. It was a decision, I would say, wrought up with my wish to do something, to leave a mark, a wish that soon found its fulfillment in a career as a writer.

At Western Michigan University, the course I took will be familiar, I expect, to many writers, in that the day-job sorts of courses for a pre-med — biology, chemistry, physics — were only half as absorbing, as diverting, as the courses in other disciplines that were required in an attempt to produce "well-rounded" souls; my first writing class fulfilled a Gen Ed requirement, as did my first and second literature courses. The second of these, indeed, was a subtle recruiting device for the English department. Called "Literary History and Criticism," the text for the class was the *Norton Anthology of English Literature*, and every year, it turned about a dozen students into English majors.

The professor was the late Robert Stallman, who knew much and shared what he knew freely (I can think of no higher compliment for a professor); at turns irascible and gentle, he was the first objective soul who ever told me I was a writer. In fact, I still (and this is fifteen years ago, now) can recall with utter exactitude how this came about, how unhappy an event it was, in the strangest of ways. I had written my first paper for the class on formal rhyming and rhythmical blank verse in some modern poets and Bob Stallman accused me, flat out, of plagiarism.

"I don't think you wrote this paper," he said to me, after asking to see me after class. "Who did?"

All I could think to say was that I had. How could I demonstrate it?

He leafed through the paper until he came to a place where I had used a few lines from William Morris, from "The Defense of Guinevere": "And feeling it shameful to feel ought but shame / All through her heart, yet felt her cheek burned so / she must a little touch it. . . ." I used to recite in my head stanzas from this poem during the long and dull hours of swimming practice, where they helped take my mind off what I was doing, which was swimming. "Tell me," Stallman said, "where the *hell* you read William Morris, then."

It would fit this essay marvelously if I said I told him "Under the little coffee table in the living room," which would have been true, but of course I didn't have such presence of mind. In fact, I mistook his point entirely; because Morris wasn't covered in the course, I assumed I had committed some grave literary faux pas by quoting him. So I might have made matters worse by blurting out, as I did, "What's wrong with William Morris?"

"Where's the book?" he demanded. "Where did you get the book?" The book was at home in Chicago, of course, on the little shelves under the windows, 150 miles away; I hadn't opened it since I was in high school, if then. But it is such a marvelously rhythmical poem, and such a sad and lovely tale, that it sticks, or stuck, in the mind. I had to tell him I didn't have it, that I had simply remembered it. His eyes narrowed. "'But, knowing now . . .'" he began. What could I say? "'That they would have her speak, she threw her wet hair backward from her brow—'"

"I'll be damned," said Bob Stallman.

We sorted things out, more or less, although it took me quite awhile to get over the terror of feeling as though I had done something . . . wrong. (He later told me that it was almost unprecedented for a student to actually know something he hadn't learned in class and that he had done me a disservice. It also turned out that he had done his dissertation on William Morris.) He became not only someone whom I admired greatly but someone I came to consider a friend.

It was Bob Stallman who asked me what I was doing in biology, when I was so clearly a writer, and it was Bob Stallman who sent me on to a creative writing class, where I first encountered the rigors and opportunities of form from within. It didn't take me very long to put two and two together: I already spent much of my time reading and writing. I had in essence already "declared" my major, although I had never said it aloud. I would write.

V

I leap ahead again here to describe what I can only call the Great Transition, when I found myself coming full circle and being a journalist. I wrote short stories and poems in college, made an equally Great Transition by going to graduate school at the University of Pittsburgh in fiction writing, where I was in the first class of the new Master of Fine Arts program. It was fairly easy during graduate school to assume that a situation permitting one to write short stories would present itself; indeed, after graduate school, I spent nearly three years teaching in a variety of marginal positions at a variety of colleges and universities in and around Pittsburgh, "full-time part-time," "part-time full-time," "temporary full-time," "adjunct this" and "adjunct that," but never anything real.

The fiction (and this will be familiar to many) was: a) that teaching gave you time to write, and b) that something would open up if you stuck with it. The reality was that I often taught five and six courses of composition each semester (one memorable semester I taught eight), which left little time to write anything but patient comments on stacks of student papers. And while there were, for example, two full-time tenure-track professors at Pitt who had begun as part-timers, there were also nearly a hundred part-timers. The odds were absurd.

I was newly married, newly settled into a big and drafty house, and enjoying life immensely, but I was not writing very much. What I was writing—a few magazine articles to bring in some money and do something interesting—was something I had not had any training for, or experience with, since high school. That I knew I could write sounds like a conceit, but it seemed more and more a fact; there was only the mildest of adjustment problems to magazine journalism, in large part because I think good writing is good writing. My mother had taught me copyediting marks, and the rest I just sort of picked up. The pay was good if one learned to work efficiently (Samuel Johnson said that nothing concentrated the mind like the threat of being hanged in the morning, and I'm also reminded of something attributed to Molière, to the effect that writers start out doing it for love, then for a few friends, and then finally they do it for money), and on the strength of a handful of magazine features, I was hired to be a writer at a Pittsburgh hospital. It had the makings of a career.

I lasted eight months. When we sold the big house, I quit the job and we moved to the country, to a house my wife and I will both always love but seldom miss.

What I had discovered sounds simple, but took some head banging (and many ten-hour days at the hospital) for me to learn: the one thing I could do well was write, but it seemed pointless to spend a life writing abstracts of articles in medical journals. I decided, for the final time, to once again become a writer, but for perhaps the first time, on my own terms alone.

I now think that writing attracts a certain sort of mind, the sort of person who wants, at some level, to be his or her own boss. At the typewriter, every sentence is the beginning of a universe, every fresh sheet of paper is an entirely new world. That is why writers angle for time of their own, why many writers don't wear very well the yoke of a day job, why I found what I find in nonfiction, a genre that fits my personality closely — perhaps uniquely. I am innately curious, and nonfiction gives me the license to go places and ask questions and watch interesting things. Nonfiction is expansive: the world, truly, is one's genre. It is participatory: rather than imagine a surgeon in an operating room or a man who carves wooden legs, I can go and find a real one, and insinuate myself into close proximity. Nonfiction is, as a field of endeavor, primarily a *sensual* experience. And finally, it is an *active* enterprise, it permits a writer to *do* something, which is make hidden worlds unfold for those who would otherwise never know something. It is no accident, I think, that the journalists I admire most — A. J. Liebling, for example — are writers who enter a world for their own, sometimes arcane, reasons and give to the reader a sense of why they were there.

I didn't know much of this, of course, when I started. I did know that the world around me interested me, and that I had a particular skill that helped evoke that world. I was helped in large measure by the sort of thing that happens to journalists — scientists, too: Pasteur once said that "chance favors the prepared mind." I met the subject of my first book.

I won't say much about Peter J. Jannetta, the marvelous and unusual and courageous brain surgeon who is the subject of *Working in a Very Small Place*, except to say that in the particular, he was made for writing about; after having my first meeting with him, I said,

"Someone ought to write a book about him," but it was my wife who said to me, "Why don't you?" I did.

I didn't know exactly how to go about it, but chance (which does favor the prepared mind) helped. I spent a year following this (extremely patient) neurosurgeon around and then wrote two chapters and an outline, which I sent to a writer friend to see what he thought. He thought so well of it that he sent it to his agent, who called me and asked if he might represent me and sell this book, which he did in a period of weeks to W. W. Norton. Where before I was simply a freelance writer, I now felt I had some sort of pedigree: a Writer. And it suits me. The book came out as well as I had hoped (absent, to my blushing chagrin, a chapter that months after the book had been printed, I happened to discover in the computer; as I say, I didn't know exactly how to go about writing a book. I do remember having to change a few things very late in the writing process, but I thought I had left out a *paragraph*); indeed, well enough for Norton to offer me a contract for the book I am working on now, about a band of solar engineers in Athens, Ohio, led by a man they call William The Beale, who are out to change the world, and the way the world uses electricity. I still write for magazines, and I love to review books, and I leap at the chance to teach a course at Ohio University whenever I can (the part-time yoke, once across the shoulders, leaves a lifelong imprint), but I am, finally, a writer, whose work is of his own devising.

I see here that I allude to a Great Transition but don't really explain it. The differences, finally, between fiction and nonfiction are mostly in the external world, I think, which is how I account for the ease of transition. By this I mean that one is seen by the outside world as Fact, the other as Fantasy, but to a writer, this distinction ought to be subtle. I *write* the same way, I imagine the same worlds, only one exists in fact, which requires a small adjustment. I was, I think, *prepared* to write about the world I live in, in a form that is seen as mostly about the world I live in. As another professor I admire greatly, William Coles at the University of Pittsburgh, says often, "Writing is an action; it is something you do." There is a tremendous amount of subtlety in these words, with their implied emphasis on "action" and on "do," as well as on the "you." Writing for me is an action; it is *what* I do.

I see here that the proportions of this essay might seem at first glance somehow skewed, in that the work I do now, the work that absorbs me and makes my professional life, only shows up very late. In a way this is fitting, because the work that I do also showed up comparatively late. It is impossible to imagine it any differently: had

I skipped, say, the three years of part-time teaching, where would I be? I likely would not have gotten that first hospital job, and therefore might never have met Peter Jannetta. Just as Tom Small, my first English professor in college, sent me to Bob Stallman, the series of steps, half-steps, missteps, that now seem to form my writer's life appear absolutely *lockstep.*

My wife, before she met me, entertained a job offer in Cleveland; whenever we visit that city, she muses on how things might have been different had she taken it. Would we have met? My disposition (to return finally to that word) is such that I of course believe that we would have; it simply would have been in Cleveland. I am as certain, as well, that I would have ended up, if not in an office over Dave Smart's barber shop in Athens, Ohio, then over a haberdasher or paint store in some equally unlikely place. But I do believe that I would be writing this essay, or something very close to it, living in what can only seem an alternative universe, one that I can *imagine*, but that I don't believe could be real. What I do now is not only real but to me, inevitable. To the extent that I can say I know myself, I know what I should be doing. It is maybe not so deceptive after all. Maybe what is deceptive is the illusion that it could have been any other way.

Books

Working in a Very Small Place: The Making of a Neurosurgeon. Norton, 1989. Paperback edition by Vintage Books, 1990. Japanese edition by Medicus, Ltd. (Osaka), 1991.
The Next Great Thing: The Sun, the Stirling Engine, and the Drive to Change the World. Norton, forthcoming.

Anthologies

"The Steel Mill" (poem). *Intro 13.* Associated Writing Programs, 1982.
"Wine Day" (poem). *Choice: The Yearbook of American Verse.* Monitor Publishing, 1986–88.
"Notes on Writing Nonfiction," "The Usual Constraints," "When Nothing Else Will Do," and "Hamburger Journalism" (two pairs of essays). *Writing: the Translation of Memory.* Macmillan, 1990.
"A Stroke of Genius" (magazine feature). *Best Sports Stories of 1990: The 46th Annual Sports Journalism Awards.* Sporting News Publishing Co., 1990.

Periodicals

More than one hundred magazine and journal publications, including sixty articles in *Ohio Magazine* (1982–91), and thirty articles in *Pittsburgh Magazine* (1986–88), as well as other publications; short stories and poems in *Three Rivers Poetry Journal, Passages North, Pennsylvania Review, Ohio Journal, Westigan Review,* and others; and seventy-five book reviews, regularly in the Columbus *Dispatch* and *Library Journal* and occasionally in the *North American Review* and the *Ohioana Quarterly.*

Jeff Friedman

Jack Matthews has published novels, poetry, essays, and plays. A self-described "philosophical sentimentalist," he collects old and rare books and thinks about the past. He and his wife have seven grandchildren, one for each day of the week. Among the awards he has received are a Guggenheim and a Major Artist Grant from the Ohio Arts Council. He is Distinguished Professor of English at Ohio University.

PILGRIMAGES IN TIME

I remember reading Joseph Conrad's novel *The Rover*, which was assigned by Miss Corbin in one of my high school English classes at North High School in Columbus, Ohio. This was in 1942, a year when Dick Keats, Rod Crist, Dan Byrd, Emerson Kimball, and I had formed a barbershop quartet which we called "The Crap Room Quartet," a name that was pretty darned daring in those days. (Obviously we remained a quartet even when one of us was missing.) We sang such golden oldies as "Dear Old Girl" and "Bird in a Gilded Cage," along with an occasional zippy topical favorite, such as the one which begins: "Now Stalin wasn't stallin' when he called the Yanks and English and began to extinguish all the vermin from the land."

Miss Corbin was a short, round, erect old lady with hair as white as spun-cake icing, aristocratic nostrils, and a wonderful eloquence in expressing genteel scorn. Her assignment of Conrad's novel brought about one of those apocalyptic moments of change we all remember. Looking back, I think that reading it inspired me to become a writer. "How wonderful it must be," I thought, "to create something like this!" It seemed to me that making such luminous realities out of words on a page was a sort of miracle, an act of magic . . . and who doesn't want to be a magician?

Actually, my reading Conrad's book was something of a miracle in itself, for it *was* an assignment, and therefore the sort of thing I wasn't likely to do. I cannot remember that the charge of doing homework was ever leveled against me. In fact, I can remember taking a book home only once during all my high school years, and that was when I was suddenly prodded alert in chemistry class one day, when Art Kiefer—a wonderfully kind teacher who once described himself as "a very tall individual with a face like a can of worms"—was talking about a forthcoming test, and I came awake long enough to realize that I had absolutely no idea of what he was talking about.

When that school day ended at three-thirty, I took two things home: my chemistry book and a certain pride in doing what students are *supposed* to do. Carrying a book under my arm felt kind of neat, and I kind of liked the feeling. Several days later when our tests were returned, I discovered I'd received the second highest grade in the class — a fact that surprised Mr. Kiefer and me, along with anyone else who might have been paying attention. The experience should have helped me realize that there really is a positive correlation between doing your lessons and receiving good grades; but *this* lesson didn't seem to take. I probably wasn't paying attention.

It was along about the time when Mr. Kiefer and I survived that experience that I was collaterally nudged into reading *The Rover* assigned in Miss Corbin's English class. Saying that it changed my life sounds a bit grand and melodramatic, but that's somewhat the way I like to think of it. After all these years, I cannot remember the plot or the characters (although I remember they frequently called one another *citoyen* — it was at the time of the French Revolution), nor can I remember the physical book — the edition, binding, or any other bibliographical feature I would take note of today. All I can remember is the general effect the story had on me. Today, if I wanted to refresh my memory, I could with considerable smugness reread the novel from my copy of the first edition.

While there would be a certain ceremonial felicity in going back to read a book that had meant so much to me, I am not strongly tempted and I doubt that I will ever return to it. Why not? Partly, my hesitation has to do with that anticipated disappointment which is the dark other side of a glowing memory. You can't go home again, and few things turn out to have justified their aggrandized translation into memory. So I feel a superstitious reluctance to read it; it seems to me that such an experience should retain its pristine innocence and purity, insulated by calculated ignorance. After all, it is through the ceremony of delimitation, or contrived inexperience, that we create our memories. "Ignorance of such things," I once read in the nineteenth-century diary of a young girl, "is part of knowledge."

Here, as elsewhere, the spirit of creativity is at war with the tyranny of the Past, and it is doubtful if the two can ever coexist entirely in peace. Nor should they, for it is out of the dialectical tension between these two forces that a sort of reality can emerge, and at times, beauty. As symbolic creatures, we are binary by nature, and find ourselves most alive and most real in the presence of otherness. What would the Past be without imagination? Or imagination without the Past? Here is my present theme.

But it is a theme best pursued by the arts of obliquity and indirection. For example, think of the Past as a distant country, where the lifestyles and mores of its inhabitants are both fascinatingly exotic and oddly familiar. There is no realm more present to the mind or more distant and uncanny. It's no wonder so many of us like to visit there in our various ways, often plundering it for souvenirs and booty in the ancient, time-honored style of raiders and pirates everywhere.

Rereading Conrad's old book would be such a foray, one calculated to recapture a past awakening, a magic moment which inspired me to write stories. Though private and interior, such a quest as this is related to that great and universal motif of the quest for some ultimate symbol — the Golden Fleece, the Holy Grail, the White Whale, and on and on. Much of my own writing has been preoccupied with this inner version of the quest, and I have celebrated it often and in various ways.

I think of this celebration as tragically heroic precisely as it is fixed, defined, articulated, and practically hopeless. So much is true of a story I published years ago, which I have only recently elaborated into a full-length play, intensifying what might be termed the motif of "The Eternal Moment." Since the play develops this idea more richly than was possible in the story, and since that idea is central not only to the plot of the play, but permeates and colors all the action . . . and since, further, it is a theme central to so much I have written, it will be useful to give a synopsis, as follows.

The play is titled *The House on Shawnee Street*, and it takes place in a small midwestern town in 1938, on Halloween Eve, in the old Hanawalt mansion, where the family's son and daughter have returned to say good-bye to their dying father, Pierce, one of the town's most important figures.

Pierce's obsessed wife Clara, however, wants her daughter June to "make up to" Dave Gardner — their next-door neighbor on Shawnee Street, and at one time her school mate — and convince him not to convert his mansion into an apartment house. This would ruin Shawnee Street and destroy it for Clara (and, she believes, for all who can understand its beauty). Pierce's and Clara's other child, Kenneth — a recent widower — has returned from Paris, where he was a correspondent for an American newspaper. He has with him his dead wife's dead dog, mounted by a French taxidermist. A sardonic drinker, Ken pets and pretends to love the dog, saying it doesn't need to be fed, walked, or treated for worms. And best of all, it can never again die.

Near the play's end — not having appeared on stage — Pierce dies in his bedroom upstairs; but poor, mad, heroic Clara conceals his death, hoping June will entertain Dave Gardner (whom she's already invited for dinner) and convince him not to convert the old Gardner mansion into an apartment house, ruining Shawnee Street. Clara's plan fails, but at the play's end, she takes matters into her own hands with spectacular effect, setting fire to the Gardner mansion and destroying it.

In one way or another, and with varying degrees of awareness, two of the play's three major characters are obsessively trying to stop time forever, to preserve some image of felicity or nobility that haunts them. And one dimension of the dramatic conflict is measurable in terms of the intersection and incompatibility of their images.

How autobiographical is this play and the story that preceded it? Now very; not in any literal sense, that is; not in terms of the key situation or characters or action. But it is a time-soaked drama, one that strangers might suppose was written by a lover of various sorts of antiques — and they would be right. Part of my enchantment with and of the Past derives from my own passionate interest in the life that has gone before.

Like many small boys, I loved all things connected with American Indians when I grew up, but I retained this interest longer than most; and today I realize that part of my fascination with their lives (I am speaking of *historical* Indians, now — the tribal Indians we read about in nineteenth-century overland narratives, for example) ... part of my fascination with their lives has to do with their being so utterly *gone*, whereas at one time they were as unequivocally *here* as we are.

Wherever they may be said to have gone, we are headed for the same place. And whatever charges of escapism, sentimentality, and a nostalgia in "wanting to return to the Past" may be made against one who feels this way, I would argue that such an idealization is precisely, specifically human, for whether we know it, or admit it, we are all essentially and inescapably symbol-using creatures; and symbols are instruments of distance, and the greatest psychological distances are temporal.

There are other sorts of stories I have written, however, in which the quest is more literal, fixed with unmistakable, unchanging focus upon some personal and private version of an archetypal moment or gesture that cannot be forgotten. Instead of trying to hold time still, these protagonists yearn to go back and in a spiritual sense recover some image that haunts them. Being literally unforgettable, such powerful symbols evoke a pilgrimage into the past to retrieve some defining element in the mosaic of self.

The need to return to this archetypal moment is profound and unique, for such moments are dense with hope and mythic promise. By "mythic promise" I mean something analogous to J. J. Bachofen's statement that myth is the exegesis of the symbol. (I find that statement itself wonderfully symbolic, therefore rich in its promise of and opportunity for exegesis.) At the heart of many of my stories, there is a fixed still point, a life-giving image, a symbol that sleeps in the dignity of silence, only to be awakened hesitantly and piously in the manner of invoking a deity.

One story that is typical in this regard is "Quest for an Unnamed Place" (*Ghostly Populations*), in which an aging married couple set out to find a lakefront tourist cabin in Wisconsin or Minnesota, which the husband personally remembers from a fishing vacation with his parents forty years before. He cannot forget one magic moment—a moment virtually without "content"—in which his parents and other adults were sitting on a lighted, screened-in porch at night, talking and telling stories; he remembers the box of light they were all inside at that moment, defying the outer darkness but admitting the cool breeze from the lake; he remembers a moment of joyous realization, an epiphany that was ineffable and puissant, remote but eternal in the way of sensed duration.

He and his wife (their children are all grown, married, and living elsewhere) get in their car and travel in search of this magic place, knowing that the actual cabin he remembers is almost certainly gone or changed beyond recognition. The story belongs to the husband; the perspective and the existential crisis are both his, although his wife shares in them. This is inevitably and deservedly so, for he is aware of what a wonderful woman she is—imaginative, sympathetic, loyal, subtle, and aware. Although their journey is mythic and powerful beyond clear explanation, they nevertheless undertake it in a spirit of zealous fascination.

As predicted, they fail in this specific quest. But there is a startling and unexpected epiphany at the very end of the story. Something very strange and mysterious and *interior* occurs. They are on their way home. It is night and he is driving. Then,

> *Two cars approached, and he glanced over at his wife, and saw that she was still sleeping deeply, in that posture of utter commitment that would leave her stiff when she awoke.*
>
> *And in that brief moment when the car was flooded with the light of the two passing cars, driven by strangers he would never know or ever see, he felt something like recognition come into his mind . . . as if the car had for an instant flashed like a screened-in porch across his memory, the black lake of night all around them, in an unknown place that might come back into his memory years later, bearing the unspeakable message of a moment's joy, gratuitous and unfathomable, coming to him only because he was watching, and for no other reason.*

Part of my pleasure in the theme of this story derives from the beautifully mature monogamous love that illuminates it — making the box of the story itself another lighted porch within the darkness — along with the shared adventure into a mystery that is both personal and enduringly human. Its quiet theme seems to me very different from the fiction that is published so widely these days, and admired so clamorously. The story is also somewhat autobiographical, for that lighted porch magically endures in my personal memory, very much as it exists in the story. Indeed, it was this memory that inspired me to write the story, just as it inspired my protagonist to go in search of its source, lost somewhere in the distant Past.

There is another story I have written which celebrates a theme central to my vision as a writer, which I have been emphasizing here. In talking about this next story, I mean to establish another thematic parallel to what has gone before, for this story also presents a variation upon what might be called "the Quest into the Past," a theme intrinsic to my theoretically rereading Conrad's *The Rover*, and to a man's seeking out a lighted porch in the darkness of the past.

I am referring to "The Pilgrimage" (*Dubious Persuasions*), a story about a dying old man who is strangely but powerfully drawn to return to a spring he remembers drinking from when he was a farm boy fifty-eight years before. The story is shorter than "Quest for an Unnamed Place," and its celebration of the quest motif is, if not more individual and more personal, at least a lonelier one. The spring at the heart of the story was part of the protagonist's youth, a time when our personal myths are created so that they may shine in our memories.

As in the previous story, the protagonist of this one is also blessed with a loyal wife. I am aware that creating such a subordinate role for these women will seem sexist to many people; but it isn't really, for I don't grade the realities of my characters. Moreover, I can write only as a man, and can see things only in a man's perspective. This does not at all rule out the possibility of other stories that could theoretically be written about this same old couple I have created — stories that belong to the *wife*, let us say, featuring the inner drama of *her* quest, in which case her husband might with perfect justice be described as "loyal." Not only do I consider such alternative versions of my story perfectly "allowable," I would tend to find them very interesting, precisely as every event is enriched by additional perspectives. But the fact is, I have not written such alternative versions; I have written only this one.

My protagonist is known simply as "Mr. Fisher." Giving him a first name would violate something in the story's point of view, although it is entirely appropriate that his wife be fully named. Her name is "Elsie," and when the story opens, she is sitting with him in the car at a filling station. They are waiting for a man named Clyde Washburn, a local stranger who was hired to drive him far back into the hills so that he can find the remembered spring and drink from it. But Elsie will not go with him; she understands that this is something that belongs to him alone.

Elsie is returned to the Twenty Winks Motel, where the old couple are staying; and then Clyde drives Mr. Fisher up a narrow, little-traveled, dangerously crooked township road, far back into the isolated brushy fields and wooded hills the old man has not seen for almost sixty years. Finally, Mr. Fisher recognizes certain landmarks and tells Clyde to pull the car off the road and park. Clyde hands him his cane, then opens an old pasture gate and helps him walk up into a field that has literally gone to seed, so that it is now thick with weeds, brush, and scrub saplings. After they've gone a little way, the old man stops and insists upon continuing alone. Like Elsie, Clyde is concerned about him. But Mr. Fisher is determined; he knows exactly what he is after and tells Clyde to return to the car. "You close the window and keep the air conditioning going," he says. "I don't want to think of you sitting there listening for me. I'll be all right."

Then, finally alone on his solitary quest, old Mr. Fisher climbs slowly and painfully through the underbrush, wondering if a beech tree might still be standing as he remembered it by the spring.

> *And indeed, after he had walked a few steps, he could see the top of the old tree jutting far above the tops of the scrub elm and honey locusts that had sprung up all over the meadow. There was a strange and sudden sadness in seeing that old tree. Perhaps it was because he had prepared himself to believe that it had died years ago, and now that it still stood it was as old for a tree as he was for a man ... and death waited for both of them, alike. As if the tree had been waiting, too, for some such moment of ceremonial recognition as this.*
>
> *But of course this was silly, fanciful. And at any rate, it wasn't the tree itself, but rather the spring from whose depths the roots of the tree had drawn life over this half-century of waiting and survival.*
>
> *Mr. Fisher stepped carefully over some thistles, tangled like green starfish in the sod, searching warily for copperheads. When he looked up once more, he saw the glossy dark ferns*

that bordered the spring. And when he took one more step, he heard a deep gulp of water as a frog dropped into the spring and plummeted toward the cold leaves at the bottom. Still, there was the little rill of water that curled smoothly and subtly down over the rocks, past the massive roots of the beech tree, and then slipped underground. Seeing such a rivulet as this, he understood how ancient men could attribute femininity to streams and rivers ... as well as sweetness and guile, mystery and the forgotten melodies of dream.

Slowly, Mr. Fisher knelt to the ground, smelling the cool mint leaves that flourished about the pool of water before him. With one hand, he dusted aside the cobwebs that lay in a delicate, transparent canopy a foot above the water. A gnat fell upon the surface of the spring, scarcely trembling the surface of the water.

And as he leaned forward to drink, Mr. Fisher saw his mirrored image turning toward him ... as if in acceptance and recognition. He looked, he thought afterwards, like a man leaning over to pray, not to drink water from a spring.

So there it is, appearing once again. If I did not have such visions as a writer, I would have no reason to write. I would hope that others can see the importance of this theme; but it seems doubtful. I think it is too greatly at odds with some of the values and superstitions of our time. Still, that's all right, after all, for even if others don't understand, the theme remains inviolate. If others are unmoved by the passion implicit in my theme, it may be because I have failed to reveal it adequately, not treating it with the great subtlety and justice it deserves. Or it may be that the fashions of our times are intrinsically, insidiously inimical to quiet and essentially private truths in a world of advertising, social consciousness, and demographic hocus-pocus.

A writer's primary obligation is to *articulate*, not communicate. Articulation expresses one's obligation to the language and the art; communication requires a receiver in a closed system of discourse. Artistic communication is beyond one's control, after all, and should be left to the media whose power is such that their hallucinations tend always to become self-fulfilling prophecies. An artist has no sure way of evoking ghosts from heads filled with other sorts of messages, many of which are, from all visible and audible signs, the pied noise of gabble glitz.

But none of that should matter. Why should it? There is no final and conclusive epistemology, and all our visions are mystical. Others may not like or understand what we do, but we do it anyway, with the dumb hope that there may be gods that exist in the silence of time — known only, it should be stated, by their past avatars . . . gods who in their own inscrutable ways will respond secretly and cunningly to our most honest expressions, assuring us that the ideas that riddle and beguile us are true and beautiful and worthy of our attention.

Who would ever think their voices might be audible?

Books (since 1981)

Dubious Persuasions (stories). Johns Hopkins University Press, 1981.
Sassafras (novel). Houghton Mifflin, 1983.
Crazy Women (stories). Johns Hopkins University Press, 1985.
Booking in the Heartland (essays). Johns Hopkins University Press, 1986.
Ghostly Populations (stories). Johns Hopkins University Press, 1986.
Perhaps the Greatest Incomparable Autobiography in the World, "Nobs" (chapbook). Northern Ohio Bibliophilic Society, 1986.
Introduction. *The Adventures of a Treasure Hunter*, by Charles Everitt. Meyerbooks, 1987.
Memoirs of a Bookman (essays). Ohio University Press, 1989.
Dirty Tricks (stories). Johns Hopkins University Press, 1990.
An Interview with the Sphinx (play). Dramatic Publishing Company, 1991.
On the Shore of That Beautiful Shore (play). Dramatic Publishing Company, 1991.
Rare Book Lore: Selected Letters of Ernest J. Wessen (editor). Ohio University Press, 1991.

Periodicals

Short stories, essays, poems, and reviews have appeared in such publications as *Gamut, Kenyon Review, London Review of Books, Mademoiselle, Malahat Review, Michigan Quarterly Review, Nation, National Review, New Republic, New York Times, Poetry, Sewanee Review, Southern Review,* and *Yale Review.*

Gerald Costanzo

Gerald Costanzo lives in Harwich, Massachusetts, where he is coach of the Hyannis team in the Cape Cod Summer Lacrosse League, and near Pittsburgh, Pennsylvania, where he edits the Carnegie Mellon University Press Poetry Series and Three Rivers Poetry Journal. *Among his honors are two fellowship awards from the National Endowment for the Arts, the Devins Award, and fellowships from the Coordinating Council of Literary Magazines and the Pennsylvania Council on the Arts.*

WHAT'S WRONG WITH THE MOON?

1.

"Sue Baseball? No Kid, that would be like suing the Church!"
— William Bendix in *The Babe Ruth Story*

I first chose language because I needed a weapon with which to defend myself. As far as I knew it had no cost and it was legal. I grew up, like most boys my age, wanting a life of athletics. Nothing unusual in that. The expectation of becoming a hero, of achieving fame perhaps. Maybe just being accomplished at something we enjoyed doing. To that end we taught ourselves what we thought America wanted us to learn: determination; fair play; dedication to a craft; the honing of mental and physical skills; that perseverance offsets a lack of natural ability; the (always undelineated) virtue of competition; and the most elusive of achievements, patience in all of this. Despite some moderate early success, it was a dream which ended soon enough. Size. Speed. Talent. The need to earn a living. There are few compensations.

I was born in the state of Oregon, and I often lament that it has not been my lot to have spent my adult years there. Its natural beauty is astounding. The Pacific coast. The rivers and forests and snow-capped mountains. I fished and rafted, spent summers in my grandparents' bungalow overlooking the ocean at Cannon Beach, and in winter climbed Mount Hood with the Mazamas. But there was an ogre in paradise. I was an abused child. For more than ten years every hour spent away from home was a reprieve. I excelled in school. I was the only one in my class who luxuriated in the major requirement of the era, reading *Silas Marner*. I excelled at games. I excelled at observing and appreciating the Great Northwest. How could it have been that my excellence vanished whenever I entered my own house?

Despite my mother's tireless efforts, my brothers and I were part of what is now called a "dysfunctional family" (a term so lightweight it bears no resemblance to the circumstance it proposes to name, so feathery in comparison to the thing itself, it could be a euphemism for the improper use of doilies). Lives go wrong. Very early I took to spending the hours at home inventing scenes and stories. I wrote them down. Little autobiographical forgeries. I succeeded in each of them, and they were my salvation. Their requirements were few. They had to be literal enough for understanding, and so clearly stated that I could believe them. A concocted life of comfort. I suppose, with all one hears about child abuse these days, I was extremely lucky, and this activity was the best that could come of that sad condition.

2.

Obviously I don't recommend the way I came to writing to anyone. And once it became an established part of my life I wish I could say it had caused me no anguish or suffering. Writing has been, by turns, a source of satisfaction and vulnerability, of accomplishment and self-doubt. If a writer's standards become more demanding along the way, as I believe they should, he cannot avoid a feeling of helplessness: the discrepancy between what he is able to write and that which he will accept as good writing. Completing a poem is, in part, an unsettling proposition. One never knows if he'll ever write another.

I can say there were excellent teachers in the schools I attended. Strict grammarians and people who loved literature. People who gave advice and support. Two of them taught creative writing in high school — something unheard of then. One, dramatic and writerly, informed us by demonstration; the other, still a close friend, simply asked us to write a lot and had important things to say about everything we wrote. I can say there are worlds to be gained in attending a college such as Harvard. I wish I'd had a lifetime to spend as a student there, though as an aspiring writer then, I remain a bit disappointed that the place had not seen fit in matters literary "to enquire into the twentieth century" yet. Grateful as I am for the background in the tradition of poetry the exercises provided me, I believe I wrote all the sonnets and heroic couplets there I will ever need to write. Then the liberation of The Writing Seminars at Johns Hopkins, where in the late 1960s we read Donald Barthelme and translations of Pablo Neruda, and listened to Robert Bly and Allen Ginsberg! The long-time director there, more a friend than we deserved, who showed us that, much as we wanted not to believe it, writing would never be a communal endeavor. It was the beginning of "survival without being a member of the club." And the generous colleague in the design department at Carnegie Mellon who taught me how to publish books by others, though it takes a long time to learn to serve poetry well.

These are the facts, a little tainted by opinion.

3.

Writers who claim never to read reviews of their work and to pay no attention to critics have to be kidding. I've been flattered by praise and stung (and yes, helped) by criticism. My poems have been called "comic" and "humorous" and "funny" and "witty" and "satirical" and work which has its base in "American pseudo-philosophy." One writer even called them "serious," and she's the one I believe. I think they are about the most serious things I know. A reviewer of *In the Aviary* put it this way: "he is at once the lecturer at the podium and the delinquent asleep at the back of the hall." Yes, that's what I was after. Is that position a comic one, or a tragic?

4.

> *The certainty of place, the certainty that we are not lost, the certainty that the world and our lives have checkpoints with names and definite directions we can follow, the certainty.*
> —Richard Hugo in *The Real West Marginal Way*

In 1945, the year I was born, there were slightly fewer than 140 million people living in the United States. The 1990 census has confirmed the current population at more than 250 million. How is it that optimism persists? Who could fail to understand the profound meaning such numbers have for the way we are able to live? Presumably, those who find being crowded into a kitchenette with twenty-six other egos, their separate needs and desires on display, a more pleasurable thing than being in there with only thirteen of them.

If there were fewer of us then, it is also true that we were more regional. Television had yet to "homogenize" America. I saw television for the first time when I was seven. Before then it was radio and the great imagining that I loved; the scenes which every program forced us to produce for ourselves. I spent summer nights on the Oregon coast tuning in whatever I could pick up: Seattle, Coos Bay, and Oakland. The mystique of place. I could imagine San Francisco and Hollywood! Later, I studied maps in order to locate them precisely. I became intoxicated by the sounds of their names: Scappoose, Walla Walla. They were places of hundreds of plausible "other" lives. The certainty. I could imagine everything.

5.

The *Oxford English Dictionary* describes the adjective "comic" by employing the words "trivial" and "fortunate."

6.

The events of our early, "formative" years continue to shape the way we feel about ourselves. They shape a writer's "vision" of the world and, consequently, the manner in which that vision is articulated. Doubtless there are "therapists" who are convinced they can free us from the past, or at least help us to "come to terms" with it. But, forty years later, I feel about my life little differently than I did when I was five: no matter how it is going at the moment, it's a burden. And writing remains a means for managing that. It's a matter of specific events and how we feel about them.

I must have been about six when my grandfather took me to visit the Indians at Celilo Falls. Their village was situated on the banks of the Columbia River just east of The Dalles, Oregon. We always referred to them as the Celilo Indians, though actually they were a small community consisting of members of the Umatilla, Yakima, Warm Springs, and Nez Percé tribes. Because of the diminishing numbers among these tribes by the 1940s, it was inevitable that they live together, and possible, one of them told me, because of the similarity of their native languages. They lived in tepees, and we used to watch them net salmon from the precarious scaffolding they had erected out over the falls which fell in three directions at that section of the river.

In the early 1950s, the government, interested in "bettering their lot," razed the tepees and constructed a new outpost of prefabricated houses. Within six months the Indians had removed the housing and reconstructed their tepees around the indoor plumbing.

The increasing need in the West for electric power brought about the construction of The Dalles Dam, which was completed in 1957. The entire town of Biggs (in close proximity to the village at Celilo, and the boyhood home of one Doc Severinsen) was carefully dismantled and moved up the mountain where it was reassembled intact. But the backwaters covered Celilo. The villagers were removed to the Warms Springs Indian Reservation one hundred miles to the south. As I remember, there was litigation, and the powers that be "sat on their hands" for as long as possible. By 1963, the year I graduated from high school, the checks had gone out. In the second semester one of my classmates began driving a new Corvette to school each day — conspicuous in that time and place. The story went that she was one-sixteenth Indian and had received the sum of $20,000 from the U.S. government for inconvenience to her race.

Today a state park commemorates Celilo. Adjacent to it is Celilo Village, a place of twenty-odd prefabricated houses built for those who insisted on returning from Warm Springs to live out their lives near the river. The villagers hosted a picnic recently, inviting anyone who remembered them to come and reminisce.

7.

What could be more deeply perplexing than leading an existence which, day to day, is marked by a combination of pathetic and humorous elements?

8.

It is only in fairy tales that anyone actually finds a needle in a haystack.

—Heinrich Boll

I had taken my first job and we were moving to a new city. I wanted to be a writer and the furniture haulers had damaged my typewriter, so you know what that meant. The first Monday found me in the local corporate headquarters and repair shop of one of our nation's leading manufacturers of office equipment. I hoisted my machine onto the counter.

"How much will this be?" I asked. "To fix the carriage return."

The short, mustachioed fellow, without a word, nodded toward a sign directly over my head which read "$25 Minimum Charge on All Work."

"That's just for the estimate," he said. "After that it's parts and labor."

"Kind of steep isn't it?" I asked.

"Well," he smiled, "last week it was $15, but IBM raised their prices and in order to remain competitive, we had to raise ours too."

Every social studies and civics class I'd ever taken said this wasn't so. I remembered arguing endlessly with the foreign exchange student from Portugal who preached the evils of capitalism. He saw competition as a wasteful duplication of effort. All those competing dairies who sent their milk trucks through our neighborhoods, wasting the gasoline and the human resources to leave glass bottles by our doorsteps. He was proud that his town was served by a single truck. The logic that his truck could ask any amount it wanted for its bottles was lost on him. And suddenly it was lost on me.

"It's just a broken spring," I said. "A little shorter than your fingernail. I can see it in there. How much for one of those?"

He looked it up.

"It's seven cents, but I gotta charge *you* more." He pointed to another sign hanging above the bench which read "Minimum Charge $10 for All Parts."

"You're going to charge me $10 for a seven-cent spring," I stated. And then, despite my usual even-tempered nature, I began to shout.

Immediately thereafter a tall man in a flowered tie pushed through the swinging doors and inquired about "all the commotion." The mustache explained it to him, and the tie proceeded to a small chest about the size of a tackle box where he dipped his tongs into one of the tiny drawers, pulled out a silver spring, and slipped it neatly into one of those teeny manila envelopes the dentist gives you to take your extracted teeth home in.

Reaching to hand it to me, he said: "And now I trust we shall never see you again."

All afternoon I worked at it, tears of frustration welling up. With an assortment of screwdrivers, with pliers both common and needlenosed, with my wife's tweezers, with mirrors. For America. For myself. I fixed it.

9.

Happy endings are defined by abbreviated lives.

10.

We were in the car. My daughter, ten, up front. My son, seven, in back. It was after dark and we were driving home. That writing is one of my continuing activities is something I had never discussed with my children. So it was with more than a little innocence that she interrupted the reverie of that spring evening to announce she had written a poem about the moon and wished (her word) to recite it to us. And then the surprising high-pitched laughter from the back seat which filled the car. Chipmunk convulsion. That little grade-school male hatred of poetry which most of us carry with us always. Call it the misunderstanding. But one *certain* in its derision. The incredulity that anyone would admit to poetry, let alone write or perform it. His mirth seemed inexhaustible, and, taken by the intensity of the laughter, its sound, the normalcy, the beauty of its naiveté, I too began to laugh.

I saw her nostrils widen. What could I say? Some things are too subtle — even for a father who loves words — to explain to a daughter in such circumstances. When she had finally had enough, she enunciated slowly and with only slight trembling, "WHAT'S WRONG WITH THE MOON? All you ever write about is Arthur Godfrey!"

11.

There is less which distinguishes comedy from tragedy than is generally believed.

12.

My children were raised in one of those "bedroom communities" so theoretically perfect that its design included a system of elementary schools within walking distance of every home. Something about entitlement. They could come home for lunch! On one of those autumn days in my daughter's tenth year she entered the kitchen, poured herself a glass of milk, and proceeded to the dining room where the day's mail, spread out across the table, included new copies of a magazine which contained two of my poems. I saw her open the journal with great care and begin to read, though not for more than five seconds, when her mother called her to her sandwich. She placed the issue back on the table and returned to the kitchen. Suddenly aware that I had been watching, she blurted out, "It's pretty good, Dad. So far."

13.

"Cloudy with showers"
—weather forecast for Portland, Oregon, October 12, 1962

On Columbus Day 1962, we experienced the greatest natural disaster to occur on the West Coast since the San Francisco earthquake of 1906. It was a Friday, the day of the game against Beaverton. Our new football coach, Mouse Davis, had installed the rudiments of what has become the run-and-shoot offense, and we were having a terrific season with only a single four-point loss on our record. It was my senior year and I was having fun playing quarterback in a system where intelligence counted as much as brawn. I had made application to the University of Chicago, Harvard, and Brown and had just received a letter from the Brown coach "wishing me luck in what just might be the championship" game. I was living on high hopes.

It had been a day of listlessness at school. At home, afterwards, waiting for Randy Burchfield, one of my teammates, to pick me up, the sun began to shine. An eerie late afternoon light. Shortly before he arrived the wind began to blow. In the distance of nearly three blocks between our house and the traffic light where we entered the main road, we were forced to stop twice to remove fallen branches in order to proceed. We thought little of it. Burchfield moved through the light, which was swinging wildly, and drove, buffeted by wind and the debris of leaves, branches, and articles of clothing, the four miles to the high school. We strode to the locker room, packed our gear, and boarded the bus.

There wasn't the usual banter among players which Davis — unlike our other coaches — always permitted on these rides. But this seemed an attribute of the game rather than of weather. As we waited, we watched the Boosters' Concession Stand blow down, and shortly after we departed, the wind demolished the grandstand and field lights of our stadium. But we had somewhere to go. As our bus approached the Willamette where we would cross over to the West Side, the trailer end of a sixteen wheeler had been smashed through the railing of the Sellwood Bridge and dangled over the water. We took an alternate route. It was like sitting in the front row of a movie house watching disaster footage. I don't know why we remained so calm, so distanced from what was happening around us. Maybe because there had been no warning. Or because we assumed it would end soon. We passed cars totaled by falling trees, houses with missing roofs, upended telephone booths, and water mains spouting like geysers. Downtown, my stepfather, on leaving his building, was blown into a parking meter which he grasped for safety then, in an instant, his hands were lacerated when he nabbed four diamond rings and glass from the shattered window of the adjacent jewelry store.

We were in the midst of a "freak" typhoon, an improbable collision of three weather patterns: the remnants of Typhoon Frieda which had nearly exhausted itself in the China Sea, and a system of unusually warm moist air from the southern latitudes which clashed with an extreme cold front from the Gulf of Alaska. The winds raged at a speed in excess of 150 miles per hour, with a velocity through Portland of about 120. The duration of the storm's passage over every point was in excess of two hours.

It was after dark and just about game time when our bus entered Beaverton. We had nearly reached our destination, but the congestion and destruction had grown so great that we were unable to continue. The driver maneuvered the bus into the parking lot of Jesuit High School and we were motioned inside. Twenty-four Oregonians died as a result of the storm that evening, some for as simple an act as going to the window to see what was happening, and having the glass explode. The Milwaukie Mustangs took shelter in a rival cafeteria until the early hours of Saturday morning. We feasted on the ice cream which was passed among us. Ice cream bars from the freezers of Jesuit High which, because the power had been off for three hours (it would remain off for nearly a week), had already begun to melt.

14.

Satire: the employment of sarcasm, irony, and ridicule in denouncing, exposing, or deriding vice, folly, abuses, or evils of any kind.

Why confirm the obvious? Because there are ogres in paradise. Because their number expands as the population does. Because the obvious is made obtuse by their language and gesture which tells us that reason is folly and, worse, that folly is reason.

My poems begin as metaphors for experience and are themselves constructed through the use of metaphors and other figures of speech. This sometimes places their subjects far from me. Autobiographical forgery. Picasso put it best: "we all know art is not truth, it is a lie which makes us realize."

15.

I've always respected those who appreciate poetry. When I went through the divorce, my poems were subpoenaed. Ostensibly to prove that I was an unstable person. But the judge, bless her heart, said it wasn't true. As a result I lost only 90 percent of everything I owned.

16.

I was selected to represent my elementary school as a candidate for Rose Festival Prince of the city of Portland. The Rose Festival Parade, held each June, is the culmination of the city's celebration of itself as our nation's "Rose Capital." The first step toward coronation occurred when my classmates and I were escorted by our fourth-grade teachers to the gymnasium where we walked slowly in a counterclockwise circle while three ladies, even older than our mothers, ogled. When the two semifinalists were announced, I was one of them. When I got home that afternoon after softball practice, my mother had received the winning phone call. She was ecstatic. A prince! Paul, the other semifinalist, had come over shortly after school because his family had heard nothing. My mother was sorry to have been the one to give him the news.

My early reign was fraught with pressures and difficulties. The next afternoon our candidate for princess, Mary Ann Doss, and I were introduced to the school. The principal was extremely proud of each of us and presented us with boxes designed to look like textbooks which were filled with rolls of assorted Lifesavers, and also with identical copies of an illustrated children's story about a horse. Then he took them back so he could present them to us again at the second assembly.

That same week my brother, a second grader, became lodged in the garbage can he had crouched into while playing hide-and-seek at recess. I remember feeling stricken by something I couldn't name while I watched from a third-story window as the two janitors carried him by the handles into the inner courtyard and began to extricate him by hammering at the rivets on the can. I was amazed at how rapidly the news spread over the school grounds. The way a tiny event in a nondescript corner with few witnesses grew to a pilgrimage of custodians with everyone watching. The prince's brother, stuck in a garbage can.

There were the rehearsals on the stage of the Hollywood Theater with the other couples from Rigler and Beaumont and Glen Haven; my mother's borrowing my grandmother's car to transport me there several evenings each week. When I stepped into the spotlight on the big day, I forgot my lines but managed to mumble something about how honored I was. Like the other contestants, I was wearing a white suit, white shoes, a red bow tie, and a rose boutonniere. My lips were highlighted with lipstick; my ears protruded more than a little; and my hair was combed up and back in the style of the time.

In the parade we rode on a float beneath a huge caricature of Johnny Appleseed made all of roses except for his tin-pan hat. We were interviewed on the radio by Uncle Bob of the "Uncle Bob and the Squirrel Cage" show. This was shortly before his death in that fiery collision of his Triumph while he was on his way to L.A. to take a new job with Disney. A blonde lady in overwhelming perfume had just taught us to wave our arms in a slow arc. "Remember," she said, "you have to keep smiling." We tossed roses to the crowd.

This happened in the spring of 1954. I have the pictures to prove it.

Books (Poetry)

In the Aviary. University of Missouri Press, 1975. Devins Award.
The Laps of the Bridesmaids. Bits Press, 1992.
Nobody Lives on Arthur Godfrey Boulevard. BOA Editions, Ltd., 1992.

As Editor

Three Rivers: Ten Years. Carnegie Mellon University Press, 1983.
The Carnegie Mellon Anthology of Poetry. Carnegie Mellon University Press, 1992.

Limited Editions

Badlands. Copper Canyon Press, 1974.
Measuring the Tree. West Coast Poetry Review, 1974.
South Moccasin. Peaceweed Press, 1974.
Wage the Improbable Happiness. Bits Press, 1982.

Anthologies

Intro 3. AWP, Bantam, 1973.
Traveling America with Today's Poets. Ed. David Kherdian. Macmillan, 1976.
The Windflower Home Almanac of Poetry. Ed. Ted Kooser. Windflower Press, 1980.
1981 Anthology of Magazine Verse and Yearbook of American Poetry. Ed. Alan F. Pater. Monitor Book Co., 1981.
The Morrow Anthology of Younger American Poets. Ed. David Bottoms and Dave Smith. William Morrow & Co., 1985.
1985 Anthology of Magazine Verse and Yearbook of American Poetry. Ed. Alan F. Pater. Monitor Book Co., 1985.
The Pushcart Prize, X: Best of the Small Presses. Ed. Bill Henderson. Viking/Penguin, 1986.
The Pushcart Prize, XII: Best of the Small Presses. Ed. Bill Henderson. Viking/Penguin, 1988.
Sometime the Cow Kick Your Head: Lightyear 1988–89. Ed. Robert Wallace. Bits Press, 1988.
Gridlock: An Anthology of Poems about Southern California. Ed. Elliott Fried. Applezaba Press, 1990.
Vital Signs: Contemporary Poetry from the University Presses. Ed. Ronald Wallace. University of Wisconsin Press, 1990.
The Decade Dance: An Anthology. Ed. Mark Sanders. Sandhills Press, 1991.

Periodicals

Several hundred poems, reviews, and articles about poetry have appeared, beginning with the *Beloit Poetry Journal* in 1969, and including, among many others, *American Poetry Review*, *Georgia Review*, *Missouri Review*, *The Nation*, *Ohio Review*, *Ploughshares*, *Prairie Schooner*, and *North American Review*.

Andrea Kochman Schnall

Lee K. Abbott has earned degrees from New Mexico State University and the University of Arkansas. His lengthy list of awards includes two Pushcart prizes for fiction, two National Endowment for the Arts fellowships, two nominations for the Pulitzer Prize in fiction, the O. Henry Award for Fiction, and a Major Artist Fellowship in Creative Writing from the Ohio Arts Council. Having held several named and visiting professorships at major universities, he currently teaches in the English department at The Ohio State University. He and his wife, Pamela, live in Worthington, Ohio.

THE TRUE STORY OF WHY I DO
WHAT I DO: AN ESSAY

All stories are true stories, especially the artful lies we invent to satisfy the wishful thinker in us, for they present to us, in disguise often and at great distance, the way we are or would want to be. Told to us in a lingo as unique as a fingerprint, they address our up-and-down, our here-and-now. They come, I think, from a desire, as irresistible as love itself, to fix on the page a moment, suffered or made up, when something—one puny thing or idea or person—revealed itself and so turned off the Boom-Boom-Boom which usually deafens us to ourselves. Happily ended or not, stories are the truth we leave behind, like crumbs, to say how we've come and what was there to see.

To be inspirational, as high minded and upward looking as the foolish half of me mostly aims to be, I have to tell you about my father—as crazed, driven, and cross hearted a hero as I have ever known. His analogues have appeared in dozens of my stories: he's the gentleman, in golf togs or business suit, throwing the epic tantrum, careening hither and thither in a men's locker or banker's office; he's the one, in the fiction I invent, with the outraged moral intelligence, the one who hectors and harangues, the one telling another (usually me, you can guess) how to behave and when to beware and what is likely to be the dry end of things we love. In fiction, he is imperious, forbidding as a Puritan God, sharp minded as an out-of-town lawyer, stiff as pig bristle, wiry and unforgiving; in fiction, the made-up landscape I am a sometime citizen in, he suffers and is redeemed (or he is not), does the wrong thing and is shamed (or is not), comes to insight and is crushed (or is not).

In fiction, given its unities and shape and its epiphanies, I comprehend my father. I know exactly what he meant when he told me that you could tell a gentleman by his handshake and his shoeshine. I know, and can articulate, what significance there is in the properly mowed lawn, what wisdom there is in the order of dried dishes. In fiction, I know—maybe as Flannery O'Connor did—why the heathen rage.

In life, however—which, messy and improbable and ephemeral, is not good fiction—I had no idea what made his world spin round and round. The facts were clear to me, not the flesh. He went to Dartmouth, I knew. He pole-vaulted cross handed. One brother died on the Bataan Death March; his sister in a boating accident on Lake Sasebo in Maine. His father went blind in the last years of his life; his mother squandered an inheritance of at least one million dollars. He was a roué, I heard, a slick-haired rake who hung out on the pier at Old Orchard Beach and went down to Miami in the winter. He married my mother, the over-pampered daughter of a Canadian insurance executive, in Harligen, Texas, while he was at gunnery school in World War II. They lived in Panama, where I was born. He ran the National Guard in Illinois, where my brother was born. He played one year of professional golf. He became a career military man, went to England, Korea, Germany, resigned his commission twice because somebody, or something, infuriated him.

If it is true, as Willa Cather says, that the "basic material a writer works with is acquired before the age of fifteen," then by the time I was a sophomore in high school in Las Cruces, New Mexico, already telling my teachers and myself that I was going to be a writer, the material I had acquired I'd got from him: a duke's mixture of soirées, of country clubs and officers' clubs, of colorful compadres named Red and Goonch and Uncle Inches — the whole of it tragic and tearful to the aggressively poetic kid I was then. My mother was a drunk, institutionalized when I was twelve; my father was a drinker. He had psoriasis on his knobby knees and knobby elbows, he smoked like the dickens, he threw a wedge at the TV, he dressed in pink polka dots for the Club Championship, he banished me to my room forever, he expected my brother and me to know the truth and speak it invariably — this was my material, a hodge-podge of goo and muck and human blah-blah-blah, the responsibility for which I was absolutely unaware of until the inspirational summer afternoon I am partly here to yap about.

Once upon a time (isn't this the rhetoric, in truth, that opens every fairy tale we survive and want to write about?), my father and I found ourselves alone at home. I want to say it was a Sunday, for in my memory the day, if not the events themselves, have a liturgical, quasi-holy "feel." In my memory, that attic atop the shoulders where everything truly felt is found, there is that Sunday light, crooked and mote filled and lazy, and that Sunday time, heavy and ever in danger of wobbling to a halt. My father, in his bermuda shorts and golf shirt, is in the TV room, drinking the rum thing he preferred; he had the habit, annoying I think now, of dumping his half-used ice cubes back in the freezer, a habit the girl who became my wife told me was disgusting every time I made her a Coke and it tasted like hooch. I am in the living room, I think, listening to records; more likely, I am reading—*Sports Illustrated*, the *National Geographic*, *Life* magazine.

My taste in those days ran to the quick, the immediate—prose of the slash-and-burn kind. *Mila 18* by Leon Uris, *The Naked and the Dead* (still an excellent book, by the way), Alistair MacClean's high-seas adventures. I saw myself writing a book like those one day—a book, conceived out of testosterone and *Nugget*-style macho, a book as pithy and direct as a dust-jacket blurb: "Mr. Abbott," the endorsement would run, "writes like an assassin. He's the 'Aaarrgghh' the yellow yammer when they spy the vast What-Not opening to greet them." I had, I thought then, no experience (this was long before I realized that Henry James was correct when he said that "experience was an atmosphere of the mind"). I was just a kid, after all. Skinny, with a flat-top and fifteen pimples, half my mind tilted toward girls, the other half tilted toward glory (which would, in the reasoning I was the victim of, get me girls).

The hours passed that Sunday afternoon as they always do when I cast myself back into the dangerous tides that are my past: the clock above the antique writing desk chiming on the quarter-hour, the father wandering between the refrigerator and liquor cabinet, Pee Wee Reese or Dizzy Dean saying in the TV room what the Dodgers were doing; the son in another room cobbling together in his fertile but screwy imagination a tale of swashbuckling and hair raising, a narrative of guns and grateful bimbos and nick-of-time derring-do. We were in our elements, him and me: one, the older, tuned to the stupid clatter of the exterior world; the other, the younger flesh of him, tuned to the twilight interior world of fetch-and-keep, of fantasy. Then he burst into the living room, eyed me as if wondering for the last time whether I was up to the burden he was about to pitch my way, and said, a little drunkenly, "Come with me."

He had been thinking about himself, it is clear now. An inventory, check mark after check mark after check mark, had been taken: three heart attacks, a fist-sized hunk of his lung removed at William Beaumont General Hospital in Fort Bliss, the yips on the putting green, Homeric-like anger, frustration at a life twisted which-away, hopes high as heaven he believed in, bitterness at being less than the hero he'd promised himself he'd be. I didn't know this at the time I followed him outdoors and into the utility rooms at the end of the carport. I knew only that he was semi-sloshed. I knew only that he was fifty-six years old, gray headed and tough. I knew he hated going to work at the post office, his job in those days, where he supervised and inspected and, unhappiest of all for him, had to tattle on those who stole money or stamps or swiped somebody's *Playboy* magazine.

"See this, Kit?" he said. He was standing in the center of the utility room, lawn mower here, gas can there, the walls hung with tools I never got the sense of. Golf clubs were in there, a bucket of practice balls, cans of oil, greasy rags, a hoe, a rake, a cheap hardware store of goodies that smelled old and used and too sweet. "You want to be a writer, huh?" he said, sweeping his arms, then pulling me after him. He snarled the word; it was sound which scorned ignorance and innocence. Against the wall, high as the ceiling, were stacked his footlockers and steamer trunks, from the Army of the United States and from the regiments that were the families of his own father, innkeeper Lyman Kittredge Abbott of Portland, Maine.

I like to think now that I knew we were coming to something, my father and me, that he was going to say words to me and I, perhaps for the first time, was going to understand him precisely. I like to think now that I was smart enough to know that I was in the presence of a truth grander than the two of us, a truth the price of which we go paying forever, a truth more dire than the knowing that we die and do not rise. This is the moment, I like to think of myself thinking then, when you discover how hard the world is, when what you've cleaved to is cleaved from you with a broadaxe.

Then he assaulted those lockers and trunks. In a fury, huffing and puffing, he snatched them down, one by one, hollering "Timber!" when the uppermost went tumbling. They crashed and banged, and I tried backing up a little, as he flung one behind him and scrambled over another to reach a third. He was hollering, you have to know, all the New England notes of his voice echoing in that now cramped room, and maybe I was some scared. This was the temper I'd witnessed elsewhere — on the golf course, behind the wheel of his Ford, in the living room when someone in the big world made a ding-a-ling out of himself. But there was more than anger here: there was pain, the particular kind of which was personal and buried deep in his bones, pain for which there is no Latin name or medicine or machine, other than fiction, to account for.

"Write it all down!" he was shouting. "Write it all goddam down!"

And it was here, from a certain X-spot in the world, 1855 Cruse, that my father, teetering from booze and the awful weight of his own life, was taking seriously, in a manner I couldn't yet, what purpose writing ought to have. Here it is, he was in effect saying. Crated and stored, cataloged and preserved, year by used-up year, place by rotten place. Here it is: the come and go of it, the building and collapse of it, the joy and weep of it. Here it is, he was saying. All the tissues and nerves and human jingle-jangle, that want and excess of it, the rigamarole and whirling, damaged creatures we are. And all you have to do, son and boy, is write it down.

Write it all goddam down.

This, I submit, is the inspirational part. If we write for any larger purpose than a simple good time—and, believe me, there is nothing at all wrong with a good time—it is, I think, because we all feel, less and more, the obligation we have to our fathers, to our mothers, to all the folks, linked by biology or not, who have raised us; an obligation, as essential to our moral natures as our hearts are to long life, to the places we were raised in and in the knowledge we learned there. We want, I hope, because there is no other way to do it, to write it down, to transform it, to set it straight. At our best, we do not write for the money alone, though money is nice; nor do we write for fame, though fame is likewise nice. We write, beginner and professional alike, because, though half-frightened, we want to know what is in the trunks and lockers we lug forward through time, what vital secrets they can be sprung to reveal.

Books

The Heart Never Fits Its Wanting (stories). North American Review Press, 1980.

Love Is the Crooked Thing (stories). Algonquin Books, 1986.

Strangers in Paradise (stories). Putnam, 1987. Paperback edition by Harper & Row, 1988.

Dreams of Distant Lives (stories). Putnam, 1989. Paperback edition by White Pine Press, 1990.

Living After Midnight (novella and stories). Putnam, 1991.

Periodicals (Stories, since 1987)

"Once Upon a Time." *Georgia Review* vol. 41, no. 2 (1987).

"Revolutionaries." *The Atlantic* vol. 259, no. 2 (1987).

"What She's Saying Now." *Witness* vol. 1, no. 2 (1987).

"The Era of Great Numbers." *Epoch* vol. 36, no. 1 (1987-88).

"Driving His Buick Home." *North American Review* vol. 273, no. 1 (1988).

"Here in Time and Not." *Georgia Review* vol. 42, no. 3 (1988).

"1963." *Tampa Review* vol. 1, no. 1 (1988).

"The View of Me from Mars." *Harper's* vol. 276, no. 1657 (1988).

"How Love Is Lived in Paradise." *Kenyon Review* vol. 11, no. 4 (1989).

"Freedom, A Theory of." *Gettysburg Review* vol. 3, no. 2 (1990).

"Sweet Cheeks." *Harper's* vol. 281, no. 1685 (1990).
"Getting Even." *Southwest Review* vol. 76, no. 1 (1991).
"The Who, the What and the Why." *Boulevard* (forthcoming).
"A Man Bearing Snow." *Epoch* (forthcoming).

David Citino

David Citino is professor of English and director of the Creative Writing Program at Ohio State University. A native of Cleveland, he graduated from St. Ignatius High School in that city, and from Ohio University. He received the M.A. and Ph.D. from Ohio State. Among his honors and awards are: a Poetry Fellowship from the National Endowment for the Arts; a Book Award for Poetry and the first annual Poetry Award from the Ohioana Library Association; a Major Fellowship from the Ohio Arts Council; the Alumni Distinguished Teaching Award from Ohio State; and other poetry awards. David Citino lives in Upper Arlington, Ohio, with his wife, Mary, and their three children, Nathan, Dominic, and Maria.

PAPERWORK

I love being a writer. What I can't stand is the paperwork.
— Peter de Vries

Whenever I am drawn to consider just *why* it is I do what I do and not something else, there being all sorts of things to do with oneself in this world, I find myself driving into the road hazard of having to admit that I cannot even say I know exactly what it is I do. And I crash into the concrete abutment of being unable satisfactorily to define the end result of all my doing, that is to say, the poem itself. It is a perilous motoring, this questioning of the self. So easily we can lose control, spin out, and roll over into a ditch by the side of the road.

Well, what is poetry? More to the point, what, or who, am I when I play the poet? While I spend many of my waking (and even some of my dreaming) hours writing or thinking about writing poetry, and more time reading it and speaking to others about it, I am certain that I could not, to save my life, come up with a definition of *the poem* that would satisfy everyone, or even one that would satisfy me. Yet I feel that I must attempt at least a consideration of the what and the who in order to explain, if only to myself, why I do the things I do (to echo, so very faintly, the Temptations).

Countless others have tried to define poetry, each attempt, it seems to me, telling more about the definer than the thing defined — and perhaps more about the poet than about poetry. Poetry is "the spontaneous overflow of powerful feelings recollected in tranquillity," says Wordsworth. And it is true that there is something in the poetic process that suggests spontaneity and overflow. Just that suddenly we are full, the meniscus of our feelings threatening to give way, and then our poetical cup runneth over. Poetry — the making of it, at least — can be messy, which is one of its chief joys for me. I arise from the desk spattered with words, shirt spotted with the marks of unanticipated bubbling and roiling, hands smeared with images, even my teeth and my fingers beneath the nails stained from the crushing and breaking of lines, face flushed with the arduous ardor of making.

"A momentary stay against the confusion of the world," Frost says of poetry. While I will grant him the ordering of experience that poetry can at times bring about, I am drawn more to the "momentary" qualities of this sorting. The making and remaking of a poem can provide the writer and reader with a momentary confusion against the stay of the world.

"Stop making sense," says the rock group Talking Heads, a piece of advice that has been offered also by a host of earthly (and unearthly) mystics through the ages, dreamers like Jesus, Blake and Whitman, Merton and John of the Cross, Joan of Arc and Catherine of Siena. Poetry can be a way of not making sense, or of making a sense that transcends the logically and rationally routine. Emily Dickinson puts it this way: "Much Madness is divinest Sense."

Wordsworth points out another crucial aspect of writing, as I see it: while it is an activity in itself, an action or process in which a body and mind and soul can engage, it is nevertheless distanced in some way from actually living, or doing. The poet does — he or she has an experience — but the having of the experience, the actual living, is somehow divorced from the writing. The writer wishes— needs! — to be immersed in life but must remain, by nature of the writing process, ever suspended from life — ever the *Poète maudit*, the accursed poet — as if he or she were sentenced over and over to long periods in the penalty box, out of the action, while the game sweeps by back and forth, back and forth. No writer has yet discovered a way to write in a sustained way *while doing*. It is a very good thing that most of us writers, for all our willingness to trumpet our prowess in any number of human endeavors involving pleasure or pain, like above all to watch.

I am reminded of the story about James Thurber, whose wife, at a party, reportedly walked up to him and growled, "Damn it, Thurber, stop writing!" The writing must be done after the living, in a sense, "in tranquillity," where and when presumably the experience is called back through the poet's memory and lived again imaginatively. The hope is then that a reader will come along and, the third time being the charm, the thing will happen again: readers all over the world can ascend Mt. Snowden with the peripatetic poet, or eavesdrop on the Thurbers at a cocktail party. (Mixing these two examples — listening to Wordsworth and his sister Dorothy bickering at a cocktail party, or ascending Mt. Snowden with Thurber, conjures up a taste of that fine absurdity — that "divinest Sense" — that poetry can provide us.)

I am one, I must admit, who actually enjoys doing a thing over and over in the hopes of getting it right, and I am one who can sometimes find in the day-to-day absurdities—in which every moment of life is also a moment nigher to death—a nugget or two of truth more valuable than the fool's gold that logic and reason too often produce.

Poetry is "the rhythmic, inevitably narrative, movement from an overclothed blindness to a naked vision," claims Dylan Thomas. Well, perhaps. I can accept "rhythmic," as even that poem written in the freest verse has something to do with language, and language is, if it is anything, rhythm. But "inevitably narrative"? I do not think that many of the poems of Dylan Thomas are narrative poems. He seems much more interested in making music or declaiming or posturing than in spinning a yarn. While I will admit that a lyric poem can be narrative as well, and a narrative contains aspects of the lyric ("Sir Patrick Spens," for example, that masterpiece of a ballad, a story spun out of song), still there is for me a definite difference—if only in purpose—between the two modes.

I will agree with Thomas that poetry does involve movement. "Perne in a gyre," Yeats the choreographer instructs the Holy Sages of Byzantium. Poetry is the dance in which we lead or are led from where we were to where we are, from what we thought then, before we started to write the poem, to what we feel now, and it is also, in a sense, a disrobing, the striptease on the runway of the burlesque house toward the crowd, a stroll or saunter from blindness to vision. Indeed, we are still today, decades after Sexton and Plath and Lowell, exposed in poetry books and magazines to far too much undressing, the emperor's new clothes displayed again and again, tons of confessional therapy, too much confusion of experience with art, and not enough poetry. "What is your poem?" we ask a contemporary poet. His or her answer? "I am hot." "I am cold." "I am horny, therefore I am." Or, something heard often these days, "I am vaguely discontented, yet nevertheless terribly clever"—and that is it. That is all. The whining I—I—I—I. "I fall upon the thorns of life. I bleed," Shelley moans to us in "Ode to the West Wind," yet while having fallen and bled (and having paused to tell us about it), he takes us in the poem of the experience far from the prison of the self; he tells us much more beside, melancholy truths about the wind and the human imagination and will, "Spirit fierce, / My spirit!"

It is true that in a sense the poet must disrobe, at least partially, in every poem, must make the flesh-and-bones statement to the world, as does performance-artist Karen Finley, smearing chocolate frosting on her body, that *here I am—this is how I really look, or how I am made to feel by a society that fears the artist or feels nothing for art.*

Shelley's statement that "Poetry is the record of the best and happiest moments of the best and happiest minds" also leaves me puzzled. The sensibility and genius that created "Ozymandias" or "Stanzas Written in Dejection, Near Naples" — a poet who can report, at the conclusion of the former poem, that "Round the decay / Of that colossal wreck, boundless and bare / The lone and level sands stretch far away" and at the conclusion of the latter poem express a wish to "hear the sea / Breathe o'er my dying brain its last monotony," seems to me to be journeying to lands that lie miles and miles from the country of happiness.

Gerald Manley Hopkins is more helpful than Shelley. Poetry for him is "speech framed . . . to be heard for its own sake and interest even over and above its interest of meaning." In order to feel one with a poet I need in a given poem to hear words that strike me as "speech framed." There dwells in the successful poem that "dramatic necessity" that Frost talks about. Poets use language, yes, but I need it to be the language "spoken by women and men" — if I may be so bold as to make Wordsworth more politically correct. A poem matters for me when I can taste its words on my tongue, or when my own mother steps in to have her say in her own voice — even if she travels all that distance and time only to tell me to eat my vegetables.

I have from time to time tried my hand at a definition of poetry. Here is an attempt from ten or twelve years ago.

A Defense of Poetry

It can't come from one wearing
a uniform. It's the bottomless ditch
filled with stagnant water keeping us
from every other suddenly bridged,
the place where together we can lie our way
to love or some next-best-thing,
the grasp of one we thought
no longer able to hold on.
It can mean running in place
over great distances. It means
no weapon flashing out to resound
loud as hell to drop the old man
stooped over the cash register,
hand on heart in the all-night carry-out
on Cleveland's near West Side,
his wire-rim glasses shattering as
his face thuds on the counter
soiled with tons of change,
the wife running downstairs

to see, holding her head with both hands
and moaning, O Stan, Stan.
It's the great astigmatism,
the hole in light and the light itself.
It resides in opals, mirrors, moons,
any body of water, other sides of walls,
eyes of old mothers lost
in nursing homes, strapped to chairs
before televisions blaring out
Saturday morning cartoons
where animals speak and humans,
whistling like bombs,
fall hundreds of stories only
to rise again. It comes
from where the wind does, a laughter
so deep inside it can't be stilled
until we will it not to be.
It's right as rain, familiar
as the sound of our name,
given and proper. It means
being alone together a lifetime.
It almost never comes in the mail.

(reprinted from The Hollins Critic*)*

Emily Dickinson's method for determining the presence of poetry, while far from a definition, nevertheless provides us with a helpful reminder.

> *If I read a book and it makes my whole body feel so cold no fire can warm me, I know that it is poetry. If I feel physically as if the top of my head were taken off, I know that it is poetry.*

There is for me something intensely physical about reading poetry. The gasp of recognition, the hurt in the throat that great beauty makes, the chill deep in bone, the standing up of hairs on the back of the neck, the goose bumps, the increased heart rate, the rapid shallow breathing of arousal into a heightened state of awareness. And there are marked physiological changes that a body undergoes when its tenant is writing poetry. I often find myself perspiring when I write, even in the coldest room, and sometimes feel when I have finished as if I have traveled a far piece. On occasion I have come from a writing session nearly spent, walking away from the desk thoroughly fatigued, bone weary. We like to call the creative writing classroom a *workshop,* and there is hard work that goes on there, the lifting, hammering, chiseling, wielding of the ax and the hoe, yet the place where we write is the real place of labor. Swift, in "On Poetry," points out the physicality of making poetry.

> *Blot out, correct, insert, refine,*
> *Enlarge, diminish, interline;*
> *Be mindful, when invention fails,*
> *To scratch your head and bite your nails.*

I do not wish to give the impression that poetry is a bodily function, or that it is something close to pornography. Good poetry is imaginative and transcendent, a leap out of the Winnebago of the flesh in which we have been traveling to face the Grand Canyon of experience; and it can be imaginative and soulful and liberating in ways that even the best pornography can never be—but the poem must involve the body, and the poet must ever be the voyeur, the words eliciting the thrills up and down the spine, that tumescence that brings a body to life up out of its own detumescence and the weight of gravity. These reactions of the body to words are too often seen by those who read little or no poetry as being somehow unseemly, because, after all, a poem must be directed only at the soul or the mind. But I feel strongly (and I know I risk venturing too close to cliché in saying this) that poetry is very much of the heart, all four chambers, the rhythm of a line the systole and diastole of a creature alive, and feeling its own bodily existence.

At the very least, the Dickinson Test gets us from the realm of impossibility—the defining of a thing as amorphous and large as poetry—to something a bit more possible, the consideration of the poet as poet, but also as human being. Hawthorne writes,

> *I don't want to be a doctor, and live by men's diseases; nor a*
> *minister to live by their sins; nor a lawyer to live by their*
> *quarrels. So I don't see there's anything left for me but to be*
> *an author.*

This strikes me as an attempt to define by negation, or aversion, or elimination, the writer's life (even though there is something of all three of these processes in the profession of writing, and even though I too am guilty of trying to define something by enumerating the various things that it is not). Still, a doctor or lawyer (or Indian chief)—even a minister—has no great difficulty with the way the world views his or her profession. After all, television soaps and sitcoms and news programs show us the work of such professionals every day. We *know* what doctors do, and lawyers, and even men and women "of the cloth." But folks do not know what poets do. There has been no sitcom involving a working poet, no "60 Minutes" exposé on poetry, Mike Wallace in serious trench coat barging in on the woman or man at the desk, the camera in severe closeup capturing the bard's darting, cornered eyes and freely perspiring forehead.

It is the snowflake or fingerprint factor—the uniqueness of each human being—that promises the singularity of each vision. As Eudora Welty puts it, tempering the cynicism of Ecclesiastes,

> *Whatever our theme in writing, it is old and tired. Whatever our place, it has been visited by the stranger, it will never be new again. It is only the vision that can be new; but that is enough.*

"I am a poet," I tell folks who inquire at PTA meetings or in supermarket checkout lines—which latter place, it occurs to me, seems a natural location to discover such an alien creature, right beside headlines like "Ghost of Elvis Sues Ghost of Liberace in Psychic Palimony Case" or "Kitty Kelly Exposed as Ronnie's Kinky Love-Slave." It took me a while to get up the courage to make this claim in public, and I still wince at my fellow citizens' unease or outright puzzlement at such a strange encounter.

When I ask *myself*, "What do you do?" as I have had to do in order to write this essay, I am really asking, I suppose, "Why?" My religious training and education—these two being, for the first eighteen years or so of my life, one and the same—still can propel me, in the attempt to solve a problem, toward the historical method (the Old Historicism, if you will). And this is true even though I have left my traditional religious beliefs back in the musty attic and damp basement of childhood.

I am in the habit of asking my students, in the writing or literature classroom, as a way of approaching the reading or writing of poems, to consider the cultural, historical roles of the poet through history. Such a look back and around might lead me now to at least a glimmer of an answer to these questions regarding my reasons for writing. Looking backward I can expect to find what others were, and perhaps the ones I was or wished to be, but these former selves might in turn provide further clues to the one I am, the ones I will be.

To the ancient Greeks the poet was *poiētēs*, which means, literally, maker. This making was conceived of as occurring in two ways. The poet takes existing materials, much the same way that the carpenter or mason or weaver or cook does, and hammers and saws and planes them, or chisels them out of the rockface and smoothes and polishes them before fitting and mortaring, or gathers and dries the reeds and weaves them into something ultimately useful, or cracks a few eggs and smashes a garlic clove with the flat blade of knife, all this just to make, to fashion something with the potential at least to endure.

I think often of my grandfather, a carpenter by trade. As a boy suddenly aware of things (at what churches call "the age of reason," although this callow age is filled with the hauntings of unreason), I stood just high enough for my head to be at the level of his workbench. I remember, along with the grand fragrances of sawdust and plane shavings and glue and varnish, his beautiful hands. They seemed, even to the little boy I was, to bear the mark of a lifetime of laboring toward some loveliness. They were cracked and scarred, and Grandfather was missing the tip of one finger and the nails of two others, the work of bandsaws and hammers and who knows what other implements of his craft.

Years later I was to learn that, in Medieval times, the skilled craftsmen, those who built the great cathedrals, were known by the nickname "blue-nails" because of the wounds they had suffered in practicing their crafts, the slips of the hammer. Grandfather Blue-nails, he was. Poetry making is a craft not unlike cabinet making (or cathedral making), and the poet must be skilled in his or her doing— must put in the time serving the apprenticeship of reading and studying and witnessing, and above all, failing, that will bring skill to the fingers. There are times when poetry hurts, when it scars, when it takes parts of us.

The second sense of *making* to the Greeks involves creation, the arising of *some* thing out of *no* thing. Where before nothing was, now there is music, now word, now meaning. "My long scythe whispered and left the hay to make," Frost tells us at the conclusion of "Mowing," a poem as much about the making of poetry (and even the making of love) as the making of hay. There is creation *and* crafting going on in that field.

(The other truth I received from Attic Greek via college days at Ohio University, "The Harvard on the Hocking," was given me by Callimachus, a librarian of Alexandria. His immortal words, prompted by his having to lug around the wordiness of the world's authors, may have something to do with my interest in poetry, that concentrated, pure use of language. Callimachus said, "A big book is a big evil." Poets tend to be both moralists and minimalists by nature.)

The Romans called their poet *vatēs*, seer, and again, at least two senses were meant. There is that visionary aspect to writing poetry, or to living the life of poetry, which is really what I am speaking about here — the poet as a seer who can be so foolish as to try to fathom the secret mysteries and correspondences of life. The poet is the priest-like woman or man who can read the entrails or hollow bones of birds or plot the course of planets and stars, in order to see into the future or the past or at the very least the present.

But the Roman seer is also an individual who does nothing more and nothing less than see, in our own most common sense of the word. He or she tries to envision the world as it really is, en route to imagining worlds better than this one. This ability to see is not limited to the sense of sight. A woman or man adept at seeing can also hear things, feel and smell and taste, as if she or he had mastered the will in order to make the senses acute to an extreme degree. Mystics from Juan de la Cruz to William Blake to Emanuel Swedenborg to Thérèse of Lisieux have reported this heightened acuity of the senses. Imagine an undiseased and unfearful Roderick Usher, for whom experience is not a harsh and metallic cacophony but a melodious and vibrant symphonic composition. Roderick could hear life and death, and came in time to know how to distinguish the two.

I find myself growing impatient with students who tell me, "But I have nothing to write about." Life is so very full, each day multihued and many textured, that the real problem is choosing the one subject from the nearly infinite number of choices. How can we not love and fear our days and nights? How can we not ache to write them?

There is much to make of a life, and out of all the other lives we can dream. And more riches can come from the spending of this one life we are given. It is the coin of our realm. The poetry is the life, and the life the poem. We *can*, Henry David Thoreau, "both live and utter it." We have nothing else to say.

The Man Who Found a Poem in Everything

Haunted — the creaky mansion
of his childhood. Shades
of bloodsuckers and saints,
drafty stanzas furnished
with the careworn and threadbare:

beribboned khaki rags
Dad wore to conquer Japan,

stamps from perforated lands,
Slovakia, Danzig, fascist Italy,
first baseman's mitt damp

with neat's-foot oil, photo
of the one who each red dawn
died in Latin and returned
at night, signed Sincerely,
Savior of the Living Dead.

He learned to throw his voice;
had a knack for finding words
he felt he had to say
under someone else's tongue/
His every line? Made to be broken.

Not yet metered out, breath
was unruly. He couldn't speak
without repeating himself,
but began to find something salty
in the bite of every sentence.

His parents grew from wisps,
chemicals fuming in maelstroms
of Big Bang, blood-bitter spumes
of primal sea, to lungfish
beaten ashore by tides, then

mammals biding their breaths in trees
for dark to kill the dinosaurs.
He adopted myths, power-mad Dad
gunning the engine, insisting
he'd have things his *way by God*

and Mom wreathing Rapunzel hair
into snakes wildly writhing.
Guilt spotted his pants
when anyone in her image
demurely crossed her long legs.

A young woman barged in, gave
herself in inspired ways
in his parents' bed at night

yet in revision he insisted
she was utterly unattainable.

He shattered her into images,
hips rounded like sea-heaves
to bear creation once again
and recapitulate phylogeny,
nipples taut at his lips,

their heaving together a fading
of borders that unmixed
his metaphors. It was her art
to knit tiny bones that set
souls to flying. They named names.

His mind was the deafening scratch
of pen on paper but he remembered
he was running out of things
to unforget. Those near him
heard music soft as the bell

at the end of typed line
or tick of broken pencil point.
Without words at last,
he'd learned to make an eternity
of the silence of his name.

(reprinted from Southern Humanities Review*)*

In Old Arabic, the poet was *sha'ir*, the knower. T. S. Eliot once claimed that American poets ought to know more. There has been a virulent strain of anti-intellectualism in American literature that has continued to the present day. Recently, the Beats in poetry and the minimalists (I would offend them by giving their appellation a capital letter) in fiction are evidence of a continued prejudice against knowledge. Knowing and feeling have for some strange reason been seen as mutually exclusive activities. I think of John Donne, of whom Eliot said, "A thought to Donne was an experience; it modified his sensibility." Eliot continues: the "ordinary man . . . falls in love, or reads Spinoza, and these two experiences have nothing to do with each other, or with the noise of the typewriter or the smell of cooking; in the mind of the poet these experiences are always forming new wholes." Lovely pun, that reference to "wholes" in the poet's mind.

Poetry can do this. It can enable us to conceive of an ordinary man, a John Doe who has fallen in love and is reading Spinoza or typing while he waits for the pot roast to finish cooking. We feel we live, we think we know.

I am one of those who feel that Modernism went too far in searching for a poetry that was refined nearly out of existence, a poem as arcane intellectual or religious artifact that could appeal only to the initiate into secret mysteries, a reader who had been on sensibility steroids for years. Look closely at a page or two of *The Waste Land* in one of the Norton anthologies. A superstructure of six or seven lines of poetry pitching above a massive, many-decked hull of footnotes, a dreadnought that plows its way through heavy seas, a container ship filled with literary criticism. I am not arguing that Eliot represents a "wrong turning in American poetry" (to use Robert Bly's phrase), for Eliot and Pound did things that needed to be done in reaction to the poets of the age that preceded theirs. I can only say that extreme intellectualism (the elevation of allusion as the most important function of the poet) was one of the reasons that countless individuals abandoned the ship of poetry in this century. Why do so many people today *not* read poetry? Perhaps because too few are willing to wade through commentary and glosses (and classes and seminars) in order to get at the poetry. Perhaps they do not wish to have the church or the priest read for and to them, but want instead to read for themselves. Too much poetry seems to reflect the actual lives they lead not at all. But still we can expect of our poets that they know, and that by reading their poetry we can learn.

American poets need to know how language works; the way poems have been made through history in their language and in other languages; and they need to know the names of things. In one of the two creation stories in Genesis, we are told that God paraded past Adam "Every beast of the field, and every fowl of the air," and, to signify man's supposed dominion over the rest of creation, "whatsoever Adam called every living creature, that was the name thereof." It is in the naming of a person, place, or thing that we come to know it, even to own it, if only for a moment. We have an obligation to have at our fingertips the names of trees and weeds and all the different finches; the names of the models of old Lincolns and Fords and of current and former rulers of this country and others. "Only connect," E. M. Forster instructs us—a valuable bit of advice for any writer. "You name it," might be another way of putting it. We must struggle to learn the words for this world. How else can we say it?

Charms Against Writer's Block

Go to the zoo. Hacksaw the bars, shatter glass,
set free every living thing, using pen and paper.

Make a novena, a devotion to the gritty wanderlust
that bites the soul: nine straight Friday nights
at the Greyhound Bus Station, watching souls
come and go, come and go — alone.

A clear night, walk outside. Look up. Never forget
how little you mean alone, how skin glows with light
it took all time to make earth, how holy you grow
by wondering.

Become in love. If already there, don't move, while
your partner grows mad with traveling. Or do,
over and over, knowing the sea's pulse and roar,
fleeing the numbing country of bone.

With friends you'd trust your nighest hungers with,
those whose words you treasure, carefully, lavishly make
a great feast: meat, herb, root, salt, fruit,
a little too much wine. Sit at table for three hours,
silent, touching nothing; then go out
and give everything to the poor.

Lean over the bed to catch the last breaths of your parents. Take
them to heart. Speak nothing but the truth about the dead.

Stand naked before a mirror in bright light
for one hour, trying to take yourself
seriously; trying not to.

With a lover at the moment of passion, look
into a mirror to see how, for good and ill, pleasure
distorts what you are.

Decide what to do with your hands.

Recalling Mallarmé, that "there was within him
that which would count the buttons
on the hangman's vest," study the death

that loops its noose about your throat. Stare down
your dankest fear, your most fragrant desire.
Breathe and breathe the song of your life.
Let nothing get by you. Write it down.
Again and again.

Other conceptions of the poet come to mind. So much of the Bible — the Old Testament in particular — is written in poetry, especially the prophetic books. Apparently there were things that could be said best through poems. The prophets heard and saw strange things. They were called to the prophetic/poetic life in terribly strange ways. Moses through the burning bush. Isaiah — that poet-adviser to kings — by getting a hot coal put to the lips he had said were too unclean to utter God's word. Hosea was told by God to marry a prostitute (a "wanton," named, of all things, Gomer) and to make her pregnant. Ezekiel — as strange certainly as any poet since, with the possible exception of Blake and Dickinson and Amy Lowell — when he appeared faint of heart and tongue-tied before God, was given a roll, a scroll. And he was told, "Son of man, eat that thou findest; eat this roll, and go speak unto the house of Israel." Ezekiel ate, and ingested the words, "and it was in my mouth as honey for sweetness," and suddenly he had things to say.

And the bards (the official court-poets of the Celtic peoples) and minstrels (the Celtic poets of the common people) were combination historians, journalists, playwrights — even public relations flacks — overall wordsmiths convinced that a song or curse or prayer or blessing could work through the utter and utterable power of words.

"We are not alone," a whole host of science-fiction B-movies from my childhood promised. I was raised, after all, to believe that an angel and a demon walked by my side, and that the foul and fuming pit of hell awaited me if I did not learn to fly right. I would sit in the dark and witness countless invasions of metal-men and green goo—oozing, drooling Martians and Venusians. (The first UFO sighting of the modern era occurred in 1947, the year of my birth.) Other times, just as the sun threatened to rise up over stone markers, I crept with the hero and heroine into fog-shrouded crypts to raise the lid on scores of rosy-lipped vampires, crucifix and stake in hand. Someone or something is watching. I do have that feeling, even today. When I sit down to write, there are voices, influences, whispers. It is history, I suppose, this haunting the writer feels. When I consider how my light is spent — as I am doing here — wondering about all things, even about wondering, I return to a series of moments from my childhood. On holidays and holy days my family paid visits to those family members who had moved out to the stony suburbs of the dead located in the heart of the city. The cemeteries, Calvary and Holy Cross, in Cleveland, contained green neighborhoods, mourning doves who-who-whoing their vigilance, redbirds trilling from the trees, and a more or less steady stream of visitors. We dressed up to go to the graveyard. It was an act of familial devotion. Here, to these neat plots, the family moved, one by one. My grandparents were peasant women and men from Italy and Slovakia. Here in American soil they found at last their inheritance, their retirement, their ultimate freedom from the harsh and humiliating strictures of class.

Charcoal Sketch of Aged Couple in Peasant Dress, Circa 1880

Their child, Father's father,
took to sea in steerage
from wild Calabria, once a kingdom
ruled by nomad Normans, who

ages before their France
were Norsemen, fierce travelers
blown like cinders from bonfires
of home by prevailing gales.

In the eyes of ancestors
staring down the wall at me
as my hand makes its slow way
across this ruled page

I recognize a northern cold,
numb and alien unease
of wanderers huddled around
their frail, windy fire,

and at the same time
the sweet heat of storied South.
I find myself this night bound
to Ohio, where all that breathed

once huddled close in caves
as outside the glacier screeched.
I feel the earth tilt and lurch

in its incessant revolution

toward winter and beyond,
sky just behind my window
a map of the history of wishing.
What comings and goings lie ahead

for my own restive children?
I feel the family disease:
blood a few degrees too hot or cold,
home both before me and behind,

the need above all else to stay
and learn the lay and language
of this adopted land;
the ache to take leave.

(reprinted from Poetry*)*

Among the kin we visited were twin brothers who had died in infancy before I was. We would make our way to their grave, say a few words, get down on our knees to pick the dandelions and crab grass, set down flowers. I recall the strange, numbing chill I got each time I looked down at the small stone of polished granite to see my own name there in stone — for I had been given the name of one of them, my big brother, my eternally infant brother. Could it be that this writing I do is a continuing attempt to speak to him, and to the others who lie beneath the earth? Am I asking them questions about the wisdom their darkness affords them? I feel at home in a graveyard, even though I have always been suspicious of overly romantic poses of The Poet, that dust-jacket figure strolling the seashore, hair riffled by brisk wind bringing scents of life's exquisite sadness, lines of a personal melancholy etched on the face — a too-sensitive frequenter of ancient ruins and boneyards.

It is important that any writer — a poet especially — not take himself or herself too seriously. The landscape of graves always pulls me back to this world. Poetry is music and dance, a making and a seeing and a knowing, a way of staving off the cold of earth, stone, and bone. It is also the grandest remembering a body can do. Something like love, I have always felt.

Reading the Graves

Running here day after day
in the stone town beyond my yard,
I'm so close to earth's pure scents,
there's nothing I can't imagine.

I move past the infant citizens:
tiny graves, briefest lives
engraved on tablets, pennies
minted and lost the same year.

For no reason at all, I think
of my afterbirth and cord —
those pieces of mother and me
that my ancestors revered

as the infant's lost brother
and fate. I can almost believe
with the old Calabrians
that our nights and days

are tied in fearful ways,
that two windy darknesses
frame each frail light,
and stepping over the sleep

of an unchristened child
can give a body grave-scab,
fatal and unalterable disease
of palsied limb and clotted lung

until earth offers its children
the one palliative
for the one and only terror —
which only earth instills.

I'm four, at Holy Cross Cemetery.
Each feast day we call on these kin
we converse with nowhere else
but in the plush caskets of dream.

At my feet under granite
lie the skeletons of my brothers,

Robert John and David John,
twins even in their new womb.
Still cornsilk-fine, their hair,
skulls in pretty bonnets.
The unlucky lungs that failed them
must be light as air by now,

their bones, not much larger
than a bird's, dressed up
in diapers and knitted booties.
What can it mean, such adult weeping?

I look down, broken-lined chaos
becoming the name I inherited when
a brother could call himself nothing.
Suddenly I can read. I can read.

(reprinted from Prairie Schooner*)*

Books

Last Rites and Other Poems. Ohio State University Press, 1980.
The Appassionata Lectures (*Texas Review* Poetry Award Chapbook). 1983.
The Appassionata Poems. Cleveland State University Poetry Center, 1983.
The Appassionata Doctrines. Cleveland State University Poetry Center, 1986.
The Gift of Fire. University of Arkansas Press, 1986.
A Letter of Columbus. Logan Elm Press, 1989.
The House of Memory. Ohio State University Press, 1990.
The Discipline: New and Selected Poems. Ohio State University Press, forthcoming.

Periodicals and Anthologies

Over the past twenty years Citino's poems have appeared in numerous magazines, including *Antioch Review*, *Chicago Review*, *Kenyon Review*, *Michigan Quarterly Review*, *New Letters*, *Ohio Review*, *Poetry*, *Salmagundi*, *Shenandoah*, *Southern Review*, and *Yale Review*; and in such anthologies as *Men of Our Time: Male Poetry in Contemporary America* (University of Georgia Press), *A New Geography of Poets* (University of Arkansas Press), and *Vital Signs: Contemporary American Poetry from the University Presses* (University of Wisconsin Press).

Eva Sanders

After studying physics and literature at Brown University, Scott Russell Sanders earned his doctorate in English at the University of Cambridge as a Marshall Scholar. His work has been supported by fellowships from the Danforth Foundation, the Lilly Endowment, and the National Endowment for the Arts. Some of his writing has been translated into German, Italian, Polish, Russian, and Japanese. He teaches at Indiana University in Bloomington, where he lives with his wife and two children.

LETTER TO A READER

Since you ask for an account of my writing, I will give you one. But I do so warily, because I have too often seen writers puff up like blowfish when they speak about their work. Writing *is* work, and it can leave you gray with exhaustion, can devour your days, can break your heart. But the same is true of all the real work that humans do, the planting of crops and nursing of babies, the building of houses and baking of bread. Writing is neither holy nor mysterious, except insofar as everything we do with our gathered powers is holy and mysterious. Therefore I will tell you as plainly as I can how I began and how I have pursued this art. Along the way I must also tell you something of my life, for writing is to living as grass is to ground.

I did not set out to become a writer. Until the age of twenty, I studied biology, chemistry, and above all physics, because my ambition was the primordial one of understanding the universe. I wished to comprehend the way of things, all things, visible and invisible, from the depths of my body to the depths of space. This ambition, along with the circumstances of my childhood, led me into the arms of science well before I was seduced by literature.

Although neither of my parents graduated from college, my father was a wizard with numbers and machines, my mother a wizard with animals and plants. My father could gaze at any structure, a barn or a music box, and see how it fit together. He could make from scratch a house or a hat, could mend any broken device, a stalled watch or a silent radio. He possessed the tinkerer's genius that has flourished in the stables and cellars and shops of our country for three hundred years. My mother's genius is for nature, the whole dazzling creation, from the ponderous ooze of stones to the bright hum of birds, from cockleburs to constellations. Under her care, vegetables bear abundantly and flowers gush with bloom. The depression forced her to give up the dream of becoming a doctor, but not before she had acquired a lifelong yen for science. When I think of them, I see my father in his workshop sawing a piece of wood, my mother in her garden planting seeds. Their intelligence speaks through their hands. Perhaps because of that, I regard writing as manual labor, akin to farming and carpentry. Everything I know and feel and think flows into words through my fingers.

I was born to these parents in October of 1945, two months after the bombing of Hiroshima and Nagasaki, so I have lived all my days under the sign of the mushroom cloud. My first home was a farm near Memphis, close enough to the Mississippi to give me an enduring affection for rivers, far enough south to give me an enduring guilt over racism. Across the road from our house was a prison farm, where I helped the black inmates pick cotton under the shotgun eyes of guards. My sister Sandra, three years older than I, taught me to read on the screened back porch of that house as we listened to the locusts and the billy goat and the cow. By the age of four I could turn the ink marks on paper into stories in my head, an alchemy I still find more marvelous than the turning of lead into gold.

My birth along the Mississippi, those forlorn black faces in the prison fields, and the country turn of my father's speech all prepared me to be spellbound when, at the age of eight, I climbed aboard the raft with Huckleberry Finn and Jim. That novel was the first big book I read from cover to cover. After finishing the last page, I returned immediately to page one and started over. From that day onward, I have known that the speech of back roads and fields and small towns — *my* speech — is a language worthy of literature. Nor have I forgotten how close laughter is to pain. Nor have I doubted that stories can bear us along on their current as powerfully as any river.

The summer before I started school, my family moved from Tennessee to Ohio, where we lived for the next few years on a military reservation surrounded by soldiers and the machinery of war. This place, the Ravenna Arsenal, would later provide me with the title and central themes for my book of essays, *The Paradise of Bombs*. The move from South to North, from red dirt to concrete, from fields planted in cotton to fields planted in bombs, opened a fissure in me which I have tried to bridge, time and again, with words.

An army bus, olive drab to hide it from enemy planes, carried us children to a tiny school just outside the chain-link fence. There were thirteen in my class, the sons and daughters of truck drivers, mechanics, farmers, electricians. At recess I learned whose father had been laid off, whose mother had taken sick, whose brother had joined the marines. From our desks we could see armed guards cruising the arsenal's perimeter, the long antennas on their camouflaged Chevrolets whipping the air. And in the opposite direction, beyond the playground, we could see horses grazing in a pasture and trees pushing against the sky.

Before I finished the eight grades of that school, my family moved from the arsenal to a patch of land nearby, and there I resumed my country ways, raising ponies and hoeing beans and chasing dogs through the woods. I helped local farmers bale hay and boil maple syrup. Sputnik was launched in the month I turned twelve, so my adolescence was feverish with the romance of space along with the romance of girls. I mixed black powder in the basement and fired model rockets from the pigpen, brooding on the curves of orbits and lips. Our neighbors were mostly poor, living in trailers or tar-paper shacks, often out of work, forever on the shady side of luck. Several of those aching people, their lives twisted by fanaticism or loss, would show up in my first book of stories, *Fetching the Dead*.

Many of the adults and some of the children in those trailers and shacks were alcoholic, as was my own good father. Throughout my childhood, but especially in my teenage years, he drank with a fearful thirst. Instead of putting out the fire in his gut, the alcohol made it burn more fiercely. This man who was so gentle and jovial when sober would give in to sulks and rages when drunk. The house trembled. I feared that the windows would shatter, the floors buckle, the beds collapse. Above all I feared that neighbors or friends would learn our bitter secret. The pressure of that secret, always disguised, shows up in my early books, especially in the stories of *Fetching the Dead*. I was not able to write openly about my father's drinking until well after his death, in "Under the Influence," the lead essay in *Secrets of the Universe*. As a boy, and most acutely during high school, I felt only bewilderment and shame. Craving order, I hurled myself into one lucid zone after another—the chessboard, the baseball diamond and basketball court, the periodic table, the wiring diagrams of electronics, the graphs of calculus, the formulas of physics. I pitched the baseball so hard I tore up my elbow; I rushed down the basketball court so recklessly I broke my foot against the gymnasium wall; I scrambled so far into mathematics that I could scarcely find my way back; I searched the teeming pool under the microscope for clues that would bind together the tatters of the world.

A scholarship to study physics paid my way to Brown University in Providence, where I spent four years feeling like a country duckling among swans. My classmates arrived with luggage bearing flight tags from the world's airports, wallets bulging with credit cards, voices buzzing with the voltage of cities. These polished men and women seemed to know already more than I could ever learn. My own pockets were empty. My voice betrayed the hills of Tennessee and the woods of Ohio. My devotion to the abstruse games of science marked me as a visionary. Fear of failing kept me so steadily at my books that I graduated first in my class. I mention the achievement because I am proud of it, but also because I have still not overcome that dread of failure, that sense of being an outsider, a hick among sophisticates. Standing on the margin, I formed the habit of looking and listening. On the margin, I was free to envision a way of life more desirable and durable than this one that excluded me. The public turmoil of the 1960s and early 1970s deepened my private confusion. Even though I am the least political of souls, during those college years I was lifted up and carried along by one cause after another: securing full rights for blacks and women, saving the environment, ending the Vietnam War. All these causes seemed utterly removed from the bloodless abstractions of physics. I began to suffocate among the crystalline formulas. I longed for the smell of dirt, the sound of voices, the weight of tools in my hands. I grew dizzy with the desire to heal — to heal my father and myself, to care for the poor and despised, to speak for the mute, to heal the very earth.

In this time of great confusion, I began keeping a journal. I strung out sentences like guy wires to hold myself upright in the winds of uncertainty. In those creamy pages, between those marbled covers, I wrote as though my life depended on it, and of course it did. Gradually I found words to address the inescapable questions: Who am I? What sense can I make of this inner tumult? How should I live? Does the universe have a purpose? Do we? What finally and deeply matters? What is true, and how can we know? I was too naive to realize that worldly men and women do not brood on such imponderable matters. I brooded. I pondered. I haunted the library, cross-examined the stars, walked the grimy streets of Providence looking for answers. Here science failed me. These perennial mysteries lay in shadow outside the brilliant circle of scientific method, immune to gauges or predictions. There are no unambiguous diagrams for meaning, and I desired meaning with an unappeasable hunger.

Pushed by spiritual hungers and pulled by social concerns, I realized in my junior year at Brown that I could not become a physicist. Then what new path should I follow? I considered history, philosophy, religion, and psychology; but at length I settled on literature, which had been calling to me ever since my sister taught me to read on that porch in Tennessee. All those years I had been living within the curved space of books. I read as I breathed, incessantly. Books lined the walls of my room, they rested on the table beside my pillow as I slept, they rode with me everywhere in pockets or pack, they poured through me constantly their murmur of words. At the age of twenty I still did not imagine that I would make any books of my own, but I knew that I would live in their company.

Another scholarship enabled me to continue my study of literature at the University of Cambridge. I sailed to England in the fall of 1967 along with my new bride, Ruth Ann McClure. I had met her at a summer science camp when she was fifteen and I was sixteen, the fruity smells of organic chemistry lab in our hair, and for five years we had carried on an epistolary romance. At first we exchanged letters monthly, then weekly, and at last daily, through the end of high school and all through college. Page by page, this girl turned into a woman before my eyes, and page by page I stumbled on from boy to man. During those five years, we saw one another in the flesh no more than a dozen times. And yet, after exchanging a thousand letters, I knew this woman more thoroughly, understood more about her values and desires, and loved her more deeply than I would have if I had been living next door to her all that while. Even more than the keeping of a journal, that epistolary courtship revealed to me the possibilities in writing. It convinced me that language can be a showing forth rather than a hiding, a joining rather than a sundering. It persuaded me that we can discover who we are through the search for words. In composing those letters, I was moved by affection — for my reader, and for my subject — as I am still moved by affection in all that I write.

Marriage to Ruth is the air I have breathed now for more than half my life. From the goodness of marriage, its depths and delights, I have learned the power of enduring commitments — to a person, to a place, to a chosen work. Outside of this union I would have written quite different books, or perhaps none at all. Even to begin telling of our shared life would be another and a much longer story.

At Cambridge, once more I was a duck among swans. Once more I felt raw and rough, like a backwoodsman trying to move in the parlors of the gentry without upsetting the tea cart or the vicar. Despite my good marriage, despite my success at Brown, despite the scholarship that had brought me to England, I still needed to prove myself. It seemed to me that all the other students were entering upon their rightful inheritance, while I had to earn, day by day, the privilege of staying there.

For the subject of my dissertation I chose D. H. Lawrence. He was another outsider, another scholarship boy, with a father given to drink, a mother given to worry, a childhood divided between ugly industry and beautiful countryside. I was troubled by much of what Lawrence wrote about women, and I despised his authoritarian politics. I grew impatient when he played the shaman or crowed about blood. Yet he knew how it feels to emerge from the hinterland and fight to join the great conversation of culture. He honored the work of

243

hands, whether of colliers or carpenters or cooks. He wrote about the earth, about flowers and birds and beasts, with something close to the shimmer of life itself. He knew that we are bound through our flesh to the whole of nature, and that nature may be all we can glimpse of the sacred. The dissertation, much revised, became my first book, *D. H. Lawrence: The World of the Major Novels*. Whatever it may reveal about Lawrence, it says a great deal about me.

On the sly, while pursuing graduate studies, I began writing stories. The earliest of them were clumsy and gaudy efforts to speak of what I found troubling in my own life — the arsenal, the bombs, the black prisoners on that Tennessee farm, the pinched lives of poor whites in Ohio, my father's drinking, my mother's discontent, the war that was devouring my generation. The stories were clumsy because I was a beginner. They were gaudy because I felt I had to dress up my measly experience in costumes borrowed from the great modernists — from Lawrence, of course, but also from Joyce, Woolf, Gide, Proust, Yeats, Pound, Eliot. For those first months of serious writing, I believed that the writer's proper stance is one of ironic aloofness, like Joyce's God, high in the clouds paring his fingernails. I fancied that the point of writing is to dazzle your readers, keep them off balance, show them what intricate knots you can tie with strings of words. I thought that real life unfolds only on foreign soil, usually in cities, and among bored expatriates.

I was saved from the worst of these illusions by reading another modernist, a Mississippian like my father, a man troubled over the legacy of racism and infatuated by the sound of American speech. Reading Faulkner, as I began to do in my second year at Cambridge, inspired me for a spell to even flashier verbal hot-dogging, but it cured me of thinking that the life I knew on back roads was too obscure or too shabby for literature. Eventually I stopped showing off, climbed down off my stilts, and tried to say as directly as I could what I had to say.

During those England years I formed the habit of rising at five or six, to write for a couple of hours before breakfast, before looking at the calendar, before yielding to the demands of the day. The world's hush, broken only by bird song or passing cars, the pool of light on the table encircled by darkness, the peck of typewriter keys, the trail of ink on paper, these became the elements in a morning ritual I have followed ever since. I wake early in order to write, and I write in order to come more fully awake.

A few of those stories, written dawn after dawn, found their way into British magazines, the very first in *Cambridge Review* in 1968, when I was twenty-two, then others in *Transatlantic Review* and *Stand* the following year. I suspect that the editors overlooked my feverish style for the sake of my characters — the Mississippi sharecroppers and Ohio prophets and Greyhound bus riders — whom they would never previously have met through Her Majesty's mails. When I received my first check, from Jon Silkin at *Stand*, I was astounded that a magazine would not only do me the honor of printing my work but would actually pay me for it. To celebrate, Ruth and I took these unexpected few pounds and went to see an exhibit of Van Gogh's paintings in London. By 1969 I was reviewing fiction for *Cambridge Review*, and over the next two years I served as that magazine's literary editor. My association with this old, illustrious journal, and my friendship with the young, industrious editors, Eric Homberger and Michael Egan, were crucial in helping me see my way toward becoming a writer.

With the small change left over from my scholarship and with money Ruth earned as a teacher's aide, we traveled during vacations all over Europe and the British Isles. For me, these were literary pilgrimages, so that in Ireland I was looking for Joyce and Yeats, in Wales for Dylan Thomas, in Scotland for Burns. Inevitably, exuberantly, I saw the Lake District through the lines of Wordsworth and Coleridge, London through Dickens and Orwell and Woolf, the industrial Midlands through Lawrence, the southern counties through Wells and James, the western counties through Austen and Hardy, all of Britain through Shakespeare. I read Balzac, Hugo, and Sartre in Paris, Cervantes in Madrid, Kafka in Prague, Günter Grass in Berlin, Thomas Mann in Venice, Calvino in Rome. Traveling with books, I came to understand that all enduring literature is local, rooted in place, in landscape or cityscape, in particular ways of speech and climates of mind.

In 1971, I brought back with me from England a fresh Ph.D. and a suitcase of manuscripts. The degree had earned me several offers of teaching jobs. (I never considered trying to write without holding a job. The jobless men I had known while growing up were miserable, humiliated, broken.) I chose to come to Indiana University because it is in my home region, the Midwest, because it attracts students with backgrounds similar to my own, and because the people who interviewed me for the job had gone to the trouble of reading my fiction as well as my criticism. They wanted me to come, they assured me, even if I turned out to be a writer instead of a scholar. Here I came, and here I have stayed. Of course I travel, I spend months and even occasional years teaching elsewhere. I hear the siren call of cities and the serene call of mountains and oceans. But I keep returning to this landscape, this community, this house, this work.

Fidelity to place, not common for writers in any part of the United States, may be least common of all in the Midwest. This region is more famous for the writers who have left than for those who have stayed. Mark Twain, William Dean Howells, Ernest Hemingway, F. Scott Fitzgerald, Theodore Dreiser, T. S. Eliot, Sherwood Anderson, Hart Crane, Langston Hughes, Kurt Vonnegut, Robert Coover, Toni Morrison: the list of departed midwesterners is long and luminous. You don't have to look hard for reasons to leave. The region has not been very hospitable to writers. Vachel Lindsay, who stayed to make his poems in Springfield, Illinois, complained of "the usual Middle West crucifixion of the artist." I think he had in mind the grudging, grinding legacy of puritanical religion and agrarian politics: art may shock Grandmother or corrupt the children; you cannot raise art in the fields or mass-produce it in factories, cannot sell it by the pound. Publishers and reviewers, most of whom live on the coasts, often regard the heart of the country as a blank space one must fly over on the way between New York and California.

The message of all those departures from the Midwest is that life happens elsewhere, in Boston or Paris, in the suburbs of London or San Francisco. But life happens here, as well. I am a witness to the fact. Fellow writers and friends in publishing have asked me, directly or indirectly, how I can bear to live in a backwater. I tell them there are no backwaters. There is only one river, and we are all in it. Wave your arm, and the ripples will eventually reach me. For the writer, for anyone, where you live is less important than how devotedly and perceptively you inhabit that place. I stay here out of affection for the Middle West — for the landscape, the people, the accents and foods, the look of towns and lay of farms, for the trees and flowers and beasts — but also from a sense of responsibility. Every acre of the planet could use some steady attention. I open my eyes on a place that has scarcely been written about. However great or small my talents, here is where they will do the most good.

Those talents did not bear much fruit during my first years in Indiana. I revised the Lawrence book, which appeared from a London publisher in 1973 and in this country from Viking Press in 1974. On the strength of my few, feverish stories, two senior Viking editors, Marshall Best and Malcolm Cowley, secured for me a modest advance on a first novel. I had been laboring on a novel called *Warchild* since returning from England, but I was at last able to complete it thanks to the generosity of Phillips Exeter Academy, in New Hampshire, where I spent the school year of 1974–75 as writer-in-residence. The hero was a young man, suspiciously like myself, who had been born under the sign of the mushroom cloud, had grown up on an arsenal, and had become a conscientious objector during the Vietnam War. In passing, *Warchild* also chronicled the decline and fall of industrial civilization and the death of nature. Thomas Mann in his late years or Leo Tolstoy in his prime might have done justice to my scheme; I could not. In all of its innumerable drafts, *Warchild* was a sprawling, operatic, rambunctious book. By the time I mailed it to Cowley and Best, Viking had been purchased by Penguin, and all the lesser contracts, including mine, had become scrap paper. After my head recovered from the pain of banging into that dead end, I realized that the world was better off with *Warchild* in a box on my shelf.

While at Exeter, in mourning for my botched first novel, I chanced to read the account of a murder that had occurred in 1813 in the northeastern Ohio county of Portage, where I grew up. A roving peddler had been killed in the woods near Ravenna, the county seat. Suspicion immediately fell on the muscular back of a gigantic found-ryman who had been carrying the peddler's goods. Two local men volunteered to pursue the giant through the woods. They caught up with him, led him back for trial, and assisted at his hanging. After the burial, three separate groups tried to steal the huge corpse. All this transpired amid skirmishes with the Indians and against the bloody backdrop of the War of 1812. The conjunction of war and wilderness, a fearful community, and a mysterious fugitive set me thinking. The account was sketchy enough to leave blank spaces for imagination to romp. The result of that work, begun in Exeter and carried on intermittently for eight years, was *Bad Man Ballad*. This novel opens with bird song and closes with human song. In between, it dances from history toward myth. The concerns of the book were not so different from those of *Warchild*, for I was still trying to understand how we had become so violent — toward strangers, toward one another, toward animals and forests and the land itself.

While reading in my haphazard way about the frontier period in the Ohio Valley, hoping to saturate *Bad Man Ballad* with the smell of history, I kept turning up curious anecdotes about the settlers. An escaped slave, a philosophical cobbler, a fierce farmer, a love-struck carpenter would be preserved in the dusty chronicles on the strength of a single flamboyant gesture. A few of these worthies made their way into *Bad Man Ballad* as minor characters; but most of them would not fit. Unwilling to abandon them once more to the archives, yet unwilling to interrupt work on my novel long enough to write full-blown stories, I began composing two-page summaries of what I found memorable in these frontier lives. To begin with, I thought I would return to elaborate these compressed narratives later on; but I soon found them to be deeply satisfying in all their brevity, with a flavor of ballads and folk tales, forms that appeal to me because they cut to the heart of experience. Over the next few years I kept writing these miniature tales in batches, until I had accumulated fifty, spanning the period of settlement in the Ohio Valley, from the Revolution to the Civil War. These were gathered into *Wilderness Plots*, a slim volume for which I feel an ample fondness, in part because it came to me like an unexpected child, in part because, although it was the fourth book of fiction I wrote, it was the first one published.

By now you may have noticed, if you are one who pays attention to dates, that long periods elapsed between the writing of my early books and their publication. This is a fate so common for young writers, and so discouraging, as to deserve a few words here. The latest of the stories in *Fetching the Dead* was completed seven years before that book appeared. *Bad Man Ballad* took five years to reach print, and *Terrarium*, my next novel, took four. By the time William Morrow gave me a contract for *Wilderness Plots* in 1982, I had been writing seriously for a dozen years, with only a single book of criticism to show for it. Dawn after dawn I forced myself from bed, hid away in my cramped study, bent over the keyboard, and hammered lines across the blank pages, all the while struggling to ignore the voices of my young children, first Eva and then Jesse, who clamored at the door, struggling to forget the well-meaning questions of friends who asked me whatever had become of this book or that, struggling to overcome my own doubts. Every writer must pass through such seasons of despondency, some for shorter periods, some for longer. Each of us must find reasons to keep on slogging.

What kept me writing? Stubbornness, for one thing, a refusal to give up certain questions, certain stories, images, and characters. The pleasure of living among words, for another thing. When I was in the flow of work, I felt free and whole. I played language as a pianist plays music, my fingers and ears captured by it, my body swaying. A good marriage also helped me keep writing. I hid my gloom from everyone except Ruth, who stood by me in the dark, and who assured me that I should follow my talent, no matter how crooked it was, no matter if the world never took any notice.

In the late 1970s, even while my books languished, my short fiction continued to appear in magazines, mostly quarterlies and reviews. For me, as for many writers of my generation, the magazines — with their underpaid editors working on shoestring budgets — have provided a training ground and a community of readers. In the years when I could but dimly see my way forward, I was greatly encouraged by a series of editors — by Roger Mitchell at *Minnesota Review*, Wayne Dodd at *Ohio Review*, Stanley Lindberg at *Georgia Review*, Robley Wilson at

North American Review, and Ellen Datlow at *Omni*.

The final item in that list may strike you as out of place. Unlike the others, *Omni* is a glossy production, pays handsomely, and publishes science fiction. After exploring the past in *Bad Man Ballad* and *Wilderness Plots*, I began pushing my questions into the future. Where might our fear of nature and our infatuation with technology lead us? What is our proper place among the animals? What might be the effects of our losing all contact with the wild? How might we keep ourselves from ravaging the earth? According to the arbitrary divisions imposed by critics and publishers, to speculate about the future is to enter the realm of science fiction. And yet, whether set in past or future, all my fiction interrogates the present, which is where we live. Beginning with a sabbatical in Oregon in 1978 and continuing for the next ten years, I wrote a series of stories that appeared in *Omni*, *The Magazine of Fantasy and Science Fiction*, *Isaac Asimov's Science Fiction Magazine*, *New Dimensions*, and several anthologies; and I wrote three speculative novels.

The first of these, *Terrarium*, arose from a nightmare image of domed cities afloat on the oceans, all bound into a global network by translucent tubes. Citizens of this Enclosure would pass their whole lives without going outside, without meeting anything except what humans had made. Set over against this claustrophobic image were the green mountains and stony coastline of Oregon, where *Terrarium* was conceived, and where a group of renegades would try to make a new life. I returned to the world of the Enclosure in *The Engineer of Beasts*, a novel whose central figure builds robot animals for disneys, the successors to zoos in those denatured cities. The central figure in *The Invisible Company*, third of my future histories, is a physicist who must come to terms with the lethal consequences of his own early discoveries, while caught in a technological masquerade inspired by Thomas Mann's *Death in Venice*.

As though I had not already violated enough boundaries by writing science fiction, historical fiction, criticism, fables, and contemporary short stories, during the 1980s I added personal essays, documentary narrative, biographical fiction, and children's books to my profusion of forms. And why not a profusion? The world is various. Nature itself is endlessly inventive, trying out one form after another. How dull, if birds had stopped with sparrows and not gone on to ospreys and owls. How dull, if plants had not spun on from ferns to lilacs and oaks. Why squeeze everything you have to say into one or two literary boxes for the convenience of booksellers and critics? Scientists and engineers speak of "pushing the envelope," by which they mean expanding the conceptual frame, or replacing it entirely with a new one. Instead of being confined, break the frame and look outside; you may find a solution there. Outsight added to insight. I also try to push the envelope. Anyone persistent enough to read my work from beginning to end will find, beneath the surface play of form, the same few enduring concerns: reflections on our place in nature, on our murderous and ingenious technology, on the possibilities of community, on love and strife within families, on the search — perhaps doomed — for a spiritual ground.

The subject of my biographical fiction is John James Audubon, a figure who combined a number of quintessential American roles: immigrant entrepreneur, real estate speculator, salesman, artist, naturalist, frontiersman, and man of letters. He was also a neighbor of mine, in geography and spirit, because he lived for a dozen years in the Ohio Valley and he formed his vision of wilderness in contact with the birds, beasts, and landscape of my region. Although I have sketched a novel about his entire life, from the illegitimate birth in Haiti to senile retirement on the Hudson River, I have thus far been able to imagine freely only his childhood and youth, about which the scholars know few facts. *Wonders Hidden* follows Audubon up to the age of eighteen, when he escaped from France to avoid Napoleon's draft and set out for America, where his name would eventually become a talisman for the protection of wildlife.

I began writing for children in 1984 following an invitation from Richard Jackson, founder and longtime director of Bradbury Press. He liked the narrative flair of *Wilderness Plots* and wanted to know if I had considered telling stories for children. Yes indeed, I replied, for in those days I was making up stories nightly for my young son and daughter. Then propose something, he said. I offered to write my own versions of the tales that lay behind twenty classic American folk songs, like "Yankee Doodle" and "John Henry" and "Blue-Tailed Fly," songs my father had sung to me when I was a boy and which I now sang to my own children. The result was *Hear the Wind Blow*, which plays all eighty-eight keys of emotion and crackles with the vernacular, a book meant for reading loud. Also for Bradbury Press, I adapted a pair of tales from *Wilderness Plots* to make two picture books, *Aurora Means Dawn* and *Warm as Wool*, and I am concocting a new story now about a backwoods peddler. Children are a tough audience, but also an inspiring one, for they have not lost their delight in the play and sound of language, their pleasure in the shapes of stories, or their capacity for wonder.

I was lured into writing documentary narrative by the quirks of my childhood and the accidents of geology. My home in southern Indiana happens to be smack in the middle of the largest outcropping of premium limestone in North America. Wherever you see gritty stone buildings the color of biscuits or gravy, from New York's Empire State skyscraper to San Francisco's City Hall, from the Pentagon to the Library of Congress, you are probably looking at rock that was quarried and milled in my neighborhood. After a boyhood on farms and construction sites, in munitions loadlines and factories and workshops, I am drawn to men and women who labor with their bodies, using heavy tools to wrestle with raw, stubborn matter. So how could I resist the quarries, with their bristling derricks, or the humpbacked mills with their perpetual grinding, or the stonemen with their shrewd eyes and skilled hands? In its original version, my portrait of these people and their landscape appeared with photographs by Jeffrey Wolin in a volume entitled *Stone Country*, and then my revised text later appeared as *In Limestone Country*.

Some years earlier, baffled in my work on a novel, I had begun writing another kind of nonfiction, the personal essays that would be collected in *The Paradise of Bombs* and *Secrets of the Universe*. The earliest of these were straightforward accounts of experiences that had moved me — carrying my infant son up a mountain in Oregon, listening to owls beside an Indiana lake. Gradually I enlarged the scope of the essays until they began to disclose patterns in my life that I had never before seen, such as the confrontation between wilderness and technology in "At Play in the Paradise of Bombs," or the legacy of a rural childhood in "Coming from the Country," or the impact of my father's drinking in "Under the Influence." Although rooted in the personal, all my essays push toward the impersonal, toward the world I share with readers; I reflect on my own experience in hopes of illuminating the experience of others.

The challenge is to be faithful to one's private vision *and* to one's place in the world, to the truth one has laboriously found and to the people whom this truth might serve. I see my writing as an invitation to community, an exploration of what connects us to one another and to the earth. I must withdraw in order to work, must close the door against my children, close my mind against the day's news. But unless the writing returns me to the life of family, friends, and country with renewed energy and insight, then it has failed. Writing for me is a training in attention, and therefore a spiritual discipline. It deepens my understanding of the ordinary. It does not cut me off from other people, but rather binds me more intimately to them.

Whether fiction or nonfiction, stories are containers. They are the pots and bowls and baskets we use to hold knowledge. To protest, as many critics do, that stories are artificial, that they are made up, is to say no more than that everything fashioned by humans is made up.

To protest that experience is scattered, chaotic, not gathered as in stories, is no more than to say that seeds and berries are scattered, not gathered as in the bowl we have filled for supper.

Writers often like to play god, proclaiming themselves the framers of microcosms. I am not making counterfeit universes; I am speaking about the actual one, of which I am a vanishingly small part. I love words, but I love the world more. I do not think of language as thread for a private game of cat's cradle, but as a web flung out, attaching me to the creation. Of course the medium is constantly debased. Television, advertising, and government have so cheapened language that many writers doubt whether it can still be used in the search for reality. But reality has never been handed to us like pebbles or potatoes; we have always had to dig it up or make it for ourselves. All of culture, writing included, is a struggle over how we should imagine our lives. I refuse to abandon that struggle to the power mongers and merchants, refuse to abandon language to the charlatans and hucksters.

Without delving into metaphysics, where I would soon get lost, I need to say that I believe that writing is more than self-regarding play. It gestures beyond itself toward all that is. The moves in writing are not abstract, like those in algebra or chess, for words cannot be unhooked from the world. They come freighted with memory and feeling. Linguists describe our ordinary speech as a "natural" language, to distinguish it from the formal codes of mathematics or computers or logic. The label is appropriate, a reminder that everyday language is wild; no one defines or controls it. Venturing into that wilderness, the writer may draw from the discoveries and inventions of all who have spoken or written; but you can never force words to mean only and exactly what you wish them to mean, for they escape every trap you lay for them.

I am less an actor than a witness. Insofar as my writing is important, it gains that importance from what it witnesses to. I have written from the outset with a pressing awareness of the world's barbarities — the bombing of cities, starvation of the poor, extinction of species, exhaustion of soil, pollution of water and air, all brands of racism, the arms race, murder, genocide, war. If I stubbornly believe that life can be good, kindness common, love durable, and nature resilient, it is in the face of this cruelty and waste. Without denying evil, literature ought to reduce, in however small a degree, the amount of suffering. Not only human suffering — also that of our fellow creatures. It is not possible to live without causing harm, but it is possible to cause less harm than we presently do.

The desire to articulate a shared world links me to the effort of science as well as to that of art. I am joined in a grand collaboration. Individual scientists, like writers, may be cutthroat competitors, out for their own glory; but science itself, the great cathedral of ideas slowly rising, is a common enterprise. The symbol for literature should perhaps be a library instead of a cathedral, but it is an equally collaborative achievement. Whether one is a scientist or a writer, the universe outshines those of us who glimpse a bit of it and report what we see. Right now we urgently need to rethink our place in nature, to examine anew our ways of living on the planet, and this need is far more significant than the careers or accomplishments of all writers put together. I believe, you see, that nature is a sacred order. By that I mean the health of our land and our fellow creatures is the ultimate measure of the worth and sanity of our lives.

I am forty-five as I compose this letter to you. I have been writing seriously for twenty years, skillfully for about twelve. With decent luck, I should continue making books for another twenty or possibly thirty years. So I think of myself as being midway in my journey as a writer. My steady desire has been to wake up, not to sleepwalk through this brief, miraculous life. The root impulse is curiosity. I wish to go about with mind and senses adequate to the splendor of the world. I wish to see the burning bush.

Writing is a labor, shot through with intervals of delight. If there were no pleasure in the sinewy turns of a sentence, the sudden bubbling up of an idea, the discovery of a path through the maze, who would keep going? I feel the need to tell you many things for which there is no room in a letter, even a long letter. Nothing I have told you here can replace my books, which live or die in the minds of readers like you, and which bear on their current of words more meanings than I know.

Books

D. H. Lawrence: The World of the Major Novels (criticism). Viking, 1974.
Wilderness Plots: Tales about the Settlement of the American Land (stories). Morrow, 1983. Paperback edition by Quill, 1985, and Ohio State University Press, 1988.
Fetching the Dead (stories). University of Illinois Press, 1984.
Wonders Hidden: Audubon's Early Years (novella). Capra, 1984.
Terrarium (novel). Tor, 1985.
Hear the Wind Blow (stories). Bradbury/Macmillan, 1985.
Stone Country (documentary narrative), with photographs by Jeffrey A. Wolin. Indiana University Press, 1985. Revised paperback edition

as *In Limestone Country*, Beacon Press, 1991.
Audubon Reade: The Best Writings of John James Audubon. Indiana University Press, 1986.
Bad Man Ballad (novel). Bradbury/Macmillan, 1986.
The Paradise of Bombs (personal essays). University of Georgia Press, 1987. Paperback edition, Touchstone/Simon & Schuster, 1988.
The Engineer of Beasts (novel). Orchard/Franklin Watts, 1988.
The Invisible Company (novel). Tor, 1989.
Aurora Means Dawn (children's story). Bradbury/Macmillan, 1990.
Secrets of the Universe (personal essays). Beacon, 1991.
Warm as Wool (children's story). Bradbury/Macmillan, 1992.
Home Ground (personal narrative). Beacon, forthcoming.

Anthologies (Selected, since 1986)

Necessary Fictions. Eds. Stanley W. Lindberg and Stephen Corey. University of Georgia Press, 1986.
The Best American Essays 1987. Eds. Gay Talese and Robert Atwan. Ticknor & Fields, 1987.
The Norton Reader. 7th ed. Eds. Arthur M. Eastman et al. Norton, 1988.
The Contemporary Essay. Ed. Donald Hall. St. Martin's Press, 1989.
The Dolphin Reader. 2d ed. Ed. Douglas Hunt. Houghton Mifflin, 1989.
Omni Book of Science Fiction: VI. Ed. Ellen Datlow. Omni, 1989.
The Prentice-Hall Reader. 2d ed. Ed. George Miller. Prentice-Hall, 1989.
The Harvest Reader. 2d ed. Eds. William Heffernan et al. Harcourt Brace Jovanovich, 1990.
Openings: Original Essays by Contemporary Society and American Writers. Eds. Robert Atwan and Valeri Vinokurov. University of Washington Press, 1990.
The Riverside Reader. 3d ed. Eds. Joseph F. Trimmer and Maxine Hairston. Houghton Mifflin, 1990.
The Art of the Essay. Ed. Lydia Fakundiny. Houghton Mifflin, 1991.
The Harper & Row Reader. 3d ed. Eds. Wayne Booth and Marshall Gregory. Harper & Row, 1991.
The Winchester Reader. Ed. Donald McQuade. Beford, 1991.

Periodicals

Stories, essays, and excerpts from novels have appeared in several dozen magazines and journals, among them *Georgia Review*, *Gettysburg Review*, *Harper's*, *Kenyon Review*, *Michigan Quarterly Review*, *New York Times Book Review*, *North American Review*, *Ohio Review*, *Omni*, *Seattle Review*, and *Sewanee Review*.

Robert Love Taylor

Robert Love Taylor was born and reared in Oklahoma City. He attended San Francisco State College and received his B.A. from the University of Oklahoma, his Ph.D. from Ohio University. Since 1972 he has taught at Bucknell University in Lewisburg, Pennsylvania, where he is also coeditor of West Branch. *In 1989 his novel* The Lost Sister *received the Oklahoma Book Award for Fiction, and in 1992 he received a Fellowship in Literature from the Pennsylvania Council on the Arts. Married and the father of two daughters, he currently lives in Mifflinburg, Pennsylvania.*

THE TERRITORY OF MEMORY

I was conceived in a cold hotel room in Great Bend, Kansas. It was January of 1941, a week or so after the death of James Joyce. The wind whined and sleet whipped against the window panes. My father, a sales representative for a manufacturer of high school class rings, usually traveled alone, mostly staying in Oklahoma, so this was a special trip. In those days the limits of his territory were not so clear-cut, and anyway you had to beat the bushes if you had a pretty wife to support. He thought my mother might've liked seeing Kansas, aside from the fact that he was low in cash and had reason to believe that she always put back a little from the grocery allowance he gave her. Having grown up in Arkansas, she cared little for seeing Kansas, but she liked the idea that he wanted to take her along. You can imagine that she might have been a little put out with him when they stopped for gas and he said, Oh, by the way, did she happen to have any cash on her. Mercy. What if she had not thought, at the last minute, to tuck that envelope in her purse. What would he have done then, not even enough gas left in the car to get them back to Oklahoma City. Well, but she had the money, thank goodness, enough for the hotel room in Great Bend too, and it must have required a good deal of charm for my father to persuade her that he hadn't wanted to bring her along just to pay the bills. For me, at any rate, it was quite a night way up there in the middle of Kansas. I've been trying to get the spirit of it into my fiction ever since.

The first of three children, the only son born to Willie Merle Wiseman and Robert Love Taylor, I was named Robert Love, Jr., and called Bobby. My sister, born a year after me, they named Carole, after the actress Carole Lombard, who had died in a plane crash not long after Clark Gable fell in love with her. My sister Carole was called Sissy, and so we were always Bobby and Sissy. Our younger sister came along when Sissy and I were starting kindergarten and first grade. This new sister was named Janis, after the singer Janis Paige. We had looked forward to her birth with great excitement, but she did not live up to our hopes and so we were not kind to her.

About ten weeks after my birth, the Japanese bombed Pearl

Harbor. I seem to remember the excitement and confusion of those days, as I seem to remember much that I could not be remembering but only imagining. My prodigious memory was much admired when I was a child, my mother frequently commenting on it in the presence of others, especially my father's parents, whose other grandchildren had already begun to amass accomplishments that needed to be seen in proper perspective.

One of my earliest memories is of the summer of 1932, after my father's graduation from high school. That summer my father traveled back to Tennessee to visit kinfolk and brought back a clock from Uncle Shakespeare's collection. I remember my father's humility before his proud uncle and the wonderful array of valuable clocks. The room was alive with ticking and chiming, and unusually warm. It smelled of furniture wax.

Take your pick, Uncle Shake said. He was a tall man like my grandfather, with sly eyes and a sharp nose and the famous Taylor bald head.

Take whatever clock suits your fancy, he told my father. Take it home as a gift to your sweet mother.

The great dark grandfather clocks were most impressive, so beautiful and grave in their handcarved cabinets. No doubt they were valuable, too, but surely they weighed a ton. Clearly it would not do to carry one of these great clocks back to Oklahoma on the bus. He could easily enough find his mother a smaller, lighter memento. But he did not want to hurt his uncle's feelings, and so he quickly looked around and saw a small mantel clock, handsome with its sloping sides, its smooth dark wood. It might just fit in his suitcase. That was the one he chose.

Imagine that, my grandmother said. He could have chosen any one of those valuable clocks and this is what he brought me, an old farm clock!

For all her teasing of my father, my Grandmother Taylor, who had been Love Thomas of Sullivan County, Tennessee, liked the clock well enough and kept it in the center of her mantel until her death. I don't know if it was she I first heard the story from or my father. Probably my father, who would have told it with gusto, enjoying a laugh at the expense of his younger self. My grandmother, pleased with the opportunity to tease her baby boy, might have repeated it at holiday dinners. It is odd that I remember the story more vividly than the occasion of its telling, odder yet that it took up residence in my mind like a memory of my own.

Another early memory is of the moment of my mother's birth. I see the house on Magazine Mountain in Arkansas, the pines swaying above it, rocked back and forth by the late September wind. The house is high up on the mountain, set back from a winding dirt road in deep shade, but through the trees you can see glimpses of the valley of the Petit Jean far below, broad expanses of green and brown, and the blue knobs of the Ouachita Mountains beyond. The long summer heat has broken and the wind carries the smell of rain. My grandmother, who had been Nancy Jane Marshall, twenty-two years old and in the throes of her first labor, cries out, and that cry echoes across the mountainside and down into the valley, where farmers pause at their ploughs and wonder was it a human sound or divine. Martin, she calls out, Martin! Clouds move rapidly across the deep blue sky. My grandfather, Martin Pinkney Wiseman, notes that at the moment of his first daughter's birth a portion of one of those clouds floats through the house on Magazine Mountain. The air is white and cool when Nancy hands him his baby daughter. What a blessing! Here is heaven. He bursts into tears, cradling the baby in his arms.

I was a quiet, well-behaved child and destined, according to my mother, to be a preacher. The sign came when she found me standing upon a large rock, talking gibberish. When she asked me what I was doing, I said preaching. This is not something I remember, though I must have been three years old.

What I do remember from that period of my life is setting off for New York. We lived in a suburb of Oklahoma City. It was a hot day — I believe it was always hot back then — and the pavement was warm against the soles of my brown oxfords as I began the long journey down Huntington Drive and up Sherwood Lane. New York was on Sherwood Lane, though you could not see it from our house because it was on the other side of the hill. I set off in the morning and expected that if I walked briskly, taking long strides the way my parents did, I'd be there in a few minutes and back home before lunch. It did not seem anything to get excited or upset about, and I did not understand my mother's unseemly behavior when she stopped me so close to my destination, halfway up the hill on Sherwood Lane. She snatched me up into her arms and carried me back home as if I were a baby and not a mature three-year-old with a clear sense of where I was going.

I never had a clear sense of where I was going, not for several decades, though I was often as certain as that three-year-old Bobby that I was charting my direction with deadly precision. So it seems to me now. But I did have more imagination than I needed. Still do, no doubt. And even if I never became the preacher my mother saw in me, I often felt stirrings of something that I could not account for.

The story of Jesus, for example, brought tears to my eyes. I felt, for a time, as if I stood in the same relation to the world as Jesus did, and that soon enough I'd be found out and nailed up. It was not that I believed myself a son of God. No, my kinship to Jesus lay solely in our mutual martyrdom. My junior high school seemed populated by the descendants of Herod. The first novel of any seriousness that I responded to — this would have been much later, in my freshman year at the University of Oklahoma — was *Tess of the D'Urbervilles*. I found myself in Tess as fervently as I'd previously found myself in Jesus. I read as many other novels by Hardy as I could find. I learned that when critics failed to understand *Jude the Obscure*, Hardy stopped writing novels, and I was strangely heartened. If I had lived in Hardy's time, I would have sought him out and shook his hand. He would know that at least one reader had understood and was grateful.

By that time I was writing myself, of course.

Music had come first. Having listlessly suffered accordion lessons since I was ten years old, learning to play by memory a string of marches, polkas, hymns, and sentimental favorites such as "Dark Eyes" and "Blue Moon," I was not prepared for the experience of hearing Bach on the huge pipe organ of the St. Luke's Methodist Church. Sixteen years old, I had gone to a recital there with my girlfriend, a member of that church. There was an organ in the Westminster Presbyterian Church, where I sang my heart out in the youth choir, and that Presbyterian organ might even have been as good as this Methodist one, but I had never heard such music from it. Perhaps the closest I'd come to this feeling was the shivers I sometimes got when I listened to my girlfriend sing. She took voice lessons at Oklahoma City University and sang coloratura soprano. But listening to her I could not have been disinterested.

Almost simultaneously, I discovered jazz. My girlfriend had an old saxophone that she loaned me and I set out to teach myself how to play it, using instruction booklets furnished by the director of the high school marching band. The band director found a baritone saxophone for me, and soon I was a member of the marching band and, more significantly, the newly formed swing band, a fifteen-piece jazzy ensemble.

In the images of Charlie Parker, Lester Young, Gerry Mulligan, and Paul Desmond I saw a spirit that I wanted to emulate. I wanted to be Gerry Mulligan, my back arched and my horn wailing. Mulligan was like Jesus and Tess, but with a dash of Billy Vessels or Clendon Thomas, star running backs for the University of Oklahoma Sooners. You improvised, quite literally on your feet, and left the demons who chased you far behind.

The pipe organist that I heard play Bach was a tiny man, bald, blind, and French, whose legs seemed scarcely long enough to reach the pedals. He did not inspire the kind of worship that Gerry Mulligan did. But once the music came forth, he seemed to disappear in thin air.

When I went off to the University of Oklahoma in the fall of 1959, I planned to major in business, like everybody else, but I brought along my saxophone, and, among my phonograph albums, I had E. Power Biggs playing Bach on some grand German organ. When my roommate was gone, I put this album on the portable stereo, turned it up loud, and felt my soul pleasantly disintegrate.

Thomas Hardy, when I came to read him that first semester, must have seemed the literary equivalent of Bach. But it did not occur to me that I might write myself, until a well-meaning friend introduced me to the poetry of e. e. cummings. I don't remember what it was in cummings I read. It might have been "I Sing of Olaf, Glad and Big." Whatever, in that poem I felt the connection between the soul of the maker and the thing made, just as I'd had glimmers of it in jazz, in Bach. Only this time, the material was language. Didn't I have access to the same language as cummings? It seemed so simple, this matter of poetry. Anyone could do it.

Pure ignorance, then, led me to write my first poem, and in that state I wrote many others. Ignorant of craft, blind to the subtleties of technique, I believed nonetheless that I was proclaiming my birth to the world. That's the way it felt to write in those days.

Halfway through that first semester, I switched my major to music and announced to the organist on the music faculty at OU my desire to play Bach on the pipe organ. She was a tall, stately woman who, unlike the blind Frenchman, looked plenty majestic enough to play Bach with strong feeling. Have you studied piano, she asked politely.

It embarrassed me to have to admit that the only instrument I had truly "studied" had been the accordion. Adding that I played the baritone saxophone surely gave me no more credibility. But if she was amused, she didn't show it. She calmly assigned me to a graduate student for lessons in the organ, and this teacher, for all her patience and encouragement, gently suggested at the end of the year that I might profit from a year or two of piano lessons. Then I would be better practiced at the keyboard and could return to the organ if I so desired.

I must have imagined that whatever I admired I could become. Or possibly I had to believe that the admirable qualities I observed in others must lie dormant in me, awaiting only the right moment to blossom forth. It was a hard lesson, forsaking music. Looking for music in my soul, I had found words. Why couldn't there be both?

I grew discouraged. My girlfriend, who had loaned me her saxophone and given me the shivers with her coloratura soprano, broke up with me. And my father, who had been paying my college bills, ran out of money and declared bankruptcy. After three semesters, then, I quit OU, left my musical ambitions behind, and lit out for the territory.

The territory was San Francisco.

I went to San Francisco instead of New York because I had seen a propaganda film put out by the House Un-American Activities Committee. The film meant to expose demonstrating Bay Area students as dupes of the Communist conspiracy, but the idea of an Un-American Activities Committee seemed obviously Un-American to me, and those students who were protesting, trying to call attention to this blatant contradiction, holding their ground in the face of powerful water hoses, looked heroic. I could not imagine such a demonstration occurring at OU.

Of course I had heard other things about San Francisco. A bohemian friend from high school — the drummer in our jazz band, the same friend who had introduced me to the poetry of e. e. cummings — had been out there. He spoke enthusiastically of San Francisco's hills and views, its blue bay and bridges, its coffee houses and jazz clubs. It had all the advantages of New York, he said, but without the grime and ugliness. San Francisco was where the Beats lived, reciting their poems to the accompaniment of jazz. I had tried to read Kerouac and found him boring, certainly no Hardy, but I admired the idea of the beats and was ready to be on the road.

The glories of San Francisco are well known and all of them true. At least in 1961 they seemed true. Everything about that city spoke to me of energy and beauty and joy. I could not get enough of it, walked up and down its hills for hours at a time, exploring every neighborhood, awestruck by the ocean, the blue bay, the cliffs, the billowing fog, the sea-flavored wind, the swaying palms and shaggy eucalyptus trees, the flamboyant rhododendrons and tulips, everywhere a spirit of inclusiveness, generosity, a kind of contained abandonment.

In San Francisco I fell among literate friends who urged on me their books and their enthusiasms. Their enthusiasms were easy enough for me to embrace: existentialism, zen, poetry, wine, low-priced ethnic cafes (Chinese, of course, and Italian, but also Basque and Filipino), flamenco guitar and Delta blues, Dostoevsky, foreign films (especially Fellini and Bergman), Kandinski and Klee, and of course the left-wing politics I'd seen dramatized in the HUAC propaganda film. With some of these friends, I attended my first demonstration, against a developing entanglement that in 1961 was obscure but, to us, ominous: Vietnam. Eggs and epithets were hurled at us as we marched in a long double-file line the half dozen or so blocks from Union Square to City Hall, but no policemen with fire hoses met us there, and I remember mainly a spirit of fellowship so cheerful and innocent it might have been Presbyterian.

I was writing constantly, calling it poetry, never more than a single draft for each outburst, and I had a sympathetic audience in my friends. One night as we sat around a tiny FM radio listening to "The Midnight Special" on KPFA, I rose to go to the bathroom and promised that I would return with a poem. I came back with a few lines scrawled on the little spiral pad I always carried for those moments when inspiration struck, and to my shame I read the lines aloud, expecting applause and getting it. Our pact was to take each other seriously. And, by and large, we were deadly serious, even when consuming large quantities of cheap wine, arguing endless Sartrean conundrums, and in blissful frenzy dancing to scratchy recordings of Ravi Shankar's sitar or the sound track from *Never on Sunday*. I loved these friends dearly, and not, I think, just because in taking me seriously they affirmed my illusions about myself. Their interests were wide-ranging and intense, serious in the best sense of the word. In their company I was educated.

At the same time I resumed my formal education, taking evening courses at San Francisco State College while working part time as a shipping clerk for a small publishing company. At S. F. State I cleverly avoided declaring a major by finding a different adviser each time I registered; that way I could take only courses that sounded interesting. A course called "The World of Symbolic Forms" turned out as good as it sounded, with readings in Erich Fromm, Joseph Campbell, and William York Tindall in the first part of the semester and then on to *The Brothers Karamazov* and *Heart of Darkness*.

To my delight, I found that you could take a course called creative writing. Handing in for assignments the poems that I would be writing anyway, I thought I was getting away with something. But in Daniel Knapp, who taught those introductory creative writing courses, I had a reader who combined sympathy and judgment. If my friends mainly applauded me, Daniel Knapp — and, later, Kay Boyle — more soberly showed me how much I had yet to learn. You've got to forget about Hemingway, Kay Boyle admonished us, if you're going to write your own fiction. This advice I found easy to follow since I had not yet read Hemingway. Another teacher, Wright Morris, fervently announced that literature and life were vitally connected, and he went on to speak of long-dead writers as if he harangued them daily. He referred to Stephen Crane with affectionate exasperation as "That Boy."

I wrote my first short stories as assignments in creative writing courses. The habit took hold. Fiction answered for something that poetry did not. It rushed in to claim the territory music had abandoned and it has occupied that territory ever since.

A commonplace in those days (perhaps a legacy of the Beats, our mid-century romantics) was that writing could not be taught. Writing—at least the writing that mattered most, the exalted arts of poetry and fiction—was the province of mystery; it cavorted with the divine. Mystery, yes, and we certainly do need all the inspiration we can get, divine and otherwise, but I'm not ashamed to say that much of what I know about writing was taught to me, and if I had been humbler in those days, less ready to believe in my own bright destiny, I would have been taught even more and would have been farther along than I am today.

One thing for sure that I might have learned from Wright Morris is that the place you come from and how you remember it matters. It is your territory. I knew that some writers made quite a to-do about their home places, but I believed that in coming from Oklahoma I had been severely disadvantaged. Ever since that abortive departure for New York at age three, I had been longing to escape from Oklahoma. When I began to write fiction, I was grateful for being in a new place, San Francisco. Now San Francisco certainly was exciting, and one day I hope to return to it in fiction, but in turning my back on Oklahoma I was condemning myself to years of imitation. Imitation can be all right, of course. I recommend it as an exercise in becoming conscious of craft. But when it remains unconscious, when all you can do is rewrite your literary influences, then it becomes a near-fatal hindrance. This is surely what Kay Boyle had meant when she said you had to forget about Hemingway. My fiction remained literary, academic, directionless, until I remembered where I was from and began to acknowledge that place as part of me.

When I began truly to remember, then I began to imagine. It seems strange to say that it might be difficult to imagine the place where you grew up. But that is precisely the problem with familiar places: they become unimaginable. As for remembering truly, well, I mean that the mind plays false with memories when it persuades you that you are in some sense beyond what you remember, distant from memory, a long ways from home.

For several summers running, my father took us out of Oklahoma. We went to Colorado, to Lake City, in the rugged, remote San Juan Mountains, where for five dollars a day we rented a three-room ramshackle house alongside the south fork of the Gunnison River. I remember the excitement of leaving Oklahoma City, the pleasing sense that the land was beginning to slope up toward the invisible peaks of Colorado — but such a long time before those blue mountains could be seen! Once there, my sisters and I repeatedly climbed on the smallest of the surrounding mountains, my father headed for the streams, dreaming of rainbow trout, and my mother, surely bored to tears, waited in that dingy house for the rest of us to return. In the late afternoon, my father always brought back a creel packed with sleek trout. He expected my mother, at least for a while, to clean his trout as well as cook them. My sisters and I, ever ingenious in avoiding chores, returned from our expeditions too tired to help. I might as well be in Oklahoma, my mother often said, and though I saw the truth of her statement and wished that she might feel otherwise, I looked to my own enthusiasms to see me through and keep me oblivious to her unhappiness.

In this way I followed the example of my father, I am sure. He wanted to leave Oklahoma behind, if only for a few weeks out of a long year spent traveling up and down the state, hauling his sample cases of class rings to one school district after another. In those deep, swift waters of the Gunnison River, he was after bigger game than trout. I failed to understand that, professed to care nothing for fishing, but it was in his spirit that I scurried up the rocky slopes of the mountains in order to look down on the distant village below. I had to come to terms with that spirit in my writing, and at the same time do justice to the truth of my mother's Oklahoma, for I had plenty of her spirit as well. Even if my mother and father would not, in the long run, be able to reconcile themselves to each other, I had to orchestrate a new union, and on common ground. That common ground was Oklahoma.

What was Oklahoma, though? How could I begin to imagine it? I began by reading Oklahoma history. No doubt this course seemed safely abstract, even academic. But the history of Oklahoma engaged me immediately, and not just intellectually. There was something else, the sounding of an emotional depth. Significantly enough, this new passion for Oklahoma history was something I held in common with my father. It became clear to me early on that just as the history of Oklahoma, with its "progress" from Indian Territory to statehood ("Tepees to Towers" was a fifties' Chamber of Commerce slogan), mirrored the history of the nation, so did the history of my family partake in the history of the state. I listened again to the stories my parents told of their lives, their families. Through the memories of my father and my mother, then, I saw how my life, all our lives, came to mean more than we could know. The self, I began to understand, was as spacious as a continent — more so, I understand now: it is a territory without borders, depthless, its history is infinite, its language is memory.

I will remember, finally, only moments:

The grayness of the Oklahoma Historical Society, grayness inside and out, the grim persistence of seekers after genealogical fact, how they labor to find the lost kinfolk, the birthdate, the wedding, the death that will at last link known and unknown. A kind of art, after all, a problem of conception.

The gravel road in Arkansas that leads to Uncle Johnny's house, the white dust billowing up behind the car, and then the sight of a two-story unpainted clapboard house that looks, in my memory, gangly, lean, gray, but with a broad front porch. Tall, leafy trees, taller than any in Oklahoma, line the dirt lane. A tire hangs by a thick rope from one of the trees. My cousin Johnny Sue's smile is as sweet as summer melons, and the barn smells of manure and hay and animal sweat.

The Children's Hospital in Oklahoma City. Seven years old, I am on the polio ward for two weeks, quarantined. The nurses have pushed my bed to the window so that I can look down into the parking lot two stories below. At first I see only the rows of cars, bright chrome gleaming in the afternoon sunlight, but then I see them, my father first, alongside the fender of his latest DeSoto, and then Mother, standing to one side, holding up baby sister Jan, and Sissy there too, all of them looking up at me, suddenly waving, smiling.

My father's study. He sells class rings but he also designs them, and here is where he does his sketching, painting, clay-modeling, often working late into the night. It is a small room that has been added onto the garage. To get to it from the house, you have to go out the kitchen door and then across the driveway. A bushy cedar almost blocks the entranceway. With the assistance of a carpenter friend, my father has made the room himself. I have watched the two men guide sheets of plywood into the teeth of the screaming circular saw. Stand back, my father tells me. Stand back, son. Now he sits at his desk in a circle of fluorescent light, magnifying lenses strapped to his forehead, and as he strokes color onto the sheet of paper he seems to hold his breath.

The garage on a summer night, musty, dark but not pitch black, on one side the DeSoto, massive and sleek, and on the other side a plethora of old magazines, newspapers, books, phonograph albums, scraps of lumber, dusty grocery sacks filled with discarded clothes, and there is my father's workbench, jigsaw, circular saw, the lawn mower, rakes and hoes and shovels randomly leaning, hanging from nails in the wall, lying on the floor. I've cleared a space and sit on the smooth, cool concrete, my ankles crossed, rummaging in the sacks of old clothes. My father works in his study, and inside the house my mother and sisters have the television on. In one of the bags I find a pair of my mother's shoes, sling pumps, high heels, and I put them on. They fit fine, I stretch my legs out, liking the way the shoes look, and I stand, a little wobbly, take a few steps, getting the feel of them, practicing, then walk out of the garage, the heels clicking on the concrete, too loud, and I hurry to the lawn. My father has watered the grass that day, the high heels sink in the softened ground, I almost lose my balance, have to get back to the street. Then it is all right, it is fine. Stepping lightly, I don't go far, no more than a block, no one sees me, and when I return to the garage I put the shoes back exactly where they were.

The warm wind, the red, rutted dirt, the weeds along the road blown almost to the ground. I'm thirteen years old and riding the Sears motorscooter, paid for with money that my mother has saved from her grocery allowance. It's a county road, narrow, the asphalt sticky like tar beneath the small tires of the scooter, and I have that road all to myself. Nobody knows where I am. The land is flat, the road stretches on and on, the great empty sky abounds. Maybe I will get somewhere, maybe not.

How easy we slip from our skin. The body is nothing to the soul.

Books

Loving Belle Starr (novella and stories). Algonquin Books, 1984.
Fiddle and Bow (novel). Algonquin Books, 1985.
The Lost Sister (novel). Algonquin Books, 1989.
Close and Distant Kin (stories). Algonquin Books, 1992.

Anthologies

"Colorado." *Best American Short Stories*. Eds. Shannon Ravenel and Anne Tyler. Houghton Mifflin, 1983.

"Later Phases of the Western Migration." *Ohio Review: Ten-Year Retrospective Issue*. Ohio University, 1983.

"Where Are Our MIA's?" *Our Roots Grow Deeper Than We Know*. Ed. Lee Gutkind. University of Pittsburgh, 1985.

"The James Boys Ride Again." *Necessary Fictions*. Eds. Stanley Lindberg and Stephen Corey. University of Georgia Press, 1986.

"Letha Posey's Husband." *Descant: 25th Anniversary Issue*. Texas Christian University, 1986.

"Mourning." *The Ways We Live Now*. Eds. Joyce Carol Oates and Raymond Smith. Ontario Review Press, 1986.

"The Spirit of Belle Starr." *Best Short Stories from the California Quarterly, 1971–1985*. University of California, 1986.

"The Tennessee War of the Roses." *New American Short Stories*. Ed. Gloria Norris. New American Library, 1986.

"Lady of Spain." *Best American Short Stories*. Eds. Shannon Ravenel and Ann Beattie. Houghton Mifflin, 1987. Also in *Prize Stories: O. Henry Awards*. Doubleday, 1987. Also in *New Stories from the South*. Ed. Shannon Ravenel. Algonquin Books, 1987.

"The Revealed Life of Cole Younger." *Editor's Choice*. The Spirit That Moves Us, 1987.

Periodicals

Seventy stories have been published in magazines such as *Agni Review*, *Ascent*, *Columbia*, *Georgia Review*, *Hudson Review*, *Iowa Review*, *Missouri Review*, *New Letters*, *North American Review*, *Ohio Review*, *Ontario Review*, *Prairie Schooner*, *Shenandoah*, *Southwest Review*, *Transatlantic Review*, and *Western Humanities Review*.

David Steingass

David Steingass has degrees from Capital University, the University of Maine, and the University of California at Irvine. He has been a Bread Loaf Bridgman Poetry Scholar and a MacDowell Colony Resident Fellow and has received a National Endowment for the Arts Fellowship, as well as the first Chandler Writing Award, in 1988, from the Council of Wisconsin Writers. He has taught at several major universities, including the University of Wisconsin, and now is tenured at the University of Wisconsin, Stevens Point and Madison. He also serves as a freelance writing program consultant and writer-in-residence for public schools and summer conferences throughout the country. He lives in Madison, Wisconsin.

TALKING TO MYSELF AGAIN

What do we want besides the brash real story, all of the ways it happened? Poem ideas in my notebooks fly stories like colored ribbon. Since one trick of writing poems is translating energy — the stories — into lines — the poem — I'll touch none of the notebooks for fear of dispelling what attracts me. I'll tell some stories whose ideas I've already sweated through into poems.

Ideas are mostly accidents, circumstances the act of writing lets wander into their own possibilities. A smile reminds me of a girl whose brother I was friends with and lost track of. When I saw his face on TV I thought of a poem, the half memory, half-surprising accident that discovery can take ("What we saw together in the woods / And took into ourselves through different eyes," from "Television Reports of Vietnam," *Body Compass*). Or, typing the title of my poem "GreatPlains," I couldn't think of the heroine's name until I mistyped "Greta."

Accident is my answer to "How (or why) did you begin writing poems?" I wanted to be a writer in high school though I didn't know what either the word or the life meant. I'd read "Fog," "Days," "Patterns," and O. Henry and Jack London stories, but I thought a poet was someone dead four hundred years: Chaucer or Shakespeare. Mostly, I studied pictures in the books which filled our house: Pyle's editions of King Arthur and Robin Hood, the *Conrad Argosy*, the *Arabian Nights*, and stark woodcuts in an edition of *Moby Dick*, seed catalogs.

Though I didn't understand my life as material for poetry I loved words, the names of things, the cadences of swearing or animal sounds, the sensations filling the farm I grew on. One-man bands are musical equivalents, lips, knees, feet, hands, head, each playing separate instruments: a conglomerate song dripping with sense like my life in backwoods Ohio. I visualized words as objects, say loaves of bread or apples, each with distinct sensuousness. Until I was eight or so my best conversations were with animals. If someone would have told me that raccoons, noggin stones, and beech trees — my favorites — lacked "humanity," I'd have known they were incapable of the perception I enjoyed daily.

from "Dialect"

... I worshipped feathers and stones,
wasp and puff ball citadels,
each turtleshell or snakeskin that measured
my hand, and hummingbird-nuzzled clefts
behind each ear. . . .

I loved splicing, knots,
plain histories the dirt wove
in my toes. I held so still
shadows climbed my legs, rode
each shoulder. I hoped I'd grow
to be a beech tree,
my shining limbs
spectacular.

One day in the woods I saw the head of a fish swimming out of a tree trunk. The woods held great gods. One of them was a silence so immense it trapped all sound but that of blood in my ears. Others were space, and distance. My father said starlight could take so long to reach earth its stars had since blown up. If that were true, I thought, what about my fingers touching mossy rocks? Are they each what they seem?

So I knew either the fish I saw or the tree was magical. I loved being able to think that way, and I glory in retaining the ability today. When I snuck for a closer look, I saw a northern pike's head nailed to the tree. While I tried to picture who would do such a thing, the fish stayed real in dreams and years later became more real through the process of poem.

The Pike King

I waited where he swam, halfway
Out of beech trunk, dripping, motionless
The way fishes pause like half-formed thought

Where weeds end. When he slid past his belly
I nailed him, half home in this world and growing
As he left his own. What better chance

Do any of us get, threading our killer
Shadows among leaves? His crown a trick

Light filtered, his fins a riffle

Wind scratched along the beech trunk,
The Pike King glistened in a gravel vein
Sifting the trunk to stream. When I found bark

Healed where he'd hung, I heard the wind
Trace wings the Pike King grew
To swim beyond our night.

It's possible I saw the Pike King the same summer I walked into woods and looked into a hollow stump for the first time. My face in a pool of water in the chill and creepy world of ferns and toads and mushrooms was different from the David I watched in the mirror each morning. Hollows and shadows and darkness made an exciting "burnish," I can say now, and a quality of romance. Was it possible, I wondered, that I was actually two different people?

Face in the Stump

The face you found mired in stump water, a dim
mirror in the woods,
wrinkles stranger each day.
Sudden as loose ambition, mud
oozes from bracken clouds straight

for your life. How did you look, those eons
before you pulled yourself through weeds?
Your shoulders still slide, fish parts
moving perfectly. Were there ever wings?
Can you remember fur's deep grace

warm on your joints? You still sleep where you land
and burn with the legend you felt
thrum the hollow stump,
a sleep you can't recall once
shaken water wakes you glistening.

The first deity I knew, outside of the woods, was a Percheron named Dick. I sat crosslegged on his back or stretched out as though I were lying on a hammock. His humid smell, the sense of power and transport beyond myself, was the physical equivalent of poetry. I felt blood and breath thud through him. Eye level with fur, I understood the edge of Dick's body as the horizon of my world.

No catalog of circumstances amazed me more, however, than that of my mother's life. Her energy seemed measureless and unqualified, her appetite for life fearless. Her benchmark never to do only one thing at a time I later labeled "double-clutching," and still use to gauge real achievement. She cooked everything from Easter lamb cakes to blood pudding when pigs were slaughtered. She sewed fur coats for girl relatives. She led the church choir, bottle-fed baby pigs, and taught grade school. Like her mother, she believed in parable and proverb ("Don't worry, David. You can't die until you eat a peck of dirt") and that people were limited in accomplishment only by their energy. I still feel her pulse of populism, her faith in New Deals, Sears' mail order, and the pressure cooker's bath to seal jars of tomatoes. She brought the dictionary ("greatest book ever written") to the table for crossword puzzles, and into my life.

The Day Lightning Called

The day the telephone bit my mother's ear
we saw her crossword take shape, and watched clouds stack
purple flatirons, their eerie smolder
threaten the sky. Heat lightning crawled
the way lines of humid rash itched
out of reach along our backs. Our green faces turned
phosphorescent. Humidity's dirtiest wash hung
our skins, air's damp fire pressed close.
Rain skittered and we shivered
under nervous sparks. When the phone rang, lightning
hooked the receiver a full hand
out of its cradle. "No," we screamed, while it rang
eight times more, "don't!"
as she picked it up. Midnight streaked our faces
dark as a seance when she said "Holy Morier,"
and shifted its haunches as though crosswords met
where lightning broke, a sky-wide party line.
Our farm gathered the sound a freight careens
down cellar stairs. "What in Blue Tunket!" she said,
as though the phone turned wacky somewhere
between anvil and stirrup. Then we saw lightning
snake its cord, try to plug its last word
straight into mother's ear. The day night called
and the tornado zoomed in at noon
my mother overheard and held her own,

telling what's what, giving back good
as each new word she got
across and down.

Among my father's accomplishments was building a barn after teaching school all day. Mother roped up tools and moved the tractor anchoring rope and pulleys which hoisted tree-trunk rafters my father nudged into slots. Too young to do anything but watch, I was reminded of elaborate cartoon gizmos designed to scratch backs or rock babies by remote control. They featured belts, pulleys, hinges with which to harness such random energy as animals' tails switching flies or dogs running treadmills after chicken heads: marvels of congealed energy. I remember my father against the wind; the sky moving behind him made everything sway and my stomach churn. Years later I looked at some of Chagall's paintings and felt in them a similar energy which gradually made this poem possible:

Threading the Sky

What did you do the day wind spoke
to your life? I saw my father fly,
cling to bark-freckled beams he inched
along air — one more tree he'd stripped
to bone. His barn skeleton rose like a gate
I felt the wind work

to open. Knees wrapping clouds,
he swayed trunks like frozen chain to airy slots
he called "threading sky." His coat billowed
like the man's above Chagall's village. The same hands
crawled their windy orbit, the splendid river
constellations trail through night. His shout

struck like the one anthem wind
could hone along beams. "Stars stand in air,"
he yelled. "You won't fall, you can't. . . ."
I felt his voice catch the wild
blues and yellows threading the sky, the purple
yearning that wove our lives.

Fifteen years later when I'd started college, our family discovered C. P. Snow's *Two Cultures*, science versus humanities (in our house, whatever science wasn't). "I can't understand poetry," my father argued to my "I can't understand electricity." We were arguing the same point, I see now, opposite sides of one issue, saying "love" to the tune of conflagration. The poetry of physics, the mathematics of language; mechanics of the universal. When my father went nuts over UFOs in the 1950s and 1960s, I understood it as poetry's revenge for saying "science is nothing without mathematics." I was unable to understand math except as people who ran around with slide rules flapping at their belts, the intellectual equivalent of linemen for the county. I've written several poems on the farmer-science teacher polarity, my wonder at the strangeness of "night" and "light":

St. Einstein's Stars

1
Each winter night
the telescope launched him from window sill
to UFOs — "St. Einstein's stars" —
my father stood bone-thin beside my bed,
relentless as a ghost
caught in starlight.

2
When he reached into night
I saw the black fields break
and fall from his hand in misted arcs.
Each tree of fantastic
feathered limbs and winged leaves
grew at his fingertips to light.

3
His hands sank to night-
colored, soot-pungent seed and cast clouds
across the meadow to explode
in summer heat. Dawn caught each seed
flying to blossom, a tiny star blazing
with dark light.

As a boy I made balsa airplane models, loom and lazy-stitched Indian beadwork; I sewed ribbon appliqué, and collected, washed, and boxed eggs, all matters of precise process. I also did nothing at all for hours besides study dragonfly wings or beech trees. Watching a dragonfly move through a tree, I'd ponder the similarities between wings and leaves, how breeze and shifting clouds affected them.

I began to sense a calm center within concentration, an almost languid heart in any perception. There was always the possibility the next dragon would forget the fly part, or clouds become what they resembled, or that I'd change into one of the forms I sensed moving around me. I learned to study colors, shapes, patterns, and to see ordinary objects in more than one way. There's great daydreaming and motionlessness about any project until things begin "to dawn," in my mother's words, in the receptive mind. I recall the day I saw turkey and chicken legs as scales on snakes' or on carps' sides, and cats' snake-like curl into cushions for naps. One of the first things I showed my son was the treeline inside a butterfly violet's blossom.

A Prayer For Children

Your child points to the treeline
crouched inside each butterfly
violet blossom. She wonders who lives
along such tiny trunks, inside the sea
of roots. He says as Aquaman
he'll talk riddles out of under-
water creatures. She squirms in his bones
they'll swim years before each fits.

I learned to improvise to make tedious jobs end. I never hear the naming frenzy in "Rumpelstiltskin" without recalling swatting flies outside the kitchen door. Naming each fallen soul I flew along the alphabet, perhaps recapping each letter's entry before proceeding:

Ann, Anna, Alice, Alan, Adam, Ajax, Ace;
Alfred, Allison, Alois, Andrew, Anthony;
Anastasia, Alcibides, Anemone, Anemone, Anemone.

I used the same process for baseball. As pitcher, umpire, fielder, and batter I bounced inning by inning from the back-stop through double headers to world series, creating stats, nicknames, personalities. Real teams never equaled the first excitement of talking to myself and hearing my voice answer the needs of isolation and aloneness.

Mark Twain called riverboat captains the last totally free and unfettered beings on earth. The river Twain knew is gone, but a poet's life still reminds me of his definition, "free" and "unfettered." His or her life, reading, and determination control the show. Nothing is more important than the hand which puts words to paper.

In this context, I want to owe no money or be otherwise vulnerable, and to hold no job to which I contribute my consciousness in routine fashion. No good comes from worrying about money, but I applaud the man who refused a substantial inheritance because "psychic maintenance of large sums of money is too great." We can't eat words, but neither can we sing with a head full of dollar signs. I take that back. A head full of decimal points and stock margins is prone to sing mostly clichés.

A poet's job is to stay alive honorably and unobtrusively while discovering a process of using language well enough to develop his notebook of ideas; that is, to transform mere being into luminous self. In Boy Scouts, for example, I cooked from scratch, mixed biscuits on the trail, chopped tomatoes for spaghetti sauce. As a poet I operate in a similar way, developing original recipes based on the "feel" of things. Poems are one-of-a-kind flavors of life.

In our society poetry writing seems to me subversive, in essence as well as in practice. Although officially championed, "individual" work — psychic exploration and discovery — is devalued in practice. By "individual," America implies something like one of many privately maintained cogs universally adaptable as business components. A poet, however, must constantly and passionately replenish the reserves of wonder. Many connections are possible, for example, among speed of light, complexion of galaxies, process of thought, and scattering of dreams through sleep. The poet departs from that connection which most compels his consciousness, and arrives at other connections apparent only through the unconsciousness. Tiny things like hummingbird eggs become important, their gem-like unexpected vibrancy establishes a fabric of innerconnection poets search out. A poet is willing to make mistakes, and plenty of them, schooled in the curriculum of accident on the way to insight.

The rewards of poetry writing are self-knowledge, a peculiar quality of thought which can balance apparently unrelated details until they begin to resemble each other through metaphor, and the ecstatic sense of organization called the poem's form. The poet also might gain respect and admiration from people whose life and/or work he or she admires, as well as an ability to appreciate the world in unexpected ways.

The difficulty of writing poems which weighs heaviest on me is a sense of the inadequacy and frailty of language robbed by our society of instant valuation and reward based often on little more than propaganda. This argument hasn't been new of course since Orwell's "Politics and the English Language," but the fact doesn't lesson its burden. Currently, for example, "Get your education — business needs increasingly skilled workers" is a saw to keep kids in school. In our society, which uses language to confuse ("education" in the sentence above) and to manipulate (advertising, politics, law, pop music, film, and novels), the process and order of thought a poem requires to be written, read, and understood (not to mention the sheer energy and psychic risk) are often too great an effort of faith to attempt. As a culture we cry out for poetry; we get Hallmark-card emotion, beer ads, hillbilly songs, and bumper stickers.

How important are poems? A single one might take years to finish and publish, and then not succeed the way it glimmered in my mind. Still, I like David Wagoner's newspaper interview comment: "Those who do without poetry should imagine their lives without music." When I build poems I think in ways which lead nowhere in "reality," but which allow me to contact the person I was before I learned to tie my shoes, the day Dick-the-Percheron stepped on my bare foot while he was being harnessed. Writing allows me to feel my foot sink harmlessly into muck again, and to use my relief to equalize other moments in my life. The product of constant sifting and winnowing of memory, poems are handmade psychic heirlooms I delight both in reliving and in living up to.

Monster

> *"I try to catch . . . the tip of the nose . . . push the bone into the brain."*
> — Mike Tyson

We shell out fifty million bucks to scream
the two-legged death to life
we'd all become, we had the nerve
to lose ourselves in the snake-eyed pool
where fear drowns thought.
                    Dazzled by strength
we feel our lizard brains grow claws
and prowl our skin. We watch his muscle glisten
like snakes thrashing in roots.
We cheer his obsession to break
what doesn't work
                    but want to be remembered
as the child who won't leave, who grows skeletal
beside the open grave. We hold breaths for life
and save from darkness what we pull from shadows.
We long to stop looking over our shoulders
and to wash the blood from our hands.

Building a poem like "Monster," I feel myself answering questions I'm not aware of asking. Any poem provides levels of monologue, a little like themes of a dream, within the context of language. I experience the sensation as an unexpected breeze on a day impossible with heat and humidity. There's something of release about the process, and of salvation.

Touching the Earth

To stand on shovels and feel the earth stumble
along my chill spine . . . nothing to tell over pears
and marzipan, each wife stripped to her best dress

and hungry for winestem-talk, a casual formality
lashing her eyes the way in the Bible
stray bushes take flame. Strangled in childhood,

her bodice careens in turmoil, peonies burst
to prowl the night, the wilderness beyond thought.
I yell for iced vodka, red onion halos,

dragon tartar. Oak leaves dance in her hair.
The buried world rubs her speech, clings the flesh
she'd translate as wax. One hand she forgot

drifts in a new shape, the unknown territory
she dreams. The old journey, the urge to lie
and swim again, to wander back lost in the dark.

Similarly, I feel poems present themselves as rewards for the occasion of pondering memories so old I can't recall life before them (so take them as foundation stones of personality), and for following their trails long enough through words that I find something I hadn't noticed. I wonder where in my reading of fairy tales and American Indian legends, for instance, feelings about twilight and woods merged so that this poem began to rise:

What Night Begins to Tell

Think of the child lost in your flesh,
the bear smell dancing his thought.
Imagine he brings you again tonight
a story he's known all his life:

the bear he saw step from bark,
the huge fur he can't understand
he feels stretch in shadow and walk
big as the woods through your dreams.

The bear who knows we are deadly
takes your sleeve in your teeth.
All you've forgot led you here
where woods still begin. Imagine.

I recall purplish humid summer twilight shadows the sun raised by fecund steam among ferns as heavy, almost, as tapestries or pelts.

Finally, poems seem to become evidence, almost relics, in the original sense of "poem" as a piling up, or an arrangement. Some of the following poem comes from my childhood sight of dew-covered watermelons in the garden as shiny striped fish (Pike King relatives, maybe); some more from old maps in which "unknown territories" held fantastic and mythologic creatures. From whatever origins, these perceptions made me realize I wanted to know more about the place I'd visualized only in dreams, a Brigadoon or Shangri-la.

from "In the Country at the End of the World"

We all begin rich, deep in dirt and gleaming
like star-nosed moles. And we pick watermelons
sleek as fish or dewy boulders, packed with flat
chocolate chips. . . .
                    In the sauna's darkness
our skins crawl to fur, our hair twists
into vines. Our fingers weave a wondrous cloth
of dark tendrils. Lizards dance all night
beds our tongues fill. Their claws shiver
beneath skin, rake stones' chill history
along our spines. Where acids flip our stomachs
synapses swirl. A mineral glisten our nerves spin
glides as fandangos the water leaves
rock to hold and light to find.

Discovering another writer's work has always felt to me like walking through a well-ordered garden. Will there be exotics like pepper grass and flowering kale? Will the ethnics — kohlrabi and brussels sprouts — be strong and quirky? What character will tomatoes, sunflowers, eggplants show? I feel privileged to experience the coding, nicknaming process called metaphor by which a poet presents his or her world. My catalog of influences would make an essay as long as this one.

In his essay "Fires," however, Raymond Carver made a particularly important comment by naming his children as influences. I scoffed, intent to keep much of what is ordinarily human out of poems, but began to feel my son influence my poems as he had my life. One day as I was kneading bread I watched him crawl through the New Hampshire house in which we lived. I noticed him gumming what I discovered was a single-edged razor blade. Though there wasn't a scratch, I had the possibilities of accident to ponder. After I tacked the blade onto my bulletin board I began to shake as I do whenever I recall the story. Years passed before his adolescence triggered these events toward meaning.

Dangerous Bread

I kneaded bread the fall you came.
Once dough worked smooth as thighs
I felt your life arc through space.
Swing close, I thought. Catch in my hands,

grow. Dough your mother said plant in steam
rose like skin you bore tight on her belly.
You seemed to say this trick is nothing —
this dangerous, All-hallows-eve party —

my treat. Your eyes held an abalone gleam
I'd seen stare from dough. The razor blade
you picked and gummed without a scratch
proved your luck, made me see whatever we do

just gets by. Each day your voice told life,
the mystery, straight from the gut.
Now you rise from my hands like the moon's
blind side swung to light.

The possible products of accident brought this poem into focus, just as the ruptured appendix I absorbed at eighteen showed me some of the power of darkness and dream, first inkling of what later I'd recognize as poetry.

The Day I Saved My Life

Once I fell sick in camp
too weak for crunchies, too far gone to care,
a sweat like skinned grapes
clustered my brow. Coach couldn't be sure
which I'd pull from best. Could I set up,

cross or pull, keep my head down and snap
out of tight spots? Pale as death, mother's face cried
through my dreams. Coach thought I faked sick
to flag a milk-run train and wander
into Cleveland at dawn. I dreamt of Jorgensen,

the Dane who turned Christine to launch my '50s
on jokes like "Men, beware the sharks in queer
waters." I spent July twisting moonlight
spread like a shroud on my bed. Each night
I threw off the lump in my gut I covered

like a dead ball. The doctor's hands made a football
"Your body must slough its own way." Proving
I could live, I lost fifty pounds
dreaming baked Alaska, dreaming all the world
chicken-fried on my plate. Liver and onion clouds,

cacciatore rivers washed my throat to slushy
drool. Each time mother read "Hurt Hawks"
I felt their talons, their fierce eyes pierce
my life. The morning I stood I blinked,
stunned like a new calf. My skin sagged loose

as redbone pelts. My heart rattled a spindly wicker
basket of ribs my stomach rolled. Each toe's joints
clunked its handful of stones tossed
down socks' argyle-ditches.
Each elbow fishtailed the blue net

my bathrobe sleeves hung. I couldn't take a step:
my feet stumbled trying to trade air
their separate ruins of flop and flounder.
I ate tuna pizza, sauerkraut with chocolate
ice cream–smothered steak —

each plate my first, all of it piled together
not near enough! I forgot the world's edge
hawks seeded in my dreams as code
poems' secret life would guide to light.
When the doc went in, he found my appendix

"gut-shot, blown by god to bits!" I felt a knot
that day, stark as spirals wound on cave walls,
twist loose to pinwheel my skull
and lodge obsidian-smooth thought
in orbit. When he clapped my back

and sang "survivor," I felt stitches net
my belly, marvelous as the colecanth risen two
million years from Indian Ocean that summer
seized my life in possibility, knit my bursting
like a burl for choices to come.

The attack came the summer after my senior high school year, the operation a year later. I'd discovered poetry in the interim and have never looked back in the same way.

One day several years later I realized I was doing the wrong work. All afternoon I walked through woods and fields. In the city I managed to avoid streets and sidewalks. That night I wrote in my notebook, "And wandered home with adventure on my feet." Not a good line, yet I felt some realization begin; the accident allowed me to understand how *what if* begins, combines with *how so*, and leads to *how thin the veneer*. Poems isolate moments of my life which link me to deeper, more remote regions of life.

Books

Body Compass. University of Pittsburgh Press, 1969.
American Handbook. University of Pittsburgh Press, 1973.
New Roads, Old Towns (chapbook). University of Wisconsin, Platteville Press, 1988.
Ratter (chapbook). Juniper Press, 1990.

Anthologies

New Poetry Out of Wisconsin. Ed. August Derleth. 1969.

Contemporary Poetry in America. Ed. Miller Williams. 1973.
New Voices in American Poetry. Ed. David Allen Evans. 1973.
Heartland II. Ed. Lucien Styrk. 1977.
Face the Poem. Ed. Franco Pagnucci. 1980.
Tygers of Wrath. Ed. X. J. Kennedy. 1984.
Anthology of Magazine Verse and Yearbook of American Poetry. 1986–87.
From the Mouth of the Crow. Ed. Allyson Bennett. 1988.
Contemporary Poetry from University Presses. Ed. Ron Mallace. 1989.
The Journey Home. Ed. James Stephens. 1989.
Transactions of the Wisconsin Academy of Sciences, Arts and Letters. Special Wisconsin Poetry Issue. 1991.
Wisconsin Review. 25th Anniversary Issue. 1991.

Periodicals

Among magazines and journals that have published Steingass's poems are *Abraxa*, *Beloit Poetry Journal*, *Galley Sail Review*, *Mid-American Review*, *New Letters*, *North American Review*, *North Dakota Quarterly*, *Northeast*, *Ohio Review*, *Poetry*, *Poetry Northwest*, *Prairie Schooner*, and *River Styx*.

HARUSPEX

The fossil record shows I attended seventh grade in Martinsville, Indiana, around 1939. There were wars, of course, and other great doings in the chancellories and parliaments, the labs and studios of the larger world.

There is a poignancy to this dreamtime in a country's life, its adolescence (all right, *my* adolescence). How long might we have slept?

In English, that year, we put together a book. I began my juvenalia with a poem about a storm, in which lightning "stuck" a cloud. My teacher, long since parsed away, thought that "stabbed" would be a better verb. Although I think now she was mistaken, I had written my first poem, learned my first lesson in literary criticism, and had felt the power of conventionality.

I was not a top student, but on graduation day, I read a poem which I had written and partially recall. The piece ended (with vamping or rap where I can't remember):

> *May the dust of countless ages of (blah-blah)*
> *Bear us up and give us the (quack-quack)*
> *Of liberation.*

It was, after all, 1944, and I was off to the wars.

A note here for those of you who flinched at my appalling pun on "passed away" above. I am helpless before such opportunities. Many delicate moments affecting crucial relationships have been threatened or sacrificed by my use of such verbal whimsy. I have since learned to keep quiet. If I appear stunned or stoned for a moment, the observer can interpret the trance as passion, even epiphany.

The war took up millions of young men and women and put them down in places they had never heard of, under stern law, asked them to die, to kill, or to be profoundly bored.

I had been no more than fifty miles from home, and then I was in Mississippi, Denver, the Panama Canal Zone, finally beached in Indiana with three hundred dollars separation pay, three amusing medals, a fishing license, and the G.I. Bill.

The carp was said to have a mud vein, which must be removed before you dined on them. The glorious Hitler war maintained and sanctified in *our* armed forces, not the SS, a rigid, often arbitrary class structure, with separate laws, courts, and punishments. The army was segregated, racially, sexually, and, often, ethnically. The mud vein lies deep.

The fifties dreamed on, under the baby smile of Ike, but nightmares began. I was an anarchist, cynical and hopeful.

Out near the high school lies the graveyard. There is a place for me, near my brother and mother. My father chose high ground, where taps could echo. The wind rocked us, his children, grandchildren, great-grandchildren. The flag cracked metallically. There were no drinking buddies. He had drunk them, and his war, under.

He went with me to the induction center. I remember him standing there, with tissue flags over his poor shave, as I marched off. Later I found out he had tried to reenlist.

My school book was Brooks and Warren. I studied with Mr. Ransom, holding his own among us rowdies. My first publication was in *The Kenyon Review*. My peers believed, or said so, that the poem should be self-sufficient, that if it needed glossing or craft interviews or the confessional, it had failed. I still feel uneasy about recalling in prose those glowing tableaux that cast these dense shadows called poems. See, even my misgivings are dramatized.

Let's get serious and boring. After service in the Air Force, I enrolled at Indiana University. Here I could list names and "influences." I met, studied with, entertained, rejected, and/or bored John Crowe Ransom, Dylan Thomas, Sam Yellen, John Ciardi, Louise Bogan, Theodore Roethke, Ralph Caplan, Stephen Spender, David Wagoner, Alan Tate, and that thin, intense, corduroy-elbow in the spilled beer, "I wouldn't let Indiana *have* my book," Ms. *et* and her sideclique, Mr. *cetera*.

David Wagoner and I were poetry buddies. We read and wrote like lapsed vegetarians at the Donner Pass. What sneers we curled for the scholars, what glossy arrogance, what fun to be young and beautiful and poets.

The writer Lillian Smith (*Strange Fruit*) came to campus and offered Wagoner, Caplan, and me a year's free residence in an abandoned motel down South. Our friends fashioned monk's robes from army blankets. Caplan, whose father was a wholesale grocer, brought canned soup to the enterprise; Wagoner had actual cash; and I had nothing.

Within a year, Caplan had a job, I was engaged, and Wagoner was married. Entertain a glissando now, of children, mortgages, promotion, rooms, emergencies, and emergency rooms. The motel shacks lean into the kudzu, operatic with bluebottle flies, and hear the recitativo that heaved and ceiling-stared from the fresh sheets before the high risers high rose in the red clay gullywashers. If there was a night song here, it might say: "I could have been Black Mountain." Caplan, Wagoner and Woods would come into the country bar, pull back the hoods from their righteous beards, and recite for their Four Roses.

One of my tasks here is to speak of gender, whether being prostatic or ovarian influences the essence of one's poetry. If I had been born Mary Elizabeth Woods, I would not have run free in the little town. The lives of girls were closed to me. Whatever they felt and thought seemed oblique, arcane, passed among them by flashed, slant glances and cupped ears. I felt I would never know half the world's knowledge, or more, if you count womb time. The war would have planted Mary deeper, as the young men rode off to Bataan, Attu, the coughing night barracks, the cruel silliness of soldiering that would change their lives forever. I would have stayed to home, likely, John, and married. I would not have the G.I. Bill, or veteran's benefits, not even a fishing license. I would not have written poetry, probably.

But, John, what impulse took that strong-faced woman, our mother, from that farm near Danville to college, a place as remote as the Bikini Islands, to study French and come home, a distinct Flapper. Was she witty, intimidating? Did she moon before she weakened and died? Was she the poet, the singer? Why don't you remember her, John Warren Woods? Don't forget me.

"Recent studies" suggest that the egg calls to the sperm. I'm working on a poem named "Returning To the Love Canal." It will settle down, I hope, into manageable local neighborhoods, but, at the moment . . . God, is the whole mammalian enterprise some Wagnerian meistersong, a protoplastic computer, singing *come, spermhead, I need a male today?* And here we are, shaving close or attending to cleavages, already tied to a mast.

The sociological record seems clear enough. Women who have accepted traditional roles have found it difficult or impossible to fulfill themselves as artists. I have never met a fulfilled artist, male or female. Martyrs, yes, causers, smugs. If we all went off to Tahiti, we would debark in Dayton. Most of us have to pay the bills, with some nuts squirreled away for the cold time. Dear ur-Egg, it is hard to break an omelet. In one of my cryptic phases, I wrote "The tool of dissection is what we dissect." It's frustrating enough to write a poem without thinking "look, I'm a man writing a poem." Or, "I'm a

woman writing a poem about a woman writing a poem." A long
hallway of repeating mirrors. The squirrel chooses a nut for his
portfolio. Suddenly, an existential inburst stiffens his tail. I am a
squirrel behaving like a squirrel. He sits his lifetime, hardening into
topiary. The ground squirrel is called a spermophile. The egg is a
hard-shelled reproductive body, a hard nut to crack, but don't it sing
good!

I have assembled two poetry selections. The first I put together at
the MacDowell Colony. My studio had a cot, a fireplace, an enormous
piano, and several long tables. I was able to lay my poems out serially,
so that one did not occlude the other. I decided that chronology was
of no importance except to literary taxidermists, who, in my case,
would be academic.

I decided to order the book thematically. One group spoke of the
vanishing life of southern Indiana in the thirties and forties. Yes, the
town seethed with all the isms that fragment societies today; but on
an autumn day, I might lie back in the high grass on Nutter's Hill, my
body at health except for a groin hearing egg-music, and wish for
nothing but the slow turn of the earth. Up what savannah might I
drift, my egg bearer beside me, her drowsy breasts diving and
surfacing in the coffee water. Through the cattails, blurred with
gnats, the sun a struck cymbal, to a cove with a burnt pier, a sense of
dread history. She would turn her green eyes, her gravid belly to me
and ask: How do you like your eggs?

In my poem "Turning to Look Back," my icons reprimand me: my
lost mother, my father, certain women, my brother, Roy, dead in
infancy (I don't know whether you lived my life / or I lived yours), and
my grandfather:

> *I don't even know where we came from.*
> *So many graves stay open too long,*
> *so many girls lie back tonight,*
> *trying to be secret rivers in the limestone.*
> *I want those days when nothing happens.*
> *Not every clocktick needs a martyr.*
> *Let my grave be a filled-in hole.*
> *Stop shoveling me out, in the black suit*
> *I bought for my laying-in,*
> *to mourn your middle age for you.*
> *Look to your own bones, John.*

I found a group of love/loss poems. "The Touch":

When I touch your body
my hand takes your whole shape.
I am beautiful
one close minute.

It is seeing
the sculpture in the stone.
It is knowing in perfect greenness
where kneeling on the earth
would make it
flower.

I isolated a few overt lyrics, quatrains, a sestina, poems of music, restraint, faint regret. Then, the political poems. I find the voice here very unpleasant, probably because I find belief hard to come by, especially when belief is involved in human behavior. One does not have to travel to El Salvador to witness human folly. An English department faculty meeting will demonstrate intimidation and compromise; the agendas based on barely disguised, long-nurtured personal animosities; turf guarding; and the feeling that, to change one course in the curriculum, one would have to change the nature of the space-time continuum itself.

But what does all this have to do with poetry? I have not cast my entrails, or anyone's, to judge the health of Poetry in our Time. Confession is good for the ego, anyway.

I don't believe that many of us, regardless of how we pay the bills, could live if we did not believe that a felicity was possible in our lonely choice, that we might, with luck and health and persistence, put our handprint on the language and the world it configures.

Books (Poetry)

The Deaths at Paragon, Indiana. Indiana University Press, 1955.
On the Morning of Color. Indiana University Press, 1961.
The Cutting Edge. Indiana University Press, 1966.
Keeping Out of Trouble. Indiana University Press, 1968.
The Knees of Widows. Westigan Review Press, 1971.
Turning to Look Back: Poems, 1955–1970. Indiana University Press, 1972.
Alcohol. Pilot Press Broadsheet, 1973.
Bone Flicker. Juniper Press, 1973.
Striking the Earth. Indiana University Press, 1976.
Thirty Years on the Force. Juniper Press, 1977.

The Night of the Game. Raintree Press, 1982.
The Valley of Minor Animals. Dragon Gate, 1982.
The Salt Stone: Selected Poems. Dragon Gate, 1984.

Periodicals

Poems have appeared in the following magazines and journals, among others: *Chelsea, Chicago Review, Epoch, Field, Hawaii Review, Hudson Review, Iowa Review, Kayak, Kenyon Review, North American Review, Northwest Review, Poetry, Poetry Now, Poetry Northwest, Prairie Schooner, Quarterly West, Saturday Review, Shenandoah, Southern Poetry Review,* and *Tar River*.

Michael J. Bugeja

Michael J. Bugeja received his Ph.D. in English from Oklahoma State University in 1985 and has taught in Ohio University's journalism school since 1986. His awards include a creative writing fellowship from the National Endowment for the Arts and an AWP Anniversary Award in poetry. He has published three collections of poems, a book of social criticism, and a writing text. He is a contributing editor at Writer's Digest *and has been recognized by students and colleagues alike as an outstanding teacher.*

THE MUSE AT HOME

*Isn't this your life? That ancient kiss
still burning out your eyes? Isn't this defeat
so accurate, the church bell simply seems
a pure announcement: ring and no one comes?
Don't empty houses ring?*
— *"Degrees of Gray in Philipsburg"*

When Richard Hugo passed away in 1982, I was a graduate student in the creative writing program at Oklahoma State University. Back then, we studied in packs, clusters of aspiring poets huddling over desks like Dickensian clerks. We wrote poems at home, refined them between classes, and then read them aloud at an apartment or house Sunday evening, potluck poets consuming gumbo and Gallo wine.

We also played parlor games. If we were supposed to interpret a poem for class, we'd toy with it like cats with a mouse, finally slaying the muse so we could explicate and examine it posthumously. One night we wrote a mock "Degrees of Gray in Stillwater, Oklahoma," each of us taking lines and liberties with the Hugo poem: "Say your hoot owl broke down, / and fronds are hanging from its tethered bill, / shards of a tattered footfall. . . ."

Punch-drunk on poetry, we were learning to mimic voices and impress our learned mentors. We meant no disrespect. Simply, we were suffering symptoms of The Workshop Syndrome and trying to heal ourselves in a comrade's house, where poems were composed, rather than in the English department, where they were dissected. Then one of us got an idea. Somehow she had procured Hugo's home telephone number — he was bedridden at the time — and wanted to give him a ring, maybe read him our poem to make him laugh or quiz him about our mentor's explication of his. Mainly we wanted to honor Hugo for his work, which we would rather enjoy over Gallo than examine over finals.

She dialed his number — his house was not empty — and spoke to a relative who told her about the poet's deteriorating condition. He couldn't come to the phone.

"We were going to tell him how much his poems mean to us," our comrade said, as if Hugo was a member of our group.

In a way, he was.

The message was conveyed. Hugo, in a feeble voice, expressed his thanks for remembering him as his life broke down in Missoula. Thereafter, it seems, we became more serious about our work. Four of our original group are still writing and publishing poems, although we have gone our separate ways and no longer keep in touch. But that night we were touched by Hugo, affirmed somehow: our way of appreciating poems made better friends than the stone walls of workshop made neighbors.

We had made a house call, and the muse was at home.

The metaphor of a house is obvious in poetry, representing a body in which a spirit resides (as opposed to *home*, a spiritual center). As we develop as poets, we inhabit several houses until we are called home as Hugo was being called when we telephoned him that night long ago. One can draw analogies to Shakespeare's "Seven Ages of Man" in *As You Like It* or Erik H. Erikson's "Eight Ages of Man" in *Childhood and Society*, depending on how many houses one wishes to possess, literally or psychoanalytically, to become whole again.

We begin life in houses of Basic Trust or Mistrust and hope to end in houses of Integrity, the warmth of our last poetic room more natural than a hospital, a workshop of Despair.

Ideally, teachers should make house calls with little black bags of pads and sharp pencils, calling on others when the usual symptoms appear. After all, poet-mentors write creatively in houses and so should instruct creative writers in them, a natural setting, the gumbo warm and the Gallo cold.

In fact, poetry and houses are paramount in typical careers. If we publish enough we apply for grants to live in houses like Yaddo, to give readings in houses like Thurber, or to take chairs associated with houses like Elliston. We pilgrim literary houses like Dickinson's at Amherst or Frost's at Derry, marveling at all that wood.

Then why do we as mentors condemn students to workshops when what we really crave as poets are houses?

Sylvia Plath, for instance, studied with Robert Lowell in 1959 in a poetry workshop at Boston University. Lowell's career can be charted by the number of houses in which he sought residence, from Douglass House at Kenyon College to Duxbury in Massachusetts, nearer his roots on "91 Revere Street." Plath reportedly learned little from Lowell in his workshop, in which, she said, students sought to curry favor with the master; however, one can also chart her high and low points by the houses she inhabited, culminating in London with a flat in a building occupied once by Yeats, her spiritual mentor.

Sylvia, at last, was *home*.

Poets and houses are historic, poets and workshops histrionic. Imagine Emily Dickinson studying in a workshop with Walt Whitman at Amherst College, taking a seat at the arc of the requisite circle; someone has rearranged the chairs so that she cannot disappear in the back.

Tonight, she is up. Her fellow students take seats alongside her and compliment Emily's work, for friendship's sake, knowing that they will have to attack it for a good grade when Uncle Walt arrives.

Emily doodles in her notebook, little hangman nooses.

Whitman appears, strokes his beard in contemplation, and asks the class to ponder punctuation, a clue to rev their critiques. Emily's eyes roll heavenward. The class hesitates, trying to please the mentor; half of them know that Old Walt violates line lengths and so might like the dashes, and the other half plays up to the journalist in him that might take offense.

Walt has a favorite, of course, a young man who uses too many exclamation marks. "Well," the student ventures, "I appreciate what Emily is trying to accomplish, but really, if she is going to rhyme so unconventionally, then she should balance that with a more traditional punctuation." He looks at Walt for a sign of approval. "Maybe not." At this point, Emily either storms out of the workshop or completes the hangman doodle, adding a long white beard on the condemned.

The absurd scenario raises questions about poetry's place — not in society but in the telephone book: an address. House or institution? Ring the house and someone says, "Hello?" Ring the latter and someone says, "English department. With whom shall I connect you?"

The irony of using Dickinson as example is her life as poet, almost cliché: the undiscovered genius huddled over a desk by a window with a view of a churchyard, a recluse who stitches poems as a surgeon stitches wounds, leaving them as legacies in a New England house.

Emily in a workshop is as absurd to imagine as Whitman in a faculty meeting. Easier to harken Dickinson at home receiving Mrs. Josiah Holland, say, to discuss the central image in Poem 712:

> *We paused before a House that seemed*
> *A Swelling of the Ground —*
> *The Roof was scarcely visible —*
> *The Cornice — in the Ground. . . .*

Or Whitman in a Civil War–era fieldhouse, bemoaning battle-deaths in "When Lilacs Last in the Dooryard Bloom'd":

> *O what shall I hang on the chamber walls?*
> *And what shall the pictures be that I hang on the walls,*
> *To adorn the burial-house of him I love?*
>
> *Pictures of growing spring and farms and homes. . . .*

Sooner or later, almost every famous poet writes a house poem that represents a leap in development or an *ars poetica*. Elizabeth Bishop, for example, often celebrates houses, as in her three beloved ones in "The Art of Losing," perhaps her best form poem. In another traditional work, "Sestina," Bishop is obliged to use "house" as the first (and thus, most important) end-word. Bishop's "Jeronimo's House," however, stands as aesthetic, a "fairy palace" and "love-nest" that, at first glance, seems abandoned. "Come closer," she implores: "You / can see and hear / the writing paper / lines of light / and the voices of / my radio. . . ."

Bishop's muse requires close scrutiny in a house whose dimensions seem askew until we adjust our eyes to the light.

Likewise Wallace Stevens describes how to appreciate his muse, the imagination, in "The House Was Quiet and the World Was Calm." In this self-defining lyric, the reader becomes the book and the summer night, "the conscious being of the book"; as such, poet, reader, and place meld in perfection. "The house is quiet because it had to be," writes Stevens, explicating his own poem in Wittgensteinian fashion:

> *The quiet was part of the meaning, part of the mind:*
> *The access of perfection to the page.*

One of the greatest "house poets" was, of course, Theodore Roethke, whose first collection, *Open House*, established him as a major voice in 1941. Again, in the title poem, the image stands as *ars poetica*, a symbol encompassing Roethke's muse, whose truths are foreknown: "My secrets cry aloud. / I have no need for tongue. / My heart keeps open house, / My doors are widely swung."

Roethke's life is an open book, as his poems attest. My favorite house poet, however, is William Carlos Williams, who lived less than two miles from where I grew up in New Jersey—my family knew him as "doctor," not "poet"—composing masterpieces between appointments on 9 Ridge Road (which linked my hometown of Lyndhurst with Rutherford and my early life inexplicably with his).

Later, as a student, when I explicated "The Young Housewife," I struggled to unlock meaning without envisioning the local doctor, probably making a house call, and the dwelling as ordinary as mine, Williams passing solitary in his car, bowing and smiling to a young woman in negligee who could have been my mother.

Wasn't this, too, my life?

In reviewing my poems for this essay, I see that "house" is also a central image in my work, chronicling my stages or ages of development.

One of my first poems, juvenalia to be sure, was completed as I crossed the Ridge Road bridge walking home from Rutherford instead of spending four bits for a bus. At the time I was living with my first wife, Barbara, an unhappy union, in an upstairs apartment of a house on Post Avenue, two blocks from my childhood house on Forest Avenue, Lyndhurst, a Sicilian enclave.

Barbara and I had recently wed in Mirabell Palace in Salzburg, Austria, where we studied in foreign exchange, living in a building on Getreide Gasse 27, a few houses down the road from Mozart's birth house and a few blocks away from Georg Trakl's birth house on Waggplatz: a romantic setting, wasted on a mismatched couple that married too young.

We thought we had escaped our environment, only to return to New Jersey penniless and confused. I could not compose poems in our house, scene of bickering and discontent, so would walk like Robert Frost, an early influence, pacing out meter as one paces out a life and slant-rhyming like Dickinson, another likely influence, remembering better days:

Young Lovers Thawing

Strolled silently my wife and I
Beside the Salzsach River;
Mitten in glove we glowed with love
In snowdrift wintry weather.

The feather in my Tyrol hat

Bent backwards with the bristling breeze;
Although I froze in knee-deep snows
I stopped and clasped her close to me.

We journeyed home that frigid night
Through wind and snow with freezing rain,
And yet I felt ice-crystals melt
When we turned up our slippery lane.

(reprinted from Pavan*)*

I recall the thrill upon finishing that lyric, knowing the marriage would probably fail but not my career as poet, because even under the most adverse conditions — homelessness — I could trust the house of memory: the mind.

Much would transpire before I could recreate the experience of living on Forest Avenue with my family, a mother who longed to be a writer and read me Ben Jonson poems instead of bedtime stories and a father who wanted me to become a journalist; if I was going to write, he advised, I should have a manly career that would support me.

Michael Carl Bugeja was a Maltese immigrant athlete and sailor who looked like James Cagney in *White Heat* and was as tough and hot tempered at times. It took years before I could depict him in poems. Meanwhile I had divorced Barbara, wed my second wife, Diane, worked as a state editor for United Press International (fulfilling his wish for me), and was a journalism professor for Oklahoma State University, studying for a doctorate in creative writing (fulfilling my own wish).

After a decade of abandoning my dream of becoming a poet, I was pursuing it now with vigor, hosting gumbo and Gallo dinners in my Stillwater house. I would write there with more power and clarity about my father, but in this early lyric, composed after a graduate-student outing, Michael Carl made a cameo appearance:

Volleyball Becomes Soccer at the International Picnic

The Kenyans can outrun anybody
But loathe volleyball. After a point
They show off. Like drum majors
Kicking in place, they bounce
The ball to an unseen lyric
Below the measure of net.

My father danced to such music.
He beat the Depression for $11
A game and all the yolk
He could swallow. I grew up
In awe of eggs, in a house
Where anything round was kicked.

How well I know that step, the scissor
That ends a performance. I fetch
The ball, hurl it for a headstart.
There's cheering. I sidestep one, two —
They're all coming at me, footwork
I'll never forget.

(reprinted from Indiana Review*)*

Thus far as poet I was able to rely on houses of memory and regret, but the specter of my father haunted my muse as I tried, futilely at first, to come to some sort of self-reconciliation after his death. Perhaps I had loved him so much that I could not forgive his passing on, despite all our conflicts. Then the house in which Diane and I lived was the scene of a burglary, calling my manhood into question, even my voice, and symbolizing how deeply the father-ego was embedded within.

The narrative below is unembellished, a *Don Giovanni*–like father-son reckoning, one of those "gift" poems seemingly dictated by the subliminal muse:

The Visit

We don't know what
He wanted: my wife
Roused from bed,
Mumbling about the knock

In the pipes, afraid
The baby will wake,
Leaves me trembling
With current I trace

To no blanket, no blue
Spark in the night,
My hands burning,
Weightless under the sheets —

Then lights everywhere,
The crashing of things,
Scream of a thief
In the house, and me

Naked, blind without glasses,
Oblivious to all but the feel
Of a presence
I loved, feared, mourned,

That overcomes my body,
Overrides it like a father
Who knows his child will fail
If something isn't done,

And something is done,
A voice I am allowed to hear
Rise from my gut,
The words pushed out

By no breath, no vibration
In the throat, the accent
Unmistakable, booming,
Bas-'tard, *out of my home!*

He ran. The door banged
Exactly three times
Before whoever it was
Gunned his engine and screeched off,

The baby crying
In the arms of her mother
Too shaken to cry, to ask
What was beyond knowing,

Anger all over us
As if a rule had been broken
On my behalf, and now someone
Somewhere had to answer.

(reprinted from Mid-American Review*)*

Soon I would have to resolve other problems besides the specter of my father. Diane had a stillbirth, an event that also brought on a bout of writer's block. I had to come to terms with our loss, and the only way, it seemed, was to enter a house of worship, a Catholic church near the English department that featured a blonde madonna above a candle stand. I would pray to the statue for words to heal my pain as well as our marriage.

One day the statue seemed to come to life in the half dark, reawakening the muse:

For the Sculptor Whose Mary I Sing to in Oklahoma

She is blond and blue-eyed as a heroine
In a country song. Even at sundown
When windows color her shawl and candles
Blink her shadow, I'd rather sing to her

Than pray. She is the last goddess
Between Tulsa and the Aventine,
Where Diana reigned until Rome turned
Holy. At least one plebeian,

Weary of lions, sang in her temple.
Maybe he strummed a fancy lute
And was forgiven, as the cowboy
Sculptor who painted Mary's face

Was forgiven for never having known
A Jewess. This much is certain:
He knew pure women, and loved one.
This is how she looked.

(reprinted from New Mexico Humanities Review)

The Mary poem represented a poetic leap, enabling me to compose related lyrics that would become my dissertation, "The Visionary." But now I was entering the awkward house of advancing middle age, with all its bravado, doubt, and, ultimately, depression. I had a dual career, completing my degree and holding jobs as a journalism professor and poetry editor for Cimarron Review, OSU's national literary magazine. As is typical with men, I neglected my family in pursuit of greater acclaim, serving the ego and jeopardizing my basic relationships in a place, Stillwater, that suddenly seemed foreign to me.

As in my first marriage, I found myself outdoors in quiet despair:

South

So I took a walk, the usual remedy, and saw
Monarchs mate on a shoot of melon, overripe,
The orchid wings out-of-place
Above red clay, and beyond the brook
Where suds flow from the development,
Goats agraze in okra: another crop
Too wizened to gather. Then the lake
With no carp to scissor the surface,
More sepia than amber and calm enough

To frame the power plant. On the way back,
However, the sun exposed that image and set
A beer keg — sunken booty — glowing
From the debris. The goats, I assume,
Moseyed to the last clumps of milkweed
By the interstate, where monarchs were
Long gone in a pattern toward Texas.
But that was all right. For a little while
I had shut her out of my mind as a man

Shuts out too many seasons. He yields
To the still life, pasture or postcard,
But not this: a robin too weak to fly
From the path or to sage to follow
The standard migration. I'll never know
Why it picked my place to loiter, the head
Jarred to one side in judgment. I suppose
I should endow a bird with wisdom. I have
Nothing better to do, standing here,
Dumb with song, unable to enter an empty house.

(reprinted from Poet Lore*)*

In an attempt to make up for lost time, I traveled back in time, taking my family to New Jersey and Austria to resurrect the empty houses of my past. We visited my mother on Forest Avenue and strolled by my second house on Post Avenue that I shared with Barbara and finally William Carlos Williams's house on Ridge Road, smiling as we passed in my car. From there we journeyed to Salzburg, visiting Mozart's and Trakl's birth houses and my former abode on Getreide Gasse. I entered old rooms and relived old pains, trying to create new memories to supplant them but succeeding only in reviving the demons of yore. Upon our return I realized it was time to leave Oklahoma, to flee from the security of tenure and the legitimacy of a poetry editorship, to find a new house; within a few months, I applied for and won another professorship teaching journalism at Ohio University.

Diane and I found a home with a Dylan-like studio in the back. I started composing again, putting the demons to rest:

Flight from Valhalla

Music! Wagnerian arias echoing at all hours
In our heads, our emptiness operatic,
Our heathen god rising suddenly against us:
A magnificent eagle with talons
Like wrists of a pianist poised to perform
The flourish of a fantasia. We want out of here.

Let us barrel with the sun, the Orient Express
Due out of Romania, Third World refugees
Welcoming us in the sullied compartments
Of a sleeper: orphans wailing inside,
Women eating onion, men breathing vodka
In our faces! Our bags are packed.

Let Mozart lie among the ruins of his requiem,
The endless entourage of child protégés
Paying mock homage at his birth place,
Or the smitten poets on a pilgrimage
Like wise men following a pagan star
To Trakl's house. Damn your sonnets and sonatas!

Let the imperial ghosts of Mirabell Palace
Haunt the halls, the gardens weed over,
The belltower peal in the cathedral,
The bishop do penance in the residence,
And Nazis resurrect on Walpurgis Night
In the Augustiner Keller! Try to stop us.

Let the fog like Merlin's fog descend

From the battle-turrets of Hohen Salzburg
And creep along the salt river,
Transmuting other lovers in its wake,
Enveloping them as they flee from Valhalla!
Herr and Frau Lazarus refuse to look back.

There comes a point when poets stop looking back and begin the work of putting their present world into perspective, entering the final house of integrity. Now we understand the influences guiding (or misguiding) our lives and so chart a new flight plan, composing poems based on insight rather than experience, giving readers what Matthew Arnold would call our best, most humane selves. Erikson, the noted psychoanalyst, says this stage of ego is achieved only when one adapts to the triumphs and disappointments of being, originating enduring ideas.

Isn't that the hope of all poets? Isn't that what Hugo realized on his deathbed, knowing his poems would endure and enlighten empty houses?

In putting my past houses in order, I was able to let them go, a process depicted in the final poem cited here, dedicated again to my father and, alas, to all male poets:

The Club House

Who knows what I did? Ask
One too many times the way
Children do for a sign probably
To prove your love. Take me fishing
In some stinkhole in the Meadowlands,
Take me to a ball game in the Bronx,

You who dived for sponges
Off the African coast and played pro ball,
Your muscular body so different from mine,
Crusader green eyes almost American
Maybe the color would rub off on me,
Immigrant child in a Mafia enclave,

My hero, father/son mystique
In every magazine now, old hat,
Hype. No one wants to overhear
The talk we never had, the carp
We never caught, the game
We never saw or played in the park,

So let us simplify the correlative
And consider the one thing
You made besides me with your body,
A club house of window and plywood,
Shelves of plank and L-joints,
Door with sliplock so I could hide

When you flew into a rage, cliché,
Too much of that already in the canon,
No need to open another vein:
Just a door. Place of my own,
Sign of your secret carpentry
As in a manger, you pagan god,

No star over our house, club of one,
No wise men to explain
Wrath of kings, why you would take
An axe to the temple, destroy
Evidence of any bond, burn it
Door by door, pane by pane,

Plank by plank in a chemical barrel,
Closest we came to a hearth.
Too bad. Who wants to hear it now?
Everyone knows the story:
Father complex. *So we have to make it
Simple and leave out the abuse, no use*

*Embarrassing the audience, smart people
Who read magazines, who think
Cosa Nostra is #8 linguine but means
"Our affair." Let us make it
Easier on the family
Swearing none of this happened,*

*I imagined it, of course I did,
And became a poet. What proof?
How many more exhibits do we need
Anyway in the canon? How many alibis?
We're a savvy lot. We have our clubs.
When we build houses, they stand.*

(reprinted from Poet & Critic)

309

Our best poems endure and are in themselves houses of ideas — love-nests, fairy palaces — whose doors are widely swung. Readers who enter find the muse at home and the world, for a short while, perfectly calm.

Books

The Visionary (poetry). Taxus Press, 1990.
What We Do For Music (poetry). Amelia Press, 1990.
Platonic Love (poetry). Orchises Press, 1991.
The Art & Craft of Poetry. Writer's Digest Books, forthcoming 1994.

Periodicals

Poetry: *Antioch Review*, *Georgia Review*, *Graham House Review*, *Kenyon Review*, *New England Review*, and *Prairie Schooner*, among others.

Fiction: *Ascent*, *Cimarron Review*, *Denver Quarterly*, *Indiana Review*, *(INTRO)*, *Kansas Quarterly*, and *South Dakota Review*, among others.

Criticism: *Alaska Quarterly Review*, *Chariton Review*, *English Journal*, *Georgia Review*, *Indiana Review*, *Mid-American Review*, *Quarterly West*, and *Southern Humanities Review*, among others.

Daniel Lowe

Daniel Lowe has received degrees from Western Michigan University and the University of Pittsburgh, where he teaches part time.

WRITING FROM NECESSITY,
WRITING AS LUXURY

I

I do not consider myself a great storyteller, which may have more to do with my modest success — that itself an understatement — as a story writer than I'd like to admit. I have never sat comfortably in a smoky room, cocktail in hand, surrounded by friends and acquaintances, and spun yarns about my life, even as I've often envied those people who are capable of such charm. Those who know me intimately tell me that I recount the details of my life rarely, and when I do, starkly. This has less to do with a desire to appear mysterious, or, worse, Hemingwayesque, than it does with a midwestern reticence that suggests I bear my troubles silently (though I doubt this is the province of only the Midwest), and, even more, the circumstances of my family that encouraged silence.

I would argue that the events of one's childhood are no more important than the many days that reside between events, and less important than the memory of both. As children, we must find ways to accommodate what will become the events of our lives through the relatively quiet, routine days (if we are blessed with many) where we attend school, play with our friends, or do whatever may comprise a "normal" childhood. Then, as adults, we must interpret both through memory, that enormously complex psychological, emotional, and intellectual apparatus which for most storytellers is their field of study. In James Baldwin's "Going to Meet the Man," a brutally racist deputy (perhaps improbably) dreams of the childhood event that led to his racism, a "picnic" where he and his sexually aroused mother and father watched a black man being burned and castrated. In a somewhat easy psychological equation, Baldwin reveals how this event and the deputy's mother and father's response to it made the deputy the sadistic torturer he is now. This is the deputy's one story. I would argue that it is the days and years following the event, where the boy had to learn to fit this atrocity alongside perhaps his father's gentleness, his mother's love, that tell the real and more interesting story.

It may be one of the mercies of childhood that we are spared the facts of our parents' lives. My mother and father were married when they were sixteen and seventeen because my mother was pregnant with my eldest sister. By the time he was twenty-one, my father had four children. I say this in defense of my mother and father in part because, an adult now, I can imagine the difficulty of their circumstances and their triumphs over them even as I'm dismayed by their child rearing. Neither had an education. Neither had money nor a source for it. I can remember my father telling me with some shame that years after he was married, he could afford to buy no more than a wastebasket for his mother and father's Christmas present, which for me forms a rather sadly funny image, if not for its pathos.

As I was growing up, my mother had very little sense of self beyond what my father provided her. I've asked her many times how she survived that period of her life, and each time she says she simply knew nothing else, which I'm sure is true of many women who raised children in that era. During this time, my father was for the most part absent, pursuing first a teaching degree, then a master's, and finally a Ph.D. in psychology. But a parent's absence makes for its own authority, and my mother and my three sisters and I felt it keenly. His presence, then, was enhanced by it. He wasn't stingy with words of praise, but he was inconsistent with them. I remember tracing a picture of a Halloween cat and telling him I drew it, then the shame over his knowledge that I truly hadn't. His anger was unpredictable. He might say nothing to you at the dinner table or, in front of family or friends, lecture you on your poor table manners. He didn't play with us often, and when he did, his games were sometimes cruel. He'd play smash hands with us, where we'd lay our hands on the table and his large, red one would come down and smack ours. Or he'd put us in rooms or closets with no light where we'd have to struggle, terrified, to get out. I learned, though I didn't know, that these were demonstrations of his power that I couldn't resist and, as the only boy, from which I could not protect my sisters. His inconsistency with words and the specter of his physicality moved in and around the walls of that house even when he wasn't there, so as I loved him I also grew to fear him.

A child who is fearful learns to watch closely for the slightest change in the air that may bring about anger (and thus a punishment), sadness, laughter, praise. I watched closely: my mother sitting at the breakfast table smoking a cigarette, working a coffee cup in her palm so that the finger ring made a slow revolution back to her fingers; my father's jaw tensing as he sat in his armchair when our play became too loud; my father's laughter when I'd take his pipe and puff from it once or twice, or when I'd try to sing "Hello, Dolly" in a

Louis Armstrong voice. Because of this watching, I became aware of a subtlety of emotion in day-to-day life that sometimes, I'm sure, wasn't even there.

My mother wasn't always an effective buffer between my father and me, since her time was so absorbed by management of our house. As is the case with a number of families, in many ways my sisters and I raised ourselves. We ran the streets with other children, our play normal enough, our rules created amongst us through games of football, baseball, and our private little wars. But so much is served to the child through the mother and father that remains a mystery. My father, receiving his education in psychology, devalued the things my uneducated mother tried to contribute. He was able to convince her (and himself) of anything, including taking family trips with the woman with whom he told my mother he was having an affair. I didn't know any of this, and would not have known what it meant at the time, but now, remembering it, I think I understood well enough. But it's one thing to understand and speak, and another to understand and have no language with which to interpret and thus defend one's self, or at least only a language that was similar to my mother's in that it was granted no validity. So by the time my parents told us they were divorcing, at age eleven I was able to look out the window on that January day and tell myself that I had to be a man now, as I recognized the silence that that demanded of me.

My father remarried six months later, which changed him in some ways radically. He became more interested in his children then, and, with his new wife, worked hard to form a different sense of family. Within three years, one by one my sisters and I left my mother's house and moved in with him. My father and stepmother, both with degrees in psychology, wanted to foster an openness amongst us. They would frequently call together family talks, through which my father's authority remained unquestioned. During family canoe trips to Minnesota, we were required to commit our thoughts and experiences to a family journal that others were welcome to read. These circumstances were unbearable to me. For so long, in family situations, I had uttered only words of which my father would approve. I had never spoken an intimate language, the language of my psychology. And if I could have, I never would have spoken it to my father. He may as well have asked me to speak Russian. I mumbled a few words during family discussions that too often brought tears; I scribbled down a few words in the journal about how we were all getting along. I lived in dazzling astonishment at my father's denial or dismissal of the unspeakable past that had preceded these years during which, later, we would describe ourselves as close.

For a long time I feared my father, for a longer time still distrusted the quality of my memory to which he had so heavily contributed. While I was in my teens, we simply did not talk about those childhood years, as if they didn't exist, or were only a means of passage to these happier years. I lived within immediate circumstances that demanded a generous memory of my family, while a larger, more distant and urgent memory pushed that away. It took years to trust that larger memory, and to distrust one's memory is to tell no stories, or at least no stories of any depth, because the storyteller lacks confidence in his tale. When I first began to write, I wrote poetry, more because I loved the sound of words than for any other reason. When I first wrote fiction at age twenty-two — an eight-page story I labored over for five weeks — I was struck by the threads of memory that had conspired to give shape to a story that was not mine, not even vaguely similar to anything I'd actually lived or done, but had somehow presented me with a form that, in terms of memory, seemed psychologically and emotionally valid.

Through my first years of writing fiction, I often used story to galvanize memory and make it legitimate, to trust it, finally. That in itself is a suspicious statement, since, of course, my sisters remember those early years much differently than I do. One need not sit through more than one grandparents' argument during a slide show to recognize that memory, for each person, is different. This in itself is interesting. But more fascinating is how memory rises from the general stew of genetics, of culture, of family and personal history to become what it always seems to be becoming. Most often, that is what I study in my fiction: the artifacts of memory, its heritage, its sexuality, its malleability, its permeability, its psychology, its utter lack of linearity. For years I held my father and, to a lesser extent, my mother under memory's harsh glare; I have noticed how that light has been perceptibly softened by my own marriage, the birth of my two sons, my divorce, and my remarriage.

Finally, I should add that I believe there can be no end to this study of memory, no final form that embraces it all. But those whose sense of it is most solidified are probably not story writers, and more likely live well rooted in the present with a strong faith in their projected futures.

II

In *The Book of Laughter and Forgetting*, Milan Kundera provides three conditions for what he describes as the "mass epidemic" of "graphomania (an obsession with writing books)":

> *1. a high enough degree of general well-being to enable people to devote their energies to useless activities.*
> *2. an advanced state of social atomization and the resultant general feeling of the isolation of the individual.*
> *3. a radical absence of significant social change in the internal development of the nation.*

Such a statement is rather glib but nonetheless applicable to an extent, I think, in this country. One need not spend too much time and money submitting to the countless literary magazines (and here I speak from personal experience) to find that many manuscripts come back unread, with form rejections, or with the simple statement that no new submissions will be considered for two years. I don't know how many M.F.A. programs exist across the country, but the number has risen dramatically over the past decade: clearly, many, many people want to become writers.

I might argue that, while each of Kundera's criteria has relevance here, the third is most disturbing to me. I have little patience with writers or artists who, because they find their own nation and culture stagnant, long to be in another place, another time, or who decide to emigrate to Czechoslovakia because "it's happening over there." I write this in late August of 1991, just after the failed coup in the Soviet Union, when I had to suppress my own idiotic longings to be in a country where things are "exciting," a conclusion born, I believe, of inestimable ignorance and some privilege. I doubt the first thing cropping up right now in Moscow is writers' colonies, though expatriates may soon begin queuing up.

It is not that I don't have sympathy for these artists, who I must assume are predominately white and comparatively wealthy. Truly the American masses are often sluggardly: witness the yellow-ribboned response to the Mideast war, where the general citizenry was more critical of the media trying to get at the truth than it was of the government's efforts to conceal it. Or witness the popularity of TV tabloid shows such as "Entertainment Tonight" or "A Current Affair," or films such as *Uncle Buck* that enjoy immense success at the expense of a moving film such as *Boyz N the Hood*. This is not a society of intellectuals, and though I'm undecided if I want to include myself in their numbers, I share some of their disgust with American government, American popular culture, and American consumerism.

The problem with such thinking, of course, is that the majority of us who consider ourselves writers and intellectuals, within and without M.F.A. and Ph.D. programs, are members of the class of people who are responsible for "the radical absence of social change" in this country, and who are, as we know, too unwilling to sacrifice our "high . . . degree of general well-being" and the relative romanticism of "isolation." To be a writer here is often to be in a position of privilege, and, depending on what one chooses to write about, one could argue that our time might be better spent working for organizations that precipitate social change, as there is no lack of these. (And certainly some writers do spearhead such organizations.) The stance that "It's happening over there" is largely a romantic one, particularly if the naive artist expects to hobnob with other artists and absorb the air of another nation's political change by osmosis and thus have his writing electrified by political circumstances.

Having said all of this, I do not consider myself a teller of stories that are overtly political. I've written a short novel, many stories, and a number of poems, none of whose purpose is to comment on contemporary society, society at large, or society in minutiae. I have not chronicled the stories of the disadvantaged because, in most ways, I haven't suffered as one disadvantaged. I am a white male from a middle-class family. I have spent very little of my writing time—already squeezed by the responsibilities of teaching writing and raising two children—constructing essays that espouse my theories for social change, or criticizing those who subvert them. I need not defend myself: one of the great canonical myths is that great and/or true art transcends political and cultural barriers, so I might simply and arrogantly argue that the stories I write attempt to do the same. I don't believe this, of course, any more than I believe in the myths of the canon. One might argue that overtly political or sociological stories are more rooted in the history they recount than are "artistic" stories; one might also argue that such stories are exceedingly didactic. But all art is didactic to an extent, and if Beauty and Truth are apolitical, certainly their observers and creators are not. The stories of the men and women on Keats's urn might alarm him, had they not been so successfully muted by the urn maker.

I am interested in such stories, but not because the telling of them will bring about any element of social change. Neither am I interested in their documentation, even though they certainly deserve to be told. I am interested finally because there is so much about the human condition that disturbs me, and, as much as anything, I write to understand it. I said earlier that I study in my writing complex memory; I also wrote about a very personal memory of my mother and father. It's a simple thing to recognize that my father's dominance and my mother's submissiveness were manifestations of the culture and society they were reared in. But that explanation doesn't satisfy me, nor does it provide a context that memory can embrace. I may be disturbed by abandonment on a deeply personal level; I may be disturbed by racism — though I don't directly know its sting — because of its immense injustice. But making these issues manifest in the story form is not interesting enough for me as a writer, even as I can value writers who do this. I am interested in what underlies these issues, what maintains them, and what their origins are. And what interests me is to keep working toward this source, whatever it may be, where ideology and psychology merge with genetics and spirituality to provide the foundation of memory, where for me real human history resides. Who knows what this source is. I don't believe I'll ever know. But how can I account for the joy in my son's face when he correctly predicts a grand-slam home run by his favorite player in a century where we have practiced genocide? I am aware of the severity of this juxtaposition but can't explain it. Which for me is the reason I write. The writers I most admire — from one as well known as Dostoevsky to another as comparatively unknown as Gina Berriault — seem to me to offer the best explanations.

And finally, this is why I keep writing, because its rewards, thus far in my career, have been only what I've described. I am aware enough of the trends of literary fashion to recognize that my stories, my novels, will probably never enjoy immense popularity, though I would certainly like them to. I have no way of knowing the occupations of the herds of M.F.A. students who have stampeded the job market in the past ten years, but presently, I'm teaching five basic writing courses at part-time pay. The president of the university that employs me just had his office renovated by the college at a price tag of eighty thousand dollars; I would have to teach forty sections of basic writing to cover that cost. Hardly a ringing endorsement for pursuit of the M.F.A. degree or the academy in general, and, as much as I enjoy teaching, had I to do it over again, I would probably pursue a different career. But I would still write stories.

III

I have often wondered why I chose language as a means of expression and communication rather than music, or sculpture, or painting. (The reason may be as simple as I was not particularly adept at the latter three.) I enjoyed books as a child but didn't consume them as had other writers I know. I was more interested in science than literature, rationality than adventure. As much as anything, I appreciated language's capacity for imprecision: a child does not need many remonstrations from her mother and father to recognize that it's easy to say the wrong thing, and that language handled delicately can go a long way toward appeasing the powers that be.

In an unhappy childhood home, a child learns to listen even more carefully to language. When a parent's anger is unpredictable, the same words spoken by him in subtly different tones have vastly different consequences for the child. I learned much later in life that my father had an extraordinary gift for words, but he didn't use many of them with me. A child needs words, of course, and the fewer he receives the more weight he attributes to those offered. The time I spent with my father was often passed in weighing these, trying to determine my father's intent. After my mother and father divorced, I learned quickly how hastily chosen words about my stepmother could bring tears or fury to my mother and retribution from my sisters. And I've written already about how, during this time, my father's imposition of a language of intimacy seemed a radical disavowal of an earlier language of separation.

As I've said, such careful listening leads not only to an appreciation of language's imprecision but a desire to master language in order to eliminate imprecision. Such a desire can never be fulfilled, of course. Each time I write I'm still aware of not having said exactly what I meant. As importantly, such careful listening creates an appreciation for the sound of language. Very early, I fell in love with the sound of language. I remember sitting on a porch swing next to my grandfather, who was singing "The Battle Hymn of the Republic" in a resonant bass. I liked his singing well enough, but I was entranced by the lyric of the song whose meaning I could not interpret but only appreciate for its sound. (Now, as an adult, to me the hymn seems rather brutal, but the words still make for fine listening.) When I read as a child, I read slowly — in fact, I still do — listening to each word. I sought meaning not only from dictionary definitions but from the sound of the words themselves. The English language is not entirely onomatopoeic, but at the time, I tried to make it so.

When I first began to write, I wrote poetry because of my love of the sound of language. At age nineteen, I read Stevens's "Sunday Morning" and thought it was the greatest poem I'd read, not because I understood it, because I hadn't, but because the language was painfully lovely. By the time I began to write stories, the language of them was self-consciously lyrical, even as their events were sometimes violent and desperate. At the time, I found the tension between these two interesting. I would write whole sentences in which characters did odd things, such as playing a violin over a lover's body, just because I thought it was pretty to say so, or I'd write sentences at the expense of semantics because I liked the arrangement of the words.

In the years of writing since then, I've learned that one does not exploit one's characters by holding them at the mercy of language, which is but one of the components of a short story or novel. As much as I used to love Eudora Welty's stories, some I like less well now because of their dependency on beautiful language. Nevertheless, I would argue that one need not apologize for one's love of language. If I admire a student's writing, initially it has less to do with the events she describes than her ability to manipulate language to tell of them. Many teachers I know feel the same way, because such a student is finally quite rare.

Which I think is an essential concern. In *The Drowned and the Saved*, Primo Levi writes, "It is an obvious observation that where violence is inflicted on man it is also inflicted on language." His point is, particularly in the concentrations camps he survived, that the violence inflicted on language in part permitted the atrocities to take place. He describes the German spoken there as "skeletal, howled, studded with obscenities and imprecations . . . only vaguely related to the precise, austere language of my chemistry books, or to the melodious, refined German of Heine's poetry. . . ." The equation, as Levi says, is simple: brutal language begets brutal acts. Clearly, nowhere was this more severely established than in the German lagers, but one can see shades of the same in our contemporary culture. My chief concern about television is that even the bastardized language that is often spoken there is sublimated by images that do not demand language for interpretation. I don't finally know what this, along with our other encounters with a truncated language, permits or prohibits us from thinking, and consequently doing.

In one of my more ethereal stories, a seven-year-old child has been traumatized by his grandfather, and, before leaving him, the grandfather whispers, "Remember there is power in every word." I believe this is true not only for the richness of a language that allows interpretation but for a devastated language that prohibits it.

IV

At its core, the urge toward the creation of form, particularly in a story or novel, is not hard to understand. Recently, the father of a close friend of mine died. The illness that preceded his death was lingering and permitted him to write a brief essay he asked to have read at his funeral. The essay ordered the essential events of his life from birth to death, each punctuated with the refrain "I'd do it all again!" Given these months, this was his attempt to shape his life not only for those at his funeral who would remember him, but because he wanted them to "read" the story of his life as he did.

On a different scale, I think this is what drives many writers, and indeed many artists, toward this grappling with form. One wants a story for one's life. Most especially, one wants to tell it. This is not to suggest that most writers write autobiographically — though this is at least partly the case — since writing is more than the kept record of memory. And it's more, too, than the desire to bring a value to one's ideas, thoughts, and experiences that others might treasure through the centuries. It is, as I've said earlier, partly a means toward understanding, and also a passion for power: to shape, if not the world, then at least one's own world, which is, despite all efforts, constantly restructuring itself and constantly being restructured by others. Amongst the many problems the writer faces, two seem to me the largest. The first is, of course, that a writer attempting to tell her story must leave out an essential chapter: the writer's death. Second, the nature of form (and language) is to defy the writer's blueprint for a story or novel, to create its own cast, and thus tell a story that emerges from the writer's life that the writer had not imagined. This experience is, for me, the exhilaration of writing; at the same time, it teaches me that what I perceive as the stories of my life are not the stories I will tell: as my writing moves toward form, I'm never sure what powers it toward its arrival as form. But I'm usually pleased when it arrives as a kind of familiar, yet unknown visitor who immediately takes up permanent residence in my home.

None of this is to say, of course, that novels, stories, or poems can't be planned, or by some miracle imagined in their entirety in a moment's inspiration. More frequently than not, a last line will occur to me before a first line, and I've worked enough in the story form to sometimes imagine the shape of a story before I've filled it with language. But the meaning of last lines and planned shapes are changed by the time spent writing. It would be truly fine to see the form of a story on paper as Michelangelo supposedly saw David in a block of marble, but language isn't so precise a tool that the writer can interpret the form of a story as it is being created.

I like to experiment with form. I think, in some ways, a writer must. No writer has an inexhaustible source of material that will concern him enough to fuel his stories over a lifetime, which is one of the reasons we have many more younger writers than older writers.

It's disheartening to write the same story over and over again; language and form lose their urgency, regardless of the size of one's readership. But it can be invigorating to tell the same story — using the same themes, perhaps, the same basic plots — in different forms, using only a different sense of language. Writing, thank God, is not solely an intellectual act, and there is a danger in making it so: one can create a quite fascinating structure that is almost wholly ungrounded in human emotion and psychology, and that is relatively void of semantic meaning. At the same time I believe one must maintain an intellectual interest in the invention of form to continue to write, or at least to continue to write well. Without the tension that exists between form, language, and the writer, I wouldn't — and more honestly couldn't — write.

I should add that the proponents of antistory, or those who write about the formlessness of life, are of passing interest to me, as is contemporary critical theory, though the latter changes so quickly that for me it remains permanently elusive. But I am interested mainly in how these ideas might be manifested in form, which is sometimes, I recognize, a profound oxymoron. By itself, the sense that life (or language) resists form is believable enough, as anyone who has spent a desperate hour knows. Otherwise, this is a pleasant bit of nihilism one might indulge in one's more self-destructive moments. But with regard to form, I find more credible a child with a lump of clay in her hands, or a physicist trying to ascertain the shape of the universe. Since I'm a writer, it's my job to be interested in theories of language and form; to dismiss them is simply arrogance. To embrace them uncritically can be simply foolishness.

I wrote earlier that I've enjoyed relatively little success in my writing career; I also wrote that the imagined promise of success was not what kept me writing. But if tomorrow an archangel dropped down from the sky and said no one would ever read what I've written, I would quit writing and spend my time doing other things. I write with the belief that eventually my stories, novels, and poems will reach readers, that these readers might be changed by them a fraction as much as writing changes me. How much of this is mere arrogance? I can't say. How much of this is a reconciliation with the death that I mentioned earlier? I don't know. I do believe that in part this is an act of faith.

But finally, how large an act of faith? There is a danger in a writer seeing his creations as so central to his life that he loses perspective on the larger acts of faith that go on about him every day. So I would like to see the romantic stereotype of the tortured, suffering artist disappear. Which is not to say that writing, for all its revelations, isn't often very painful. But how can I worry about a world that may not house my stories when I've found the difficult faith to believe in a world that will house my sons when there are other children who don't eat? If one asks for faith in one's stories, one should ask with all due humility.

Anthologies

"The Harlequin" and "The Harlequin: Autobiographical Sources" (story and essay). *The Writing Room: Keys to the Craft of Fiction and Poetry.* Ed. Eve Shelnutt. Longstreet Press, 1989.

"Albert Einstein, Plumber," "An Elderly Woman Resists Falling in Love," and "Self-Consciousness," along with essay on sources. Ibid.

"Heritage" and "Heritage: Autobiographical Sources" (story and essay). *Writing: The Translation of Memory.* Ed. Eve Shelnutt. Macmillan, 1990.

"A Commentary on Some of the Autobiographical Works of Elie Wiesel" and "The Wiesel Commentary: Sources" (essays). Ibid.

Periodicals

"Severance" (story). *Wisconsin Review* (1982).

"Night" (story). *Rhode Island Review Quarterly* (1984).

"Heritage" (story). *Montana Review* (1986).

"Jump-starting a Hearse" (poem). *Mill Hunk Herald* (1986).

"Albert Einstein: Plumber" (poem). *Long Pond Review* (1987).

"Opening Day: Four Poems." *Spitball* (1988).

"Leavening" (story). *West Branch* (1989).

"Three Poems for My Father." *Nebraska Review* (1990).

"Late Winter" (poem). *Nebraska Review* (1990).

Dick Allen

Dick Allen has won poetry writing grants from the National Endowment for the Arts and the Ingram Merrill Fellowship Foundation, in addition to the Robert Frost Fellowship in Poetry, the Mary Carolyn Davis Poetry Prize, and the San Jose Poetry Prize. In 1985, his Overnight in the Guest House of the Mystic *was a National Book Critics Circle Award Final Nominee. He has been selected for reading on both the Connecticut and the Ohio poetry circuits. He was educated at Syracuse University and Brown University and currently lives in Trumbull, Connecticut. For many years he has held the Charles A. Dana Endowed Chair of English and been the director of creative writing at the University of Bridgeport.*

ONLY WHEN LOVE AND
NEED ARE ONE

Talking with Poets

Gossip is most of it, a barrier of thorns and small berries
Cultivated to disguise a wall,
False entrances and gates with shallow courtyards behind them,
And sometimes a few gypsies slowly dancing in firelight
Or swinging pails as they take a path down through the forest
To an old mossy well. Small heaps of masks,
And costumes with puffy sleeves or threadbare blouses
Lie beside the moat, are rummaged through
As often as not. But the poets seldom talk
Of forays they've taken; although they are always riding
In and out, mounting or dismounting, holding
The traces, wiping their brows and calling
For strong drink and friends, their verbal reports
Are sketchy, reluctant. No, they would rather laugh
Than speak of high rooms and the maiden's cot,
Books on stone shelves, what shackled prisoners
They may have been shown. . . . Yet if all this sounds
Too romantic, consider the cop coming home
To his house in the suburbs, how he pretends
There are no city streets until he walks their shadows;
Or the bored-to-death businessman,
The void he plunges daily, rising out of it
Like a circling, wounded hawk, blood under his nails
And in his throat, seeking Lethe
In television comedies or children's homework grades;
Or the doctor who vanishes
Into a nightmare of tumors, splintered bones,
The cardiographic line of a dead horizon,
CAT scans and mottled skin, before she finds herself
Whispering for the mercy of an airplane above layered clouds,
Flirtation, oblivion. . . . Still if only the poets
Would cease in their talk of grants and reputation,

Reviews, or lack of them, readings, teaching loads,
Editors and enjambment, then on an autumn evening
When the wall is a looming thing of masonry,
Bulwarks and turrets, and a king walks by himself
Under limpid banners, how I would love to hear
(for I have read their books, and like you marvelled),
Of the way they find Blue Sailors by a country road,
Wander in Sibelius, or how they've taught their lines
To study a landscape starting with morning sunlight
Coasting the grass. Talking with poets,
I could be enthralled by cries of Russian wolves,
The smell of vanilla flavoring in an open brown bottle,
What happens when they look at statesmen's eyes —
If only they were not so distrustful, so afraid, so exhausted,
So bent on saving themselves for the perfect man or woman
Who will listen to their voices in another time
More living to them now than these roses, these open palms.

(reprinted from The Hudson Review*)*

In a footnote to a chapter called "Focus," in *The Examined Life*, Harvard philosopher Robert Nozick writes, "What we presently focus upon is affected by what we are like, yet over the long run a person is molded by where his or her attention continually dwells. Hence the great importance of what your occupation requires you to be sensitive to, and what it ignores *de jure* or *de facto*, for its pattern of sensitivities and insensitivities — unless a continuing effort is made to counterbalance this — will eventually become your own."

Like most present-day poets, my "occupation" until I left graduate school was that of a student. As such, essentially free of most imposed duties until I was twenty-four, I studied, read, experimented, and tried to learn my craft. Yet I had realized, even before high school, that my becoming a poet was in many ways caused by the shaping forces of a domineering mother and an acquiescent father who were locked in a relationship fulfilling her need to control and his to be controlled, regardless of my being caught in their web. My mother, the middle daughter of a compulsive gambler, had an overwhelming need to create and maintain the illusion of everything in our family being perfect. Appearances meant everything to her. No one in our family got sick, no one ever failed, no one was not up to any task, no one let anyone else down. We were never to waste time, but always to be actively working, analyzing, planning, reading, putting our best faces forward.

Indeed, at sixty-five, my mother had a face-lift. It was kept a secret between my father and her until her death ten years later. She refused to acknowledge she was dying when everyone around her could see — in a terrible weight loss — how she was failing. She kept up the illusion that everything was normal until she was carried to the ambulance, kicking and screaming.

To live in a household controlled by such a person, it was absolutely necessary for other members of the family to become extraordinarily sensitive to her moods or we would be punished by her silent, clenched-fist anger. Responding to her, just as the children of alcoholics do, I learned empathy. Not to be empathic was to be shut out.

My father, as the late-child baby of my grandmother Allen's family, married a surrogate mother. He was content to have my mother pay the bills, push him to write Americana and historical books and articles he'd rather not, live at the fringes of their modest income in perpetual debt while all the time buying more unnecessary possessions — and, whenever they had a little extra money, to give it away, as my mother's brothers and sister and their families were always to think the Allens were doing well. Of course, there were plenty of benefits for him. Her urging pushed him to a worldwide prominence in his field far beyond his modest early ambitions. Left to himself, he would have puttered his life happily away in research-library basements. He was free of clothes selection, bill paying, planning ahead, most usual adult-male responsibilities for those of his generation; she expected him only to have a decent job. After work and on weekends, with mind uncluttered, he could research and write and enjoy life as a "good boy." He followed the path of least resistance; if his mother-wife wanted something, he would be talked into it. I remember him arguing with her only one time, when I was about seven, after she'd snooped into one of my secret desk drawers and I'd complained. My father took my side, but she threw dozens of dishes against the kitchen walls in a hysteria of being opposed. He left the house for two days before she forgave him. Yet in repayment for his not standing up to her, she would protect him with her usually everlastingly rational mind (reason and will power will take care of everything), and she could figure her way out of almost every problem they ever faced.

As a product of this household, like my father, I was "free," or so it seemed, to follow my student occupation. I was free, waited on, protected, to remain in many ways a child. And since more than anything, my parents — although both with only high school educations — read and talked, words being their staff of life, I naturally read and talked. Knowing my mother loved the poetry she'd memorized in high school and often recited to me, I began to write poems.

I found in poetry, in poems my parents never knew about, both another world and another self. The other world was one of honesty and expression of truths not allowed in our house. The self I found in poetry, in the lives particularly of the Romantics, was one my parents would only shake their heads at: embarrassing, irresponsible, unconventional, risk taking. Increasingly, as I grew older, I came to find that I could only fully connect to the real world of flux and passions and mistakes, and to my real feeling self, through poems.

Like many male poets of my generation (virtually every male poet I know claims he has had a dominate mother), I came to maturity fissured. On the one hand, my long occupation as a student was inevitably aiming me to make my life as a professor, protected by the mother-university just as my father was protected by his mother-wife. As a professor, I would fulfill my mother's expectations, be respectable and successful.

On the other hand, my poetry would keep me in contact with the real world and my real self. If I could reach those true places where poetry led me, I could feel one with Keats and Shelley, Byron and Dylan Thomas, Sylvia Plath and Anne Sexton — in touch with the elemental, creating and shaping. When I wrote, I was a poet, not a son, a husband and father and college professor. "For [your occupation's] pattern of sensitivities and insensitivities — *unless a continuing effort is made to counterbalance this* — will eventually become your own."

II

In recent years, many have written eloquently about the "silences" and "the lost years" of older women writers — the years they were expected to devote to child raising and homemaking and subservience to the frequent moves of the breadwinning husbands. It was once a disgrace to a man if his wife worked. But while not taking away from the problems of women writers, they were not the only victims of their times. I am concentrating here on the situation of male writers prior to the late 1960s, the last subjected to the division of roles.

A heterosexual male of my generation (I was born in August 1939 and came to relative consciousness following World War II) was expected to marry young, have children young, become an early success in his occupation by devoting most of his working attention to his job, buy a house, put aside savings, perhaps take on a second job to create more savings, and the like. There was to be no financial help from his wife and none wanted. If he could keep moving up (better house, better cars, better schools, savings for the children's college expenses), he would also increase the prestige of his wife (who might be known as "the corporate wife" or "the faculty wife").

I accepted this role as natural. I was married five days after my twenty-first birthday, one year before my graduation from Syracuse University. My wife, Lori, and I had the first of our two children three years later, at the end of my second year in Brown University's Ph.D. in English and American literature program. At twenty-four, I began teaching full time in the English department of what would become Wright State University, in Dayton, Ohio—five courses a trimester and another two in summer school, for a total of twelve courses a year or thirty-six credit hours. Simultaneously, I helped found and then became editor-in-chief of *The Mad River Review*, a small national literary magazine; advised the school's undergraduate literature magazine; ran its visiting writers program; even—for one year—was in charge of the school's public relations. For two summers, I taught writing at the Indiana Writers Conference.

If you accept that you should be devoted to your work, fulfill all your responsibilities, teaching is a life that can easily absorb your energies. I have always been an involved teacher, giving as much attention to the weakest of my students as the finest. My compulsion always to do my job well doubtlessly stems from following my mother's need to keep up appearances, to never let anyone down, and to empathize with others I can't shut off.

But, regardless of my success in teaching at Wright State, and similar accomplishments at the University of Bridgeport, this enormously time-consuming profession never seemed to me the real one. Teaching and administrative work was what I did to make a living. Actual reality was only in the few weeks of holiday vacation, two one-semester sabbaticals, and the few summer months when I could write: "my continuing effort . . . to counterbalance." Some of my students might be upset to read this. "You mean that wasn't really you who was teaching?" However, most writers in my profession as well as in other professions would understand. We learn early to work in the outer world as facsimiles of ourselves, and many of us remain undetected throughout our lives, even through our mid-life crises. For most men, only in drugs, drink, sex, and sports is there a being in touch with the elemental feeling self. Drugs, drink, sex, and sports give us permissible ways to feel. Yes, male writers and other artists have their writing to put them in touch with themselves, but even they live in two worlds. "If you would really know me, regardless of how well you think I talk or teach," I've often heard myself saying, "read my poems."

Frost's lines from "Two Tramps in Mudtime" come to mind: "My object in living is to unite / My avocation and my vocation." I have found this impossible to do. Frost, as is well documented, was for the most part an irresponsible college professor. His great poems may balance his disservice to his ordinary students. Yet there is much in me that shudders at his dissociation from those students and their lives. I have chosen what sometimes threatens to be disastrous for my poetry: to put my students' needs before my poems — a not uncommon choice for the majority of American poets who, because of the circumstances at their less-than-prestigious schools, work fifty or more hours a week at their jobs during the academic year. Certainly part of me feels victimized. But the alternative seems to be to let myself become less human. How does one turn away from the freshman who can't spell, from the young writer who, with a little extra praise, can be encouraged to tell those stories we all need to know? Some of my teachers — Carol Fisher, Professor Woolsley, Albert Menut, Arthur Hoffman, Daniel Hughes, Harmon Bro, and others — changed my life by giving me extra attention and encouragement. I feel compelled to follow their example. And raw talent? How can I not spend extra hours on a student manuscript which has in it potential genius — or talent above the ordinary — or even that manuscript which reveals to its writer a new and true direction her life might take? It sounds egotistical to say this, but I am truly helpless before good writing, compelled to urge it in its own direction, not in mine.

Still, I try to wrest my own free time the best I can. My telephone is unlisted. I am a terrible correspondent, since when I finally get to answering letters, I write epics. Lori's and my social life consists of attending — almost never giving — three parties a year, three visits to or from friends, and a few holiday visits with immediate family. During the academic year, I can only manage reviews or essays and some revision work on my poems. The "counterbalance" is a ruthless, obsessive-compulsive plunging into poetry for two or three summer months of writing twelve or more hours a day, trying to bring poems to a draft stage where they "lock." Then, I live with these poems for the next one to five years (in some cases, ten to fifteen), revising and shaping until I finally feel they're ones I can submit. For me, this is the only method by which I can find my way, year after year, and now decade after decade.

III

Is this any way to live? Obviously not. Yet, with some variations, I think the pattern is fairly representative. For male poets of my generation and I fear for too many of the following generations, poetry is something stolen from what we have let society and ourselves define as our major duty in life: being responsible, money-making successes, doing our jobs well, supporting our families well. Not many of us are what used to be called "bohemians." And, unlike novelists, we have no glimmer of hope that we might one day support ourselves by our chosen form of writing. Most American poets are university teachers, an abundance of them teachers of creative writing. Only in our time have so many poets been able to claim so much reward from a world outside poetry; what was previously a marginal existence for writers now becomes relatively comfortable and seductive, when "what your occupation requires you to be sensitive to, and what it ignores" applies to the endless fascination and opportunity the university provides. And as the college professor's duties and responsibilities increase and deepen, it becomes more and more difficult for writers to find our way back to the true poetry. We lose focus. Commonly, we keep too many irons in the fire. Good at so many things, we become best in none. The only way to survive as a writer, we half realize, is to get more time, more time. However, to do this we must become less in the eyes of the outer world than we perhaps feel we can afford to be, turning our backs on so much that needs doing and then living with the guilt. And if we do not pull away from responsibilities we have assumed, and do continue to write poetry, the result is likely to be only those smidgens of little lyrics that have filled the periodicals of the last fifty years, composed without an inkling of how true poetry always has a universal meaning.

Then again, if poets do pull away, we may become spoiled, cut off from daily knowing the stresses and exhaustions of men and women outside the profession, and our poetry may carry within it a false understanding of ordinary human existence.

IV

At the core, true writing is only possible when one can freely respond to all that summons and surrounds him, hear the cicadas and crickets, notice the various shades of green in the forest, spend hours staring into a woodland pool, see the pattern of headlights on a distant superhighway, read and meditate on books, hear a Bach symphony over and over until it has entered the being, write a single stanza a hundred times until it comes as right as if plucked directly from the air. Somehow, the writer escapes from time, from feelings of impending responsibilities, and drifts where Ted Hughes's "Thought-Fox" can find him. Each summer, I try to find my way back. I write hundreds, thousands of mediocre lines, "left-brain" lines, dozens of poems that are mainly exercises. What I am trying to do, I realize somewhere along the line, is get in touch again with that other world, that other self I've left behind for so long. Finally, a month or two into the process, it seems to happen: a line rings right, a connection is made, a rhyme is true to meaning. I am changed and feel again. Sporadically, the drafts of the poems come and I'm able to be in touch with what I know subconsciously but not consciously. If I'm lucky, by the end of the summer I have a few good poem drafts. But each poem, if it is eventually to become one I will submit, must be like the piece of a hologram, in some way containing all I know or feel within it, all of which I am capable. Writing, creating, I am free to be a complete human; my spiritual vocabulary has increased; those feelings and thoughts I've so poorly expressed in conversation or during teaching are phrased the way they should be; I've solved a form or I've formed a new one.

Then it's September and I'm lost again.

This cycle has shaped what my art is most often about: the unending struggle of the modern human to find an authentic life in a future-shocked world that is trying to overwhelm him; the struggle to make sense of this dichotomy; the struggle between duty and freedom, maintaining appearance and abandoning it. This poem is partially illustrative:

William Rimmer: Flight and Pursuit

> I saw two men in flight and in pursuit,
> Stone castle walls around them and their bodies bent
> As if they were the same. They were not the same
> But in the leaning shadows of my dream
> First I wore a dagger and a sash —
> I fled the Lord's white lash;
> Then a curving sword, a hood across my face —
> I sped through darkness of His headlong chase.
>
> I could not gain; I could not lose. We stayed
> Near, not closing nearer. I could hear the wind

Roaring through the turrets, fleshing out the flags;
Beggars' hands reached up from beggars' rags,
Doorways turned to rooms; we sped through rooms
To other doorways — eyes, hands, bare thighs numb
As gods in bas-relief. The rooms went on and on;
Neither of us stumbled as we ran.

My mind, like all minds, sought a single room without
Another doorway; or, another world beyond it.
In either place I could have turned and drawn
My dagger from my sash; I could have shown
The face beneath this hood. But as we passed
Each portal, sandals burning, thinking it the last,
One more, one more. His sandals raced before
And followed me across each stone slab floor.

(reprinted from Flight and Pursuit*)*

I have been obsessed with the struggle in other ways. My generation of poets was taught by what are now known as "academic" poets, but it was influenced during undergraduate and graduate years by first the Beat poets and then the "uncooked" poetry of the early 1960s. This has resulted in an intense struggle between eloquence and decorum and the need to spontaneously express raw and awkward passion. Ironically, this tension seems to mirror my own tensions. On the one hand, I want to reveal that I know myself as often self-pitying, power craving, angry, egotistical, and to explore the implications of this real self in my poetry. On the other hand, I love the grace and elegance of carefully phrased language, meter, and rhyme, and the mysteries of the barely revealed. The latter "self" is more socially acceptable, more "publishable," less clumsy. Yet if I hide the frightened and grasping baby self, I am dishonest, posing as what I am not, my poetry apt to be too much facade. I am lost about what I am supposed to do, to be:

The Mystery

for Prof. Israel Kapstein

Of course we hound it with words. To give it up
to the trees and flat meadows
or the farmhouse that for thirty years has seemed
about to topple into its deserted yard
would be, as Kapstein said, boring.

It is ours by right: both of long hunting
   and birth into knowledge. We have known
such moments! Such moments when the hills turn gray,
   and the wind has seemed to settle into itself
and it seemed to be solved, it seemed to be solved!

The moments of love: the hand across your own
   so briefly in time; the glance across a table
through candle flames like tiny leaves suspended
   in the soft darkness of a restaurant where each
wall is blue or mirrored. Such moments

the mystery seems to deepen and we follow it
   down, down, down until there is an end
to words, a living coral reef
   faintly glowing, extending to the ocean floor's
horizon, luminous fish like flattened raindrops twirling.

II

We cannot leave it alone, said Kapstein, even
   supposing we could, always it would be waiting
in the moment before you cross the room and look
   from the window to the sunlit hills you knew
would be sunlit, or the ordinary stars in heaven.

And the butler did not do it. From the start
   we were not misled by the Master's careful words
and the sweeping gowns of his ladies. We suspected
   something in the twilight, beyond the elms
and the light a moving picture of itself

on the outskirts of the garden. O, the mystery
   is bound to resist us, Kapstein said, our invention
of words that draw closer, curtain in the wind
   blowing in the farmhouse, footsteps in the yard,
what is discovered of our lives when we discover

how close we can draw, how near we can come
   without fainting. It is the gunshot
muted in the parlor; it is the room
   locked with a body inside; it is the clue we follow
like those hounds forever and not quite yet closing in.

(reprinted from Overnight in the Guest House of the Mystic)

V

Each year, it has become more difficult to search mysteries. Wordsworth wrote, "The world is too much with us, late and soon / Getting and spending, we lay waste our powers." The lost years, the silence of male writers — and increasingly this will be the case for women writers who, freed from some of the demands of child raising, are now taking on official responsibilities in the workplace — comes from this being overwhelmed by the nominal demands of life: "What we presently focus upon is affected by what we are like, yet over the long run a person is molded by where his or her attention continually dwells."

The poet becomes so much a teacher that she can no longer stop applying the critical mind to her own work at its inception, rendering the art too conscious. The poet becomes the responsible spouse and parent, his attention so much on his family that he cannot think and feel much beyond it. The poet develops such a strong sense of institutional loyalty that when she has free time, her mind and even her imagination increasingly return to how she might further benefit her institution. The poet, as he ages, gets overly anxious to achieve recognition, finding that his essays, his reviews, his anthologies bring him more recognition than his poems. The poet looks around her at people with less or equal education and sees she could make more money. She spends her summers teaching at writers conferences (or running them), her thoughts dwelling more and more on handling her annuities, the equity in her house. The poet, reading again the work of a major writer, realizes and with great self-courage admits that his work is ultimately minor confessional verse, that he has lost the connection with universal themes and sensibilities, that "where his or her attention continually dwells" has molded him so well it's impossible to escape.

"Getting and spending, we lay waste our powers." Or we tap other ones, much less dependent upon the fragile and complex sensibility, the empathy, the freedom, and the imagination poetry must draw upon. Life has overwhelmed us, as it does most, and atrophied what abilities we had.

Or perhaps it is for the best, and those taken up by life more than art will be reborn on a higher plain.

If it turns out I write genuine poetry, it is because when I cannot write, I literally cannot feel completely real. Persistence in writing poetry in our times almost always stems from some psychological need. Even in my most left-brain months, I keep sensing that the real world is magic and mystery and craziness and billowing sorrow.

This knowledge is there on the edge of consciousness. I wish to know the other world and be in it and speak from its saving truths, learn its stories, counterbalancing the daily lies and capitalistic motivations with its images and insights.

Most college-professor poets, myself included, live ordinary lives. What I have written about in this essay is the plain truth about the ordinary, the nonheroic, the daily griefs and pains that men, particularly, seldom speak about. It is unseemly to allow the private self full reign, to admit—as women have recently stressed while we gather their lost diaries and unpublished works—that illnesses, deaths, breakdowns often come in unrelenting waves for men too, and we flounder, often overwhelmed, as these are added to the numbing daily tasks. I think of one wonderful poet who has retreated to a stereo room, and of another who now devotes most of his life to serious jogging. Neither could cope with the constant pressure to maintain responsible careers and caring lives and still write demanding poetry. Like them, I also have too many lost years.

Or a number of us have pretended to be Dylan Thomas. The generation that preceded mine drove too many of its members to celebrating madness, thinking (somewhat correctly, it turns out) that the vanishing readers of poetry would only return if they were motivated by their *People*-magazine interest in poets' tragic lives. I am not very interested in myself, in writing confessional poetry.

No, that's not quite all of it. Autobiographical explaining tends to neglect objective reasons for why poets write, particularly nonconfessional poets.

I write because grotesque sunflowers stood in the Coshburn's garden when I was seven, and my fear of them paralleled a nation's terror during World War II. I write to capture the American faces I saw as I hitchhiked across the country when I was nineteen. I write to understand and perhaps to give others some understanding of how Meister Eckhart and Lao Tsu live in us; to protest the killing in the Persian Gulf and the massacre in Tiananmen Square; to tell stories of ambition and love; to create music and chants; to chart, to prophesy; to give devotions.

I write to set the sacred and the profane in one circle, to bring modern science to literature, to share grief and joy, to make phrases and stanzas and poems that may—because of how they're phrased and imaged, because of their metaphors and similes, their rhyme and rhythms—stay in others' minds, be a source of insight or comfort or wisdom for them, as the lines, stanzas, poems of Whitman, Dickinson, Frost, Yeats, Stevens, Rilke, Berryman, Williams, Lowell, Wilbur, Plath, Brooks (and Homer and Dante and Goethe and Pushkin and

Borges and Akhmatova), and hundreds of others have been for me.

I write because one day, in an eye doctor's office in Syracuse, New York, John Donne finally spoke to me from a Modern Library Edition. I write because without words we do not know what we are, and that we live at all.

Books

Anon and Various Time Machine Poems (poetry). Delta, 1971.
Science Fiction: The Future (editor). Harcourt, 1971. Rev. ed., 1982.
Detective Fiction: Crime and Compromise (coeditor, with David Chacko). Harcourt, 1974.
Regions with No Proper Names (poetry). St. Martin's Press, 1976.
Looking Ahead: The Vision of Science (coeditor, with Lori Allen). Harcourt, 1976.
Overnight in the Guest House of the Mystic (poetry). Louisiana State University Press, 1984.
Flight and Pursuit (poetry). Louisiana State University Press, 1987.
Expansive Poetry: The New Formalism and the New Narrative (editor). Crosscurrents, 1989.

Selected Anthologies (since 1987)

The Writer's Handbook. The Writer, Inc., 1987.
Contemporary New England Poetry. Vols. 1-2. Texas Review Press, 1987–88.
Anthology of Magazine Verse/Yearbook of American Poetry. Monitor Books, 1988.
Expansive Poetry: The New Narrative and the New Formalism. Story Line, 1989.
Contemporary Authors Autobiography Series. Gale Research, Inc., 1990.
An Introduction to Poetry. Little, Brown, 1990.
The Best American Poetry: 1991. Collier Macmillan, 1991.
The Norton Introduction to Literature. Norton, 1991.
The Norton Introduction to Poetry. Norton, 1991.
Formal Introductions. Aralia Press, 1992.

Periodicals

Hundreds of poems, essays, and reviews have appeared in many magazines and journals, including *American Book Review*, *American Poetry Review*, *Antioch Review*, *Atlantic Monthly*, *Beloit Poetry Journal*, *Boulevard*, *Carolina Quarterly*, *Chronicles*, *Cimarron Review*, *Crosscurrents*, *Hampden-Sydney Poetry Review*, *Hudson Review*, *Kenyon Review*, *Manhattan Review*, *Michigan Quarterly*, *Minnesota Review*, *Mississippi Review*, *New Criterion*, *New Yorker*, *North American Review*, *Ontario Review*, *Paris Review*, *Poetry*, *Prairie Schooner*, *Prism International*, *Salmagundi*, *Saturday Review*, *Southern Review*, *West Coast Review*, *Western Humanities Review*, *The Writer*, *Writer's Digest*, and *Yale Review*.

Herbert Woodward Martin

Thomas Acita

Herbert Woodward Martin holds degrees from the University of Toledo, Middlebury College, and Carnegie Mellon University. He is professor of English and poet-in-residence at the University of Dayton. He was recently a Fulbright Lecturer at Janus Pannonius University in Pécs, Hungary.

FIRE, WATER,
THE ASHES OF MEMORY

——

Let me try and explain this strange title. Why? Because titles are meaningful. We begin by naming things which are important in our lives: our toys, our children, our relatives, the people we meet: ordinary and special. The act of naming helps us to access language; it helps us to remember the familiar and to store the painful. I think I tell you this truth about myself because last night as I was working on the first draft of this essay I inadvertently touched the wrong computer key and all 580-plus lines disappeared from the screen, and fifteen minutes of pleading, praying, and pressing of keys retrieved absolutely nothing. The pages were all consigned to that vast memory bank of experience and lessons learned.

Now the task is to begin again, to rummage through the smoldering ashes hoping to find a memento of some excellent event, and something fused together from this fire which will help me to remember to be careful in the future, and to find a space where I can meditate in peace and recall in joy, a place where my senses can evoke memories in their full array of colors, textures, rhythms, sounds, tastes, and smells.

Place, space, and time are important for me. A particular place, with the necessary inactivity around me so that the imagination can play, and a specific time which I can use to call on the muse to appear. This is invocation; it is magic; it is also calling forth by name and memory the imaginative dreams which may touch some other individual's mind and heart.

For me the act of writing is a difficult task; it can also be an exhilarating one because I am trying to create a viable life and tension on a flat piece of paper, as well as voice, anger, gesture, place, time, and character, all on a flat surface, 8 ½ x 11. And when a reader or an audience responds positively, that is my first reward. When I send the piece out and some anonymous editor responds by accepting the work, that is my second, and when a letter arrives from an unknown reader, that is my third. Each time I write I learn something different about my craft; each attempt is a new beginning.

Since this essay is essentially about memory in general and mine in particular, let me say at the outset that memory is deceptive, perhaps even defective, but is mainly what I have to rely on. Why do I say this? I say it mainly because after I have endured an experience — joyful or painful — when I retell it, I start inventing, I start turning the screw of the tale to make it more mysterious, more suspenseful, more succinct. It is as if I am putting the essence of the story in a vial to be preserved, and in doing so I alter, change, and revise so that it becomes almost unrecognizable from the initial occurrence. This is called revision in the world of the creative, and this for me is an interesting point because the word *revision* means to re-see, to see again, to experience again, in effect to do it over. What we do when we do it over is to strengthen some moments which seem lax, and loosen others which seem too tight. In effect, creative writing is the altering of reality. The best that a creative writer can do is to approximate reality, to represent it as closely as possible.

I do not mean to suggest that the human memory has no accuracy, but I think that individuals are given to altering and changing to make the stories they tell more effective, and in that respect they are like all creative artists who are desperately trying to package the essence of life in the shape of an egg. I do not mean to suggest that creative people are liars, it is simply that they have an overabundance of imagination and are always trying to envision the possible. Imagination is the one element which frees us from the bonds of gravity. It allows us to break free; it allows us to fly; it allows us to dig deep into the earth and to fly beyond this galaxy into other galaxies. We are for all intents and purposes demigods; we are always inventing in our own image, with our own particular speech rhythms, and in many instances with our own personal gestures.

With my imagination I learned early in Alabama to entertain myself as well as join in the entertainment with other children in the neighborhood. It is those adventures with the use of words, the smallest part of which is a syllable, that I have returned to in my middle life. Also by this time in my life I know the necessity and importance of voice. Voice is similar to point of view because it is related and determined by a particular perspective. It is also related to memory, taking into account, factually, that no two individuals will see or report an accident in the same way. So voice and point of view are vital to creative work, and one of the reasons why is that it allows the reader to distinguish one writer from another and one character from another. Here is an example of voice and characterization. The poem is called "My Mother's Voice." It is not my mother in particular but rather a collective sense of black mothers. It is also a poem about writing, as well as about good and bad magic. Observe for a moment the opening.

Lawd chile, I done told you a million times
Them words you is fooling around with don't make
    no sense.
Them words is the Devil's work.
You better leave them alone! You hear?
Here you sit from morning to night
Writing down what you think is right.
Who ever told you,
You had the right to decide bad and good?
It ain't worth the time of day,
'Less it's going to bring you some silver
And I don't see how it's possible for anybody
To be paying you for something
You done scribbled down like chicken scratch.
And don't go telling me nothing 'bout
What or how much money white people make.
You ain't white!
And I don't want to hear nothing 'bout no fame.
Attention ain't no good when you're dead.
Don't make no sense,
And further more it don't make no never mind
How much you scream or how long and wooly
You let your hair grow, or how many baths you
    refuse to take.
If you ain't got no money, you ain't got nothing
    to say.
And I din't have to go to no fool college to learn
    that!
I done been walking through this world and
    learning
Since I knowed exactly who I was.
So if I tell you a hen dips snuff
Go search for the box.
Boy where is you going?
You better come back here and listen to me.
Lawd, Lawd these children are going to be the
    death of us all,
Not that we ain't given them plenty of kindling
    wood.

There is intent behind this combination of words. First, it is an attempt to characterize a mother's displeasure and nagging. With a few cultural changes and, in some cases, none at all, she could become anyone's mother. We have all heard this kind of similar advice despite race, religion, sex, and nationality. Mothers are always trying their best to get their children to become something that they think is safe, and will make a better life for them. These are not bad values; they simply, in most instances, are not their children's.

Second, the intent here is to use "words" in the same way that perhaps only black mothers use them. The rhythms and the phrasing of the lines help to delineate, I hope, her character. We all have different speech patterns, and as soon as I had tuned up my ear to hear those specific differences I took another step toward becoming a better writer. But the use of "word" in this poem denotes another context. Words represent magic and secondarily illusion. "Let there be light, and there was light." This is a vital creative imperative; every writer works within this tradition, and belief in God (whether a he or a she) has nothing to do with the process. Nor am I suggesting that writers are gods.

Words in this case have both negative and positive values, despicable and divine, subtle and blatant, and the warning to stay away from them rings true as motherly advice. Beside the fact that writing, in this poem, does not seem to be a worthy activity, it is also one in which almost no one makes any money. This mother is not interested in what white people achieve, nor their fame. She wants to see positive results while she is alive and able to enjoy them. Money is the result of hard work for her, not fame and certainly not radical protests. She has learned this in "the school of hard knocks." Still her reflective remarks at the end seem to condone what this child will do, realizing that she, and all other parents, are in part responsible for the world as it exists, and that if their radical children destroy it, it is, in part, due to their own making.

For me this poem is about finding out who you are as much as it is about discovering what you can do in this world; it is about ambition. It is a key to how I listen and attempt to record. I try to hear as naturally as possible, and that entails getting the sense and the speech patterns right. When I was an undergraduate, I wrote the typical long Eliotic great poem, I sent it out every day, and it was sent back every day. It had mistakes in language and grammar, the kind that are not supposed to be there. It was then that Dr. Ernest Gray said to me, in the hallway of the university one day, that if I wanted to be a writer, I needed to learn the rules of grammar before I could break them, because, I suspect, I would have some logical reason for doing so. It made sense after I calmed down my sophomoric arrogance and thought about what he had said. Besides, he was a considerate man who cared for his students both black and white when it was only fashionable to care for the latter. So, I thought he would tell me nothing wrong. All of this is to say that the double and triple negatives which appear in this poem may be wrong grammatically but they are correct in the context of this poem because that is how this particular lady talks. She may exist somewhere in reality, but as far as I know I have never met her completely, only in bits and pieces here and there.

Another story which may be, in part, apocryphal occurred at the same university where I had submitted some poems as a prerequisite to membership in the Blue Key Society. I heard that the judge said of my poems that they were the worst things she had ever read. Needless to say, I was not admitted to the Blue Key Society. In a matter of days I was writing small, clear poems which I hoped could be understood in any state of the union. So the comment, true or false, was another important juncture in my development as a writer. However much I was frustrated by the moment, I also learned something important about writing. Communication is the germ of what I learned. It is in many ways related to intent or intention in writing. Writers give birth to ideas which they want to communicate to others. Clarity and preciseness are the basic underpinning of communication.

If I return all the way back to my childhood, I remember the tall tales that were told about coach-whip snakes that could bite their tails, turn themselves into wheels, and overtake any escaping human being, and with body and tail bind them up, and with that same vicious tail drain all the blood from an individual. In these stories human wit and intelligence were always being pitted against animal wit and intelligence. Almost never did the human win or escape. Now I ask you, how was I to go, after hearing such stories, quietly to sleep? These stories were compounded by my cousin's ability to create his own form of terror where "Bloody Foot" was always climbing up the back stairs to our bedroom to kidnap us and then devour us from head to toe, all the while licking his bloody chops in delight. Was it the vividness of my cousin's imagination, or was it my gullibility? Whatever it was, he was effective in getting me to feel the fear he wanted to communicate. There was another time when my cousin desired action because everyone was quiet in the middle room watching the fire and relaxing. Billy, for no reason that was ever given, screamed out, "Herbert, your feet are on fire!" Cousin Louise and Uncle Ad grabbed blankets and began wrapping me up in them. Suddenly they realized that my feet were not on fire and then it was Uncle Ad's turn. He said, "Boy, is you got good sense?" I think my cousin meant no harm; he simply needed active people around him, not sedentary ones. I think the family still laughs at this story when it is told.

I was the dependable child and so I was sent to town with the money pinned to the inside of my undershirt which was not to be removed until I was face to face with the bill collector. I was always told to get a receipt. As I now suspect, it was cheaper for me to go to town on the bus than it was for an adult. Pennies must have counted in those days and so I was sent on the errand.

One final memory from the South. Once, a week before Easter we were all identified by a local white family as being the culprits who had thrown rocks at them, causing minor injuries. The fact of the matter is that we were all at church practicing our Easter speeches. It seems as if the white family was intent on revenge for I thought they could surely see the differences between the people who had aggravated them and us. Still, no matter how much we or our parents protested we were found guilty by the attending police and our parents were instructed to beat us with the ironing cord. My mother stood firm in bed, recovering from an operation, saying: "Get a switch from the tree outside. That's what God made those trees for." Even though I was spared the whipping, our Good Friday came early, for Jesus could not save us since he was preoccupied with his own troubles. Still, I cried with the others. Was this a test of our spirits, our resolve not to be troublesome? Right now the trees are rustling outside and I wonder where all those people — black and white — are. Some no doubt are still alive, some dead, some with children of their own, some with renewed and fortified prejudices, some reformed with no prejudices at all, some with newer crosses to bear, some with better visions, all far removed from me, but not the experience located somewhere beneath the scar of memory.

I tell you these things because I have only in the last ten to fifteen years looked at these events and begun to try and make poems from them. I hasten to say that many of them have been altered and some others invented. They are not all about me even though they have passed through my imagination. So I would hope that every reader would read my poems separate from my life.

I went to the Bread Loaf Writers Conference three times, once to the Antioch Writers Conference, and once to the Boulder, Colorado, Writers Conference. Chronologically, the Antioch Conference came first. It was there that I met W. D. Snodgrass, whose reputation had been established with *Heart's Needle*. Anne Sexton was there too, along with Judson Jerome. In Boulder, I was fortunate to study with Karl Shapiro. The first time I went to Bread Loaf I was on a Waiter Scholarship. We had to work three meals a day and then we went off to classes if we could feed the patrons and clean up rapidly. I remember two individuals from that period: Samuel R. Delany, who has become an innovative influence in the world of science fiction, and Dave Margolis, whose sister helped me find a job during that first fateful week I stayed in New York City. John Medelman, who was then a Bread Loaf scholar, gave me a ride in his VW all the way from Middlebury to New York City. He left me at the front door of the 34th Street YMCA. I have not seen these latter two individuals since that time, but their kindness has remained with me, and I still watch for their names.

The second time I came to Bread Loaf I was on more confident footing. I was a scholarship writer and had no duties except to speak with other younger student writers who were just beginning. I think my good fortune was largely due to John Ciardi, then director of the conference, who understood better than anyone else my need to be confirmed as a writer. I am sure it was through his good offices that I received that scholarship. Miller Williams was my critic, and he encouraged me to go ahead with my first book. He is the only poet who gave me permission to disagree. That is an excellent privilege. It allows you to state your intentions in a nondefensive way and continue to learn.

This time I lived in Cherry House with eight to twelve other men. My roommate was the poet Alvin Aubert. He had only one book out then, but he has since done considerable and remarkable work, including being the founder and first editor of *Obsidian*, a magazine devoted to black American writing and criticism. It was he who encouraged me to seek out Miller Williams. One other memorable person who lived in that house was William Kotzwinkle. He had written a children's story of exquisite charm, "Marie," I think it was called. Soon after the conference it was published and later included in his first book of short stories. He impressed me because he was quiet and stayed to himself. Later I discovered that he was not only in love but engaged as well, and he had finally decided that this was the summer to wed. He asked me to stand up with him as best man, and I quickly agreed. He also asked me not to mention it to any of the other guys in the house, no doubt because they would tease him. Though I never broke the promise, the secret was somehow discovered. I tell this now because it points to a characteristic which I have never altered or thought to change. If you tell me a secret, I keep it. I place it so far back at the end of my long-term memory that I almost forget. I am not committed to gossip. I owe that summer to John Ciardi and his faith in my work, not only for the friends and memories I made, but for the special confidence he offered in his own quiet way. He had a first-rate eye and ear for gifted writers and promising work.

To illustrate how fearful I was in New York, those first months in the Village when I went to poetry readings, I read under a pseudonym. The name I chose was David Dave. The names belonged to my father and grandfather respectively. I thought I might be laughed out of not only the Village but existence as well. I had heard about the Beats from the media and I thought I knew how that group frowned upon academic forms of poetry. Well, no such thing occurred. After I had read, a written invitation was passed along to me asking me to join a local writers' workshop. Among the promising writers were Carol Bergé, Susan Sherman, Taylor Mead, Diane Wakoski, Jackson MacLow, Marguerite Harris, and Ree Dragonette. There were others writers frequenting the Village at that time: Calvin Herton, Raymond Patterson, David Henderson, Lorenzo Thomas, Ishmael Reed, and Bob Dylan, who took up the guitar and began singing his poems. Dylan succeeded us at the Thirdside because Ree got us thrown out for referring to the coffeehouse as "the third side of death."

Having begun this essay, which is in many respects about myself, I realize that my worst habit now that I am "mid-way through life" (a Dante echo) is revising too much. This is at once a good and dangerous characteristic. I am now in the process of teaching myself when to leave well enough alone. This is a difficult lesson to learn. Too much revision destroys spontaneity; too little revision leaves work in a semi-unborn state. I hope for better each time I begin, aiming for a piece with no cracks or seams. I suspect that the best I attain is somewhere in between a work that is too girdled and one which has no girdle at all.

Let me say here and now that I am suspicious of writers who say they do not revise. I had some ideas in my head when I began this particular essay, and I wrote them down in a random order, and then I lost that version. So I had to begin again. For all intents and purposes, when I started again I was on the second or third draft, depending on how one counts. One thinks, which is a version; then one writes, which is another version, and then one makes huge or slight changes, which result in another version, because, I suspect, as my mother used to say, "You want to put your best foot forward." It is the artifice one is after, the magic of the effect; it is the visual realization constructed and brought to life on a flat sheet of paper. When your readers believe implicitly that what you have placed on a sheet of paper represents a part of reality, you have achieved a goal. Of course when you begin the next piece, you begin, as it were, all over again, not knowing if you will fail or succeed. Fear is a white sheet of snow. Will it survive? Will you see the chance beauty there? Will others see the same beauty? Can you, with accurate sleight-of-hand, show it to them? This is the work of the writer; it is my work, and many times I sense that I can do nothing else better. It is in a sense like a religious calling. So more or less I am in the business of condensed emotion, the preservation of humanity and all that is good about it. What is particular about my vision is that my good may not be someone else's, and their sense of morality may not be mine.

I think when we work with language we invoke the world of magic. For the Judeo-Christian world the "word" is central: "Let there be . . . and there was. . . ." So in a sense when I wrote in "My Mother's Voice" the lines "Lawd chile, I done told you a million times . . . / Them words is the Devil's work," I was satirizing the process by which writers create. Writers are like demigods. They too create out of chaos, out of nothing. They create out of their imagination that which did not exist in exactly those proportions or dimensions before. That is, in itself, magic. This is the world of the poet/writer, and it is the world I inhabit no matter how mad or dangerous it may seem to others.

Let me once more return to my infancy. I was born in Birmingham, Alabama, and much of my fears of water, policemen, and dogs come from living in that city. My life began in 1933. I am one of six first cousins. Only one of my paternal aunts chose to have two children; all the rest had one. Everyone in my father's generation is gone except two aunts; I hope against hope that I have inherited their genes.

My mother, as far as I was informed, was one of three children: two girls and one boy. Her brother and sister were older; they left home early and returned only once, when their mother died. After the funeral she never saw them again. I think of Etheridge Knight's great poem "The Idea of Ancestry."

> . . . *There is no*
> *place in her Bible for whereabouts unknown.*

It is this perception that demonstrates the mark of greatness. Knowing that new perceptions are possible, given time and thought, I get up daily with renewed strength and confront the fear implicit on a blank sheet of paper.

My father and mother came to Toledo, Ohio, in 1916 and 1947 respectively. I followed my mother six months later in the winter of 1948. I remember the conductor coming through the train and announcing: "We have just crossed the Mason and Dixon Line." Settling back into my seat I thought to myself, That's that! I didn't look back for almost twenty years and could not have guessed then that my formative years were already set in concrete and hardening. And as I have said earlier, it has only been in recent years that I have begun to mine the wealth contained in those experiences.

It is a wealth of imaginative detail which has lain untapped in my mind. I guess I have always had a comic flare for the folksy dialect and black vernacular, because I remember Robert Hayden being very amused when I lapsed into speaking that way. I also remember Dudley Randall warning me to be careful because of the way dialect seemed to affect Paul Laurence Dunbar's career. I think that Randall gave me the warning because, even though Dunbar needed and was pleased with William Dean Howell's endorsement, I think he ultimately felt trapped because he could not sell his standard English poems as quickly as he could the dialect pieces. There is still a belief that dialect means ignorant and uneducated. It is an unfortunately false signal. A new explanation needs to be put forth about the origins and development of black dialect in America. So I backed off as if the fire were too hot, but I still played with it from time to time, as children will do with the fire of imagination when no one is looking.

In the early days I remember my father was fascinated with detective stories, science magazines, and other pulp magazines. My mother was engrossed in the Bible. More important, stories of heroics and daring were told in the middle room in the evening as we sat by the fire, sometimes listening to "Amos and Andy" and their antics, or to "The Inner Sanctum," which generally terrified the women and children.

These days I want to make sense out of the images I create. I think that I want to make the reader feel passionately some of the things I have felt. I want this despite the fluidity and changeability of words. I think this may mean making accurate and even sometimes severe choices between the words I first think about and the words I write down.

I realize that I am limited by what I think a reader might want to know about my life, and indeed by what questions an interviewer might ask. No interview can attain all the answers one might desire, and that may be the reason why writers sometimes grant several interviews during a lifetime. Point of view is important with each writer because it points to material from a perspective different from any we have ever considered before. No two writers think exactly alike. It is possible to perceive and identify with another position because it is similar to your own, but each writer must possess his or her own specific voice.

Voice is as identifiable as a fingerprint. We know the writer by the distinctive voice. Shakespeare, Mozart, Michelangelo, Van Gogh, Walker, Faulkner, Welty, all have recognizable voices. The point here is that no writer really wants to sound like another writer. Voice may be related to style, because style is related to an individual writer as well as year, decade, and century. Sometimes styles reappear as they do in dress, but since language is in continual flux, they do not seem to reappear in terms of definitions or styles of speech. Style is again an integral part of approach: how one begins, how one narrates, how one describes, how one combines. The technique of writing is like a recipe; the ingredients are all the same but the combinations and the order make the difference. Thus we produce many similar dishes with differing effects on the palate.

In a recent letter to me, a Hungarian student made several statements about language and meaning which made me rethink my position on writing.

> *I have always loved the way you read aloud poems, but sometimes I do not have critical ears — it must be terribly wrong that that makes me miss the point. Reading delivers the receiver important materials through the eyes. But reading only to yourself and to a public are totally different. The first one can be achieved by acquiring proper pronunciation, intonation skills, but the latter one needs significant practice in timing. . . . If I read to myself, there is no need to care [for] stops of breaths, breathing in and out, falling and rising intonation. . . .*

The small quarrel I have with my former student is that I think he touches only part of the truth about reading and meaning. Whether you read to yourself or to a public audience, the reader must always consider the pauses, the rise and fall of rhythms, pitch, intonation, and timing. Reading carefully to oneself can be practice for a public reading. Reading well in your head as well as aloud ensures "that you will not miss meaning." All of the above component parts are the spices of meaning. They are all necessary to obtain meaning. If you ignore a comma or period or question mark, you have ignored an important signal of meaning. Imagine the chaos if one paid no attention to the key signature, the rests, the rhythmic dynamics of a musical composition written before this century? Those markings are there for meaning. They are not to be ignored and certainly must be heard in the head of composer, conductor, and performer alike or the entire process is for naught. Thus I would suggest that a good reader reads well aloud as well as in one's head. My finest teachers in this respect were W. H. Auden, Dylan Thomas, and Sir John Gielgud. I ran the gamut of extremes between their reading styles. I learned something else about music and phrasing from singers, musical compositions, and the old black Southern preachers. These are the technical influences in my life. There are too many poets from past centuries for me to name, and I admire many of my contemporaries for their use of language and their vision. There are many poems by some of them that I wish I had written. Finally I must confess that I will appropriate from any discipline or genre any effect which seems to work in print. I try to bring music to my lines; I try to give them shape, motion, and color. I try to imitate what a critic must mean when speaking about the music of poetry—the combination of syllables and words which communicates certain sounds and makes a particular music. Tone is essential to all writing because it, too, implies meaning. We never, or almost never, misunderstand the tone of a parent or teacher; it is identifiable. The same is true of the good writer and the excellent artist.

My years at SUNY at Buffalo were a mixture of ups and downs. The first two years of course work were horrendous, but I struggled with every demon who saw fit to confront me. For the most part, I won with a certain amount of dignity. I remember Gary Brodsky, who struggled as much as I did, fearing C's around every bend. Meat hooks, we called them, that would fling us into the wilds of the country, without a degree, if we were not careful. In those days, I confess, a 9-to-5 job without papers to grade or preparations was very inviting. We survived because tradition (Jew and black) demanded it of us.

My mother had a stroke near the end of that first year. I was ready to throw in the towel and go home and take up my duties. She had seen me into manhood; I could see her into comfortable old age. That stroke was the beginning of the end, although my mother's will was not conquered until twenty-one years later when she finally succumbed to cancer. It was during those years that I began the long series of "W. Poems" which have in some sense become a poetic autobiography. That first poem was commissioned by Joseph Fennimore the composer and was published by Quincey Troupe. The last of that group recounts the final months of my mother's life, when we learned that her cancer was terminal. I was reminded of Etheridge Knight, whose doctor reportedly told him: "I am afraid your cancer is terminal, Mr. Knight." He replied quickly and to the mark: "I am afraid life is terminal, doctor."

My mother lived long enough to see her granddaughter. She lived long enough to see me president of the senior class at the Bread Loaf School of English, to see me receive my degree, and to travel to Pittsburgh to see me get my doctorate. That was an interesting day; I got to sit next to Richard Wilbur, who was being given another honorary degree. Then the years went painfully quick, and now she rests from the labors of this world. Much of what I have become is because of her encouragement and indefatigable will, and as an inheritance, I pass it on to my daughter.

Only two other women have buttressed my career with belief and encouragement. They were Irene Neuman, affectionately my "New York Mother," and Sarah S. Bissell, who, like Dr. Grey at the University of Toledo saw me as a good student and never as separate or incapable. When I teach I try to imitate the visions of Grey and Bissell, to pass on what they gave unstintingly to me, to others.

For me, then, there are two ingredients necessary when I am trying to make poems: experience and imagination. The line between these two elements is very thin and even sometimes indistinguishable, so much so that it should be impossible to tell where experience ends and imagination begins. This is true when the mixture is exactly right. Perhaps this is true when you consider that each time you tell a story after an initial incident has occurred, embellishments in voice, gesture, character, dialogue, and even atmosphere take place, for one learns with each telling to adjust and tighten those moments which are working best and eliminating those which do not contribute to the desired effect. I try to learn and understand what my fingertips might meaningfully have to say. I try to hear what the grass and water whisper to each other. I try to watch as the daylight and nightlight bathe each other. I try to taste the perfumes of the air and smell the gloriousness of the world, which is always there at the bend leading to the next universe.

Someone is left out of this thumbnail sketch, but then someone would be left out of a three-hundred-page autobiography. When you condense, that is the failing. Something or someone gets left out, but that makes for another story, another book, another time.

Books

New York the Nine Million and Other Poems. Abracadabra Press, 1969.
The Shit-Storm Poems. Pilot Press, 1973.
The Persistence of the Flesh. Lotus Press, 1976.
Paul Laurence Dunbar: A Singer of Songs (monograph). State Library of Ohio, 1979.
Forms of Silence. Lotus Press, 1980.

Anthologies

10 Michigan Poets. Ed. L. E. Grinke. Pilot Press, 1972.
The Poetry of Black America: Anthology of the 20th Century. E. Arnold Adoff. Harper's, 1973.
The Urban Reader. Eds. Susan Cahill and Michelle Cooper. Prentice-Hall, 1971.
Afro-American Literature: An Introduction. Eds. Burrows, Lapides, and Hayden. Harcourt Brace and World, 1971.
Peace Is Our Profession. Ed. Jan Barry. East River Anthology, 1981.
The Cornfield Review: An Anthology of Ohio Poets. Eds. David Citino, James Bertilino, and Alberta Turner. Ohio State at Marion, 1984.
Glass Will. Ed. Joel Lipman. Toledo Poets Center Press, 1988.
A Milestone Sampler: 15th Anniversary Anthology. Ed. Naomi Long Madgett. Lotus Press, 1988.

Essays

"Paul Laurence Dunbar." *Book of Days.* Ed. C. Edward Wall. Pierian Press, 1987.
"Carter G. Woodson." *Read More about It.* Ed. Carla J. Kohoyda-Inglis. Pierian Press, 1989.
"How 'The Deadwood Dick Poems' Came into Being." *The Writing Room: Keys to the Craft of Fiction and Poetry.* Ed. Eve Shelnutt. Longstreet Press, 1989.

Periodicals

Poems have been published in the following journals: *Beloit Poetry Journal, Black American Literature Journal, Broken Streets, Centennial Review, Cottonwood, George Washington Review, Grand Street, Images, James White Review, Late Knocking, Mississippi Mud, Pied Pipe, Ploughshares, Poetry, The Great Lakes Review, Strand, Up Against the Wall,* and *Vincent Brothers Review.*

Videos

Paul Laurence Dunbar. Twentig Productions, 1984.
The Eyes of the Poet: Paul Laurence Dunbar. 1991.

Recordings

The Poems of Herbert Woodward Martin. Library of Congress, 1976.
"Six Songs." *The Music of Joseph Fennimore.* Albany Records, 1989.

Steven Bauer

Steven Bauer received his M.F.A. from the University of Massachusetts and teaches literature and writing at Miami University in Oxford, Ohio. A fiction writer and poet, he has won the Peregrine Smith Poetry Prize, the Strousse Award for Poetry, an outstanding teacher award from Miami University students, and several fellowships and grants. He lives in Bath, Indiana.

BECOMING A GARDENER

I have been gardening for the past four days. The weather, which for weeks had been unseasonably hot and humid, finally broke and presented me with a stretch of cool dry weather, so I allowed myself the pleasure of digging in the dirt. I find that kind of digging easier than this other kind. I am more patient with soil and seeds than I am with words; I am more forgiving when something fails to flower or bear fruit.

I've been building a large perennial bed for almost a decade now, and the progress has been steady, if not always easy. It generally takes three years for the bare-root twigs or tender shoots which arrive via UPS to resemble the glorious pictures in the mail-order catalogs, from whose plantsmen I order the species more various than the sparse stock available locally. I don't know why, but perennial gardening isn't practiced much around here, certainly not when compared to the growing of vegetables and annuals, and so what I've learned I've learned on my own. It has taken a while, trial and error mostly, to understand which plants will thrive under the conditions my part of the middle West provides — fierce drying winds in late spring; humid, often scorching summers; lingering falls; generally mild winters, with too-occasional snow, and every now and then a calamitous drop to sub-zero temperatures and a wind chill which pushes the cold's effect down to forty below. Bee balm does well here, and hollyhock mallow. These flowers are so tough — indeed, so invasive — that barely anything I or the weather can do seems to faze them. Even now the bee balm pushes against a mature stand of heliopsis, threatening to choke it out. Daylilies flourish, too, and yarrow.

Other genera do poorly. The azaleas that in spring light up northern Florida, where my parents now live, do not like eastern Indiana. I have a small group clustered by the north side of the house, but they struggle; one or another dies each year and is replaced, and none seems to grow bigger or stronger. Two years ago, enamored of a photograph of *Crocosmia x 'Lucifer'* which resembled brilliant flames hovering over a mass of sword-like fronds, I ordered three and planted them in a prominent spot, and received for my effort a few thin leaves which looked more like whip-grass than swords. Delphinium, which the nursery catalogs proclaim "the queen of any perennial border," prefers a different kingdom than mine.

When my wife and I were in New Zealand last November, the roadsides were littered with lupine, their strong, five-foot stalks covered with purple and yellow pea-like blossoms. As we drove we discovered entire valleys, their rivers dried to a trickle, carpeted with a profusion of bloom so thick that to look at it gave me a pain in the chest, somewhere below the breastbone. But here? For years I have been trying to coax a small stand of lupine, and with little success; a plant will grow to mature size and then, for no reason I can discover, its leaves dry at the edges, until they look like shreds of grocery bags, and then the whole plant withers and dies.

There are lessons for me in gardening, lessons I could profitably transfer to my writing, but up until now I've been unable to. I'm continually enraged when something I start, full of hope and promise, a vision in my mind more ravishing than any full-color photograph in a gardening catalog, simply will not take root and flower. I refuse to learn from my experience about what grows well in the soil of my unconscious. Though I possess an imagination which sees striped bees bubbling up out of a pail of fresh milk as evidence of serious ill in the kingdom of Balistrodde, where the king, a man who has never been warm, is deforesting the land to feed his ever-present fires, I do not value this vision, as — in the beginning — I didn't value those plants which needed no special nurturance or husbandry. Thus I abandoned a novel called *The Seven Months of Winter* at somewhere near a hundred pages. It includes the following, in which the king, having sent his seven ministers into the hinterlands to bring back signs of the impending winter's fury, is given a small glass vial to reassure him:

> *The king took a finger and dipped it in the pollen. As he touched it, it seemed to melt, to coat his finger with gold leaf, and when he placed it on his tongue, the attar of roses filled the Great Hall, so the odor of horse and sweat, the pungent smell of woodsmoke disappeared. Before him, as if growing out of the carpet and the heavily hewn stones beneath it, the king saw banks and banks of roses, their centers heavy with gold dust, nodding in a breeze which was no breeze. At that moment the sun hit an angle above the earth which brought its roundness visible for the first time that day from within the Great Hall, throwing an elongated fan of fire across the company. The pollen in the king's hand disappeared. He felt a slight sting, as if touched by a bee, and a wisp of smoke*

*smelling of roses left the king's palm. There was total silence in
the hall as everyone watched the smoke until it dissolved; then
the logs began again to crackle.*

In that moment of transformation and stillness lies my talent, but
I've chosen to turn my back on it in favor of the grittier odor of horse
and sweat and woodsmoke.

For years I've given most of my attention to the mainstream
realistic fiction which doesn't come easily to me, but which seems to
have a monopoly on reviewers' consideration; when I finally coaxed
out such a novel, it was not the exotic cultivar I'd hoped for, but
closer to a weed. There is hope for me, though; one lesson I've so
clearly learned from plants is patience — patience on the scale of
years. There are visions waiting to be had, many words still waiting to
be written.

Both my parents worked, in a way, with words. My mother was
secretary to the principal of our local elementary school and spent her
days behind a typewriter. My father, employed by the Paterson
Evening News, was one of the last stereotypers in the United States;
he took me to work with him once, when I was preparing a fifth-
grade project about newspapers, and he showed me how he made the
curved stereotype plates fastened to the great rotary presses seen in
so many movies of the thirties and forties. I watched him,
Hephaestus of the world's events, as he poured molten lead into a
matrix of wood and rag pulp, a mold formed by heavy pressure against
the formal locked rectangular type-galleys prepared by the linotype
operators. This process was known as "hot" type, and with the
advent of computers and "cold" type, my father's occupation became
as functionally obsolete as the manual typewriter and carbon paper.

But though they worked with words, my parents weren't readers; in
fact, only once can I remember either of them with a book. That
book was Jim Bishop's *The Day Christ Died*. Bishop had bought my
paternal grandparents' house in Sea Bright, New Jersey, and my
father had dinner with him after the closing, where he was presented
with an autographed copy. I never picked up this book: I had loved
the Sea Bright house, with its third-floor bedroom I slept in and its
dormer window with a clear view across the seawall and expanse of
beach to the gray and heaving Atlantic, and I hated the man who had
taken it away from me.

As I remember, there were fewer than ten books in our house in
northern New Jersey, and all but the Bishop belonged to my mother's
stepmother, who lived with us. Tielhard de Chardin's *The Phenomenon*

of Man. Thus Spake Zarathustra. Will Durant's *The Life of Greece.* William H. Prescott's *History of the Conquest of Peru.* When she was not in the backyard poking about in her two narrow perennial beds, this grandmother sat alone in her room in the house's converted attic, sipping a tumbler of rum and thumbing through dense pages of philosophy and history. On Saturdays she put up her feet and listened to the Metropolitan Opera, brought to her by Texaco and introduced by Milton Cross. To me, she was an inspiration. She had only an eighth-grade education yet now was reading French theologians and listening to Rossini. Her brother Wiard, an architect, lived in Holly-wood and was married to Edith Head, the costume designer; stories filtered east of their having Alfred Hitchcock over for dinner. She had a friend in Denmark whom I never met, a woman I referred to as Aunt Elsa. Someday I would get to Hollywood and swim in the indoor-outdoor pool set in a grotto surrounded by hibiscus; someday I would go to Copenhagen and see the statue of the Little Mermaid in the harbor.

Though I never got to California or to Denmark as a child, I traveled to Tahiti and Panama, the Fountain of Youth and Guadalcanal, by way of the books I read. The one thing on which my parents could be absolutely counted during those years was to take me to the library whenever I asked to go. Florham Park was too small for even a high school, so my parents drove me to Madison, the neighboring town, where, like a fortress, the public library commanded the north end of Main Street. I'd been in it once with the mother of a friend, who took us into the hushed dim interior when she was returning some books, and I longed for my fourteenth birthday when I could enter it unaccompanied, whenever I wanted.

It was a stone building with a formidable flight of steps leading to a heavy double-hung door; across a marble parquet lobby stood a mahogany circulation desk behind which brooded a bespectacled dragon. It had a turret, a dank basement, and a reading room lined with massive oak tables, each one surrounded by sleek oak chairs with scrolled arms. Best of all it harbored what appeared to me at the time to be a structural impossibility. Sets of tightly curling wrought-iron stairs led to the library's open second story, a floating world where the fiction was seemingly hung from the roof, with no visible ground supports, an enormous wall-less loft, with a floor made of glass panes, inches thick, through which the haze of the ground floor could be dimly seen as the surface of a lake can be sensed from ten feet below the surface.

But this land of promise was not for children. *Butterfield 8* and *From the Terrace* and *Peyton Place* were shelved on the open stacks, so the

Library Board had decided on fourteen as the proper time for the issuance of a lending card. For the time being, I had to be content with the Children's Library, which stood across the street in a grim little storefront, with an unwashed plate-glass window covered with flyers and the Scotch tape remnants of their ancestors, the very poor relation to the castle across from it. My mother or father would pull up before the curb and sit there with the motor running. Neither of them ever chided me or told me to be quick about my selection, but neither of them accompanied me inside either, as did the parents of other boys and girls. I was on my own. My mother or father simply sat out front, in the burbling getaway car, while I went about the task of pillaging the shelves of their booty.

The Landmark Series, for example: in my memory there were hundreds of volumes, about various historical events and personages, brave strong men and women who did remarkable things. I should know everything there is to know about history, but I cannot remember a single title, much less a single piece of information — those books went through me without leaving a trace. Then there was the adventure series about the two brothers who wound up in places as foreign as opera locales, as they went about having a Volcano Adventure or South Sea Adventure. But the Children's Library seemed to me a pale place, finally, and when I would literally stagger out to the car, a stack of books tottering between the brace of my arms, there, across the street, stood the Public Library, its turret's slate-roofed spire knifing the late-afternoon sky.

Perhaps this drastic architectural disjunction, symbolizing as it did for me the separation of "children's" books and "adult" books, helped give me such a distorted sense of the value of mainstream fiction. In school, I was well ahead of my peers, at least according to those standardized tests which determined "reading level," and so was steadfast in my desire for the books I thought adults read. With no one at home to guide me in my pursuit of what this meant — and I was too proud to ask questions of librarians or other strangers, thereby exposing my ignorance — I turned to such cultural arbiters as the Book-of-the-Month Club, whose advertisements were everywhere. This earnest wrong-headedness made me yearn for Leon Uris's *Exodus* and James Michener's *Hawaii*, books I believed held the secrets of mainstream culture. How else but through reading was I going to rise above the provincial blue-collar life into which I'd been born?

These habits of thought die hard. Though I'm no longer so naive, I am still reflexively drawn to the *New York Times Book Review*'s early December edition which clears its throat and through pinched lips pronounces the "year's best." (How, I wonder, can I read these two hundred titles before January 1?) Though many of my favorite contemporary authors—Mark Helprin, Ursula LeGuin, Martin Amis—appear on this list, would Melville and Faulkner have made the cut, compiled as it is from one idiosyncratic review? And these writers I wholeheartedly admire are still a far cry from the writers of so-called mainstream fiction. They are, by and large, fabulists: Sutpen's Hundred, the great white whale, flying horses, enormous babies, the myths and songs of a culture which hasn't yet evolved.

The books I should have been reading as a child, and which were lavishly available in the Children's Library—the Pooh and Alice books, *The Hobbit* and *Lord of the Rings*, *Treasure Island*, even *Huckleberry Finn*—I disdained as being "below" me. They were easily available; they were for "babies." I chose, instead, the Children's Library's versions of the books I aspired to—"realistic" texts about World War II or Lewis and Clark, or the adventurous brothers (the children's equivalent of Ludlam or Deighton). Jim Hawkins and Frodo, Alice and Eeyore, had to wait until I was an adult.

If I blundered about in my reading, I began writing for the wrong reasons altogether. Though I seemed to possess, with little work on my part, an inherent understanding of the ways in which sentences were constructed, I did not begin to write because it gave me pleasure, or because it was a tool for exploration, or because I wanted to write a book I wanted to read.

I began to write because I wanted approbation. And not in a vacuum—no, I wanted the approbation of Mrs. Miller, my freshman high school English teacher. There was a chasm at home I could no longer bridge, no longer wished to; my parents were lost in their private furies and miseries, their war of the Four Roses, and I was busy pretending I was in no way like them. I told myself I'd been adopted and hadn't been informed. But this common-as-dirt fantasy didn't go far enough. The fact was I felt like an alien; I felt like a creature from Mars. I wanted a reason to feel so abnormal.

As I look back on it now, Mrs. Miller was an unlikely crush. She wore her hair high and teased, in something I only later came to realize was the style of Jacqueline Kennedy; she wore so much makeup that her eyelashes looked like rusted crimped wire. She had bow-shaped lips, painted crimson. While I was busy shooting up to my current height of well over six feet, she was a diminutive woman with the hands and feet of a geisha.

But who can fathom love? At the time, I wanted more than anything for her to notice me, and though I doubt whether I would have had a similar crush on her had she been my chemistry or geometry teacher, I had at my disposal the requisite ability: she told me I wrote very well.

In eighth grade, Miss Gordon had attempted to teach us the intricacies of syntax through sentence diagramming, a practice which seems to have gone the way of home milk delivery. My students now claim never to have seen the horizontal line slashed by the vertical, separating the subject and predicate, or the intricate series of slants under them, like the street map of a demented housing development. But back then, Miss Gordon would stand, arms crossed on her chest, and bark out a sentence which we, having been divided into two teams, would rush to the blackboard to elucidate. *The young boy in the red cap hit the baseball so hard it disappeared. Boy* to the left of them; *hit* to the right of them. Volleying and thundering, we placed *baseball* on the special space after the predicate reserved for direct objects, we placed the subjectival prepositional phrase in its proper subordinated position, we realized that *hard* was an adverb, modified by the adjective *so*. What to do about *it disappeared*?

But the next year, as I sat in Mrs. Miller's classroom, she suggested we diagram this: *It was a rich cream color, bright with nickel, swollen here and there in its monstrous length with triumphant hat-boxes and supper-boxes and tool-boxes, and terraced with a labyrinth of windshields that mirrored a dozen suns.* Twenty-seven years later, I can't read the description of that car without feeling a shiver between the shoulder blades. The point was, Mrs. Miller didn't really want us to diagram that sentence any more than she wanted us to take apart the humming engine under the cream hood; she didn't want us to become experts on subordinate clauses or to learn the rhythms of what we would all, in a fit of syntactic sophistication, later come to call the periodic sentence. No, she wanted us to luxuriate in the language the way Nick Carraway was about to luxuriate in the back seat of Gatsby's "green leather conservatory." She wanted us to swoon.

I swooned. If she was to be the high priestess of art, skipping hurriedly over *Cheaper by the Dozen* and *Mama's Bank Account* in favor of a languorous stroll through *As You Like It* (the school board–approved Shakespeare for ninth graders), I would be her acolyte. If the poetry of Edwin Arlington Robinson made her momentarily put one of her petite hands to the string of faux pearls at her neck, then I would write poetry, faux as it turned out to be. Had the unconscious been discovered by 1962? Not in that classroom tucked away in a regional northern New Jersey high school. A whole cult developed; I soon found myself rubbing shoulders with three other smitten boys who sought Mrs. Miller out for private attention. I was the most shameless of the lot, writing poem after poem for her, presenting them for her scrutiny and the flattery of her red pen. The poems, of course, were tortured and dark — metaphors startling in their obtuseness leaped from my brain in a regular frenzy. She took every one seriously; she was nothing if not encouraging. I found the comments, fastidiously written in looping cursive, a kind of love letter.

What I am trying to say here is that for me, writing (and I was now determined to be a writer) had nothing to do with writing: I was after product. It was product after all which was returned to me with Mrs. Miller's sweet scent. I became a perfect poetry machine.

And for years I went on producing, creating products; when they were finished — stories, poems, novels — I sent them forth like so many voodoo dolls of myself, to be worshiped or to be stuck with the sharp pins of criticism or rejection. The hours at the typewriter were agony, since there was no pleasure in the process. All my energy was centered on the product: the response to this next one would change my life.

Surely a part of me knew that what I was doing was skewed, and from this knowledge grew the double-headed serpent of guilt and fear. And as I continued, in one form or another over the years, to write for praise and love, the guilt and fear came to overpower me, so that I felt nauseous whenever I thought about sitting down to write. Fear of success, my wise friends told me; fear of failure, I told myself. But it was neither of these, finally. It was the fear and guilt which derive from inauthenticity. When one writes for praise, or money, or the adulation of strangers, one poisons the well from which the writing itself comes. Sooner or later the sickness unto death sets in, and writing is no more possible than flying. And then where are you, when you are no longer capable of producing the objects which bring you water, and light, and air, and life itself?

Like writing, gardening is a solitary pursuit. It requires a willingness to experiment, sometimes to act on impulse. The most carefully planned garden — plotted on graph paper, as the books suggest — must finally bow before the hard realities of confronting a blank space of earth with a shovel, rake, and trowel. It demands faith — that the carefully sown seeds will germinate, the plants, through proper cultivation, flourish. It takes imagination — trying to envision the effect, three years from now, of a mass of shepherd's crook planted in front of a stand of loosestrife. It requires an enthusiasm for tasks some might consider unpleasant or boring: weeding, watering, dead-heading. It demands a readiness to be ruthless. Some weeds are tempting (wild yarrow, for example, whose foliage is feathery and delicate, but whose umbels are dirty white and bedraggled; worse, by the time it's bloomed, its wildly ambitious root system has strangled everything around it). Particularly zealous plants must be pruned back in order to give the faint hearted enough sun and air, and some few must be constantly savaged (one's darlings) to keep them under control. Mostly, it takes a willingness to spend an inordinate amount of time on one's hands and knees, like a supplicant.

Sophomore year (*Julius Caesar*) I had Mr. Teichert, a tall and earnest man who seemed bewildered to find himself before a classroom of squirming adolescents. After my experiences with Mrs. Miller, who had praised my vibrating soul when I handed her a poem using a pile of frozen sand as a metaphor for conformity, Mr. Teichert was a disappointment. But I was stuck in a rut, and so I continued to write poems and present them for approval. These were left on Mr. Teichert's desk, offhandedly. And they were duly returned, though not with the breathtaking speed of which Mrs. Miller was capable. (As I remember, I'd slip a poem into her small hands at noon and receive her homage at the close of school.) Mr. Teichert was a good deal more desultory both in terms of getting the poem back to me and in terms of his response. Instead of Mrs. Miller's annotations and exclamations, Mr. Teichert, without fail, for an entire year, placed a small "95 — See me" in pencil in the upper right hand corner of each poem. I never did "see" Mr. Teichert. I mean, what was the point? I didn't want a percentage; I wanted words as a mirror in which to see myself. Still, I was comforted by the knowledge that I was only fifteen and writing almost flawless poems. Surely by the time I was eighteen and a freshman in college I could master those five points separating me from perfection.

I kept writing, though more or less without a specific audience. Junior year (*Macbeth*) I was taught by Miss Usher, a severe woman whose Scottish accent made her sound to me as though the words were escaping from her lips against her will just as she had surely escaped, at the last moment, from Poe's story. Tall as a pike, with jet-black hair, she lacked Mrs. Miller's neediness and Mr. Teichert's befuddleness, and perhaps I obscurely understood that my adolescent effulgences would not be received so kindly into her long-fingered pale-nailed hands. Senior year (*Hamlet*) I was allowed entrance into the most elite class at my high school, the Humanities Studies Group. This was presided over ("taught" conveys neither his magisterial knowledge nor his sardonic wit) by Mr. Keisman. Short, compact, and balding, though he was only in his early forties, Keisman was a doctor; while some of our other teachers had received a master's degree, Keisman had a Ph.D. from Columbia. Even so, we were admonished always to call him mister.

Under the spell of our own astounding luck, we never questioned why he continued to teach on the high school level. (Later, to my chagrin, I learned the degree was in education rather than English.) He always wore three-piece tweed suits, always; and across the front of his vest, his Phi Beta Kappa key glittered. Now were I to find someone so attired, I'd find him arrogant at best, even ridiculous. But at the time, when the key seemed destined to unlock the door to a place I wanted to go, when the key was held by Mr. Keisman, I was properly awed.

Keisman's class was a whirlwind of organization. We started with the Greeks. Keisman lectured on the city-state and resulting wars; he read part of *The Iliad* aloud to us in Greek. We read Plato and were lectured on the "other" philosophers; we studied sculpture, spending as much time on Pheidias as we had on *Macbeth*. We learned the fundamentals of post and lintel architecture and how, inevitably, this evolved into the Parthenon. We chanted *Doric, Ionic, Corinthian*; we read *Oedipus Rex* and *Antigone*. By June we'd limped into the Middle Ages. Though this clearly sounds like Western Civ fare, let me emphasize what a revelation it was for the son of a blue-collar family in a relative backwater.

But it was also a high school English class, so Keisman wrote rules on the board; we learned the difference between *number* and *amount*, *continuous* and *continual*, *between* and *among*. We learned that *suave* and *epitome* were not pronounced *swavay* or *epitoam*. We were given fifty new vocabulary words a week: *coruscate, hirsute, jejune, soporific*. If Mrs. Miller had been for me the high priestess of art, Keisman was a demigod. Pure knowledge flowed in his veins; if I could have, I'd have arranged for a transfusion.

While I had wanted Mrs. Miller to think me sensitive and aware, I wanted Keisman to think me *erudite, discerning, puissant*. My diligence and desire were rewarded; that year I received the not-very-much-coveted top-of-the-class prize. I still have it, a copy of A. E. Hotchner's *Papa Hemingway* in which is written, in the finest calligraphy, on the pea-green front endpaper, "For intellectual integrity in the Humanities Studies Group." This was a new meaning of the word *integrity*: n. the vaulting ambition to be loved and respected.

Armed with my new erudition, and my copy of the Hotchner—such irony!—I went off to Trinity College in Hartford, Conn., prepared to have my poems universally admired. At my first wine-and-cheese party, I looked wildly around for a slice of American, the only kind I thought existed. I discovered quickly enough that there were lots of words I didn't know — *Brie* and *Port-Salut*, *Pinot Noir* and *Chardonnay*. Surprisingly, no one much wanted to hear my well-rehearsed speech about Pheidias. To end this part of the story, let me just say that the college literary magazine rejected all the poems I submitted to it, and when I wrote a condescending review of it for the college paper (oh, bad mistake!), the editor of the magazine wrote a cool, controlled letter to the editor of *The Tripod* suggesting that perhaps my aesthetic judgments had been affected by my disappointment. So much for *integrity*; so much for being loved and respected.

It continues to embarrass and amaze me how naked and alike we are, all living things, animal and plant, in our earliest desires — to be protected, to be cared for, to be fed, to be given room to grow. If these desires aren't met when we're infants, or if they're thwarted, or if too much is asked of us (and I suspect one or more of these conditions is true of everyone's life), we're enraged, and frightened of our rage, because we understand, inherently, how powerless we are in the face of these gods who refuse to give us what we need. Those desires, unfortunately, don't shut up, like polite little children should, but go underground, continuing to clamor for satiation.

We turn elsewhere, looking blindly for those needs to be satisfied in friends, lovers, teachers, spouses, psychiatrists. There was Mrs. Miller with her teased hair and her looping red pen; there was Mr. Teichert with his implicit promise of perfection. There were my friends whose approval I pursued with the dedication of the fanatic. While at Trinity I joined a fraternity for a while, and there was the class of 1968, two years ahead of me — George Fosque, Lew Goverman, Rod Cook, and many others — and when they graduated, I lost interest in the fraternity, and quit. In the years after college, when I finally went to California, there were Barbara and Charles Minor, whose children Pam and Pat were respectively my lover and my best friend. And in graduate school, at the University of Massachusetts (after discovering that if I stayed in California's gold country, whose cerulean skies and fig trees and cold wild rivers demanded all my attention, I could forget my ambitions as a writer), there were Maxine Kumin and James Tate, as well as other apprentice-writers like myself.

My poems began to be published, and that brought some pleasure. But now I wanted more: a book, a teaching job, an NEA grant, famous drinking buddies. Most of all I wanted to be adopted by a great man.

In the summer of 1978 I was awarded a working scholarship to the Bread Loaf Writers Conference. As most people know, Bread Loaf

positions itself as the oldest and most elite of the summer conferences; it prides itself on the most distinguished staff, the most
elegant surroundings. For easily impressed me, it was irresistible —
part summer camp, part cocktail party, where standing in a group
just out of reach were the people one had dreamed of meeting all
one's life, a whole cadre of mentors. The problem was that the strict
hierarchy which governs Bread Loaf works to keep the plebes in their
place, while the aristocracy retires to a cottage across the road, for
drinks and the kind of conversation which would (I thought, if I could
only get close enough to hear) change my life, if not the course of
American literature.

But if Bread Loaf mostly isolated the famous, it also offered the
opportunity to hear them lecture about craft, and one morning I
wandered into the Little Theatre, a converted barn, to listen to John
Gardner talk about the novel. I hadn't read any Gardner then, but
who needed to? I'd read about him. He'd been on the front cover of
the *New York Times Magazine*, with his mane of white hair and his
potbelly and his gnomish smile, his pipe and his motorcycle and his
black leather jacket. He had taken on the literary establishment,
chiding his fellow writers in *On Moral Fiction* to make writing matter.
Gardner had not, at that point, published *The Art of Fiction* or *On
Becoming a Novelist*, but he knew their contents intimately, and in
slightly over fifty minutes he proceeded to give us, rapid-fire, a précis
of, as he put it, "everything you need to know to write a novel."

I was thunderstruck; I took furious notes. But mostly I found
myself nodding in agreement to a series of admonitions and injunctions which made perfect sense to me. The fiction writer needed "to
create a vivid and continuous dream in the mind of the reader," he
said. I remembered those days when, home from the library with my
tottering stack of books, I repaired to my room where the world
disappeared for two or more hours while I dug the Panama Canal, or
fought at Bull Run, or went on a volcano adventure. When my mother
called me for dinner, it was almost like getting the bends, surfacing
too quickly from such a depth, up to consciousness and out of the
dream. Gardner said much more as well — about how to get a plot in
motion, for example — and I wandered out again, when the Bread
Loaf bell rang, elated and frightened, my head spinning. The director
at U. Mass. had decided for me, when I'd wanted to take both the
poetry and fiction workshops, that I was to be a poet, but I still
wanted to write fiction, and now I thought I knew where to start.

I had a fellowship the following year to the Fine Arts Work Center
in Provincetown, eight months without the distractions of the kind
of work the world means when it asks, "What do you do?" While in

California, on a walk at dusk, I'd seen the moon rise through a stand of far-away trees, and though it made swift progress, it hesitated, longer than was possible, when it reached the top limbs, as though it were trapped there. Taking the basic thrust of Gardner's lecture, I used that image as the starting point, and began asking questions: If the moon were indeed trapped in a tree, how did it get there? I discovered a great horned owl, who wished to rule the world in total darkness, who had sent a legion of ravens to capture the moon. Since the world (according to Genesis) had been created in seven days, I wondered if it might not also be destroyed in a week's time, in a book with seven chapters. In a number of sketches Pam Minor had made of Pan, e. e. cummings's "goat-footed / balloonMan" from "in Just - / spring," I noticed a satyr, whose tenuous stance between the animal and human worlds might allow me some interesting possibilities. I was extraordinarily lucky that the first line appeared to me as in a vivid and continuous dream: "It was just past midnight, and the air was filled with wings." From this I unraveled a novel called *Satyrday*.

The following summer I returned to Bread Loaf with the manuscript in hand, and this time asked to be paired with a fiction writer rather than a poet, as I had the previous summer. I asked for, and got, John Gardner; I was sick with trepidation. When Gardner approached me in the Bread Loaf dining hall and said, "You've written a wonderful novel," I heard the angels singing. The world burned red at the edges; in the distance a wild wind bent the trees low. All sound drained into a point in the floor between my shoes. I'd found, at long last, my mentor.

Immediately I began work on another novel, this one written completely with John in mind (how far I'd come from Mrs. Miller!). Whereas *Satyrday* couldn't have been written had I not attended his lecture, when I wrote it I had never spoken to the man and thus was able to achieve a degree of sunlight in which to work. But now I toiled away in Gardner's shadow.

With my plants I've come to learn which prefer shade (astilbe, prunella, lily-of-the-valley) and which need sun, full sun, eight hours of it. I'm convinced that writers require full sun. Those who work in shadow fail to thrive; their leaves turn yellow and droop, their buds are small, and if any come to blossom, the blooms are pale. Imitation may be the sincerest form of flattery, but for a writer trying to do something other than hone his or her craft, imitation, appropriation, or a desire to please can be as bad as an infestation of aphids, those tiny insects who suck away a plant's juices causing the plant to lose its vigor, become stunted or distorted, even die.

John didn't want to be my mentor; he didn't want to be anyone's mentor. He saw his responsibility as far greater—letting as many people as possible know the secrets about writing he'd toiled to uncover, trying to keep writers honest, injecting a little uneasiness into the often cozy stratum where they sit, preening and congratulating themselves and one another. At Bread Loaf, for example, he sat in the Barn, the conference's great common room, during the second week, a time when the other staff were meeting individually with writers or repairing to Treman for a Bloody Mary. He'd already held his meetings, during the first week, and now he sat, inviting anyone at all to come to him with a manuscript. While most staff had ten to fifteen conference members, John took on all comers.

But he had no choice in the matter: he was my mentor because I'd made him so—in a way, I invented him, endowing him with powers and abilities far beyond those of mortal men. Ironically, *Satyrday* is, among other things, a novel about a fifteen-year-old boy, raised by a satyr, who searches for his real patrimony. What I didn't understand at the time was that the novel hadn't been written to please John but had pleased him anyway. Nevertheless, I was determined to write an "adult" novel, to show him what I was capable of. *Satyrday* had just been practice, a fantasy. Now, like the second brother in the Grimms' tale, I was determined to bring home something of real value: a gold-speaking donkey.

When Gardner died, in September of 1982 in a motorcycle accident, I was suddenly robbed of my imprimatur and the magic password *Bricklebrit*, and the donkey stopped speaking. It took me eight more years, eight futile years, to finish the book, which remains, as of this writing, unpublished. Although I continue to be interested in the original concept, I've become increasingly convinced that it went awry because I wrote it for the wrong reasons, and because it was the sort of story which didn't flourish in the soil of my particular experience and unconscious. I paid no attention to the fact that Gardner was, finally, a fabulist (look at *Grendel* and *The Sunlight Dialogues*, at "Vlemk the Box Painter" and *In the Suicide Mountains*, even the great *Mickelsson's Ghosts*). I paid no attention to the advice he'd given me: "Don't be afraid to exaggerate; look at Dickens; look at Disney." I was back in fourth grade, gazing longingly at the adult library with its shelves of books of the month. I wanted to play with the big boys and girls, whose parents were readers, who had Phi Beta Kappa keys. I didn't want to be stuck in the grim Scotch tape–defaced storefront with the books which last the ages.

During those years the novel became increasingly hard to write, though I finally finished it and then refinished it, again and again.

(What did publishers want? If I knew, I'd have given it to them.) Slowly I came to some understandings. I discovered that the voices that clamor for attention and love can be acknowledged, and quieted, even turned to positive use. I learned by going where I had to go.

I met my wife, a novelist and nonfiction writer, at Bread Loaf in 1980. She had grown up loving the Children's Library books I had ignored (she's read *The Lord of the Rings* seventeen times), and she had read and loved *Satyrday* before we'd really met. For years she's tried to push me in the direction of fabulism and I've resisted her. (Why didn't she write fantasy, I wanted to know, if she thought so highly of it? She, after all, wrote the kind of books I wanted to write. She would if she could, she told me; but it was an ability not everyone had. This was difficult for me to believe, since I seemed to have it.)

As well, I became a gardener. When we bought our place, an abandoned and dilapidated 1910 farmhouse, the land was a forest of head-high weeds. The people who had owned it before us had buried their garbage on the property, and everywhere I dug I uncovered shards of glass, shattered pottery, crushed cans, bits of wire, the occasional rusted and broken farm implement. What a story the garbage told! Though I wasn't sure I wanted to read it.

I started small, with petunias, pansies, and marigolds, those dependable, practically foolproof annuals one can buy just about anywhere in the spring. With Liz's urging, the memory of my grandmother's well-tended beds, and the description of the border Liz had loved outside her mother's home in Vermont, I began to learn about perennials. For a rank beginner this was a challenge, since it involved mastering yet another language — *herbaceous, floribunda*, the word *border* itself, *umbel* — before I could begin deciphering the books and catalogs that would teach me where to start.

Frustrated, I plunged ahead, illiterate. My first pronounced success was with lilies (bulbs were less intimidating than "herbaceous perennials"), planted too late, and without any thought, but *did they bloom*! I moved them to make room for doronicum and rudbeckia and echinops, and now they have a bed of their own. Each fall, just when the academic semester was moving into high gear, the boxes arrived from White Flower Farm or Wayside Gardens, and I'd plant my latest inspirations, sometimes hurriedly, after discovering that if they lived through the winter, they'd survive transplanting the following spring. One year the plants arrived on a Wednesday, and on Thursday we had the earliest snow on record, three inches in the second week of October. What a winter this prophesied! I consulted the rose's pollen: no problem. I planted on Saturday, after the snow had melted. I became not a talented gardener but an assiduous one, who makes up in time and energy what he lacks in foresight and basic common sense.

Now I can see that my struggle has been, among other things, a struggle about class. Because I aspired to more than my parents had — more knowledge, more "culture" — I was vulnerable to a host of false and pernicious ideas about sophistication. I valued not what I had or what came easily to me, but those things just out of reach, the frail perennials which do not grow here, but which the culture told me to value. It has taken me a while to prize those plants which thrive with little help, and not to think of them as common or not worthy of pride. In this, perhaps, I've been merely an American, wanting those things that others have, scorning what is mine by birth and constitution. I need to remember that though I have gotten many plants from high-toned nurseries, several of my absolute winners — coreopsis and dianthus among them — have come from local discount stores.

So tomorrow, I will start over as a writer. I will get out the manuscript of my unfinished children's book *The Cat Who Loved Water*. It begins:

> *Long ago, in a village not far away, there lived four cats, born in the same litter. Three of them had green eyes and orange coats and white paws, and their names were Hoot-malalie, Flumadiddle, and Gigamaree. They lived in different houses with different masters and mistresses, but they looked so very much alike that sometimes Mrs. Biddle, who harbored Hootmalalie, would call "Here, Hootmalalie," when Gigamaree passed by. And sometimes Mr. Mayapple, the man who fed poor Gigamaree, would call "There you are, you orange cur!" when he saw Flumadiddle. And sometimes Miss Gagney, who fussed and fiddled over Flumadiddle, would yell at Hootmalalie, "I just saw a mouse you missed last night!" which would badly hurt Hootmalalie's feelings, because he was an excellent mouser, even though Flumadiddle, Miss Gagney's cat, was lazy as a summer's day.*

I will try to write for the pleasure of it, for the sound of sweet words placed carefully next to one another, as I've learned that coneflower and heliopsis planted together make a fine show. I will try to remember who I am and where I'm from, to dig more slowly and pay more respectful attention to what I uncover. I'll try to start small and allow the work to fill the available space. I'll move things around, note what grows well, and watch what develops with a critical eye. I'll remind myself that not every start reaches fruition, that failure is as honorable as success, so long as the process is understood for what it is — an exploration into the realms of the possible.

It won't matter who comes to see my garden, though if anyone does, I'll be pleased to show them, and I'll hope they will take some pleasure from it as well. I'll lose myself in process. There is always a new gardening space.

And who knows? If I'm patient and lucky, perhaps I'll stumble on a weird cross-pollination, or discover a strange admixture of form, color, scent not suggested in any gardening book I've read. Perhaps I'll finally teach myself that the only reason to write — the only reason for any art — is the serious play from which spring those reasons we go on living: self-love, self-respect, self-confidence, and the hope of creating for others an environment which nurtures, protects, challenges, gives joy.

Books (First U.S. Editions)

Satyrday (novel). G. P. Putnam's Sons, 1980.
The River (novel). Berkeley Books, 1985.
Steven Spielberg's Amazing Stories (stories). 2 vols. Charter Books, 1986.
Daylight Savings (poetry). Gibbs Smith, 1989.

Anthologies

"All My Life" and "Reclaiming the Family." *Gritloaf Anthology*. Palaemon Press, 1978.
"Stopped in Memphis." *Anthology of Magazine Verse and Yearbook of American Poetry*. Monitor Books, 1980.
"Marconi Station, South Wellfleet" and "Ring-Necked Pheasant." *Anthology of Magazine Verse and Yearbook of American Poetry*. Monitor, 1984.
"Intro to Poetry." *Discovery of Poetry*. Harcourt, Brace, 1986.
"White Cedar Swamp." *The Forgotten Language: Contemporary Poets and Nature*. Gibbs Smith, 1990.

Periodicals

Nonfiction

"A Conversation with Alan Dugan" (with Jason Shinder). *Antaeus* (Autumn 1982).
"Farmhouse Blues." *Home* (October 1986).
"Teaching Creative Writing." *Mississippi Review* vol. 19, nos. 1-2 (Spring 1991).

Poetry (since 1986)

"The Man Who Knew Too Much" and "Intro to Poetry." *Prairie Schooner* vol. 60, no. 1 (1986).
"Vagrant" and "Grass." *Prairie Schooner* vol. 60, no. 4 (1986).
"Hint of Spring." *Missouri Review* (Spring 1987).
"Out Here." *Oxford Magazine* (Spring 1987).
"Evening." *Indiana Review* (Summer 1988).
"White Cedar Swamp." *Southwest Review* (Summer 1988).
"Digging the Grave." *High Plains Literary Review* (Spring 1989).
"Reading." *High Plains Literary Review* (Spring 1989).
"Wild Waters Wave Pool, Ocala, Florida." Arts Indiana *Literary Supplement* (1990).
"Gleaning" and "Harvest." Arts Indiana *Literary Supplement* (1991).

Roberto Celli

Jim Barnes earned his graduate degrees in comparative literature from the University of Arkansas and teaches in this field at Northeast Missouri State University. He is also editor of The Chariton Review. *He has received the Pushcart Prize in poetry, a translation prize from Columbia University, a creative writing fellowship from the National Endowment for the Arts, and other fellowships and grants. He and his wife currently live in Macon, Missouri.*

ON NATIVE GROUND

I

I was five years old the last time I heard the mountain lion scream. That was in Oklahoma, 1938, when times were hard and life was good — and sacred. But a year later the WPA had done its work: roads were cut, burial mounds were dug, small concrete dams were blocking nearly every stream. The government was caring for its people. Many were the make-work jobs. A man would eat again, while all about him the land suffered. The annual spring migration of that lone panther was no more. The riverbanks that had been his roads and way stations bore the scars of the times, the scars of loss.

In my mind the rivers must always run free. But in truth today I do not recognize them. They are alien bodies on a flattening land where everything has been made safe, civilized into near extinction. Sounds of speedboats drown out the call of the remaining jays and crows. The din of highway traffic carries for miles now that the timber has fallen to chainsaw or chemical rot. Green silence in the heavy heat of summer afternoons is no more.

The Fourche Maline River and Holson Creek flow through much of what I have written. I suspect they were always there, even back in the mid-1950s when I wrote my first bad short story and my first bad verse. My sense of place is inexorably linked to these two streams and to the prairies and woods between them.

I was born within spitting distance of the Fourche Maline, on a meadow in a house that no longer stands. A long clump of gnarled sassafras and oak rises out of the meadow a short mile northeast of Summerfield, in the hill country of eastern Oklahoma, where the land was once heavy with wood and game. Nobody knows why the clump of trees was not cut down when the land was first cleared for the plow. Once there was a house a few feet east of the trees. The broken tile of a well long since filled still rises a few inches above the earth. But you have to look long, for the tall grass hides it like the night. I cannot remember a time when the house stood there. My mother says that, as a child, she lived there for a short while at the turn of the century when her parents first moved up from Texas. But she does not recall the house, nor why it ceased to be.

Maybe the maker of the house knew why the trees were left in the middle of the field. At any rate, the trees are still there and are not threatened. Local legend has it that they once guarded a rich burial mound, but now no mound rises among the trees. Instead, a musky sink in the middle of the clump shows the scars of many a shovel and many a firelit night. The story of one night in particular sticks in my mind, though I was much too young at the time to know of the night at all. But like bedtime ghost stories, some things told again and again when you are young and lying with your brothers and sisters on a pallet before the hearth of the fireplace later illuminate the dim, unremembered years. It is the story of how my brother outran a horse.

Before I could stand alone, we lived on the lane that borders the east edge of the field where the trees still stand. My brother was nearing manhood and owned a horse and was a night rider. He learned that three men, neighbors and good-for-nothings, planned to dig in the trees. He asked to join them. He longed to prove himself a man. They had visions of gold and told him there was money buried there.

So when the October moon was dark, they gathered in the clump of trees and hung a lantern over the chosen spot. There was frost on the limbs of the sassafras and oaks. My brother broke first ground, and a hushed moan moved through the still tress. He dropped the shovel; later, strange pieces of bone-red matter began to show up in the dirt at the edge of the pit. While all were gathered about, another moan, much louder than the first, moved through the night — and my brother leaped out of the dark pit. But the good-for-nothings held him fast and howled with laughter as one of their cronies strode into the circle of the lantern's light, drunk on erupting mirth and bootleg whiskey. Everyone had a good laugh at my brother's expense. And he laughed too.

But the laughter was short lived. A deep, low moan — ghostly but unmistakably human — rolled up from the bowels of the black earth. There was for a moment, my brother recalls, a stillness like doom upon all of them. Then everybody was running, running: the good-for-nothings were running, the original moaner was running, my brother was running, all the beasts of the field. A great shadow passed beside my brother. It was a horse. The moan persisted, even over the sound of thumping boots and racing hoofs. Now my brother passed the horse, and burst through the barbed wire fence at the edge of the field with one wild bound. He flung himself down the lane and plunged through the doorway of our house and hugged himself close to the dying coals in the fireplace. An hour passed before he began to cry.

Several days later my father filled in the pit and brought home the lantern, dry of kerosene, the wick burned to a crisp.

The clump of trees in the middle of the field was the hub of the universe of my childhood and my adolescence. We always lived within sight of the field. And after the field became a great meadow, I found several days of bone-breaking work each summer helping a cousin bale the tall and fragrant lespedeza that had been urged to grow there. But never did I seek the shade of those trees for my noonday rest. For me, they were too ghostly, foreboding, sacred. In my mind's eye I could see beyond all doubt that here was the final resting place of the broken bones of some great Choctaw chief. He had made it just this far west. He had come within sight of the blue Kiamichi range to the south, which was to become the last home for his dispossessed people, and had fallen dead on the spot from a homesickness of the soul. Among the sassafras and the oaks he had been buried with all the pomp and honor that was left to his migrating children. For me, the spot was inviolate.

And thus it has remained. Only recently have I had the courage, and the reverence, to penetrate the gnarled clump of trees in the middle of the meadow. I went there in midafternoon and sat as motionless as I could while the sun dropped well below a long, low line of trees far to the west. Sitting there, I tried to grasp something I could not name, something I knew was gone forever. I could not invoke it. I did not know its name. Once, just as the sun went down, I heard a hawk cry out high above the clump of leafless trees. Perhaps there was a moan. But I did not hear it.

Named by the French who early explored eastern Oklahoma, the Fourche Maline is by literal definition and observation a dirty stream, though one which once teemed with all the life that water could possibly bear. It was home to some of the world's largest catfish. I have seen mudcat and shovelbill taken from the river, on bankhooks or trotlines, huge fish that ran to more than a hundred pounds each, their hides so scarred and tough you had to skin them with wire pliers or Vise-Grips. Bullfrogs loud enough to drown a rebel yell, turtles big as washtubs, and cottonmouths all called it home, dared you to enter their domain. I can remember bear tracks on the shoals, mussel shells bitten in half.

The Fourche Maline was always a sluggish river, at least for the last twenty-five miles of its course. Though its head is in the western end of the Sans Bois mountain range, where ridges are still thick with government-protected scrub pine and savannah sandstone, and the water begins pure and clear, it is soon fed by farms and ranches with runoff from cornfields and feedlots and by worked-out coal mines as it snakes its way eastward to join Holson Creek. I can recall a time when the Fourche Maline cleared in early summer even as far as its mouth, and the water of the deep pools tasted of springs. Now the river runs ever more slowly, if at all. Its life grows stagnant out of season.

Conversely, Holson Creek — named for Holson Valley, from which it heads northward — was in the past a clear, fast-running stream. It flowed through the pines of Winding Stair and blue mountains, through pastureland thick with native grasses, among stones that seem still today old as the sky. When I remember Holson Creek as it was in my youth, I smell the odor of water willows, sharp in the summer, and hear the sounds of barking squirrels, of rapids and small falls, the banks rich with a treasure of arrowheads.

But now both rivers are slow, dammed. Where they meet, mouth to mouth, a lake begins. And for miles back up both streams it is difficult for the eye to discern movement of water, except in flood time, and then there is no guarantee which way they may run.

The land and streams are changing. Even what is protected pollutes: in the wildlife refuge, near the confluence of the Fourche Maline and the Holson, there are so many deer now that tick fever has thinned even the equalizing coyotes and has put salt fear into the veins of poachers, who once knew — who once were, right along with the coyotes — the true balancing force in nature.

Though fishing is sometimes fair, gone are the days of the scream of the mountain lion, the days of the big catfish. No one has seen a bear track in forty years. I doubt you could get snakebitten if you wanted to. But I am a child of the past. I live it in my waking dreams. The white clay banks along the Fourche Maline still hold their lure and the lore I assigned to them. I dug caves there. I danced the old songs. I attacked wagon trains or, on the other side, killed Indians. And once in a rare sundown, I realized that here in the bottomland stood the only native holly tree I knew of anywhere in the great wooded valleys between the Sans Bois mountains to the north and the blue Kiamichi to the south. The holly tree is gone, victim of the backwater of the Corps of Engineers. When backwater rises, is held like a cesspool for weeks on end, all flora and fauna rooted to place die. Even a simple child knows this.

What's more, and the hell of it all: I see but little hope; rather, mainly dissolution of river, of land, and thus spirit. You can see it plain on the faces of those who have witnessed, have lived, these civilizing years. Their faces are not lined without cause; there is something in the blood that needs rivers free, forests and prairies green with promise. Maybe lack of fuel and the death of automobiles will help, but I doubt it; I know people who will hike ten miles or more carrying a six-pack just to be able to throw the cans into a stream to see how long they will stay afloat while they are pumped full of lead.

We have been called a nation of tourists. But I suspect, deep down, some of us somehow know where home is — and what it has become.

II

Home for me will always remain the Great Southwest. That the Southwest is a rich cultural region few will deny. But what its boundaries are is a moot question. For William Bartram in his *Travels* in the early 1700s, the old Southwest was Alabama, Mississippi, Louisiana. But this did not last. In later years Washington Irving showed us Arkansas and eastern Oklahoma as Southwest territory. Cherokee Sam Houston took us to Texas. The Santa Fe Trail opened up New Mexico, and the region expanded on to California. Useless to argue boundaries.

But there are things in my lifetime I cannot help associating with the term *Southwest*. My grade school geography and history classes taught me that Oklahoma, Texas, and New Mexico were the Southwest. My high school library had one book that was passed off as Southwest literature — J. Frank Dobie's *Coronado Children*, a book that made me dream of buried treasure from the Brazos River to the Superstition Mountains. He made it all come alive — that feeling for west Texas and Oklahoma — and he did through his characters, the spinners of tall tales, Coronado's children.

The cultural Southwest means always for me Indians, their land and their customs and their languages. The Native American languages are going fast. It is no small wonder that they have held out this long. There are mighty few Yuchi speakers left today. Ten or twelve years ago I believe there were some two hundred acknowledged Oklahoma Yuchis living, and of those perhaps four or five native speakers. How many languages we have lost! The Yuchis, who came from Georgia with the Creeks in forced migration, are virtually no more. That great tribe believed that they came from the East, across a great water — a belief that seems borne out by the so-called Metcalf stone that was unearthed in Georgia back in the 1960s bearing characters from the Phoenician alphabet.

Some years ago I spent several hours with one of the few remaining

383

Yuchi speakers, listening to her and trying to transcribe a few phrases of the language. I remember her saying that the typical greeting in Yuchi is "Wa-hin-gi?" (Where are you going?) or "Sen-ga-le-la?" (How are you?). She spoke of many things Yuchi: I tried to transcribe. Several days later we met, and she greeted me with "Sen-ga-le-la?" Wanting to appear miraculously fluent, I replied, with the only phrase I could remember then, "Yubo-ah-tee-tee-onde-de-tah," which means "I want an orange." She laughed long and hard, then said, "You must try harder." Words I try to hang on to.

Tomorrow we will be able to count the fluent Choctaws on one hand if something is not done today. I was raised in Choctaw country, LeFlore County, and count myself one-eighth *Chahta*. I was raised on the language and the foods, practically all that was left us then of the culture. I have eaten *chongkus chom pooey* (pork backbone boiled in hominy) and *tom fuller* (meat and cornmeal cooked in a corn shuck) and hickory nut soup — to my infinite delight. But now these have passed away like so many other things Choctaw. In a few years Choctaw will become a rare language. I hate to see that happen, but it is bound to come to that unless something more is done. I can recall the day when "Halito, chin achukma?" (Hello, how's your fat?) was a familiar greeting in eastern Oklahoma, around Talihina and Summerfield. You will find few replies to the question today.

I am proud of the Choctaw blood I carry, and I am equally proud of the Welsh blood in my veins. But I object to the term *regional writer* or *ethnic writer* or even *Native American writer*, though it may apply to a number of us in a general sense. I don't think I could be called a Kiamichi poet or an Oklahoma writer by any far stretch of the imagination. In my work, place names are important, but they are usually important not because of any geographical sense but because of the names themselves. "Antlers," for example, in "Stopping on Kiamichi Mountain" (*The American Book of the Dead*), carries with it the name of a very old town in Oklahoma but also a pretty good-sized rack of horns. So if I use "Antlers," it's because I can get mileage out of the image as well as the place name. I feel good about many place names in Oklahoma and elsewhere: the *sounds* are good.

I object to terms like *regional* or *Native American* for art and artist. As a magazine editor and a lover of good literature, I don't care who writes the poem, where it is written, or what it is written about. Whenever the universal grows out of the specific and vision is achieved, you can tell yourself here is art and it should be preserved. Such a work is, for example, N. Scott Momaday's *House Made of Dawn*. I doubt anyone would call Momaday a Southwest writer (true, by birth he is largely Native American); his novel deals with the people and the land of New Mexico, but also Arizona, Oklahoma, southern California. It is a book of vanishing Americans in all their many faces, many skins; it is a book that documents the failure of a way of life, ways of life, the failure of the individual, of society, of religion, of myth. It is a book that touches the human heart and head and universalizes the human struggle to survive, to prevail, in this hopped-up turned-on world. The message is as clear in Momaday's work as it is in Ralph Ellison's *Invisible Man* when Jack the Bear finally realizes that to survive we must change, must reject, must affirm, must love, must hate; we must know that ambivalence is the condition of being human and that we are subjects of loss.

Momaday is hardly *just* a Native American writer. I know of no fuller expression of loss in contemporary American literature than the Sermon and the Peyote Ritual of *House of Dawn*. The celebrants know what is to be done — the world as it is must be admitted, affirmed, but also remade, recreated. The four blasts of the eagle bone whistle to the four great corners of the world. In the beginning there was a sound, a single sound at the very center of the universe. In the agony of stasis, sound comes, the first word and — if we are lucky — the poem as world, the world as poem.

There are several contemporary writers that I associate with the Southwest — that is, Oklahoma, Texas, New Mexico — though I do not see them as *regional*. Then I ask myself: Is Albert Goldbarth a Southwest writer, a Southwest Jewish writer? He has been living, writing, and teaching in Austin, Texas, and has recently done good (weird) work with the character of Sam Bass. Is Speer Morgan, from Fort Smith, Arkansas, a Southwest writer hiding out at the University of Missouri? His fairly recent *Belle Starr: A Novel* would seem to say yes. But here he comes with a novel called *Brother Enemy*, a work set in a Caribbean banana republic. Is Speer Morgan a Caribbean writer? Or is Winston Weathers a Southwest writer in scholar's disguise at the University of Tulsa? He is of Osage heritage, but his works go far beyond both Osage country and Tulsa.

There have been many, many anthologies of Southwest literature and Native American literature to tell us just who are the American Indian writers, just who this and who that, along with pedigree. And their will no doubt be more. But we must not be misled. The writer is first a writer, second a Native American, a black, a Chicano.

There may be works about a place, about a people, by a writer native to the area; but none of this gives anyone the right to catalog or label the works *regional*, *Native American*, *black*, or whatever. Is Ralph Ellison, born in Oklahoma City, a regional writer? Is his work to be listed as black literature only, when it is so universal that it is horrifying? Is his *Invisible Man* a product of his Southwest heritage (Hey, boy!), his Southern heritage (I yam what I yam), his New York heritage (Sibyl, you been raped by Santa Claus)? A writer, whoever he may be, if he believes in art as art, will bring everything to bear upon his art, ethnic or otherwise. The work of Ralph Ellison, N. Scott Momaday, J. Frank Dobie — all are larger than the cultural and geographical boundaries we might try to fence them with.

III

In Defense of Sobriety and Lying

A few years back I submitted a manuscript of poetry to a well-known university press. In four or five months the manuscript came back with words of praise, generally; but it seems the book was rejected because, as the editor put it, the work was "unrelentingly sober." Well, I think maybe the editor who said that did not like poetry of images, poetry filled with the sense of loss yet with an affirmation of that loss. Unrelentingly sober — I hope not because I don't occasionally have a sense of humor. If I've entirely lost my sense of humor, then I'm not of much worth. It's a dangerous thing to do or have done. Sober, unrelentingly sober, too, because when I get an image going or a metaphor working, I will try to carry it throughout the poem and weed away anything that is extraneous, anything that's not tightly connected to the major image of the poem. That is why, for example, in "Elegy for the Girl Who Drowned at Goats Bluff" (from *The American Book of the Dead*), water, stone, and bone are carried throughout the five stanzas:

> The sun strikes water like soft stone,
> oblique and torn by surface waves.
> Below, in the still place of stone,
> the slow fish nuzzle through the caves
>
> you seldom know are there at all
> and rest among the drowned girl's bones.
> Above, the bluff is too brittle
> for a date in stone. The long day downs,
>
> and she alone records the passing.
> You think you know her now, the scream
> that cracked the bluff, the siren song
> that wails its way into the dream

you sometimes have. Dark water.
Darker still the night. You wait
for the water to take the sky, for
the floating moon to turn stone white

as the skin of dead fish. You know
she sees you stranger to this place,
her empty eyes wide against the night,
her empty hands, her empty face.

Of course, you can kill an image by overworking it. I try not to do this; I try only to stay true to the image through the poem. I am always trying unrelentingly to succeed at that particular task. And the effect is usually a sober one, in opposition to the drunken one or the dizzy one, which would be failure, in my view.

I have no theory of poetry. I feel no need for one. But I do have complaints. Looming large today is the Poet-as-Speaker. Surely here at the end of the twentieth century, by this time surely, we must understand that the poet does not speak. The poet creates a voice, and that voice speaks.

La Plata, Missouri: Clear November Night

Last night in La Plata an avalanche of stars
buried the town in constant light the way the red
coalburners on the Santa Fe used to send fires

climbing night and falling back again, burning sheds,
hay, carriages, whatever was set along the track.
An avalanche of stars, last night the Leonids

fired every farm with ancient light, curdled milk
in Amish churns, and sent dogs howling through field
and tangled wood. Never was there such a night like

this. Lovers sprang from one another's arms, reeled
away from lurching cars and thoughts into a state
of starry wonder no human act could have revealed.

As if by common will, house lights went out. The late
work left, families settled out into the snow
unaware of cold, unaware of all except that state

which held us all for those long moments. We saw
and saw again the falling stars course Bear and Swan,
take field and farm, take all, and give it back as though

a gift given was given once again. Our lawn
on earth was full of promise in the snowing light.
Earthbound, we knew our engine on a rare November run.

(reprinted from La Plata Cantata*)*

Confessional poetry? No way! It is high time the poet quit lying about his poetry. It is high time critics stopped being cretins. There is no such thing as autobiography or biography. One cannot write one's life, or anyone else's. It is impossible. The greatest biography is fiction; the greatest autobiography is lie. One has to take a few facts here and there, make transitions between, and hope somehow to capture the essence of the thing or person one is writing about. Essentially, poetry works the same way, because for each poem there must be created a voice to carry that poem — a speaker, not the poet, to say what is to be said. The best poetry is dominated by speaker and image, image and speaker. The voice is the fiction (the lie) in respect to the poet's life. The poet may be using a few facts that belong to his experience, but he has to expound these facts in a certain way to create a universal. He must *think* he is speaking, and he must make it real. Momaday does it in *House Made of Dawn* (pure poetry throughout); Ellison does it with Jack the Bear; Bobbi Hill Whiteman does it in her work, as do James Welch and Joseph Bruchac and Ernest Gaines and Garcia Lorca. For the writer the experience is not real in sense of fact. He uses whatever he can to enhance the initial fact or image that he is working with. The fiction, the lie, is a mixture of anything, many things, that the poet cares to stir up that will make the poem work as art.

From the total experience of the poem comes an experience of the speaker, and it is in this combination of fact and lie that Truth stands. If it means something to you, if it affects you, it is a certain truth. If it makes you see, if it makes you realize, if it makes you grow, then it is somehow true. Great truths have come out of lies. All great analogy comes out of Plato's relating the vision of Ur or the story of the Cave, and we learn something about ourselves from such fiction. For me, then, only fiction (only lie) is the greatest of all truths. In all honesty, I can say I have never learned anything about the world and its importance by reading a newspaper, that bastion of daily fact. But believe me, I learn, *I learn*, today when I read and reread Momaday, Ellison, and our other good ethnic or otherwise contemporaries.

Books

The Fish on Poteau Mountain (poetry). Cedar Creek Press, 1980.
Summons and Sign: Poems by Dagmar Nick (translation). The Chariton Review Press, 1980.
This Crazy Land (poetry). Inland Boat Series, 1980.
The American Book of the Dead (poetry). University of Illinois Press, 1982.
A Season of Loss (poetry). Purdue University Press, 1985.
La Plata Cantata (poetry). Purdue University Press, 1989.
Fiction of Malcolm Lowry and Thomas Mann: Structural Tradition (criticism). Thomas Jefferson University Press, 1990.
The Sawdust War (poetry). University of Illinois Press, 1992.

Anthologies (since 1987; poetry unless otherwise noted)

Editor's Choice II: Fiction, Poetry & Arts from the U.S. Small Press. The Spirit That Moves Us Press, 1987.
Harper's Anthology of Twentieth Century Native American Poetry. Harper & Row, 1987.
I Tell You Now: Autobiographical Essays by Native American Writers (essays and poetry). Ed. Brian Swann and Arnold Krupat. University of Nebraska Press, 1987.
Anthology of Magazine Verse and Yearbook of American Poetry. Monitor Books, 1987–89.
From the Heartlands: Photos and Essays from the Midwest (essay). Ed. Larry Smith. Bottom Dog Press, 1988.
Dancing on the Rim: An Anthology of Contemporary Northwest Native American Writing. University of Arizona Press, 1990.
Decade: Poetry and Commentaries 1980–1990. New Letters, 1990.
The Decade Dance: A Celebration of Poems. Sandhills Press, 1991.

Periodicals

Poetry, translations, and essays have appeared in the following publications, among others: *Agni Review, Amicus Journal, Chicago Review, Concerning Poetry, Confrontation, Dacotah Territory, Denver Quarterly,*

Georgia Review, *Greenfield Review*, *Louisville Review*, *Melus*, *Memphis State Review*, *Midnight Lamp*, *Mississippi Review*, *Mundus Artium*, *Nation*, *New Letters*, *Nimrod*, *North Dakota Quarterly*, *Northwest Review*, *Paintbrush*, *Panache*, *Poem*, *Poetry East*, *Poetry Now*, *Poetry Northwest*, *Prairie Schooner*, *Quarterly West*, *South Dakota Review*, *Southwest Review*, *Texas Review*, *Three Rivers Poetry Journal*, *Translation*, *Tri-Quarterly*, *Webster Review*, and *Xavier Review*.

Tom Andrews

Tom Andrews received a philosophy degree from Hope College and an M.F.A. from the University of Virginia, where he was awarded a Hoyns Fellowship. In 1984 he received the Academy of American Poets Prize at Oberlin College, and in 1989 his book The Brother's Country *was a winner in the National Poetry Series Open Competition. He lives in Lancaster, Ohio, and teaches at Ohio University.*

THE SELF-AVOIDING RANDOM WALK

The new geometry mirrors a universe that is rough, not rounded, scabrous, not smooth. It is a geometry of the pitted, pocked, and broken up, the twisted, tangled, and intertwined.

— James Gleick, *Chaos: Making a New Science*

There is a mathematical process, useful to physicists and probability theorists, called "the self-avoiding random walk." A physicist friend once explained it to me as a succession of movements along a lattice of many dimensions, where the direction and length of each move is randomly determined, and where the walk does not return to a point already walked on. This process, my friend explained, was especially helpful in the study of turbulence. I was visibly delighted.

My friend looked confused. "You studied randomness in school?" he asked, earnestly.

What delighted me was that the process, as my friend described it, gave an account of randomness without blunting its unpredictability. The process honored randomness. Like John Cage's chance operations, it participated in, incarnated, the randomness it sought to evoke. That it was useful to certain scientists startled me. The implication was that those scientists were learning what Cage and others had discovered long ago: that cooperating with chance led not to "a bloomin' buzzin' confusion" (in William James's phrase) but to unexpected ways of seeing the world, of letting the world be present to us.

Discussions of randomness in poetry often end with an assertion that poems offer a vital imposition of order upon chaos. Certainly when I began writing poems I did so in part to fulfill my hunger for a convincing order to my experience. Yet the more I wrote the more dissatisfied I became with the ordering impulse behind my poems. As the poet Gregory Orr noted in "The Interrupted Scheme: Some Thoughts on Disorder and Order in the Lives of Poets and the Lives of Poems,"

I think it's fair to say that poetry exerts a powerful attraction on people who have an intense consciousness of disorder. The

> *art has an enormous reservoir of ordering principles and historical models which it offers the individual as he or she enacts "the difficult balance" of making sense of the world. However, the very ordering powers of poetry can represent a possible danger. What if, in the complex interaction between the poet and the poem, the poem comes to represent* only *an ordering — what if its order suffocates all wildness in the process of offsetting the psychic imbalance of the poet?*

In my early poems I was limiting what was possible, suffocating "all wildness," in order to satisfy my need for order. In time, though, I realized that my "intense consciousness of disorder" was not the point. Something greater was taking place. Writing brought me into a process not unlike the self-avoiding random walk: my mind became alert to unpredictable associations and juxtapositions, receptive to words' strange interactions, their echoing eruptions of meaning. This process seemed to have nothing to do with me, or my personality, or my particular consciousness of disorder. I began to understand what Pierre Boulez meant when he said that the motive behind all his music was "the search for anonymity."

I'm fascinated by those moments when one's vision is mysteriously enlarged, when possibilities open up into areas where before one found only a humiliating dead end. I'm also fascinated by what precedes those moments. Let me backtrack a little to give you an account of one such moment.

During my first year at Hope College I used to collect quotations from my reading and pair them in contradictory fragments on the wall beside my desk. Soon my wall became a nearly mural-sized collage of these pairings:

> *It is the transcending of our own individuality, the sense of the sublime. — Schopenhauer,* The World as Idea

> *I rarely lose sight of myself. — Valéry,* Monsieur Teste

My intent was not to undercut the writers' visions but to leave them in free and unexplained collision. I was learning, clumsily, something about how sudden shifts in context can release unanticipated meaning and feeling from traditional sources. More crucially, I was learning to let go of my intentions.

My wall was more exciting to me then than the stories and plays I was trying to write. Hope College was a Christian school where I had gone for preparation to become a minister or, better, a Christian writer, an apologist for the faith like St. Anselm or Cardinal Newman or C. S. Lewis. Besides formal apologetics, I wanted to write stories and plays that would make people see beyond doubt that the divine and the human intersected in the person of Jesus Christ. Then, I thought, my life would be justified in the eyes of the Lord.

I was, however, in big trouble. Secretly (from whom? God?) I loved comic writers such as S. J. Perelman and Woody Allen. St. Anselm's ontological argument for the existence of God quickened me with its beauty and simplicity, but a line like "I've got Bright's disease, and he's got mine!" or "He is perhaps best known for his experiments in behavior, in which he proved that death is an acquired trait" embodied a mystery no less fascinating to me but more habitable. I was unable to reconcile this tension. The only reconciliation I would consider was to try in my stories and plays to lure readers with wildness and humor only to drive home the fact of the Incarnation, the bad faith of which didn't occur to me. My trouble was, I preferred the wildness and the humor to the sermon.

I persisted in my folly. Not to the point of wisdom, no doubt, but long enough to begin to understand how constricted, how spiritually corrosive, were the limits and protections of the faith as I practiced it. At that time I was reading some the great Christian mystics: Dame Julian of Norwich, the author of *The Cloud of Unknowing*, the Thomas Traherne of *Centuries of Meditations*. To my astonishment, I recognized in certain passages an energy and a delight in surreality that I'd found in, say, S. J. Perelman! *Centuries of Meditation* was particularly remarkable:

The World is a Pomegranate....

... every soul is an Infinite Centre.

And the soul is a Miraculous Abyss of Infinite Abysses, an Undrainable Ocean, an inexhausted fountain of Endless Oceans.

As pictures are made curious by lights and shades, which without shades could not be: so is felicity composed of wants and supplies; without which mixture there could be no felicity. Were there no needs, wants would be wanting themselves, and supplies superfluous; want being the parent of Celestial Treasure.

This was unlike any Christian writing I'd encountered. The best things, Traherne wrote, were "the most obvious and Common Things": "Air, Light, Heaven and Earth, Water, the Sun, Trees, Men and Women, Cities, Temples &c." It was a revelation, this uncensored and playful expression of desire by a Christian. It was like the moment in Robert Bly's poem "Listening to Bach":

> There is someone inside this music
> who is not well described by the names
> of Jesus, or Jehovah, or the Lord of Hosts!

Strangely, reading the mystics brought me back to delight in *this* world — the palpable, the sensual, the "most obvious and Common Things." I'm still dumbfounded by the odd trajectory. Soon, artists took up where the mystics left me, with a desire to create something out of my newfound astonishment. I began glimpsing Bly's "someone inside" everywhere in art: in Miró and Max Ernst, Erik Satie and Steve Reich, Lydia Davis and Guy Davenport, Charles Wright and Jean Valentine. Music, painting, writing: I exploded with curiosity. For the first time, I allowed myself to experience art without bypassing it in the search for its "worldview." The freedom of it! The mysterious quickening life in it! I've never recovered from that experience.

Perhaps the best account I know of such an experience is one given by Thomas Merton in his *Asian Journal*. After seeing the towering Buddhas at the monastic complex of Polonnaruwa in Ceylon, Merton wrote:

> Then the silence of the extraordinary faces. The great smiles. Huge and yet subtle. Filled with every possibility, questioning nothing, knowing everything, rejecting nothing, the peace not of emotional resignation but of Madhyamika, of sunyata, that has seen through every question without trying to discredit anyone or anything — without refutation — without establishing some other argument. . . . I was suddenly, almost forcibly, jerked clean out of the habitual, half-tied vision of things. . . .

My approach to art had been precisely to "establish some other argument" when confronted with work that challenged my limited understanding of Christianity. Now I was ready — when looking into, say, Max Ernst's collage-novel, *La Femme 100 Têtes* — to be "suddenly, almost forcibly, jerked clean out of the habitual, half-tied vision of things." It was also during this time that the poet Jack Ridl, who teaches at Hope, encouraged me to try writing poems. With Jack's help I discovered that through poems I could participate, if I allowed myself, in a spirit of receptivity and generosity, "filled with every possibility." Some time later I wrote "Song of a Country Priest," a poem which tries to articulate my sense of "seeing through" my limited Christianity "without trying to discredit anyone or anything."

Song of a Country Priest

"Naturally I keep my thoughts to myself."
— Bernanos, Diary of a Country Priest

April 4. Wind hums
in the fireweed, the dogwood
drops white skirts across

the lawn. From this window
I've watched the pink shimmer
of morning light spread

to the sky and the blond
grass lift the dew. You
in whose yet greater light,

etc. My prayers grow
smaller each dawn. Each dawn
I wake to this landscape

of thyme, rue, a maple
whose roots are the highways
of ants, cattails down

to the river. I rise
and look and learn again:
I believe in my backyard.

I can mimic the sway
of weeds in wind. I can
study the patience

of tendrils. God knows what

I am, a rib of earth?
a hidden cloud? I am

old now. I am a priest
without believers. I counsel
leaves, fallen petals, two

bluejays and one shy wren.
In my book of Genesis,
the serpent says, "You can't

tempt me with green
peppers, yellow squash,
the ripe meats of Eden.

I'm looking under my
belly for the next meal.
I'm lying beside a dirt

road in West Virginia,
waiting for a pickup
to stir a thick cloud

of dust into my mouth.
I will never hunger.
I will live like this

forever — inching with
rhythm across the dried
dirt, pulling myself

like a white glove through
meal after parched, ecstatic
meal . . ."

Perhaps my blasphemies
have saved me. Perhaps God
reads between these lines,

that whiteness touched
by no one. I'm ready
for Him to settle my

body like an argument;
my ashes can settle
where they will. God could

fall like an evening sun
to say Eat dust
with the serpent, crawl

on your belly. He could
say the earth is a secret
told by quartz vein and

nothing else. Tonight
in the thin dark He could
whisper the sky is the

earth, the stars are foxgloves,
quince blossoms, white flames
of trilliums, and I am

flaring and vanishing
above them. I'm ready.
I would believe it all.

(reprinted from The Brother's Country*)*

"Perhaps my blasphemies / have saved me." To my mind now, the poem is a farewell note to myself as a would-be minister and a greeting to myself as a would-be writer—or if not a writer then at least someone "ready to believe," someone wishing to remain open to wonder.

You see the contradictory impulses at work in this brief narrative. Joyce Carol Oates, in her essay "Beginnings," writes of "two general theories about the genesis of 'art'":

> *— It originates in play: in experiment, improvisation, fantasy; it remains forever, in its deepest impulse, playful and spon-taneous, a celebration of the (child's?) imagination.*
> *— It originates out of the artist's conviction that he is born damned; and must struggle through his or her life to achieve redemption. By way of art.*

Progress in writing, for me, has meant the gradual acceptance of the former impulse and the simultaneous forgoing of the latter. Of course it's messier than that. Perhaps both impulses are so intertwined that it's impossible to ferret out one without dragging the other along. "Without Contraries," wrote Blake, "is no Progression."

Still, I can trace in my writing a movement toward the condition of not-knowing, of trusting the playful and improvisational impulse Oates writes of. I am not suggesting that this is the right movement for someone else; it is simply the movement that has made poems possible for me. The notion of the poet caught in a romantic *agon*, struggling "to achieve redemption," feels false to me when I acknowledge how accidentally and surprisingly my poems come into being. That's why the self-avoiding random walk interests me as an image of the writing and revising process. It suggests an openness to accident, to wildness. To me it also suggests an openness to the scabrous and tangled lives we lead.

Earlier I remarked that a desire for order suffocated my first poems. "Song of a Country Priest," though important to me for the reasons I mentioned, suffers lingeringly, I think, from this suffocation. A poem that pleases me more is "A Language of Hemophilia," which closes my book, *The Brother's Country*.

I wanted "A Language of Hemophilia" to embody, as nakedly as possible, the disruptive process of a poem's coming into being. I had in mind a poetry of jarring ellipsis and interruption: George Oppen's "Of Being Numerous" was a model, as were Beverly Dahlen's *A Reading* and John Ashbery's experiments in *The Tennis Court Oath*. I wanted to include "found" language — quotations from medical texts, advertisements, overheard conversations, etc. — and to leave them in unexplained collision with more conventionally lyrical voices, recalling the pleasures of collage I'd discovered so clumsily as an undergraduate. Here is the first section:

1

Blood pools in a joint
The limb locks

'Acute hemarthrosis'
'Thromboplastin generation'

Hear a language force
Intimacy with
Itself, the world

With *and* of, *as in skin's turning*

Henna, oxblood, roan, russet

Bruise-blue, color of no jewel

'The secret is locked
 Inside
The structure
 Of the chromosome'

Perhaps I should say at this point that the disruptiveness of the poem mirrors my own experience with hemophilia. The poem begins with the moment of crisis: "Blood pools in a joint." In a sense, the rest of the poem is a recording of the competing languages — and the states of awareness they provoke — that surround and inhabit me during a bleed. These languages are spliced, altered, combined, layered, and repeated throughout the poem. Here are two later sections:

13
"Clotting time — 40 minutes (normal 5 to 10 minutes)
Clotting retraction — good
Prothrombine consumption — 15.5 seconds (normal over 20
 seconds)
Prothrombin time — 17.5 seconds (control 14.5 seconds)
 Recalcification time — 8 minutes (normal less than 180
 seconds)
Thromboplastin generation tests with the patient's
plasma and serum and alternately substituting normal
plasma and serum confirmed the diagnosis of classical
hemophilia."

14
"We read most of these words and numbers
Uncomprehendingly,
As if they were hieroglyphics"

A day, a day

Recurrences through which
'I' assume

'You'

Thistle, keyhole, spittle, crow

Glide, sample, knot, cheek

*"In four years, 84 hemophiliacs have contracted AIDS and
56 have died. A new test to screen donated blood for
AIDS virus lowers the risk, but genetically engineered
factor VIII should carry no such risk at all and also be
much less expensive. Alan Brownstein, the head of the
National Hemophilia Foundation, sees the race to produce
it as 'capitalism at its finest.'"*

Blood pools in a joint
Hear a language force
Firn, mere, cyme, hydrant

Assembling such "unpoetic" material, especially medical termi-
nology, in a poem was liberating. I was like a child who "says 'tree,'
'moon,' 'mountain' and thus orients himself," as Günter Eich once
remarked. The splicing and layering of languages was part of my hope
for a structure faithful to the mind's actual engagement with experience, its possibilities of attention. I don't think "A Language of
Hemophilia" was successful finally—what poem is successful to its
author?—but it opened ground that I hope to explore further.

As these comments about "A Language of Hemophilia" suggest, I
don't want to deny the ordering possibilities of a poem. Still, the
word *ordering* troubles me in this context. *Orienting*—following Eich's
remark—is more accurate, I think. Writing helps me enter into the
complexity and unpredictability of the world's presence. The effect
is of being oriented, not of ordering.

Certainly hemophilia is a chaotic experience. As it happens, I have
the disease as a result of a "spontaneous mutation" in one gene on
the X chromosome. I think of it now as my particular stake in the
notion of participating with randomness. It's one thing to understand
with contemporary physicists that chance is at work in the foundation
of the atom. It's quite another to understand and proclaim with
Antonin Artaud that "Chance is myself." Poems, I'm beginning to
learn, make that more difficult affirmation possible.

Books

Hymni the Kanawha. Haw River Books, Ltd., 1989.
The Brother's Country. Persea Books, 1990.

Recent Poems and Articles

"Yellow Grass" (poem). *Virginia Quarterly Review* (Spring 1989).
"Glimpses into Something Ever Larger: On William Stafford" (essay). *Field* (Fall 1989).
"The Hemophiliac's Motorcycle" (poem). *Field* (Fall 1989).
"Three Purgatory Poems" (poem). *Kenyon Review* (Fall 1990).
"Second Winds: On Li-Young Lee's *The City in Which I Love You* and Marcia Southwick's *Why the River Disappears*" (review essay). *Westminster Review* (Fall 1991).
"When Comfort Arrives" (poem). *Westminster Review* (Fall 1991).

Herbert Scott

Jim Powell

Herbert Scott teaches in the writing program at Western Michigan University. He has received a Pablo Neruda prize from Nimrod *and best poem awards from* Poetry Now *and* Quarterly West. *In addition, he has won fellowships from the National Endowment for the Arts, the National Endowment for the Humanities, the Michigan Council for the Arts, and the Michigan Arts Foundation.*

DAILY BREAD

Poetry is a response to the daily necessity of getting the world right.

— Wallace Stevens

I

She remembers
her mother

a white flame
in the dark house

bringing anise
in hot milk

evening prayers
in flannel gowns

her mother bending
above the bed

like a pitcher
pouring

porcelain cups
steaming

their licorice
breath

My mother's mother, Addie Copeland, rode into Oklahoma Territory on April 22, 1889, the day the territory was opened for settlement. For a fifty-dollar filing fee one could stake claim to a quarter-section of land (160 acres). Addie Copeland, age twelve, and her father Andrew rode to Guthrie, the territorial capital, in central Oklahoma, all the way from Vermillion County, Illinois, where there were too many Copelands, to claim a homestead. Soon the rest of the family would follow, leaving several hundred acres of rich farmland behind for a much smaller spread of hilly land which had to be terraced to keep the topsoil in place, land marked by clusters of scrub oak, red-clay ravines, and dry creeks, inhabited by rattlesnakes and copperheads, but also by bobwhites and whippoorwills.

The first year in Oklahoma was tragic for the Copelands. Addie's sister Ora died of galloping consumption, and her brother Eugene of diphtheria. Margaret, her mother, broken by these deaths, died shortly thereafter leaving Addie to rear her younger brother Arthur and the baby, Stanley. During the next three years the farm in Illinois was sold to help the survivors in Oklahoma survive. The loss of that land, the last vestige of her childhood, would always remain a symbolic, bitter event for Addie.

At eighteen Addie became a schoolteacher. At twenty-three, in 1900, she married Jay Pickard, a man twice her age; a native of New York and graduate of Ann Arbor Law School, Pickard had come to Guthrie to practice law in the capital of the territory. Addie was a beautiful dark-haired, gray-eyed woman barely five feet tall who never weighed more than a hundred pounds even during her several pregnancies. Three of her children lived beyond birth: John (b. 1901), Charles (b. 1904), and Betty (b. 1906). My grandfather, Jay Pickard, after a few prosperous years, watched his practice disappear. The political and business base of the territory had begun to shift to the oil cities of Oklahoma City and Tulsa. Here, family history is in dispute. Perhaps Jay Pickard asked Addie to leave the farm, move to Tulsa where he could renew his practice, and she refused, unwilling to leave the land, the one thing one could trust to have value, and the graves close by. In any case, Jay Pickard mortgaged the homestead, left town to look for opportunities elsewhere, and never returned. In the novel Addie wrote, which she gave me to read, in script, when I was thirteen, the wayward husband returns, on his last legs, crawling up to the shingled, vine-encrusted house on hands and knees to beg forgiveness. But, sadly, he dies on the front lawn, never to be forgiven, while inside the betrayed family sleeps peacefully. Addie, in real life, left with three young children to rear, convinced the First National Bank of Guthrie to lend her the money — although she had no collateral — to start a dairy. She called it "The Pollyanna Dairy."

II

I am still in love with Addie Copeland. By the time I knew her, her hair was gray as her eyes. Her left leg was bowed as a hand sickle, painfully, from a disease that softened the bone in her lower leg. She could milk six cows twice a day at the age of seventy and could spit like a farmer. She had worked hard her whole life but had never let labor for sustenance become her whole life. She surrounded herself with things that pleased her, such as lovely lamps, her walnut secretary, an oriental rug. She played and sang at the piano every day, and she loved to read. Her bookcases were filled with novels and nineteenth-century poetry. She had a copy of *Ben Hur* autographed by General Lew Wallace, who had visited her home. At 4:30 A.M. she would drink her tea from a Havilland china cup before going to the barn to milk. Before taking the milk to town she would don her hat with the black veil that fell just below her eyes, and pull on her pigskin driving gloves. She was also an inventor. I have two of her patent applications, including one for what would have been the first directional turn signal for automobiles. She wrote poems and stories and one novel. And she told wonderful stories about her childhood in Illinois, about the early years in Oklahoma, about her own children. Her stories were so wonderfully textured, so brilliant in their detail, that I can still see many of them. No actual events in my childhood are more real to me than those stories my grandmother told. I am certain that this is where my interest in becoming a writer began.

While I was growing up I spent my summers on my grandmother's farm. I baled hay, harvested oats and Kaffer corn, milked cows, mended fence. One summer I worked as an apprentice gravedigger in the cemetery that had originally been part of the homestead, the cemetery where the Copeland family is buried. My grandmother believed in hard work, but summer afternoons between one and four when it was too hot to work in the fields — except during harvest — I was given two options. One, take a nap (impossible in 100 degree heat), or, two, sit on the screened east porch sipping iced tea while memorizing poems from *America's One Hundred Best Loved Poems*. The decision was easy. I didn't even hate the poems, not even "America for Me." In fact, I liked "The Wreck of the Hesperus." At 4:00 P.M. it was time to hike out to the east pasture to bring the cows in for the evening milking. After supper we would sit on the lawn and visit while waiting for the lights to come on in town two miles away. Saturday afternoons if I had finished my weekly mowing of our full acre lawn we would drive to town for the movie at the Melba and a pint of Terrell's chocolate ice cream on the way home (black walnut for my grandmother).

All that I suppose I know about women, about writing, about life, begins with Addie Copeland.

> *The woman snapping beans*
> *from the oak rocker*
> *on the east porch*
>
> *is the one*
> *I would marry,*
> *but I am only four,*
>
> *sitting at her feet,*
> *a fly swatter*
> *across my lap.*
>
> *Now I see her rise.*
> *Her chair begins to sing*
> *its own diminished song,*
>
> *her skirts drift by,*
> *winging my face.*
> *I climb from the floor,*
>
> *follow, swinging the fly*
> *swatter, back and forth,*
> *innocent in the buzzing air.*

III

> *My father raised bulldogs on Pickard street*
> *Our neighbors learned to hate us . . .*

My father, Herbert Hicks Scott, was born in 1897 on an Ozark hill farm near Plato, Missouri. He was the seventh of thirteen children. The Plato school district offered only eight years of schooling. After my father completed the eighth grade he remained at home for five years to help his parents with the farm and the younger children. At eighteen he sold his horse Dan Tucker for a stake and walked out of the Ozarks to work the summer wheat harvest in Kansas and

Oklahoma and to enquire about the location of a good high school. Someone told him that Beggs, Oklahoma, had a new high school. After the harvest he walked to Beggs, secured work and lodging in a general store, and in the fall entered the ninth grade.

> *One night someone slipped into our garage*
> *to tap in the heads of a new litter with a hammer.*
> Like a cook cracks eggs.

> *You always think you know who does something like that.*
> *The unemployed brothers who live across the street*
> *and down with their mother, next door to the house*
> *of the young girl bitten by a black widow spider.*

After graduating from school in Beggs, my father moved to Norman to attend the University of Oklahoma. He graduated Phi Beta Kappa, married Betty Pickard from Guthrie, a small town fifty miles north, and the two of them began a family: first, Ann, then Sue, followed by Herbert, and finally Addie. My father was a quiet, shy, gentle man, but so emotional and tender by nature and so wary of those emotions, he always held himself at a distance and remained a mystery to me throughout my childhood.

> *My father brushed the bulldogs' coats for hours,*
> *his quiet Saturday ritual,*
> *trimmed their thick toe nails,*
> *taped their ears into roses.*
> *As if any human labor could make them beautiful.*

My mother was the disciplinarian. My father never trusted himself to mete out punishment, nor was he present when it took place. Mother was the tough though fair drill sergeant; Father was somewhere offstage. I don't think it ever occurred to any of us children to question this arrangement. Mother was the solid, dependable, predictable, reassuring force. Father was the elusive, mysterious yet equally dependable and comforting presence guarding the borders of our existence, a presence who loved us very much yet could barely bear the closeness of that love.

My father's bulldogs became intermediaries. We always had bulldogs, as many as twenty-one of them at one time, one or more singled out as family pets: Crodie and Pepper the two I remember best. We all loved the bulldogs. They were an integral part of our family.

So my father, shy in sexual matters,
took me to the garage
to watch him breed the bulldogs.

Those hushed evenings, my father's arms
around the bitch holding her steady
as Crodie circled, coughing, sniffing,
until his cock hung slick and limber.

My father, finally, taking the pendulous cock in his hand
to work it in before the fist-sized knot could form.

The times as a child I was alone with my father were few and filled
with silence, yet each one is clear and reverberates still.

Driving to dog shows late at night with my father
through Oklahoma, Kansas, Missouri, the wing
windows of the Pontiac cranked open,

a stream of air across our faces,
ice-cold coca-colas from late-night diners
or vending boxes at filling stations.

Riding in silence through the dark passage of country,
smelling the languid, unclothed land, pungent,
like the body at night, opening, the held heat rising

IV

She says
her lean evening
prayers
for the flesh
fingers dipped
in Pond's
cold cream
blessing
her face
before the birdseye
maple dresser

children tucked
asleep
beneath the rim
of wind-whipped
sheets.

My mother is her mother's daughter, strong, a survivor. I can't know how difficult it was for her to have had her father leave when she was a young girl, to have never seen him again. Or how painful it must have been for her to have been sent away from her mother for a year to live with an aunt while her mother spent all her energies keeping her son John alive. (He had swallowed laundry lye at the age of two which closed his throat. He could not swallow food or liquid again for thirteen years. He wasn't expected to survive, but by sheer force of will his mother kept him alive, feeding him through tubes and letting him chew meat then spit it out to keep his jaws and teeth strong. At the age of fifteen, while sucking on ice cream for its flavor, John felt a small cool trickle go down his throat. In another year he could take nourishment normally, but the toll on the family of those years was high).

This summer at eighty-five my mother moved from Illinois to Texas. Drove herself, alone, the thousand miles, and enjoyed the trip. My mother has always had the ability to actively enjoy life, to never be defeated by its harshness.

When I was seven I contracted undulant fever, a severe case which did not go into remission for seven years. I missed most of the second grade, so weak that my legs would go out from under me when I tried to walk. I spent much of that year propped in bed, my mother beside me in a chair, reading to me. She must have read all the Oz books, and many of the dog stories of Albert Payson Terhune. This is what I remember of that year. Not the debilitating illness, but the joy of listening to my mother read. It must have been a long and difficult year for her, but I was never allowed to understand that.

I was a quiet yet troublesome child. I don't believe I spoke much. I listened to my older sisters, my mother, my grandmother. I kept things to myself, was shy, was always in love with older women, with Rosalie Long, our babysitter, with Betty Jean Armstrong, my sister Sue's friend. No one noticed that I was shy or quiet or in love, since I was a good listener, a good watcher, and a good keeper of secrets.

I was in awe of women, stunned by their accomplishments. My mother and grandmother governed my world with such judicious authority, such knowledge and ability, that it never would have occurred to me to question their wisdom.

Yet I was, as I said, troublesome, but almost unconsciously so. My rebellions were usually quiet, perverse, self-inflicted wounds that came about either because I saw no sense in something I was required to do or simply that I was concentrating too hard on something I fancied to pay attention. My grades in school were wretched. I usually did well if I liked the subject (English) and poorly if the subject didn't interest me (almost everything else).

One major contributor to my perverseness, my questioning—for which I am thankful—was the exposure to the opposing political views of my grandmother and my father. My grandmother was a committeewoman for the Republican party who campaigned for Wendell Wilkie, among others. My father was a New Deal Democrat who believed the Republicans had nearly destroyed the country. I took politics very seriously and stayed up late into the night listening to the national conventions and the returns on election night. How was I to reconcile the diametrically opposed positions of these two vital forces in my life? I learned to puzzle over absolutist positions rather than accept them, and, as my mother did during the political skirmishes between her mother and her husband, to keep my own counsel.

I remember childhood in images and scraps of spoken language. What rises through all, what gives strength, foundation, desire, to my writing, to my life, comes from Addie Copeland, Herbert Hicks Scott, Betty Pickard Scott. Certain things can't be named. They have to be "hinted at." Yet we spend our whole lives trying to name them. Central subjects in my writing are family history, a coming to terms with human existence in relation to the life of the planet, an examination of our history as a nation, trying to account for the failure of our dreams, the pervasiveness of our willful ignorance. . . .

My father lived ninety-two years, a man happy in his marriage, his work, his children. My grandmother lived on the farm she loved until her death at ninety-three. In fact, she shot a man when she was eighty-nine who was trying to scare an old lady off her isolated rural property. He was trying to frighten the wrong woman. My mother at eighty-five is still vital, still looking forward to her life, loved and loving.

Books (poetry)

Disguises. University of Pittsburgh Press, 1974.
Groceries. University of Pittsburgh Press, 1976.
Durations. Louisiana State University Press, 1984.

Limited Editions

The Shoplifter's Handbook. Blue Mountain Press, 1974.
Dinosaurs. Hoffstadt & Sons, 1979.
As She Enters Her Seventieth Year She Dreams of Milk. Bits Press, Case-Western Reserve, January 1982.

Essays on Writing

"For the Living and the Dead: A Consideration of Three Poems." *The Writing Room: Keys to the Craft of Fiction and Poetry*. Ed. Eve Shelnutt. Longstreet Press, 1989.
"Keys to the Writing of Poetry." Ibid.

Anthologies

"Late Fall, Setting Traps," "Passing the Masonic Home for the Aged," "The Man in the Closet," "Spring Commences," "Excavations," "The Apprentice Gravedigger," "Picture Puzzle." *Down at the Santa Fe Depot: 20 Fresno Poets*. Giligia Press, 1970.
"The Beekeeper's Wife," "Babies," "Picture Puzzle," "The Apprentice Gravedigger." *Just What the Country Needs, Another Poetry Anthology*. Ed. Dennis Saleh. Wadsworth, 1971.
"That Summer." *Poems One Line and Longer*. Ed. William Cole. Grossman, 1974.
"The Fear of Groceries," "Boss's Dream," "Butcher's Dream," "Checker," "The Clerk's Dream," "Cracked Eggs," "The Lost Aisles." *The Third Coast*. Eds. Hilberry, Scott, Tipton. Wayne State University Press, 1976.
"Breakfast at Aunt Hattie's." *Been Here Once, Cafe and Hotel Poems*. Ed. Mark Vanz. Dacotah Territory Press, 1979.
"Help Is on the Way," "Letter from a Working Girl," "Butcher's Wife." *A Geography of Poets*. Ed. Edward Field. Bantam, 1979.
"Hams," "Coffee," "Relief Locations Manager," "Canned Goods," "The Night Crew." *Going for Coffee: North American Work Poems*. Ed. Tom Wayman. Harbour Publishing, Fall 1980.
"The Meeting." *Fathers*. Eds. Mark Vinz and Grayce Ray. Dacotah Territory Press, 1981.
"The Other Life," "Old Woman in the Desert." *Modern American and Russian Literature*. Gnosis Press of Columbia University, 1982.
"The Apprentice Gravedigger." *Writing Poetry*, by Barbara Drake.

Harcourt, Brace, 1983.

"Fathers of Desire." *Love Stories and Poems*. Ed. Roger Weingarten. Fiction International, 1983.

"The Rapist Speaks to Himself," "The Derelict." *Chelsea: 25 Years*. Ed. Sonia Raiziss. (Fall 1983).

"Early Love," "Achilles' Heel," "The Man Who Would be a Mother," "Fathers of Desire," "The Woman Who Loves Old Men." *New American Poets of the Eighties*. Eds. Jack Myers and Roger Weingarten. Wampeter/Poetry International Press. Fall 1984.

"Passing the Masonic Home for the Aged." *Pocket Poems*. Ed. Paul Janeczko. Bradbury Press, 1985.

"Relief Location Manager." *Language at Work*. Holt, Rinehart and Winston of Canada, Ltd., 1986.

"Early Love." *The Music of What Happens*. Ed. Paul Janeczko. Orchard Books. Franklin Watts, Inc., 1988.

"Hearts," "My Father's Bulldogs." *Contemporary Michigan Poetry*. Eds. Delp, Hilberry, Scott. Wayne State University Press, 1988.

"The God That Keeps Us Alive." *Passages North Anthology*. Ed. Elinor Benedict. Milkweed Editions, 1989.

"A Brief Reversal," "My Father's Fortune," "That Summer," "Evening Dawn." *Preposterous: Poems of Youth*. Ed. Paul Janeczko. Orchard Books. Franklin Watts, Inc., 1991.

"Morning, Milking." *A New Geography of Poets*. Eds. Field, Locklin, Stetler. University of Arkansas Press, 1992.

Periodicals (since 1987)

"Oklahoma Pastoral," "Grandmother, Waiting for the Mail." *Nimrod* (1987).

"A Brief Reversal." *Passages North* (1988).

"Everything's Already Been Said," "Wolf," "A Tintype of the Black Walnut." *Celery* (1988).

"The Husband," "The Sea of Despair," "Invocation," "Neighbor." *Black Warrior Review* (1988).

"If It Lasts." *The South Florida Poetry Review* (1988).

"The Minister," "She Dreams a Letter from Her Son." *Caliban* (1988).

"My Blind Grandfather." *Zone* (1988).

"Evening, Milking." *Shenandoah* (1989).